The Writer at Work

To my good friends and colleagues
over many years

D.I.B. Smith

&

MacD.P. Jackson

C.K. Stead

The Writer at Work

Essays

University of Otago Press

Published by University of Otago Press
56 Union Street/PO Box 56, Dunedin, New Zealand
Fax: 64 3 479 8385
Email: university.press@stonebow.otago.ac.nz

First published 2000
Copyright © C.K. Stead 2000
ISBN 1 877133 95 7

Printed through Condor Production Ltd, Hong Kong

Contents

Introduction *9*

1. New Zealand – Reviews and Reminiscences

Janet Frame, Janet Clutha and Karl Waikato *17*
Lady Chatterley's Glover *29*
Mansfield as Poet *33*
We Were Drinking the Honey of the Flax Flower *35*
Katherine Mansfield as Colonial Realist *38*
Ngaio Marsh *43*
How to Read Curnow *45*
Honest Lauris, Honest Iago *49*
Keith Sinclair – His Story and Ours *51*
A Life of Sargeson *55*
The Making and Unmaking of a Maurice *60*
Eric McCormick – The Scholar Ambulant *66*
Gregory O'Brien and Andrew Johnston *70*
Mansfield's F.O. *73*

2. Four Public Lectures

Narrativity, or the Birth of Story *79*
Nationalism, Regionalism and the Tradition in
   New Zealand Poetry *93*
English in Our Schools *102*
English in Our Universities *114*

3. Meanwhile in the World

Barry Humphries – Contemporary *129*
Stephen Spender – Inside the Great 'O' *138*
Ezra Pound's Rapallo *145*
Ezra Pound – A Storm in His Luggage *152*
Craig Raine – A Celebration *157*
Allen Ginsberg – King of the May *161*
Another Contemporary – Thomas Keneally *165*

Ted Hughes, Sylvia Plath and the Ironies of
  Literary Reputation *170*
E.E.Cummings – Petal by Petal *173*
David Malouf goes Elliptical *180*
The Death of a Book *184*
Theroux's Naipaul and New Zealand's 'Malcolm' *189*

4. Thinking Aloud – Thinking Allowed?

The View from Mt Eden *197*
What I Believe *200*
Remembering the Fifties *207*
Second Thoughts on The Death of the Body *209*
The Treaty and the Emperor's Clothes *211*
Why Do I Like It Then? *214*
Te Papa – A Linguistic Approach *217*
Left, Right, Left ... *219*

5. In Conversation

With Harry Ricketts, 1985 *225*
With Dennis McEldowney, 1991 *232*
With Fleur Adcock, 1991 *247*
With Terry Locke, 1996 *260*

6. The Scholar Persists

Shelley's Constantia *271*

Index *282*

Acknowledgements

My thanks to the editors of journals in which some of these pieces first appeared: (New Zealand) *Evening Post, Landfall, Listener, Metro, Stage and Radio Record,* and *Sunday Star*; (United Kingdom) *Commonwealth,* the *Independent, London Magazine, London Review of Books, PN Review, Times Literary Supplement, Verse*; (Australia) Australian Broadcasting Service, *Scripsi, Sydney Morning Herald*; (France) *Le Nouvel Observateur*; (Germany) *Chelsea Hotel, Merian.*

Thanks also to the universities and institutions which invited me to lecture and entertained me as a guest – University of Canterbury (John Garrett Lecture); the University of Otago in conjunction with the Australasian Universities Languages and Literatures Association; the Alexander Turnbull Library; the University of Tübingen; the University of Stockholm; Georgian Court College, New Jersey; and St John's College, Oxford.

Introduction

In 1986 I took early retirement from the university to write full time. Even before I enrolled as a first year undergraduate I had thought of writing as my vocation, and knew that, if it was to be in New Zealand, there would have to be employment as well. Teaching was to be my work – school-teaching, I imagined; so academic success, a lectureship, a senior lectureship, a professorship, were all pluses – unexpected bonuses. I wrote fiction when I could, criticism because it was a natural extension of my scholarship and teaching, and poems when they decided to be written. It was a better life than I had ever supposed would be available to me. Doors opened, not only in New Zealand, but everywhere in the English-speaking world. After teaching in an Australian university, and post-graduate work in England, I had come back to New Zealand in 1960 because I was a literary nationalist – something that no longer means a great deal to me, but which then seemed full of glitter and promise. My two mentors – Allen Curnow and Frank Sargeson – were my examples of what a New Zealand writer should be and do. Dan Davin, on the other hand, whose desk in Oxford I had seen covered with New Zealand maps, reference books and newspaper clippings, represented the expatriate writer trying to hold onto his subject as it slipped away from him.

Decisions of that kind, to stay or to leave, mattered a great deal in those days. The distances were vast (five weeks by sea), travel expensive relative to everything else, communications between 'here' and 'there' slow. We were still a colony; and the fact that New Zealand intellectuals (I mean myself) asserted we were not, only served to demonstrate that the break with the 'mother country' was not yet complete. The stridency, the insistence, were part of the completing.

When I compare my own beginnings as a writer with those of my daughter, Charlotte Grimshaw, I see the magnitude of the change. A young writer begins now knowing there are, and have been, New Zealand writers of consequence, that there are local publishers competing for New Zealand books, that those books are bought, read, discussed and studied in our schools and universities, that there are grants and prizes for writers and lending right payments for use of their books in libraries. There is, quite simply, an industry. None of this was so four and five decades ago. Not everything about the change is good, and I will be found from time to time in this book remembering nostalgically the days when our writers were hardy independent souls who stood alone, officially unrecognised, making their own small public and their own fine books. But it would be absurd to complain because the present is less than perfect. New Zealand writing has arrived. It flourishes. Three – or to borrow from E.M. Forster – two, cheers for it!

Increasingly over my years in the university there was a conflict between what my work required of me and what I wanted most to be doing. Fiction, in particular, was difficult. I needed a long run at the first draft of any novel. Without that, the fiction always seemed to break into sections – the one I wrote last summer, the one from the year before that, the one I was writing now. I was always pasting over cracks, and seeing them through the paste.

After I reached forty-five I slowly removed myself from teaching. I stepped down from my chair and took a three-year research fellowship, during which I wrote a critical book on Pound and Modernism, edited the short stories of Maurice Duggan, put together a collection of my own critical essays – did, in other words, all the things I had proposed doing when I applied for the post – and still at the end of it had six months in which to write my second published novel, *All Visitors Ashore*. After that, in what were to be my last three years of teaching, I instituted Auckland University's first class in creative writing (poets Greg O'Brien, Chris Price, and Andrew Johnston, film maker Garth Maxwell, writer and journalist Tim Wilson, and a number of others, all passed through it unscathed) and prepared the ground for the final severance. At the age of fifty-three it was done. I took off in August 1986 to teach at the Yeats Summer School in Sligo, and stayed on a couple of months, writing and meeting literary friends. Already, during those three years on the research fellowship, a pattern had been established of nine or ten months of the year at a desk in Auckland, and two – occasionally three (and once six) – abroad in England and Europe, and sometimes North America.

A desk was kept for me in the Auckland English Department, and a mail box. I was Professor Emeritus; I had life membership of the senior common room. But I found I seldom went near the place. It belonged to my past. And in any case, though I had colleagues there who were, and would remain, my very good friends, the university was changing in ways that seemed alien. From one side, political pressures for social amelioration were determining outcomes which should have been reached on academic grounds; from the other, commercial considerations, equally alien to the idea of a university, were reshaping tertiary institutions and their relation to society at large. It was as if two enemy armies had set aside their differences while they closed on the territory which they would divide between them while remaining implacable opposites. If I had been a cartoonist I would have represented the university in those years as a nut about to be cracked. One head of the nut-cracker would have been Roger Douglas, the other Geoffrey Palmer. Since that time things have got worse.

As for English departments, which were my professional concern: in New Zealand, as everywhere in the Western world, theory was gradually replacing practice as the dominant force. Scholars continued to write literary history, critics to distinguish and dissect; but they were becoming subdued, nervous, lacking in confidence, fearful of being 'out of date' (as if there is a use-by date on knowledge and intelligence!) – either ashamed or resentful. Theorists, on the other hand – neo-Marxist, feminist, anti-racist, post-colonialist – were noisily dismantling the canon, denying all authority to what had been called the Great Tradition, and replacing civilised literary discourse with an occult language available only to the initiated, while behind their backs Commerce, which 'in theory' they deplored, was quietly taking over the institution that employed them.* No place illustrates so often and so clearly as a university does the fact that wisdom and high intelligence are not necessarily, or even often, co-incident.

In this climate, it seemed to me, the best of literary journalism became more than ever important. Writers for the literary papers were answerable to readers who could choose to go elsewhere. Their job was to write at once intelligently and intelligibly; to bring literature to life, and life to literature; to exercise, extend and entertain lively minds. A literary paper addressed itself still (even if the notion was now widely rejected by the theorists) to the common reader. And among the very best papers offering that kind of writing in the English-speaking world was Karl Miller's† *London Review of Books,* for which I wrote over a period of about fifteen years.

The pattern of my working day after I left the university was almost invariably the same. The morning – in fact until at least 1 p.m. – was spent on my major project (usually a novel, but sometimes poems, more recently a movie script). In the afternoon I might return to the major project, but tried as far as possible to keep that time for secondary work – reviews, literary articles, public lectures, a column – whatever of that kind I was currently doing to supplement my income. It is this secondary occupation that has provided the material from which the present book has been pieced together.

But it has all been reconsidered, much of it revised, some rewritten. Things have come out and things have been added. Some pieces are entirely new, or so unlike their first appearance as to count as new. The intention has been not simply to aggregate discrete items, but rather to select, arrange, make

---

* Within a week of writing this I read in the newspaper that the University of Auckland was amalgamating certain functions with the Auckland Institute of Technology 'in order to protect its market share'!

† Karl Miller, a dour and clever Scot whom I think of as the Eeyore of the British literary scene, had been in turn literary editor of the *New Statesman,* then of the *Spectator,* and finally editor of the *Listener* before taking the Lord Northcliffe Chair of English at University College London, where he invited me to spend a leave in 1977, lecturing in the Modern Literature course. When he began the *London Review of Books* in 1980, Miller asked me to write for it. Twelve years later Mary-Kay Wilmers, deputy editor and chief backer of the paper, used her position of financial power to edge Miller out and take his place, after which, although I continued to write for it, I felt it lost something of the special flavour and distinction Miller's brilliance had given it, becoming more academic and predictable.

connections while eliminating major overlaps, and to thus shape the whole into a book with a personal character that offers (as the title indicates) a picture of the writer at work – reviewing books, reflecting on writers he has known, giving occasional lectures, offering opinions on public matters. As a book it is, then, somewhat unusual, lying somewhere on the border between literary criticism and literary autobiography.

In Part 2, 'Four Public Lectures', there is a good deal of opinion, strongly stated. The teaching of English, I argue, has a profound influence on society as a whole and is, or should be, a matter of national interest and concern. But that argument is conducted within a literary and academic context, which is my area of professional expertise. Writers, however, live in the world, not just in literature. And though it will be found that I insist on the distinction between what is literary and what is political, the two interact.

Throughout my life I have been, intellectually if not always actively (as the French would say) *engagé*. Politics for me began in childhood, in my family (I joined the Labour Party at the age of seven), and has never ceased, though it hasn't consistently found public expression; and because conflict is more newsworthy than a well-turned sentence or a well-told story, this engagement has from time to time given me attention that has only a tenuous connection with fiction, poetry and literary criticism.

I never minded vigorous debate – in fact I enjoyed it; and during the years of my involvement in protest against the war in Vietnam, or during the 1981 Springbok tour (to take the two most public examples), it didn't greatly worry me that some people would gladly have seen me strung up from a lamp post. They were not *my* people. I had my constituency, so to speak; and when the local chemist couldn't let me pass his shop but had to come raging out to tell me that if we let communism win in Vietnam it would soon sweep down through the Pacific and take us over, that was a little comedy which made my day.

During the 1980s all that changed in a way I should have foreseen but which came as a shock. I expressed public doubts about government policy in relation to Maori issues and issues of gender equity, and all at once the roof fell in on me. I discovered why, or rather how, the apostate is hated with greater ferocity than the enemy. Arrested in 1981 on Hamilton's Rugby Park I had felt like Daniel emerging from the lion's den. Now it was as if Daniel had demanded better working conditions for lions. I had lost one constituency; and if I had gained another, it was either silent and invisible or, seen and heard, was not, on the whole, one I would have chosen.

The battles which followed were unpleasant; though, looking back, the statements of mine which gave most offence all seem moderate in tone and rational in argument. There was my suggestion that the representation of Maori texts in Ian Wedde's *Penguin Book of New Zealand Verse* was more wishful than historically accurate. There was my questioning of whether the Treaty of Waitangi should be given the constitutional force which first the government, and then the courts, were according it. There was my conservatism on matters of teaching English language and literature, and my questioning of the place of te reo Maori in that teaching. There was the argument over my part in the 1990 purchase of a London flat for New Zealand writers, and the *Frontline* programme which followed. There was the fuss about the *Faber Book of South Pacific Stories* and the withdrawal of four writers after they had signed contracts for the inclusion of their stories.

These matters were not all – or not obviously – connected. But what was continuous, I felt, was my new identity as an apostate, which manifested itself most clearly in my repeated questioning of how 'equal opportunity' and 'positive discrimination' could ever be reconciled. My insistence that no positive discrimination on the basis of race or sex could ever be made without a negative discrimination on the same basis seems to me as true and unanswerable now as it was when I stated it. I don't, and didn't, say one should never swerve from a moral principle; but I did, and do, say that the swerve, if made, needs to be recognised for what it is – needs to be discussed openly, justified, and made, if at all, with great caution and care. Apartheid, after all, was positive discrimination in favour of a racial minority – the Whites.

What I had looked for was open discussion. What I got most often was abuse. If I should ever write an autobiography I would have to find a way of dealing with these conflicts without seeming either to complain or to recant, neither of which I would wish to do. I mention them here because a few of their occasions and echoes will be found in the present book, chiefly in Part 4, which I've called 'Thinking Aloud – Thinking Allowed?' Not to represent them at all would be to give an incomplete picture of 'the writer at work'. But it is important to recognise that these debates, which have had such disproportionate public attention, are properly represented by the space they get in this collection – a relatively small proportion of the total. I was, I am, I will remain, primarily committed to the English language and its literatures; but I live in the world, I have opinions and a voice, I am temperamentally predisposed to doubt official statements and policies, and I believe in debate. If there is a programme, a campaign, an undeclared war going on in this book, it is not in favour of this or that policy but in favour of open discussion, without cant and hypocrisy, without stridency and without fear.

Insofar as this is a book of literary criticism (and in large part that is what it is) it is the first I have published since *Answering to the Language* in 1989, and I see no reason why the final words of the introduction to that book should not be repeated here. Saying that I was addressing myself to the common reader, I concluded:

> For that reason I think there is no important difference in tone, in vocabulary, or in the demands they make, between my academic papers and my reviews for journals. I am not interested in arcane dialogue. I would like, where possible, to be understood.

Part 1

New Zealand

Reviews and Reminiscences

Janet Frame, Janet Clutha and Karl Waikato

I first met Janet Frame early in 1955 when she was living in the disused army hut in Frank Sargeson's garden that had been his home until his bach was built, and had since been occupied for brief periods by Maurice Duggan and Renate Prince. (The next after Frame would be Kevin Ireland.) I was twenty-two. Janet was thirty but in many ways seemed much younger, having spent most of the previous decade in psychiatric institutions after being diagnosed as schizophrenic. That long incarceration had increased rather than alleviated the extreme shyness and sensitivity which had caused her social problems and self-destructive tendencies. She had had over two hundred applications of ECT (electro-convulsive therapy) and had been selected for a leucotomy (severing the frontal lobes of the brain) when the medical team dealing with her case discovered that some of her short stories had been published as a book and won a prize. The question then arose whether it was right to interfere so radically with a brain that could produce prize-winning fiction.

So the surgery that would have destroyed her creative powers and personality was averted. Her treatment was changed and she was soon released. But she carried with her the 'guilt' of knowing that others did not have books to save them; and the bitter knowledge that she had been robbed of eight crucial years.

By taking her in, providing a place where she could live and write, Frank Sargeson, she later said, saved her life. It was there she wrote *Owls Do Cry*, her first, and in New Zealand probably still her most widely read, novel.

On one of my early visits to Sargeson's house that year, before I had met Frame, he read to me over lunch, and then showed me, what he called a poem, not telling me who the author was, and asking what I thought of it. I was immensely struck by a sort of child's-eye freshness and clarity in the images (one of which, I remember, was 'pepper-pot breast of the thrush'), and I told Sargeson I thought the lines were poetry but that together they were not a poem. He laughed and was satisfied with that, and told me he had extracted the lines from the opening pages of a novel being written by his

---

A short article commissioned by the German magazine, *Merian*, appeared (in German) in August 1996. In rewriting and expanding it I added extracts from letters I wrote to Frame, and about her to Frank Sargeson, copies of which were sent me by Frame's biographer, Michael King. In its final form it was joint winner of the *Landfall* Essay competition for 1999 awarded by University of Otago Press.

new guest, Janet Frame, and was sending them to his London publisher, John Lehmann, editor of the *London Magazine.*

Janet was at that time intensely shy and withdrawn, a shadowy figure who, the first couple of times my wife, Kay, and I visited in the evening, came into the room and listened silently and withdrew. But as the visits continued she was drawn into the conversation. After a few weeks we were four friends, entirely relaxed together. Frame was writing her novel; Sargeson was working on a play; I was an MA student, but also writing a verse play in a modern setting structured on Racine's *Andromaque*;* Kay was a librarian and a great reader. My reading was governed by my studies; but Sargeson took Kay in hand, plying her with books and discussing them with her when they'd been read, rather as Ezra Pound did with young protégées.

We talked about books and writers, and about ourselves. There were reminiscences, verbal games, jokes, gossip. We swam together and went for walks. Once the four of us went to a literary party together. We'd been there I suppose ten minutes when Sargeson noticed that Janet was missing. She hadn't been able to cope with so many people, and had run home.

On another occasion we took the bus along the eastern bays of the Hauraki Gulf to swim at a beach overlooked by a headland in which there were gun emplacements. Frank wreathed himself in seaweed, used a stick as his pipe, and did a Pan-dance in the shallows, lifting his knees high like a figure on an ancient urn or bas relief. Suddenly the guns boomed over our heads. The army was doing a practice shoot out to sea – blanks, no doubt, but the sound was huge. Frank dropped his pipe; Janet shrieked, panicked (did anyone make the etymological connection with Frank's dance?), rushed from the water and had to be soothed and reassured.

In 1956 I took my first university job, in Australia. Letters came from Sargeson. Frame's novel was finished and had been accepted for publication. That was a great step forward; but she was not an easy living companion, and he was steering her now towards travel overseas. Along with others called upon by Sargeson, we sent a few pounds to help with her fare.

Two years later we were living in England. A small scribbled letter came from Janet telling us that she had been unable to cope with life in the big city and had checked herself into the Maudsley Psychiatric Hospital. She asked would we visit her. Sargeson had been asking for news of her, and in a letter dated 28 January 1958 I gave him an account of our visit, part of which went as follows:

> But I'm really writing to tell you that we drove up to London (through snow and ice, like the lad who was inclined to vice …) on Friday night, and talked to Janet for almost 2 hours on Sunday morning.

---

* It was never published or performed, though it impressed Sargeson. Decades later, and of course quite unaware of my youthful attempt, my Oxford friend Craig Raine wrote a modern verse play (called *'1953'*, and set in a fictional Italy after a Second World War which the Axis Powers have won) structured on the same French original.

We called on Saturday but she got frightened and of course wouldn't see us. I talked to the nurse who said she is there voluntarily, and that she gives notice every so often that she is going to leave. However, as she hasn't anywhere specific to go the doctors always talk her out of it. She sometimes packs her bags and even sets off, but then comes back the same day. She is allowed out in the daytime. They know she writes, though she denies it to the nurses.

I went back and asked the nurse if there was any chance of seeing her on Sunday, as Janet had sent a message saying she wanted to talk to us but was just too scared. Apparently Janet saw me come back and decided I looked so scholarly and harmless there was nothing to be frightened of. I rang on Sunday morning and the sister said J. would see me.

This time we were admitted to her room. She was in bed with the blankets up to her neck and wearing dark glasses. The old extreme shyness had returned. She wanted to see us, but she was hiding. My way of coping with this was just to behave normally and wait for the fear to pass, which it very quickly did. In no time the blankets were pushed down, the shades were removed, she was sitting up, she was out of bed, and the three of us were joking together, back on the old footing of good companionship.

We heard a lot about her adventures in Ibiza, after which, she told us, she had come to London because she 'wanted to see everything in a cold light'. She had finished a novel about Ibiza ('all very *Daily Mail* and no good at all') and begun another which she couldn't get straight. There had been 'a traffic jam' in her head, which was the cause of her present troubles. She felt that everyone was waiting for her to publish something more after *Owls Do Cry,* and this pressure wasn't helping. I went on in my letter:

> She also said that speaking Spanish almost all the time [in Ibiza] made her respect English much more when she came to write in it, and that it improved her writing and made her much more conscious of how she was using the language ... (She was reading a book on semantics when I arrived.)

Visits continued, though infrequently while we were living in Bristol; but then we moved to London, and a letter I wrote to her on 8 May 1959 catches something of the tone of our encounters:

> I was going to come and see you again this weekend, but have to go and see my friend Don Smith* race at White City (he is a greyhound), and to an objectionable luncheon (not to be confused with a lunch) on Sunday. So it will probably be the following weekend ...
>
> They hung Marwood this morning, which is, I believe, the law taking its course (or coarse) – a process which various magistrates, Sir Reginald Manning Bullshit, Mr Butler, and our Gracious Sovereign Majesty, Eliza II, are all regretfully,

---

* D.I.B. Smith had been a fellow student in the MA class at Auckland and was later my fellow professor there. He was having a brilliant season as a half-miler in Europe, and the following year ran for New Zealand at the Olympic Games in Rome.

almost tearfully, powerless to prevent. Isn't it terrible that such things as the law are allowed to roam our streets, taking their course ... But then what can you do? You can't hang the law. It is good to feel one lives in a country where everything possible is done in such circumstances.

It was around this time that she changed her name by deed poll and became Janet Clutha, which had the odd and appropriate effect of turning her original name, the one which appears on her books, into a pseudonym. Replying to her note telling me of the change I wrote, 'You are indeed fed by the cold snows and flow deeper and more powerful than any other among the hot rocks. I am still ambling in green pastures.' And I signed myself Karl Waikato.

In August of that year Sargeson, who had been trying to extract a manuscript of new work from Frame in order to make a case for further support from the Literary Fund, wrote:

> I just can't get anything out of Janet, though it's heartening to hear she may now be in receipt of some sickness benefit. But I seem to put a foot wrong every time I write to her – all told, everything her friends do for her seems only to make her more guilt ridden and miserable.

By September he was briefly in a mood to wash his hands of her:

> You shouldn't worry about Janet ... It's sad and hopeless and too great a burden for any of us ... It's not that she won't co-operate. She can't.

It was at the Maudsley that Janet came under the care of an enlightened young doctor, R.H. Cawley, who was to become her personal friend. Interviewing Frame, Cawley soon recognised that he was dealing with a brilliant and subtle mind. He said he would like to speak to someone who had known her in New Zealand, and she suggested I write to him.

When we met, Cawley asked me first did I think Janet was 'mad'. This, I have since thought, was more likely a test for me than for her. I said I thought her completely sane – in fact knew her to be – but that (speaking metaphorically) she was lacking one layer of protective skin, and this was a lack which had been made worse by her incarceration at a time when young people need to be out in the world learning social skills and defences.

Cawley told me that Frame was their most interesting patient, that all the qualified staff had taken an interest in her, and that they were divided between those who thought the New Zealand diagnosis of schizophrenia was correct, and those like himself who believed she had none of the standard classifiable mental illnesses. He also told me he considered the number of ECTs she had been subjected to in New Zealand had been 'barbaric'. Cawley's later account, and Frame's autobiography, make clear that the hospital's final verdict ruled out schizophrenia.

Reflecting many years later on Frame's problem, or condition, Cawley suggested it might have been described as 'an identity crisis or an existential dilemma'. It was, he said, 'something very real, unnervingly elusive'. The way out of it, he could see, was to be found in her writing, and in the identity that would bring. He encouraged her, as Sargeson had done, and her next book, *Faces in the Water,* a direct account of her experiences as a psychiatric patient, was dedicated to him.

But things in London clearly got worse for her before they began to get better. On 4 March 1959 I wrote to Sargeson:

> I've had your letter (18 Jan) some time now. One reason I have put off writing is that I meant to see Janet again first. I just have to admit to myself that I have been putting off the visit – there is always a reason of course, but I could have seen her by now if there wasn't some inner reluctance holding me up. Not that it is painful in any noticeable way seeing her. But maybe she is an uncomfortable symbol for the mind to assimilate – very gay, not in the least sentimental, her criticism of everything exceptionally sharp and objective, detached, and her hair standing out straight all round her head (no doubt electrified by what is below its roots). And now in a locked part of the hospital. She said the last time we visited that she had been 'high' and was locked up for the time being – the time being how long I hate to guess. She pointed vaguely to some marks on her wrists … I hope this doesn't distress you too much. She hasn't changed at all, and is just as frighteningly sane as ever.

Early in *Faces in the Water* Frame writes, 'I was put in a hospital because a great gap opened in the ice floe between myself and the other people whom I watched, with their world, drifting away through a violet-coloured sea. I was alone on the ice.' In clear cool lucid prose she recounts both the distress of a mind overcharged with images, unable to process reality as fast as it came in through the senses, and the day-by-day happenings – brutal, mundane, funny, sordid, terrifying – of life in a psychiatric hospital.

By now people in the literary business were beginning to notice her work. One was Mark Goulden, who became her publisher when she emerged from the Maudsley period. Frame was, he would later declare in his memoir *Mark My Words,* one of only two writers he had dealings with whom he considered to be geniuses. (The other was Dylan Thomas.) But he believed she needed help and direction as a writer. He provided her with a flat in Kensington, gave her several best-seller novels, and recommended that she drop her off-beat manner and dark subject matter in favour of something more conventional. Goulden records that the novel she then wrote began wonderfully (by which I think he means conventionally) 'with every prospect of developing into a great book'. But before it was finished Frame had returned to New Zealand, and when the completed manuscript arrived 'we were back to the old depressing atmosphere of mad people and doom and despair'.

Frame went her own way – the way of the 'genius' that Goulden had been prescient enough to recognise and foolish enough to think he could take charge of; but she later took a small revenge by describing, in her autobiography, her first meeting with him. 'I sat in the deep easy chair and thought, so this is my English publisher. I thought he looked like a bookie or a "spiv".' Nor did his wife escape punishment:

> I took the lift to the top floor, rang the bell, and was admitted by Mrs Goulden, tall, dark, regal, with a remarkable resemblance, I thought, to the Queen of Spades in a film I had lately seen, *The Manchurian Candidate.* She wore black and had an air of having lived inside her skin as if it were a house, polished, prepared daily, with herself the mistress in total possession. She was not an immediate person; there was a porch, an entrance hall where one waited to be received.

—

Sweetness and light. But then came 'that story'.

Published in 1963 but written earlier, it was about a brilliant young man who married a beautiful young woman and lived a romantic life on the beach writing poetry. But (to make a short meal of its twenty-five pages) he became an academic, wrote critical reviews of his rivals, lost his talent, and went bald, while the beautiful wife became motherly but had no children, and they were left with the 'fear' that would 'devour their lives'. It was not a very good or successful piece of fiction, but that was not what concerned Frank Sargeson when he read it. The problem was that many many details were derived from the life and doings of the Steads. It seemed like a curse on them, a malediction.

Frank considered it (he later wrote to me) 'an insanity'. And he felt sure I would see it because I'd been appointed to edit the second World's Classics *New Zealand Short Stories* (he had recommended Dennis McEldowney but Dan Davin had over-ruled him) and would be reading all recent collections. So what was to be done?

My recollection is that Frank more or less frog-marched the wicked girl to our house for dinner-and-apology – though we, Kay and I, had no idea what was going on. There was no spoken apology, just a constrained (and therefore unusual) atmosphere until they were leaving, when Janet dived deep into her bag and extracted a boxed set of her two-volume collection of stories published in New York. It was her own set with her name crossed out in each copy and replaced by 'Now inscribed to Karl, Kay and Oliver [we had by-passed the story's jinx and produced our first child] with my good wishes and apologies'. Apologies? I was still in the dark – until I got to the last story of the second volume. My immediate reaction was hurt.

Then came a letter from Janet – a very beautiful letter on ugly yellow paper. The first page explained that the story was not really about me. The second acknowledged in effect that it was. 'Perhaps I voiced my fears, perhaps I tinged them with feminine jealousies and hopes.'

I was still reeling from the surprise of it all, and my response was entirely polite but chilly – unforgiving. Her response to my response was a single sentence, blazing with anger. I threw it in the wastepaper basket.

For two years we didn't meet. Then I was invited to Dunedin by the Otago student literary society, and stayed with Charles Brasch. We went to visit Janet and the story was never mentioned. It was over, gone, understood, signed off.

Her room looked over a deep valley, and she said, in her Marilyn Monro voice, that she liked to watch the armies of the rain marching to and fro across it. Charles smiled his custodial smile. It was the sort of 'literary' thing that made him happy, and I remember thinking at once, but not saying, 'You should get out of here, Janet. You can't cook without salt.'

I have a photograph of the three of us outside Charles's cottage at Broad Bay on the Otago Peninsula, taken by Ruth Dallas – Janet sitting, smiling straight at the camera from behind the safety screen of dark glasses; Charles clinging fruitily to a verandah post and smiling down at her; me leaning back against another post, pencil thin and formal, with a goatee beard, looking like a Viennese doctor or a revolutionary Russian.

The following year I met Iris Murdoch for the first time, and wrote to Sargeson:

> I.M. reminded me in some ways of Janet, though on the surface far more formidable and commanding. But I detected the same disbelief in the world around her, the same dislike of being the subject of attention and dislike of not being it, the same apparent diffidence covering an enormous self-consuming ego.

—

In 1972 I was the second Winn-Manson (as it was then called) Mansfield Fellow in Menton. Janet followed two years later. When she had completed her time there an article by Anton Vogt appeared in the *Listener* complaining of the conditions in which the Fellow was expected to work. Formerly a Wellington poet and Teachers' College lecturer, Vogt had left New Zealand in the 1960s with great éclat, announcing (also in the pages of the *Listener*) that he would never return to our benighted shores. This was a vow he kept, and he had recently moved to Menton where he helped Janet, and later other Mansfield fellows, find their bearings. Though his complaints about the Mansfield room below the Villa Isola Bella were overstated, they weren't without foundation; but I felt strongly that these problems shouldn't be aired publicly. The fellowship was still precarious, and might vanish. Improvements should be worked for out of sight. In the meantime I wrote an article for the *Listener* which I called 'A Room much Maligned'. It was accompanied by a photograph Marti Friedlander had taken of me in the room, and I made my recollections as up-beat as I could, recording (truthfully) that my experience in Menton had been positive and stimulating.

In what for her was a rare – in fact probably unique – venture into public controversy, Janet wrote a letter to the editor backing up Vogt and mentioning her 'yellow urine bucket'. Soon afterwards, as if by way of appeasement, she sent me a clipping about the Yeats sisters, found in a book once owned by Richard Le Gallienne which she'd bought in Menton. My reply to this was jaunty, faux-Mansfield and meant to amuse, I suppose because that was my mood of the moment, but also because I wanted to make a point without seeming heavy handed or unduly censorious.

> Dear fellow Fellow (or fellow former-Fellow),
>
> How nice of you to send the Yeats clipping of 1939 – thank you very much. I am chirpy this spring because I am sonneteering at a prodigious clip and in fact will direct one at anyone's eyebrow at the drop of a hat …
>
> What a grumpy ungrateful old party you sounded in the *Listener* (*they* wet my books, *they* got my name wrong) – we old boys and girls of L'Ecole Winn-Manson are supposed to front the world with a smile and a song. Buck up there Clutha, shoulders back, girl!
>
> I have a 'new' old desk in my shed, and a brass lamp, and some pear blossom (freckled) and an Indian mat, and here I am writing the best sonnets in the world …
>
> Who resurrected Vogt out of his European grave? I thought we had heard the last of him.
>
> Well, my dear, I must simply *fly* back to my knitting.
>
> Goodbye sweet aureole.
>
>   Karl
>
> PS And just WHAT (pray) is a 'yellow urine bucket'? To which noun does the adjective attach?

There was no answer, and a long silence.

—

But towards the end of that decade Janet and I must both have been in a mood to look back. Writing to her in August 1979 about *Living in the Maniototo,* which I was about to review for the *Melbourne Age,* I said:

> I had an idea in the weekend that you and I should write a novel together. I would write the first 20 pages and send it to you and then you would write the next 20 and send it back. I thought I (it would be first person – two characters) would be Curl Skidmore; you would be Cecelia Skyways. Frank would figure as Melior Farbro, or the old master. The first 20 pages would be devoted to what happened and didn't happen at Farbro's place 25 years ago. I have ideas about how it would go on.

We were both to be in Wellington soon and I suggested a meal together.

Janet agreed about the meal. Much more surprising she wrote, 'That's a good idea to write 20 pages each of a novel. Frarbro's Place [Frarbro was Janet's spelling]. Seriously, that time should be recorded before it's forgotten.'

I remember that we met and had the meal together at The Settlement in Willis Street. But did we talk about the novel? Or had I already gone too far with it to want to share it? I only know that then, or a little later, it took hold of me, took off, took its own course, and couldn't be shared, not even with a master craftsperson who knew as thoroughly as I did the foundation of fact on which any such story would be built. It was written very fast; and then, once completed, was something I couldn't bring myself to re-read. It was consigned to an iron trunk and remained there until some time in 1983 when I met a London publisher, Carol O'Brien, who knew some of my work and asked whether I had a novel to offer her. I said I had one, but couldn't bring myself to read it. 'You don't have to read it,' she said. 'I'll do that.'

In 1984 *All Visitors Ashore* came out with Harvill in London. And meanwhile Janet had written the second volume of her autobiography, *An Angel at my Table,* which in its later chapters deals with 'Farbro's Place', acknowledging the companionship, friendship, love that existed among four people there at that time. 'The friendship of Karl and Kay,' she wrote, 'filled my life giving me at last a place in my own years, for I felt I had lost so many years that I could not determine my "real" age.'

But far more important at Esmonde Road was what Sargeson supplied to all three of us – something which came also (in those days) with a university education in the humanities, but from our mentor came with the extra charge of passion, and with the hands-on sense, almost, of an apostolic succession. Of her reading under Sargeson's guidance, she writes:

> There is a freedom born from the acknowledgment of greatness in literature, as if one gave away what one desired to keep, and in giving, there is a new space cleared for growth.

The dedication to *An Angel at My Table* includes Frank Sargeson, Karl and Kay Stead. The dedication to *All Visitors Ashore,* which came out in the same year, reads *To whom it may concern.*

—

Le style, c'est l'homme – or if it isn't, something is wrong.

Making one of my regular visits to Esmonde Road a dozen or so years after I was first in the same room there with Sargeson and Frame, I found the old man ready for me with a grin of pleasure and a small book on the counter/bench across which he dispensed tea or lemora. The title was revealed – *New Zealand Short Stories* by Joan Stevens – but he held something over the four-picture illustration on the cover while I had to guess which writers were represented. There was Mansfield of course, and Sargeson himself. The other two (and this was what had pleased him so much, and the surprise for me) were Frame and Stead.

The Mansfield story analysed was 'The Daughters of the Late Colonel', Sargeson's was 'An Affair of the Heart', Frame's was 'The Reservoir', and mine, 'A Fitting Tribute'. What seems interesting now, looking back, is that, though Frame and I both owed so much to Sargeson personally and professionally, we owed him next to nothing in terms of style. My story was a fantasy of a kind which made a complete break with Sargesonian realism.

Frame's was one of those stories in which a child's literal focus on reality affects language itself, giving it a sharpness usually associated with poetry:

> The Reservoir was the end of the world ...
>
> 'The Reservoir!'
>
> The damp smell of the pine needles caught in our breath. There were no birds, only the constant sighing of the trees. We could see the water clearly now; it lay ... in an almost perfect calm which we knew to be deceptive – else why were people so afraid of the Reservoir? The fringe of young pines on the edge, like toy trees, subjected to the wind, sighed and told us their sad secrets.

Frame's work is all based on her sense that language is a paradigm of reality, a precarious magical structure continually threatened with breakdown. In an interview she said of one of her novels:

> I wrote it as a result of a visit to the dentist in London. He was very vague. He went to the window and he looked out and there was a patch of blue in the sky. He said, 'What I wouldn't give to be in Sussex!' Then he said, 'Rinse whilst I'm gone.' I hadn't heard anyone say 'whilst' and it was that word that prompted me to write the whole book.

An anecdote of that kind is always told by Frame in a tone that seems to tremble on the brink of laughter. Her voice and articulation are bell-clear, almost child-like, and key words are hesitated over, as if she and her interlocutor should pause to marvel over the huge pretence they are engaging in, behaving as if they can hold chaos in check by the device of linguistic communication. The same sense of marvelling at itself, at times mocking itself, pervades the best of her writing. It represents, I think, a scepticism native to post-colonial societies, where national identity is insecure and the social imprint faint. Add Frame's mental history to her New Zealand background and, with the accident of literary genius, you get this vivid sense that reality is itself a fiction; or that our grasp upon it is no more than a linguistic convention or pretence.

It's a view perhaps not properly described as despairing nor tragic, though it can seem at times intensely black. There is pity for victims. But beyond that there is a sort of universal dark laughter. Nothing else seems to Frame finally appropriate – and she takes pleasure in it. Above all she loves language ('Rinse whilst I'm gone'), loves literature, loves poetry. It's as if she's saying, How marvellous, when our fate is so terrible, that we should have such toys! The great nineteenth and twentieth century anthology of English poetry, *The Golden Treasury of Songs and Lyrics,* and the collected works of Shakespeare, must have been the reading in her formative years that made the most durable impression, and their influence is everywhere in her work. Again and again, when Kay and I were helping Carin Svensson with cruxes in her translation into Swedish of *Living in the Maniototo,* we were able to locate the source of phrase or image or echo in *The Golden Treasury.*

Frame's other mode is satire, where she seems to want to punish the world, and especially the world of 'sanity' and bourgeois certainty, which so misunderstood and damaged her in her youth, and withheld love from the woman it declared to be 'mad'. In this mode there is a bitter wit which can often be self-defeating because it diminishes her fictional characters, and consequently the world they inhabit, to the point where the reader's belief in them is undermined. Her novels characteristically veer between magic and satire, with islands of realism between.

Frame has always been respected by the literary community who know her work. In America her novels have customarily received serious and very public attention in magazines like *Time*. But she had no great commercial success until the publication of her three volumes of autobiography, collected under the title of the second, *An Angel at my Table,* the name given also to the Jane Campion movie, which won awards at Cannes. Here was revealed, in the recollections of her early years, the extremes of her experience – the wonder of books and language, the shame of poverty, the horror of the accidental deaths of her two sisters, the mental breakdown.

But Frame's overriding purpose in writing the autobiography seems to have been to clear her name, so to speak, of the stigma of madness – to show in particular how she came to be wrongly diagnosed as schizophrenic. This is a subject which research may show she simplifies a good deal, since diagnoses of her case were always various and contradictory; but there can be no doubt that the long incarceration of her youth was needless, and the treatment brutal and unhelpful.

Recently I was visited by a German student who had been travelling around the country talking to literary and academic people about Janet Frame. She came to me last and I gave her my impressions, based on my knowledge of the person and my reading of the work. Just before returning to Germany she wrote me a card in which she said, 'Our conversation was very positive to me because you are the first person I have talked to who speaks of Frame, not with pity, but with respect for her brilliance, and appreciation of her sense of humour.'

This made me aware of the extent to which the New Zealand literary community (which has, in recent years, repeatedly, and not unreasonably, nominated her for the Nobel Prize) has got into the habit of speaking about Frame, not just uncritically, but in hushed and reverent tones, as if we were gathered at her bedside. Her talent is huge beyond praise; but I'm sure she would prefer to be honoured for her strengths rather than pitied as a victim.

—

Janet has lived in many houses over the years, always moving on, while Kay and I have stayed at the same address in Parnell. Once, driving up from Wellington with two of our children, we called on her, I think it was in Palmerston North. What I remember is her sitting room. It must have been quite large but it was full of furniture. Janet led us around the edge of it, as if through a path at the edge of the woods, to a gas heater in a very small cleared space where we drank tea and ate chocolate biscuits and talked about the past. At the front of the house was the room where she worked. Special cladding had been put over the outside to keep out noise. I remembered Sargeson telling us that Proust wrote in a cork-lined room.

The last of her houses I saw was in Avondale before she moved finally (but in three stages) back to her roots in the South. It had a huge pool table which she was planning to replace with a desk of similar proportions. At the back the land sloped down through pines to a tidal creek, all mud and mangroves and crabs at low tide, brimming at the full. She said if only she had a row boat she could go to the supermarket by water. I wrote a poem about it.

In 1992 when I was reviewing a book in which Graham Greene recorded his dreams,* I became more than usually conscious of my own dreams, and took notes of two, one of which was about Janet and went as follows: I was one of a large group of New Zealand writers at tables on a stage, watched by an audience also made up of New Zealand writers who would soon join us. After some speeches there was music and we were to get up and dance in pairs. I didn't want to, and resolved I would not.

Soon it seemed that everyone on the stage was dancing, and I was conspicuously alone at a table near the front, watched disapprovingly by the writers in the body of the hall. I looked around and saw that there was someone still seated – it was Janet – and I remembered she'd written me a letter in which she asked, 'Will you dance with me at my End of the World Party?'

I got up and went over to her, we began to dance, and (in the way things happen in dreams) the stage was suddenly empty, and there was no one in the hall. Janet was still Janet, but she was also another red-head I once knew, a girl called Thelma, a brilliant dancer with whom, as an undergraduate, I used to go dancing at the Civic Wintergarden in Auckland. The lights were very bright, the music was a waltz, the stage was now enormous and expanding, the hall completely empty.

On and on, unseen, Janet/Thelma and I waltzed.

---

* Graham Greene, *A World of My Own: A Dream Diary*.

Lady Chatterley's Glover

I knew Denis Glover over many years, mostly at a distance, and never very well, yet my memories of him are sharper than those of people I have known much better – I suppose because they tend to exist as discrete scenes, with dialogue. He was an actor, always determined to be centre-stage, and he gave himself memorable lines. Here are three examples:

1. Coming out of a poetry reading into one of Christchurch's colonial-neo-faux-Gothic cloisters, Glover, unsteady on his feet, throws himself back against a wall and delivers in his colonial-neo-faux-English English, 'A hearse, a hearse, mey kingdom for a hearse.'
2. Glover, drunk, at one of those Wellington PEN 'national' AGMs of the 1970s, barking from the back of the room, when the Chairman calls for nominations for Vice President, 'Ay nominate Princess Anne's horse.'
3. Three of us on a panel in Auckland, Allen Curnow regrets the numbing effect Mansfield's overseas fame had for a long time on NZ Lit. and recalls a journalist describing her as 'the only peacock in New Zealand's literary garden'.
   I interject, 'Pea-*hen*.'
   Glover corrects: 'Pi-*ha*.'

This curious mix of the satiric and the surreal is typical of Glover's writing, his talk, and his carry-on – as when he applied for the Mansfield-Menton Fellowship saying that if granted it he would work on a collection of prose pieces to be called Lady Chatterley's Glover.

Glover was very heavy, and in his later years his legs were not up to their task. Once Lauris Edmond and I had to ship him from a PEN end of year party to his flat on The Terrace, where the party was to continue. Supporting him on either side, we got him from her car to his door where the key, he told us, was under the mat. Trying to hold him up while bending knees to reach the key, some engineering ratio of weight to whatever was breached, and as disparate a trio of poets as it's possible to imagine was brought together in a heap on the threshold.

Booze has a lot to answer for. Of the three or four significant literary drinkers I have known, Dan Davin functioned the best – though I've heard it said in Oxford that his drinking prevented his getting the top job he aspired to

---
A review of *Denis Glover: His Life* by Gordon Ogilvie, in *New Zealand Books,* May 1999.

in the Clarendon Press. Maurice Duggan was by far the darkest, the most seriously depressed by his habit. Glover was at once the worst and the most cheerful. He made scenes and sometimes wanted to fight, but he seldom harmed anyone but himself. What I found distressing were the intimations (more than confirmed by the present book) that this was a man in the process of destroying himself. Physically, professionally, creatively, socially, Denis Glover appeared over the years to be committing suicide in slow motion, resisting every attempt by those close to him to stop, or at least slow, the process.

After the war he staggered from job to job, sacked, suspended, reinstated, sacked again. When he left Christchurch in 1954 he had lost or left everything – his first wife and only child, the Caxton Press which he started and the Pegasus Press which had followed its example, the Banks Peninsula Cruising Club from which he'd been banished for non-payment of dues, and the Navy Volunteer Reserve, which was trying to recover money he owed the mess funds. He left debts everywhere, including six months' rent, and had misappropriated cash donated by friends for a stone on the grave of his old-salt hero, Mick Stimson.

With Khura, his de facto second wife, he left for Wellington and a new life, much like the old except that he now had an alcoholic playmate. The 'Sings Harry' sequence (and Harry, it occurs to me, was the name of the father who had left Glover and his siblings in their childhood) are looking-back-with-regret poems; and 'Fool's Song' which, slightly revised, became their epigraph, appeared first, Ogilvie tells us, in a letter to Glover's long-lamented wartime lover, Dorée Elkind:

> All my beautiful world is gone.
> Heigh ho for a biscuit,
> And a buttered scone!
> For a dog loves his biscuit
> And a man his buttered scone.

Dorée was a clever, educated woman who might well have known, as I'm sure Glover did, that in eighteenth century literature to 'have a buttered bun' was to have sex with a woman who had just had it with someone else.

There was a time at Paekakariki when I remember Glover and Khura together seemed hospitable, sociable, picturesquely bibulous; but by the end there is no other word for it than degradation. The stories of Khura's death and funeral in this biography are pure Ronald Hugh Morrieson.

At intervals after the war, until she terminated their correspondence in 1967, Glover had written asking Dorée Elkind to come and join him in New Zealand. Dorée, it appears, continued to love him but knew him too well to agree. So when Khura died he called on his abandoned first wife, Mary, suggesting she should rejoin him. Wisely she declined, as did librarian-bibliographers Olive Johnson and Margaret Scott, who were, each in turn, invited to apply. Janet Paul was then wooed, and hesitated long enough to paint the poet's portrait and cause a new vein of lyricism to open. When she declined finally, Glover turned to Lyn, ten years his senior, who became the devoted mother-wife, nurse and drinks-monitor of his final decade.

We all came to think of Glover as 'old', when in truth he was merely damaged. In a 1995 interview with Gordon Ogilvie, Lauris Edmond speaks of helping Glover make a selection of 'not very good stuff': 'It was an old writer gathering up bits and pieces'. I'm sure it didn't occur to her that when she made that remark she was seventy-one, while the Glover she was speaking of had been sixty-one. The 'old writer' she was remembering had been so blasted by booze, so wasted by it, his age in years became irrelevant. People interviewed by Ogilvie recall his being able to hold the thread of an idea in conversation as if that were a remarkable achievement.

Like every poet whose temperament tends towards the Apollonian, Yeats liked to romanticise the Dionysian, the Bohemian, the dissolute; but he knew the waste of energy it represented. Writing of Dowson and Johnson, his alcoholic associates in the Rhymers' Club of the 1890s, he reflects of poets and artists:

> Our fires must burn slowly, and we must constantly turn away and think, constantly analyse what we have done, be content even to have little life outside our work, to show, perhaps, to other men, as little as the watch-mender shows, his magnifying glass caught in his screwed-up eye.

Glover in his younger days was boxer, rugby player, mountaineer and sailor; and the war gave him the chance to show real heroism under fire. He took great pride in all this, a pride he found difficult to deal with, because he'd inherited that curious British snobbery which prizes modesty above achievement. Like Fairburn, but with even greater claim to it, he liked to think of himself as a man of action, a 'neo- Elizabethan', one who disdained the prissy, the fussy, the arty, the girly and the gay.

Artiness can be a great bore; but so can heartiness, its bully cousin. What kind of 'work' is required in order to get the best out of oneself will differ from person to person; but without application of one kind or another, time, energy and talent go to waste. Frank Sargeson's life certainly didn't lack colour, sociability, stout political engagement, or rebellious fun; but he taught by example that writing was work, and that it called for patience, diligence, sobriety, and a basis of good order.

Ogilvie twice quotes me saying that in Glover are found 'some of the sharpest scenes and some of the purest songs in our poetry', and I doubt that anyone would want to argue; but I would add that these treasures, of immeasurable and permanent worth, are few and small, and come, for the most part, early in his career. After that, Glover became a character, a clown, a versifier, something of a charlatan, sometimes a disgrace.

What this book brought home to me most clearly was that his great achievement, apart from 'Sings Harry' and the like, was the Caxton Press –

not just to have set it up, but to have established a local tradition of choosing work solely for its literary quality, and publishing it in books that were finely printed and excellently produced, while sustaining the press financially through job printing. It could almost be said that New Zealand literature, as distinct from random items of literary work published in New Zealand, had its beginnings in that enterprise, far removed from the operations of international commercial publishers which dominate the current scene. Glover and those who worked with him had no one to answer to, no shibboleths to respect, no anxiety about giving offence, no dues owing to anything but the search for good writing and the faith in its efficacy and worth.

This, along with his part in helping Charles Brasch to establish *Landfall*, and his role as Allen Curnow's closest literary collaborator during their Christchurch years and beyond, makes Glover one of the three or four founders of a national literature. Heard at this distance, the note that was struck in the New Zealand writing of the 1930s and 1940s rings bell-like and clear, and Glover deserves all honour for his part in it.

There is an anecdote somewhere in this biography of Glover-in-decline, with his blasted face and collapsing legs, tottering up to a woman he didn't know at a literary gathering and asking whether she would like to go to bed with him. Her reply was an emphatic, 'Thank you, *No!*', to which Glover returned, 'I just didn't want you to feel *left out*.' To Rex Fairburn he wrote:

> I wish I didn't smoke
> I wish I didn't drink
> I wish I didn't poke
> I wish I didn't think
>   But then I wouldn't be
>   Yours faithfully, D.G.

Every Court must have its Fool, whose job is to release the comic irreverence and impiety which are in all of us, but which we collectively agree to repress. For this task he is primed with booze, rewarded with protection and indulgence, and at the same time punished with buffets. Denis Glover had the temperament and talent for the task and carried it out with gusto.

Postscript: For no good reason, but perhaps going on appearance, Glover once decided that I was Jewish. He wrote asking me to confirm this, saying he hoped it was true because he was a keen Zionist – all of which was perhaps no more than an excuse for sending me his latest limerick:

> There was an old 'Ebrew of Auck
> Who was madly affected to pork.
>   He knew what he did
>   Was forbid to a Yid
> But he brandished a knife and a fork.

Mansfield as Poet

To anyone who values Mansfield for the best of her finished fiction, and perhaps even more for the sense, in her posthumously published letters and journals, of a wonderful talent committing itself absolutely and recklessly to the business of writing, the excesses of the Mansfield industry can be irritating and distracting. Without that industry we would not have in print a great deal of the best of her work; but without it we might be able to enjoy her quietly, untroubled by the feeling that there is a New Zealand brass band and a troupe of academic axe-grinders noisily claiming her under the window.

The centenary of her birth in 1988 was marked by interminable libations, lucubrations and re-dedications in Wellington. One product of these was the present edition of her poems, selected by Professor Vincent O'Sullivan.

'Mansfield's poetry', the blurb reminds us, 'has only been known through a handful of anthology pieces ... O'Sullivan has made a fresh selection. The result is an edition which shows Mansfield's poems in a completely new light. It can now be seen that she was innovative, as a poet, to a degree which has never before been recognized.'

Publishers have to sell their books, and I don't suppose O'Sullivan can be blamed for this nonsense; but in the Introduction he does point out that he has restored 'the spontaneity of her own erratic punctuation', and suggests that this scrupulous editing, replacing the 'cosmetic' job done by John Middleton Murry in the 1920s, will make a significant difference, helping to overcome 'that sometimes anaemic image of "Mansfield the poet" ensured by Murry's selection'.

I don't find this to be the case. The problem is that Mansfield, a keenly intelligent and sensitive reader of the great poets, didn't treat her own poetic talent with much respect. She made it too often the vehicle for moments of weakness or whimsy. Her great strengths – of character, of observation, of intelligence – she reserved for letters, journals and fiction.

There have been half a dozen poems worthy of serious attention, and of those, two in particular have been rightly favoured by anthologists (including O'Sullivan). One is the formal sonnet about her brother killed in the First World War – a poem as tight, unflinching, strong and clear in its feeling as the

---

A review of *Poems of Katherine Mansfield*, ed. Vincent O'Sullivan, in the *Times Literary Supplement*, 2 February 1990. This review elicited an angry letter from the Professor of English at Victoria University, Roger Robinson.

best of Wilfred Owen. The other, 'To Stanislaw Wyspianski', is a romantic rhapsodic Whitmanesque piece in which Mansfield speaks out as a woman and a New Zealander, and in which one can see a talent not yet disciplined by pain, but not yet curbed by it either.

For the rest there is a great deal of charm, some examples of the Mansfield wit, and increasingly the sense of a physical decline which robs her poetry of its native vitality. At her best, in prose or verse, Mansfield has the ability to speak right out of the middle of the note. But her poems look increasingly bruised and defeated. The spring goes out of their step. In the end she is simply sorry for herself. She has every reason to be, but it doesn't make for the best use of her talent.

O'Sullivan pads out his selection by including early prose sketches which she called vignettes, and which by way of justification he calls prose poems. These have the effect of reinforcing one's sense that there is hardly a book to be got out of her poetry; and also of showing how much stronger she can be in prose.

The one poem in this collection which is new to me and strikes freshly and forcefully is 'The Ring', which O'Sullivan's note tells us is 'an obvious pastiche of Robert Browning's "A Woman's Last Word"', but which, if it does owe something to the Browning poem, significantly changes its metre:

> But a tiny ring of gold
> Just a link
> Wear it and your heart is sold
> ... Strange to think!
>
> Till it glitters on your hand
> You are free
> Shall I cast it on the sand
> In the sea?
>
> Which was Judas' greatest sin
> Kiss or gold?
> Love must end where sales begin
> I am told.
>
> We will have no ring, no kiss
> To deceive.
> When you hear the serpent hiss
> Think of Eve.

We were Drinking the Honey of the Flax Flower

The Moriori were a Polynesian people who arrived on the Chatham Islands, from what we now call New Zealand, probably about the fourteenth century. From that time until 1791 they never saw other human beings. The world was their islands and the ocean. For food they had ample birds, fish and sea mammals, and rather poor supplies of edible plants. For warmth they had seal skins and woven flax. Since no big trees grew they could not make ocean-going canoes; but their wash-through rafts, buoyed by kelp, sat low in heavy seas and served local purposes well. They conducted ritual fights to resolve differences, but fighting to the death had been forbidden by their mythic ancestor, Nunuku, and the prohibition was obeyed. Life was hard and mostly short. They were said to be 'a very tapu people'. They were about 2,000 in number, occupying 100,000 hectares of land.

Their first encounter with Europeans was a mixture of warmth, excitement, misunderstanding, and finally a skirmish. Thereafter, strangers were welcome.

In the early 1800s whalers and sealers arrived and the gradual destruction of the seal population was a serious blow to the traditional economy of the islands. On the other hand, pigs and potatoes were introduced. Like all Pacific peoples, the Moriori had little defence against European diseases, and by 1835 the population had decreased by about one-fifth to 1,600. If, like other Polynesian cultures, they had been colonised by Europeans, it's reasonable to suppose they would have suffered serious damage and losses from time to time, but that as a people they would have recovered and survived. In the 1830s they were described as 'cheerful, full of mirth and laughter', living at ease and in harmony with a handful of European settlers.

In 1835 two hapu of Ati Awa Maori, displaced from their lands in Taranaki by wars with the Waikato, decided to invade the Chathams. They had thought first of Norfolk Island or Samoa, but settled for the Chathams because one of their chiefs, Matioro, had visited and knew what to expect. They chartered a ship to take them over the 870 kilometres – first one lot of 500 men, women and children; then a second of 400. Safely landed, they began to takahi – walk the land to claim it as their own.

> ... the invaders ... curtly informed the inhabitants that their land had been taken and the Moriori living there were now vassals. ... when some of the Moriori

A review of *Moriori: A People Rediscovered* by Michael King in *Metro,* November 1989.

men began to contest this process and argue back ... they were disinterestedly slain with tomahawk blows to the head. Fifty years later the horror had not dissipated, and the Moriori remembered who those initial killers and their victims were. 'Matahi Tepoki murdered Hikimanu, Ketu murdered Mahe, Kirihi murdered Kananga ...' (pp. 60–61)

The Moriori now called a council of about one thousand men. They met in the most sacred place on the island and argued about what should be done. The young wanted to fight; the old said Nunuku's law was a moral imperative and could not be broken. The elders prevailed. The invaders would be offered peace and friendship and the island would be shared.

Almost at once the Maori began killing Moriori. Men, women and children fled into the bush and were pursued and slaughtered. Many were eaten. Some were kept alive to be eaten later. The remainder became slaves who could be worked to death, starved, beaten, traded or killed. Husbands and wives, parents and children, were separated. Marriage was forbidden, as was the use of their own language. At least three hundred were killed in just a few weeks; and during the next two decades a further 1,300 died in conditions of humiliation and servitude. By 1848 Bishop Selwyn, on a visit, estimated the Moriori population had shrunk to 268. By 1870 it was down to 100.

Europeans pitied the Moriori and continued on good terms with them, but until 1863 there was no effective power on the island that could enforce the repeated injunction that the Maori should release their slaves. When at last it was enforced, it was too late. Damage had been done on such a scale that as a people the Moriori would not recover. Genocide had been effected.

In 1870, assisted by one or two European settlers, the remaining Moriori appealed to the Native Land Court for the return of their land. By this time most of the Maori had returned to Taranaki but they nevertheless contested the matter. They were by now experienced in dealing with the Court, and claimed a legitimate intertribal conquest. The Court upheld this against the Moriori remnant, who received only a few small allotments.

By the turn of the century there were only twelve Moriori left; and in 1933 the last 'pure-blood', the amiable Tommy Solomon, whose brief biography forms Michael King's final chapter, was buried.

Since then the Moriori have been commonly described, on the say-so of those who saw them at the time of their decline, as a people much inferior to the Maori; or it has been asserted by Maori that they never existed. It was to counter such distortions, and to put the facts on record, that those still alive of part-Moriori blood, who wanted also to reassert that part of their heritage, asked Michael King to write their story. He has done it well. It is a piece of our history every educated New Zealander should know.

What is to be said for the Maori whose method as colonisers was humiliation, slavery and genocide? King points out that death or enslavement is what they would have handed out to any defeated enemy; and what they would have expected if defeated. It casts a grim light on the uncertainties of pre-European Maori life, and serves as a warning to anyone inclined to romanticise it. But King adds:

> What was *different*, however, was that the adversaries were *not* Maori. The Moriori were subject to a different customary law, unacquainted with the conventions of Maori warfare ... Moreover the victims ... had nowhere in the Chathams to which they could escape. For them this sequel to the Maori invasion had all the unreality, all the physical and psychic horror, that it might have had for non-combatants dropped into the same circumstances in the late twentieth century. (p. 66)

After their decades of oppression were over the few Moriori survivors were able to put together lists of the names of hundreds killed. They remembered it all vividly. 'November must have been the month,' they recorded, in sentences at once compelling and poignant, 'for we were drinking the honey of the flax flower when they landed at Whangaroa.' That was the end of honey for them, and the beginning of their end as a people.

King's book is well written, thoroughly researched, finely produced and copiously illustrated. It honours appropriately, and gives a voice to, the Moriori dead. To watch how it is received in New Zealand, especially among radical Maori and their academic support group, will be instructive.

Katherine Mansfield as Colonial Realist

Our history is a colonial and post-colonial history, and our literature is likewise colonial and post-colonial. That is the fact and in some ways it is a brutal fact. It is not only the colonised who are the victims of colonialism; the settlers are victims as well. Once the early sense of freedom and opportunity passes there is commonly, I think, and especially among intellectual and literary people, a sense of loss, isolation, insignificance, subservience, inconsequence. So there's an urge to get out of the colonial condition; a desire to be a free-standing independent nation. Yet where the line is drawn between colonial and post-colonial is always vague and arbitrary, depending in some degree on the particular rhetoric it happens to be serving.

In colonial literature aspiring to be post-colonial, realism inevitably dominates. The colony brings with it, and maintains contact with, the parent culture; but that culture doesn't fit perfectly the new circumstances. Also, if permitted total dominance, the parent culture will sap morale and reduce confidence in the local product. The balance between maintaining living contact with the literary tradition, going back in our case at least to Shakespeare, and 'making it new' on our own ground, has been the difficult task of New Zealand writers.

But it has to be said also that there is a great gain for writers in knowing that there is a job to be done; that not just the individual ego but history itself is requiring that a literature be written; and that the colony, or new nation, offers stories which haven't been told before, and circumstances which are new.

It's often said that Mansfield's New Zealand stories are her best; but it's not often remarked that there are two quite distinct New Zealands to be found in them. One is the middle-class, respectable, intelligible-to-Bloomsbury New Zealand of 'Prelude', 'At the Bay', and other like stories; the other is the harsh colonial New Zealand of 'Ole Underwood', 'Millie', and especially 'The Woman at the Store' – stories which foreshadow a whole line of New Zealand fiction that came in the 1930s, forties and fifties. These early and abandoned Mansfield experiments in colonial frankness caused Elizabeth Bowen to remark that their 'flavour and vigour' raise the question of whether Mansfield, if she had stayed at home, could not have become 'a regional

---

This extract from the John Garrett Lecture, delivered at the University of Canterbury, 12 July 1989, was published in *Commonwealth,* Special Issue, No. 4, 1997.

writer'. 'Did she,' Bowen asked, 'by leaving her own country, deprive herself of a range of associations, of inborn knowledge, of vocabulary?'*

I think the answer to that is Yes, she did – though of course we have to acknowledge that she gained a great deal as well. I'm sure it would be wrong to say that the polite Burnell family stories are untruthful. But they represent only as much of the colonial truth as was palatable to a British readership of the time; and one has to say that in the long term that was simply not enough not if New Zealand was to find and understand itself in works of the imagination. Frank Sargeson and his contemporaries in the 1930s and forties had to take up in fiction where 'The Woman at the Store' left off.

There is plenty that can properly be called realism – or more simply truthfulness, fidelity to the real – in the Burnell stories; but it is found chiefly in the human relationships and in the evocation of place. Against the background of a physical location vivid in its particularity, Stanley and Linda Burnell are made to act out their roles in such a way that every word, every silence, every gesture, subtly reveals more than itself. After forty pages we know as much about this couple as we might expect to learn from the reading of a whole novel.

Where truth is carefully shaded out is at the edges, in the broader social context. V.S. Pritchett complained that these were stories lacking a social background.† I think in saying that, he was scoring a competitive, an English, point. He was saying, 'Well, she may be clever and so on, but she lacks a decent-sized subject because she isn't one of us. She grew up in the wrong place.'

I am suggesting something rather different: that Mansfield refused to let the whole canvas be seen because she didn't trust English readers (and by now that was her audience) not to react, for example, in a class manner, which would be inappropriate. The point about the woman at the store is not that she's 'working class'. It's that she has no identity left – class identity or any other. She has been demoralised, and barbarised, by the loneliness and the desperate rigours of colonial life. She is her husband's victim; he has become her victim; but both are victims of that terrible twilight New Zealand where (the young Mansfield wrote) the savage spirit of the country walks abroad and sneers at what it sees. This was something she could not trust Bloomsbury to understand; and so, when considering what might be used in a collection of stories, she told John Middleton Murry that of course she could not allow 'The Woman at the Store' to be reprinted.

But although there is this prevailing aura of respectability in Mansfield's best-known New Zealand stories, there are also glimpses of the colonial reality

---

* *34 Stories by Katherine Mansfield*, selected with an introduction by Elizabeth Bowen, 1957.
† 'Who are these people, who are their neighbours, what is the world they belong to? We can scarcely guess.' *The New Statesman and Nation,* 2 February 1946.

out there beyond the immediate stage on which the Burnells act out their lives; and by that I don't mean the poor family whose breadwinner is killed in 'The Garden Party' and to whom Laura takes the leftover cakes – because the 'poor', and leftovers, were perfectly familiar to Bloomsbury. By glimpses of the colonial reality I mean odd things that might easily pass unnoticed – Jonathan Trout, for example, talking to Linda Burnell, admitting his reluctance to go back to the office where he works as a clerk, staring at the beautiful sunset and saying, 'It's all wrong, it's all wrong … It's not the scene, it's not the setting for … three stools, three desks, three inkpots and a wire blind.' There you have the sense of a gap between the local reality and the imported model, which is what so much of the post-colonial experience is about - something that Maurice Duggan describes as 'a discrepancy between the real and the written'.

Or think of the figure of the servant girl Alice going to visit the storekeeper, Mrs Stubbs, in 'At the Bay'. In one sense this is pure English comedy, based partly you could say on class snobbery, though because its direct antecedent is Dickens, the underlying feeling is warm-hearted and charitable. But what adds something different and unEnglish to the comedy is that it's built on the contrast between Alice's notion of 'manners' and the stage on which she's acting. The heartless Beryl thinks Alice looks 'a guy' – and so, one suspects, does Mansfield, though she hugs it to herself and relishes it. But Alice in this atrocious get-up, which includes white gloves whose fastenings have caused rust stains, is making her way along an empty New Zealand beach towards a store which has a long line of bathing suits hanging on the verandah, a window full of sand shoes, and a sign on the roof that reads 'MRS STUBBS'S'.

> Alice did wish there'd been a bit of life on the road though. Made her feel so queer, having nobody behind her. Made her feel all weak in the spine. She couldn't believe that someone wasn't watching her. And yet it was silly to turn round; it gave you away. She pulled up her gloves, hummed to herself and said to the distant gum tree, 'Shan't be long now.'

Then there's the perfect little snapshot of colonial social history in 'The Doll's House', where we learn how the New Zealand Company's plan for Christchurch and Port Nicholson of a society which would preserve traditional British class stratifications is already falling apart.

> For the fact was, the school the Burnell children went to was not at all the kind of place their parents would have chosen if there had been any choice. But there was none. It was the only school for miles. And the consequence was all the children of the neighbourhood, the Judge's little girls, the doctor's daughters, the storekeeper's children, the milkman's, were forced to mix together.

Superficially this looks like a story about class, but really it's about how class – real class – doesn't exist any more; there's only the pretence that it does. 'The line had to be drawn somewhere', we're told. 'It was drawn at the Kelveys.' The Kelveys – one family! – have to do duty as the underclass.

Class in the colony has become as unreal as Alice's 'manners'. 'It's not the scene, it's not the setting', Jonathan wails, for stools and desks and inkpots. And it's not the scene or the setting for true blue class distinctions. As Allen Curnow was to write of the new nation, 'It was something different, something nobody counted on.'

Or again (still thinking of Mansfield the colonial realist) one might call to mind the scene in 'Prelude' when the duck is beheaded. The Irish writer Frank O'Connor wrote that it was for him 'one of the most remarkable scenes in modern literature'; but he was also shocked by it and deplored it because it seemed to him 'written in complete suspension of the critical faculties'.*

In considering that scene and O'Connor's reaction to it we have perhaps a good example of the colonial consciousness confronting the civilisation from which it came. I suspect that among people of my age and older in New Zealand it would be difficult to find anyone who didn't have memories from childhood of avian executions very like the one Mansfield describes in that scene; and among such people the shock is of recognition, not of moral outrage. Poultry was not something bought dead in a shop. It was something that happened in the back yard. Such a person will want to ask O'Connor, What criticism did Mansfield suspend? Was O'Connor, when he wrote that comment, imagining that poultry sold in shops died of natural causes? My point is that here again we have, momentarily, Mansfield the colonial realist; and in O'Connor's shocked reaction we can see that she knew what she was doing when she drew a careful line around her scenes and didn't allow too much beyond the Burnell family to appear.

But the scene or the moment I want to consider finally is not in quite such an obvious way a moment of realism. Rather, it's a moment that has symbolic significance for the development of post-colonial literature.

In 'The Doll's House' the Burnell children have been told they may bring any of their schoolmates to see the doll's house – any except the Kelveys. The Kelveys must be excluded, otherwise the pretence that class proprieties and distinctions still apply would be exposed.

Bossy big-sister Isabel clearly approves, and obeys the edict. Kezia, the incipient artist, does not. She is the one who has observed the Kelveys. She knows they're human, and badly treated, and she longs to share the treasure with them. So she invites them in after school; but Aunt Beryl catches her and drives the unwelcome ones away.

In the final scene the Kelveys are down the road sitting on a big red drainpipe, recovering from the shame and humiliation:

> Presently our Else nudged up close to her sister. But now she had forgotten the cross lady. She put out a finger and stroked her sister's quill; she smiled her rare smile.
>
> 'I seen the little lamp,' she said softly.

---

* *The Lonely Voice,* pp. 139–40.

Then both were silent once more.

That's the end of the story. Why does it end with the image of the lamp? Why is the lamp, which has also attracted Kezia's attention, so special? Here's the relevant passage earlier in the story when the children have just received the doll's house:

> But what Kezia liked more than anything, what she liked frightfully, was the lamp … The father and mother dolls, who sprawled very stiffly as if they had fainted in the drawing-room, and their two little children upstairs, were really too big for the doll's house. They didn't look as though they belonged. But the lamp was perfect. It seemed to smile at Kezia, to say, 'I live here.' The lamp was real.

I think of the doll's house as an image of the colony. The colony is playing at being a real society, with real class distinctions; but in truth it's like the doll's house, where you have to suspend disbelief and pretend not to notice that things don't quite fit together and that the dolls are too big for the rooms.

In this story there are two sets of eyes which see the truth. One set belongs to Kezia, the other to Else Kelvey. Here we have an early example of the idea that comes up also in the literature of the 1930s, that the artist and the outsider are natural allies; they alone see clearly and recognise what they see. For Isabel the doll's house is only an instrument of social power; and for the others a place in the queue to see it is a sign of social status.

Many years ago M.H. Abrams wrote a book called *The Mirror and the Lamp,* structured on a distinction between two kinds of literature – mimetic and didactic. Mimetic literature represents, and its symbol is the mirror. Didactic, or in its more exalted forms, visionary literature tells us not what is but what ought to be. Its symbol is the lamp.

I'm not suggesting that Mansfield is making use of such symbols; but it happens that one of them is there. The lamp is valued by Kezia, and noticed by Else, because it seems, of all the things the doll's house contains, the most authentic, the truest representation, the only perfect mimesis. The maker of the lamp 'held a mirror up to nature' and got it right. 'The lamp was real.'

So it's as if in Abrams's terms the lamp has become the mirror and the mirror the lamp. In the colony the most visionary thing is simply the representation of reality. Before anything else we must discover how to tell the truth about ourselves. When we do that, we become real to ourselves, and no longer colonials. In their view of the doll's house, Kezia Burnell and Else Kelvey are our first realist critics.

Ngaio Marsh

In 1949 when Ngaio Marsh was well established as one of the four 'Queens of Crime' (the others being Agatha Christie, Dorothy L. Sayers, and Margery Allingham), Penguin and Collins reissued ten of her novels, one hundred thousand copies of each – a million Marshes in one go. The *TLS* had 'no doubt' that she was 'among the most brilliant of those ... transforming the detective story from a mere puzzle into a novel'. The author, officially fifty but in fact fifty-five, and just arrived from New Zealand, appeared expensively and stylishly dressed at cocktail parties, receptions and interviews, and 'decided to help the British export drive by ordering a new Jaguar for use while she was in England'.

She had first travelled to England at the age of thirty-three, but her visits now were made – always by sea – at regular intervals. In England she said she 'came alive'. But home was New Zealand, and she always went back to her house and garden in the Cashmere Hills above Christchurch, looking across the Canterbury Plain to the Southern Alps. She was the first to resolve what was seen then as the New Zealand writer's dilemma – either expatriation, or remoteness and isolation – by living and working at home while keeping herself professionally present in London.

She had many talents. In her early years she was one of a group of Christchurch artists which included two of our most significant painters, Evelyn Page and Louise Henderson.

Among theatre people Marsh is remembered with honour. She was a brilliant producer, especially of Shakespeare, and worked for the establishment of professional theatre in New Zealand. She encouraged Allen Curnow to finish the first of his verse plays, *The Axe,* and saw it produced. She helped numbers of young actors make a start as professionals either at home or in England; and she encouraged and influenced at least two of our major playwrights, Bruce Mason and Mervyn Thompson.

As a writer she was admirably professional – thirty-two crime novels between 1934 and 1982; an autobiography, a play, film and television scripts, two books on play production, and an amount of journalism. Her view of the writer's trade was unromantic:

We worry and fumble and rehash. At two o'clock in the morning we get

---

A review of *Ngaio Marsh: A Life* by Margaret Lewis, in the *Times Literary Supplement*, 5 April 1991.

marvellous ideas and at eight o'clock the following evening we recognise ... the nonsense they are. We have awful sessions when nothing goes right, and brief but blissful sessions when everything seems to go well ... We do not work in a light-hearted, carefree fashion, all for fun. We do not wait for inspiration. We work because we've jolly well got to. But ... we toil at this particular job because it's turned out to *be* our particular job, and in a weird sort of way I suppose we may be said to like it. (p. 64)

I recall seeing her in 1952 or '53 adjudicating among student theatre groups competing as part of a universities Winter Tournament. She was already famous – and impressive: tall, stylish, good-looking, with a deep voice and an accent we thought of as English. Her comments at the end of each production were direct, incisive, intelligent, practical, encouraging, giving the impression that we were involved with her in a collective enterprise.

She made a very good living, received a number of awards and honours culminating in a Dame-hood, and completed her last book shortly before her death at the age of eighty-seven. She had neither abandoned New Zealand nor let it cut her down to size – a singular and salutary achievement.

Was it all, then a Big Success? Yes, and no. One has wondered what secrets might lie behind the public façade. The secret which Margaret Lewis's biography reveals is perhaps the saddest – that there were none. Ngaio Marsh was for most of her life an isolated, rather lonely woman who felt herself to be living on the margins. An only child, at once fostered and constrained by intense parental love, she was emotionally dominated by her mother, and in her fifties still looking after her ailing and possessive father.

As an older woman she cast herself in a satisfying and useful half-mother role with a succession of young men who were her theatrical protégés; and at the age of fifty-eight fell deeply but platonically in love with an emigré Estonian, married and possibly homosexual, with whom Margaret Lewis suggests she achieved 'a meeting of minds such as [she] had never enjoyed before'.

But timidity in her private live was reflected also, I think, in her work. It was her mother who especially encouraged her writing; and very early Marsh's ambition was to write 'a serious novel about New Zealand, and ... a detective story as an exercise in style'. When her mother read the draft of her first detective novel she told her daughter that she'd been unable to put it down; but Marsh commented later, 'I don't know to this day whether I imagined an overtone of regret in her voice.'

The regret was probably her own. The 'serious novel' was never written, just as the richer possibilities of life remained insufficiently explored. And though she resented the sort of snobbery that paid reverent attention to pretentious and insignificant 'literary' work while slighting hers, she probably knew the conventions she worked within were both a security and a limitation, preventing her from discovering the full range of her talent.

But she was a notable woman, a true professional who earned her successes and deserves our respect.

How to Read Curnow –
A Note on 'The Parakeets
at Karekare'

My discipline in what follows will be (after the initial indulgence of this page) to write only of the poem, not of the man, because for me to begin to write about the Allen Curnow who has been in turn my teacher, mentor, colleague, and neighbour-across-the-street over a period now approaching half a century, would be to embark upon a fragment of autobiography. But I will offer just one anecdote.

When I was a second-year student Curnow was my tutor, and didn't observe the usual convention that the purpose of tutorials, however difficult to achieve, was conversation. His were mini-lectures. On one occasion the subject was Shelley's *Epipsychidion,* and having read the poem with great interest and attention, and also a booklet about Shelley by Stephen Spender, I was (quite untypically of my behaviour at that time) keen to have my say. Curnow's close and, as always, fascinating reading of the poem had gone on for twenty minutes or more when I caught a brief pause into which I jumped with, 'Spender says the poem collapses at the end.'

Old Lizard Eyes blinked, surprised by an interruption to the smooth flow of his thought. 'What? What does he say?'

I repeated it.

There was a chilly pause, and then: 'Oh why doesn't Granny Spender get on with her own knitting.'

Now let us attend to Curnow's knitting: 'The Parakeets at Karekare.'*

If you read him for yourself, for the pleasure poetry can give, which in his case is of the highest order, there's no need, nor is it necessarily desirable, to 'balance all / [Bring] all to mind'. But once you become critic, propagandist, teacher, or even celebrator of his eightieth birthday, the requirements change. You must tell yourself what is happening before you can begin to tell anyone else. You must give an account of yourself as reader.

There's a temptation to linger on meanings. They are unavoidable; but they tend to obscure the action of language which, because it conspires with meanings, can become confused with them, but is at least in part independent, and is possibly the most clearly distinguishable poetic element. Certainly the 'meaning', if it can be said there is one, is not the poem. And where there are – as is often the case in Curnow – two or more meanings present in a word or

---

VERSE (Scotland) Vol. 8, No. 2, Summer 1991, special issue – 'Allen Curnow at Eighty'.
* From *You Will Know When You Get There: Poems, 1979–81*, 1982, p. 41.

phrase, it's not aggregation which alone explains our sense of enrichment (1 + 1 = 2) but rather the enhanced sense of language in action. It's for that, even more than for the meanings themselves, that these linguistic double helixes are worth unravelling – but only, I think, or mainly, as a confirmation that there were good grounds for our pleasure in the kind of reading that was not obliged to file a report.

Karekare (pronounced somewhere between *carry-carry* and *curry-curry*) is a real place, of course, and there are parakeets there – Australian immigrant rosellas. But what does the title do for the ear? How does it play? 'The Parakeets at Karekare'. Like so much in poetry of this kind, it needs to be said over and over until 'meaning' is shaken through the sieve and the grains of sound are exposed. Then one recognises what the ear has been registering – the nine vowels, all *a* or *e*; the pattern of ...*ar-a* ...*ar-e* ...*ar-e*; and the three beautifully spaced hard *k*s – all of that packed into four words. It's a title that should have alerted the sensitive, or sentry, ear, setting it slightly on edge. There is even, buried in it, the sound of 'Keats at Karekare'. Is this to be Curnow's 'Ode to a Nightingale'?

> The feathers and the colours cry
> on a high note which ricochets
> off the monologue of the morning sun
> the long-winded sea, off Paratohi posturing
> on a scene waiting to be painted.

Now we can see that the poem is already partly saying what it is doing, which is to 'describe' the bird presences (flight / colour / sound) not by description but as an object may be said to 'describe' an arc, by moving through it, acting it out, being it. The rosellas fly in a flock, fast, twittering and squawking as they go. As so often in Curnow, a colloquial phrase is buried for the mind to register, possibly without being aware of it: 'the feathers fly'. But 'fly' has become 'cry'; and because it's not possible to distinguish feather from its colour, nor bird from the sound it makes ('How can we know the dancer from the dance?') feathers and colours do it together and at once – fly and cry – 'a high note which ricochets / off the monologue of the morning sun.' The sun is repeating itself ('off the mon ... of the morn ...'), just as the sea is 'long-winded' (though it is that, one should add, in two senses, the prevailing westerly on this coast blowing across twelve hundred miles of open ocean from Australia.)

And now –

> Scarlet is a squawk, the green
> yelps, yellow is the tightest cord
> near snapping, the one high note, a sweet-sour
> music not for listening.

Yes – rosellas are scarlet, green and yellow; and here the poem pretends to find equivalences, in the parakeets' sounds, for each of its colours – the squawk, the yelp, and a sound that is all tension like something about to snap. Mixed up in there are also suggestions of a yell, a chord, a snap, even perhaps a yap. And at the same time the aural patterns continue separate from, or in addition to, this cluster of potential meanings: scarlet / squawk; yelp / yellow – the poem's own 'sweet-sour music', parallel to that of the birds.

But it's soon over:

> The end is
> less than a step and a wink
> away as the parakeet flies.

As the parakeet flies is as the crow flies – a straight line – and they are fast. Their chatter is suddenly cut off.

> Darkness and a kind of silence under
> the cliff cuts the performance,
> a moment's mixture. Can scavenging
> memory help itself?

The moment has been such a brilliant mix of colour and sound, but so brief, it becomes an analogue for all experience: lost, and left to memory the scavenger. The question asked is rhetorical, but double, and the answers are opposite: yes, and no. 'Can … memory help itself?' – i.e. can it take from the moment? Yes, it can. 'Can … memory help itself?' – i.e. stop itself / do otherwise? No, it can't. So not only is memory able to take and keep; the moment has been so vivid, it has no choice – it must.

Where then does all this action – sight, sound, and the compulsive registering of the senses – leave the simple ego, a poor helpless container for so much, who has set off only to walk to the beach? For a few lines this person is permitted a voice. He is frankly puzzled at what his senses and the occasion have conspired to do to him:

> What do I imagine coloured words
> are for, and simple grammatical
> realities like, 'I am walking to the beach'
> and 'I have no idea what the sky can mean
> by a twist of windy cloud'?

For a moment we are given the 'simple' scene that was 'waiting to be painted', perceived by the simple mind, and simply expressed. And though its simplicities have been thoroughly subverted, this moment of rest is also a moment of beauty. Here, as reader, one can only speak of the poet's sure touch, his tact and his tactics, which seem to cease to tease the mind with complexities of sense and recognition, while in fact restating them.

But now we must go back finally to the paradoxes:

> What's the distance between us all
> as the rosella cries its tricolour
> ricochet, the tacit cliffs, Paratohi
> Rock in bullbacked seas, my walking eye
> and a twist of windy cloud?

The richness of saying here, more than its meaning, is in the thing said. We are back with that central Curnow preoccupation – the certainty that there is a reality out there, and that we perceive and share it, and yet at the same time the recognition that in the absence of 'God', the certainty rests insecurely on the time-bound, fleeting perceptions of 'the walking eye', which must serve here for all the senses, and represent in turn the walking 'I', that invention we call the self. The whole experience, and the much that is made of it, is so precarious, it might be (in another colloquial phrase we may choose to hear mumbling off-stage or in the next room) 'all my eye'.

The poem has had to gather and mix them – observer and observed, the rosella's tricolour ricochet, the cliff, the rock, the bullbacked seas, the twist of windy cloud. And although only the cliff is 'tacit' in its special silence, all are 'tacit' in the sense of 'understood', 'taken for granted', 'given', because by the time memory and language have begun to work on them they are no longer there in the disposition which made them and their moment unique.

As Keats concludes, having lost the nightingale's song 'in the next valley-glades',

>Was it a vision, or a waking dream?
>Fled is that music – Do I wake or sleep?

Honest Lauris, Honest Iago

The first two volumes of Lauris Edmond's autobiography gave us her childhood and youth, marriage and motherhood, the early days of her late literary career, and the beginning of the end of her marriage. This third volume completes the death by slow degrees of the marriage, and the rapid rise of her poetic reputation, culminating in invitations overseas, the award of the Mansfield Fellowship, and her winning of the Commonwealth Poetry Prize, all of these semi-public events running parallel with the private life of (as she describes herself) 'an emotional and sexual adventurer, looking to improve on the muted and conservative experience of the past'. (p. 86)

In these private-made-public sections of the book the names of two of the key players are changed (improbably) to Edward Green and Chester Wadsworth. No doubt Edmond's husband, had he lived, would have wished all their names, especially his own, might have been changed, but he died somewhere, it seems, between the publication of the previous volume and this one, and so was spared the pain of discovering himself again cast in the role assigned him in part two – failed husband and failed headmaster.

There have been times when I have taken great pleasure in Lauris Edmond's company – in person, as on the page; and there are sections in this book (especially the account of her sojourn in Menton) where I feel the same pleasure, and can understand how readers who have enjoyed the first two volumes will enjoy this one even more. There is certainly no decline in interest; and this deserves mention, because autobiographies are commonly good on childhood and youth, where distance lends enchantment and erases irrelevant detail, and then lose focus as they near the present.

Edmond writes intelligently, though there's a tendency to gush and be starstruck, smitten – to overreact and overwrite. She has a sense of humour, but little wit or style (the qualities that save Katherine Mansfield and Sylvia Ashton-Warner in their personal writing). 'She and I talked *endlessly* about our values … She was *wonderfully* illuminating … Occasionally we remarked, a bit *shamefacedly* … All this interested me *intensely* …' The italics are mine, of course, but the adverbs are hers, and all in less than half a page. They are authentic, in the sense that if you know the woman you can hear her voice in them. But isn't it one of disciplines of good writing to eliminate one's weaknesses?

A review of *The Quick World* by Lauris Edmond, in the *Sunday Star,* 19 July 1992. (Lauris Edmond died early in 2000, aged seventy-five.)

Behind, or beyond, style lies the difficult question of truthfulness. Of course there must be a point of view, and it must be the writer's. But the reader must be made to feel that essentials are not being withheld. If you are an uncritical reader – and there are enough of those to make a book like this commercially secure – you will take it all at face value. If not, you will feel, as I do, a disbelief which interrupts and undermines enjoyment in the narrative as it unfolds.

Describing her first experiences as a member of PEN, she writes, 'Each [meeting] represented a glorious adventure into the high life of the creative intellect, a journey of distinction taken in the company of other guardians of the cultural health of the nation.' And of visits to a pub afterwards: 'The companionship was warm and ripe ... I returned to my office ... hearing still the sharp, surprising, rude or funny echoes of the conversations ... impressed by every word.'

By what rhetorical device would you increase the reader's sense of this high society of the intellect? How better than by introducing a serpent? So: 'When Karl Stead came to one of our meetings representing Auckland members and told us we were power-hungry, we sat and stared at him, mystified and hurt.' (pp. 39–40)

Mystification and hurt ('deeply distressed and completely mystified' – p. 200) are precisely what Edmond will later tell us she felt when her own children turned against her. This pretence at incomprehension is the method by which she keeps her readers in the dark while extracting sympathy. Even if the serpent didn't say exactly that (and of course he didn't) why would he have come into her PEN Eden and said anything remotely like it? That the issue was Auckland's ten-year battle to wrest PEN from the total control Wellington writers then exercised and turn it into a truly national and representative body, remains unexplained. But thirty pages on we read that in 1977 an international PEN Congress was held in Sydney, and the 'local centre' suggested she and Bruce Mason should represent it. That was how PEN worked in those days, and those who profited by it were extremely resistant to change.

Similarly we are never told exactly what it was that angered her children; but anyone who saw a letter to a Wellington newspaper by two of her daughters, dissociating themselves from her account of family matters, and complaining about reviewers who, ignorant of the facts, described the second volume of their mother's autobiography as 'honest', will have a fair idea.

Edmond insists more than once that she has been not just a good mother but a superior one, and is consequently 'mystified' by her children's revolt. Comforting herself after much thought, she concludes that they must have favoured their father because he did what parents are supposed to do and simply went into a decline, while she in her later years achieved independence and a public identity. That they might have felt she had done less than justice to Trevor Edmond's good name is a possibility she doesn't allow herself – and so doesn't give her readers the opportunity – to consider.

Keith Sinclair – His Story and Ours

Professor Sir Keith Sinclair was testosterone incarnate. He had, I think, the quickest, and at times the most combative, mind of anyone I've known. Too quick sometimes; it was both his strength and his weakness. He could work through huge quantities of historical material without losing either his own sense of direction or the emerging picture. In party or common room conversation he played simultaneous chess, often giving offence by recognising where one's laborious sentences were heading, answering before they were completed, and throwing something into another conversation he had tuned into. He also remembered what he had appeared not to have listened to, and responded with a new thought days or weeks later. He remarks in his autobiography, published a fortnight after his death, that he learned his bad conversational habits in a family of ten lively children.

As a person, and I think as a scholar too, he was competitive, exact and exacting, industrious, impatient; but also oddly modest. It was surprising how often he expressed surprise. Things were always coming at him fresh. His interest was always alive. He sometimes seemed insensitive in his dealings with people; but he was not ungenerous, and was easily moved to tears.

He made his name as an historian, but his first love was literature; or it might be truer to say that his first ambitions were literary – to be fiction writer and poet. 'I had a clear idea of who I was and of my goals … by the time I was twenty. First of all, I had a burning desire to contribute to the making of a New Zealand literature – I was a literary nationalist.'

Sinclair published no fiction, though as a young man he tried to write it; but he made a name for himself in the late 1940s as one of the new post-war poets. He characterised the Curnow-Brasch-Glover-Holcroft writing of the 1930s and forties as 'South Island Romanticism', and rejected the notion that 'the plains are nameless and cities cry for meaning' (Brasch), that ours was 'a land of settlers with never a soul at home' (Curnow). He liked to joke, mocking that sort of mountain romanticism, that he and his Auckland contemporaries Kendrick Smithyman and R.McD. Chapman were 'the Mud-flats school' of New Zealand poetry. Later, when Chapman had stopped writing poetry, I was added to the group and we became the three K.Ss, also referred to by

Half way Round the Harbour: An Autobiography by Keith Sinclair, reviewed in the *Times Literary Supplement,* 7 January 1994. This review has been combined with parts of the obituary I wrote for the *New Zealand Author*, 7 August 1993, extended and revised.

James Bertram as' the Auckland Metaphysicals'.

Love and landscape brought out the best in Sinclair as a young poet – a lyric strain, and an acute sense of place and history; but his ear was uncertain. In his *Penguin Book of New Zealand Verse,* Allen Curnow wrote:

> Sinclair uses a fairly conventional syntax, but many of his words seem placed with a kind of careful absent-mindedness, lest he should compromise his meaning. He lets his limitations be seen, and they are considerable.

Knowing my admiration for Curnow, Sinclair asked me what I thought this meant, and I had to say (truthfully) that I found it opaque, indeed impenetrable. I didn't add what I supposed to be the case, that it was Curnow's circumspect (and in this case not altogether satisfactory) way of indicating a clumsiness, a lack of finesse, that characterised even the best of Sinclair's poems.

And he didn't grow and develop as a poet, didn't read it or study it enough to extend his range or his initial notion of what it might be. His first two books seemed full, if not of promise, at least of possibility. The later ones are technically disappointing, intelligent but pedestrian, lacking a higher register, a stylistic overdrive.

His nationalism, which he would have thought of as an achieved independence, a cutting of the last imperial apron string, seems to me still a phase, though a very late one, of colonialism, because it relied on assertions of superiority. Of himself as a Second World War soldier, and later sailor, he writes, 'We thought Englishmen small and completely lacking initiative. The lower class spoke such foul language they made us sound like Boy Scouts. I wrote [in letters home] that they were locked in a class system divided by a gulf they could not bridge in a generation.' And he adds 'Class was and is the medium in which the British swim. Where else does a man, on meeting another, look him in the tie?'

But nationalism gave all his work, literary and historical, a point of view, a point of intellectual focus which was not intellectual or abstract in origin, but strongly rooted in a love of the most down-to-earth of Kiwi pursuits. His early life, spent largely out of doors on the bays and tidal reefs of the inner Waitemata, laid down the pattern for all his later recreation. He loved boating, swimming, fishing, diving for scallops, making fish-head soup; and all these activities continued throughout his life, from his holiday bach at Waiuna Bay on the Coromandel Harbour. As a young man he had been athlete, rugby player, boxer, and his keen interest in sport also continued throughout his life. Sinclair intellectualised New Zealand's popular mind so that what he had to say reached over and beyond the academy.

He wished, he says, 'to encourage a New Zealand literature and history which would do away with [colonial] feelings of inferiority'. If this required, sometimes, short shrift with Poms, that was a pardonable rhetoric, of a kind which never prevented him from enjoying at every opportunity the best, academically and culturally, offered by what had once been the homeland.

He had no respect at all for Marxist doctrine, but his political loyalties remained with Labour, and the campaign against New Zealand's involvement in the Vietnam war made him for a time an activist. In 1969 he stood as a parliamentary candidate, and some of his friends joined, or rejoined, the party to become involved in door-knocking and campaigning. Among photographs pinned above my desk is one by Marti Friedlander of the two of us walking on Takapuna beach the day Marti's election publicity photographs were taken of him. Keith won the Eden seat for Labour on election night but lost it a few weeks later when special votes were counted.

As a non-historian I will risk suggesting that there have been four Pakeha ways, distinct enough despite exceptions and overlaps, of viewing New Zealand history since European contact. First come the imperial stories in which the challenge, adventure and trials of exploration and colonisation are recounted, and in which the Maori figures often as the noble savage, mainly welcoming, but unpredictable.

Next come the settler accounts (not, of course, necessarily published) in which London, the imperial power trying to balance the needs and costs of settlement against some sort of fairness to the indigenous people, is seen as another, and sometimes the major, obstacle to progress. Here already the Pom is beginning to be identified as alien, often a self-important busy-body insensitive to settler needs and circumstances. In this phase the Maori have fallen into two basic categories – facilitator ('friendly'), and obstacle ('rebel').

We are well into the twentieth century before there is a third stage, the recognition, seen for example in Sinclair's *The Origins of the Maori Wars* (1957), not just that there is a distinct Maori view of events, but that the complete picture requires it to be investigated, given credence and mana, and held in proper balance with that of the Pakeha. Parallel with that goes the recognition that those whom Sinclair called, in a later book, 'the native born', represent a European consciousness differently shaped and significantly distinct from that of first generation settlers.

Fourth comes the kind of history which predominates at the moment, in which the Maori view is given the high moral ground, and the imperial power is seen as only marginally less self-serving and culpable than the settlers and their greedy progeny our forebears, who are represented as robbing, bullying and cheating the native people out of land and livelihood. This is a view so universally acceptable, both in and beyond New Zealand, that the injustice it does to a majority of lives that have been lived in these islands since 1840 passes for the moment unnoticed; but my guess is that it won't wear well over time.

Sinclair belonged to the third phase, the only one which offers anything like a balanced and rounded account of our history, and goes any distance towards doing justice to all. He was not alone in his distinction, but he was the most notable historian of his generation; and despite changes in intellectual fashion which don't altogether favour his work, he is likely to prove the most important and durable recorder of, and reflector upon, New Zealand's first one hundred and fifty years.

Keith Sinclair's death made me realise that he has been a part of my interior landscape for all of my adult life – first as teacher, then as colleague and friend. He was much more gregarious than I, and found my avoidance of social rituals (lunch in the common room, for example) odd, and probably chilly. But I have vivid recollections of raucous, funny, and ultimately drunken social occasions with him and Maurice Duggan and our wives; and my times with him in Coromandel gave me the background/landscape for large parts of my first novel, *Smith's Dream*.

In (I think) 1966 I went with Keith and his brother Jack (later Professor of Medicine at Auckland University Medical School) to watch a Lions–All Black test at Eden Park where in 1950 I had watched Jack, then New Zealand mile champion, run for New Zealand in the Empire Games. As we walked along Keith reminisced about their childhood. Other children had bread and butter; the Sinclairs had bread and dripping.

Jack grinned. 'Yes,' he agreed. 'But it was good dripping.'

Clearly it was! On another occasion, a dinner at the Sinclairs' house, something was said on the subject of Pacific literature which Albert Wendt, newly appointed to a Chair of English in Auckland, found unacceptable. Wendt rose from his place and indicated that he was leaving. Keith asked him why.

'I'm a Samoan,' he said loftily.

Keith came back at him instantly. 'You're a Professor of English, for Christ's sake. Sit down. Get used to it.'

In an age that fosters lip service, compliance, cant, Keith was a person of total, sometimes brutal, authenticity. I admired him almost as much for his social transgressions as for his academic distinction. He was brilliant, brusque, outrageous, alive. He made life in New Zealand brighter, more colourful. He was one of the very few at any one time who keep us intellectually on our toes.

A Life of Sargeson

There's a scene in the Jane Campion movie *An Angel at my Table* when Frank Sargeson goes to meet (I think) Janet Frame's relatives who have arrived by car at his gate. He is shirtless, and carries a bottle in one hand and a glass in the other. This, I suppose, is the film-maker's notion of 1950s bohemia, and about as accurate as it would have been to put Sargeson into jeans and sneakers. He did wear sandals and shorts in his garden; he did believe it was healthy to expose one's body to the sun. But he would never have greeted strangers without his shirt.

There was a formal quality. He cared about appearances, and occasions. I used to notice when I was visiting that if there was a knock at the door he would duck into the bathroom and check himself in the mirror before answering it. When he went to town he always put on a tweed jacket and woven tie. Michael King quotes Eric McCormick: 'I also remember his skilful performance as a host: the ease with which he produced a delicious concoction of tomatoes for his swarm of unexpected guests; the slight – the very slight – air of formality he imposed by addressing us with unadorned surnames; the adroitness he displayed in guiding conversation from speaker to speaker, topic to topic.'

That is *le vrai* Sargeson.

Michael King's credentials as a scholar and writer meant that in writing Sargeson's biography he was sure to do a proper professional job. The question was whether he would catch the true Sargeson flavour, so particular, subtle, individual – by turns sharp, salty, fruity, sweet-and-sour, and just occasionally poisonous. On the whole I think he has; but reservations will follow.

There are some parts of the book, towards the end, where King has been almost overwhelmed by the material – too many new names and minor events coming too fast; too many voices clamouring to be heard. To use a favourite term of Sargeson's, 'focus' is lost – but never for long. What keeps it unified is the predominance of Sargeson's own voice, from letters and autobiography. Where there is no reason to distrust him, his own words are best, and King is right to let him speak for himself.

On the other hand, where the documented facts and Sargeson's retelling manifestly diverge, King takes up the burden of the story – most notably in the matter of his criminal conviction in 1929 for a homosexual act. Sargeson's

---

A review of *Frank Sargeson: A Life* by Michael King, in *Landfall* 191, Autumn 1996.

strategies of concealment and falsification (including an eighteen-month rustication, and a change of name) confirm what is King's major point: that this – the shock of being caught, the shame of public exposure, the family humiliation, the loss of job and professional status – was the shaping event of Sargeson's life.

Sargeson's own biographical notes always mentioned that he had qualified as a solicitor and then turned his back on the bourgeois life in favour of the life of art. What he concealed, even from most of his friends, was the way in which the bourgeois life had turned its back on him. It is a fact that explains a good deal, including his outbursts (not always without reason, but often wildly disproportionate) against public institutions like the university, his paranoia about the police, and his suspicions and imaginings which often seemed excessive and just occasionally mad. He had changed his name from Norris Davey (he told me that when he played hockey at school he was nicknamed 'Dainty') and recreated himself as a writer; but he was living with the memory of a horror, and the fear that it might revisit him. Quite apart from its literary importance, Sargeson's life is an exemplary story, a reminder of the cruelty of the collective will.

King's narrative makes plain how unfair Sargeson was to his church-going 'wowser' parents. His father supported him in his crisis; his mother, it seems, gave the conveniently dizzy impression of thinking the conviction must have been the result of a horrible misunderstanding. They gave up the use of their Takapuna bach, and later their plans for a retirement home there, in order to give their son a place to carry on his chosen career. Often, when Sargeson couldn't pay the rates, his father paid them. For this the parents got the kind of thanks Harold Beauchamp got from Katherine Mansfield, who lived off her father's money and described him as 'the richest man in New Zealand and the meanest'.

Sargeson's resentment was particularly against his mother; and it was elaborated into, or found common cause with, a social theory that New Zealand was a destructive matriarchy – a view as common in the 1950s among literary and intellectual people, and as shallow, as its opposite which now prevails. I remember how shocked we were, a young couple fresh from the suburbs, when Sargeson told us that when his mother died he would dance on her grave. I wouldn't be shocked now, but would think, rather, 'For this there has to be a cause.' The cause was shame, and frustrated love. His mother could not love the son he was, only the son invented for her personal comfort and social convenience. The parents too were victims of that social will; but as he saw them they were also its instruments.

Sargeson disliked the term 'gay', and the stereotypes that went with it. When the sense of a liberation began he was too old to want to come 'out'. He was even, I think, partly locked into the social pattern that saw homosexual acts as sinful, and danger as an aphrodisiac. Take away the sin and the fear, and part of the pleasure might go too. Certainly he was excited by urinals, and loved the undercover world of codes, signals, recognitions; and King is right to link this with his aesthetic, where there was always a sub-text, never made explicit. A world in which everything was open and declared would have been alien to him. 'Don't pretend to yourself that you are anything but what you are', he wrote to his lesbian friend Peter Dawson. But the crucial words are 'to yourself'. In the same sentence he acknowledged that as things stood in the present, 'social pretence' was 'necessary'.

To a heterosexual friend, Alec Pickard, he wrote, 'If the heart is moved it is a fact that can't be got over – something has to be done about it – & for me that "something" has always been ... positive rather than negative.' But in his letters to Pickard his homosexuality was concealed. Giving his sexual preferences an old-world literary flavour, he pretended to be excited only by 'servant girls & prostitutes'.

The biography makes one more keenly aware of how Sargeson's literary reputation hung fire, took fire, sputtered and seemed almost to go out, and then flared at the last. The stories of the 1930s and forties in which, after so many false starts, he at last found his true voice, made a strong and enduring impression. Here at long last was (in Curnow's phrase) 'the New Zealand thing, the regional thing, the real thing'. Then came the hiatus of the 1950s – only one short novel, *I For One,* published in that decade, while he laboured at plays and at *Memoirs of a Peon.* And then, after 1964, an extraordinary crop of thirteen books in fifteen years, some of them reprints, but nine written after the age of fifty, seven of those nine after the age of sixty.

The writing of *Memoirs of a Peon* was his second great breakthrough. There he discovered a first person narrator quite other than himself, a bookish sexpot, but hetero, who could retell the anecdotes and adventures of Sargeson's old friend Bake, and at the same time could be slyly made the vehicle for some of the author's own. The further discovery, made in extending *Up Onto the Roof and Down Again* into the first volume of autobiography, was his application of a Proustian method to the events of his own life. Autobiography was a special kind of *fiction*, in which you were permitted to make yourself the central character.

King quotes Sargeson writing to Dawson asking whether there was a waiting room in the Tauranga railway station, open all night, because he intended to write that he spent the night there! And to another saying he couldn't swear that everything in his autobiography really happened. King shows how the story about the period spent on his uncle's farm, and its significance in his life, is used as cover for the real fact of a retreat from the public humiliation of the criminal conviction. He recognises too the huge gap between fact and autobiography when Sargeson writes of his great love, the deregistered jockey and horse trainer Harry Doyle, 'it is not untrue to say that he stayed [at Esmonde Road] for 36 years.' It was quite untrue. Except for the last four years of his life Harry came and went, but was mostly notable for being somewhere else.

But I think King doesn't recognise just how far Sargeson went in inventing and making free with facts. In *Never Enough,* for example, the third volume of his autobiography, there is a wonderful connecting passage about a farmhouse, nikaus, and a giant kauri. They are seen first, early in the book, by the young Sargeson travelling north by slow train with his friend Frank Gadd. On the last page, fifty years later, the same scene recurs, rediscovered. The house turns out to be that of his new friend, M., and though the nikaus have gone, the giant kauri still stands, preserved on his property.

King writes that Sargeson 'believed he was looking down the same valley' at the scene that had moved him so many years before. That of course is what the book says. But my recollection is of Sargeson telling me how he had invented the first sighting – hugging himself almost, not at the thought of a deception, but at the beautiful shape it would give to his story; and on reflection one can see how much it is a part of the narrative strategy, and how unlikely it is that the first sighting would have been remembered in such precise detail half a century later. Such strategies are an essential, and neglected (I mean by critics) element in the art of storytelling. Their 'truth' is emotional and imaginative, not literal; but they are traps for the historian and biographer.

Likewise King takes on trust statements about Sargeson's poverty and lack of earnings, which it seems to me were always exaggerations, and sometimes mendacious. Frank was secretive about his Civil List pension, less than truthful about royalties, guilty at having no dependents, and determined at all costs to be poor. When royalties and benefactions came his way in the 1970s he concealed or obscured the facts, and gave money away by the bucketful in order to keep up indigent appearances. It was a subject on which at the time (though it was none of my business) my feelings were finely balanced between irritation with Frank and extreme distaste for his parasites – not only M. and 'little Jimmy', but also the Greek family who 'bought' the Takapuna house left to Sargeson by his aunt.

The broad picture King has given is right; his industry and tact have been immense; and if I have a complaint it is only a mild one. About the characters and reputations of the huge cast of literary people who pass through these pages, King's eye seems to light infallibly on those things in the documents which confirm what is popularly thought to be the case. Where the evidence suggests otherwise, it seems to be passed over. It's not that one asks a biographer to go looking for trouble; and there are sensitivities to be respected. But life is full of surprises and so, surely, should be a book which takes us through half a century of our literary history.

On page 385, for example, King writes of the 'close and harmonious' relationship between Sargeson and Charles Brasch. 'Frank was at all times protective of Brasch when he heard criticism of his poetry, his editorial policies at *Landfall* … or his qualities as a human being'; and he goes on to give an example of Sargeson reproaching me for some harsh things I said about Brasch after being visited by him in Menton.

In fact Sargeson was worried about my remarks going on record (something which didn't bother me), not about the remarks themselves; but that is not the point. The point is that Sargeson was not 'at all times protective of Brasch', and King ought to have known it – did know it. Fifteen pages back he quotes Sargeson writing in a letter, 'Literature is infinitely greater than life, and confronted with such work we are all arch-traitors if we don't sink personal differences to acknowledge greatness when it confronts us.'

King uses this quotation to illustrate how Sargeson often appealed to high principles when he fell out with fellow authors; but he gives no indication that the letter was referring to Brasch. In fact (it was to me, so I have been able to check) it was about a poem of mine published in the *London Magazine,* which he very much admired and which he believed Brasch had slighted: 'I wrote back the most devastating letter I have ever written to C[harles] – even if devastating only by implication. The implication that Literature is infinitely greater than life, and confronted with such work we are all arch traitors if we don't sink personal differences to acknowledge greatness when it confronts us … I await Charles' reactions with trepidation – he could be in no doubt that I was saying on this occasion "You are a traitor".' And after remarks about Ron Mason's admiration of the same poem he added, 'Of course with Charles it *was* personal.'

I also notice that on a page of a notebook of mine from which King quotes a quite separate anecdote (so he must have read the page) I record Sargeson saying that James Bertram's promotion of Brasch as the major New Zealand poet was 'absurd'. 'Brasch simply didn't have a fine enough *mind* to be a major poet,' Sargeson said.

The Making and Unmaking
of a Maurice

Keats said if poetry comes not as easily as the leaves to a tree it had better not come at all. Mozart wrote his 'too many notes' as if it was hardly different from breathing. Shakespeare's workmates, Heminge and Condell, said he wrote so fast he 'never blotted a line'. The same is surely true of Dickens.

That is one kind of composition, springing from confidence in the medium and from an inner harmony. Another kind, quite different, is described by Yeats and exemplified in his manuscripts:

> A line will takes us hours maybe;
> Yet if it does not seem a moment's thought,
> Our stitching and unstitching has been naught.

Everything about Maurice Duggan was deliberate, orderly, composed – until order broke down, after which he was the Lord of Misrule. It wasn't just his desk and his papers that were in perfect order; so were his bookshelves, his house, his garage, his garden, his tools. Colleagues in advertising described his immaculate dress, his cheeks shining from what Henry James called (and I remember Maurice liked the phrase) 'the matutinal steel'.

Duggan's voice and articulation were a conscious replacement of the accent of his childhood and youth. Socially he was charming, considerate, modest, witty. His letters (and because of this I disagree with his biographer that he was a notable letter writer) were cleverly over-composed, as if several drafts had preceded the final version. Most of his fiction was worked and reworked, revised, recast, abandoned, born again.

The opposite side of this orderly person was a boozing rager of monumental proportions. The writer who kept his literary papers in such meticulous order was the alcoholic who burned them up in one lost weekend. The generous host and guest became the fight-picker and recluse. The loving husband and father was also the man who told his wife when she became pregnant that she should jump off a bridge, and who once assured his school-age son that they were not related.

Somewhere between the order and the disorder, it seems, there existed a very small space in which Duggan's best work was done. He could never reach it by the will alone. To get there he needed a combination of the right

---

A review of *To Bed at Noon: The Life and Art of Maurice Duggan* by Ian Richards, in *Landfall* 195, Autumn 1998. See 'Barry Humphries – Contemporary' in Part 3 of this book for a brief account of Duggan meeting the creator of Dame Edna Everidge.

personal circumstances and the excitement of another writer's work. His three literary propellants were Joyce, Nabokov and Beckett; and measuring by the relative importance of what resulted, I would say the latter two were the truly important ones. Duggan's early Joycean work, fine in its way, is somewhat overborne by the echoing presence of its model and master. With Nabokov and Beckett, on the other hand, Duggan didn't just imitate. He discovered, through them, how to invent the self-on-the-page he wanted to be.

We all like to think in terms of cause and effect, and Duggan's is a life which invites it. He lost his mother in childhood and a leg in adolescence, the one damaging his faith in female love, the other damaging his sense that he was worthy of it. At the age of thirty he contracted tuberculosis of one lung, then later of the other. He suffered what were diagnosed as 'endogenous depressions', and made an attempt, very nearly successful, at suicide. By the time he reached his forties he was seriously alcoholic. He committed himself more than once to a mental institution, and was twice committed against his will, once receiving a course of ECT, and once dragged there by police, shouting and resisting. In his early fifties we are told he had finally beaten the alcohol, but the finality of the cure was hardly put to the test. He was diagnosed as having cancer, and died in 1974 at the age of fifty-two.

If one thing leads to another there are ample 'reasons' for the course his adult life took. It's perhaps hard to imagine him pushing himself through all those preliminary years of what must have seemed like failure – all those endless drafts and redrafts, those huge efforts towards a novel which always broke into fragments – if a life of action had remained possible for him. But to think in terms of causality is probably misleading, and in any case irrelevant.

In Duggan's orderliness, one feels, there was an element of self-repression, as if he'd been too well drilled in a belief in the will. He tried always too hard, and when he failed, wrote himself a report that said 'Should try harder'. The tussle to maintain order within himself must have been huge; and when the soul broke out of its dark airless workroom, the mayhem was correspondingly destructive. The losses, the humiliation, the pain, of his early life, together with the strict Catholic schooling, no doubt made these inner conflicts more extreme.

A writer doesn't have to leave a large oeuvre to be important in literary history. Everything Coleridge wrote is considered to be of interest, but would it be if he hadn't written 'Kubla Khan' and 'The Rime of the Ancient Mariner'? Fewer than half a dozen poems make Marvell a classic. My view of Duggan is that his place in our literary history is more like that of a poet than a fiction writer. He will never have anything amounting to a 'public'; and what's likely to prove durable is a relatively small part of the total work – chiefly 'Along Rideout Road that Summer', and 'Riley's Handbook', together with perhaps half a dozen shorter pieces kept alive partly because of their own singular merit, but also because they are by the author of those two classic works. This may seem unduly conservative; but I am talking here about long-term literary survival, of which there is never going to be very much.

I remember when 'Riley's Handbook' first appeared in *Landfall* another of the Maurices – Maurice Shadbolt – visiting from Wellington, stayed the night with us in the little two-storeyed house we rented close to the Auckland Domain. He borrowed our copy on his way to bed, and in the morning came downstairs whistling. Duggan's story was unreadable, he declared, and ate a hearty breakfast on the strength of it. My own view, which I'm sure he saw as yet another example of the academic wank he was about to satirise in the character of Derek in his novel *Among the Cinders,* was that if, one hundred years hence, there should be a continuing interest in our literary history, most literary work which grabbed immediate attention would be forgotten, or looked back upon as quaint relics of a long-lost age, while 'Riley's Handbook' would still read like living language. That is still my view.

It was written towards the end of 1960, Duggan's year on the Burns Fellowship at Otago University. He had been enjoying his time there, which he chose to describe, in a letter to Keith Sinclair, as a domestic 'cease-fire', an escape from the 'wicked attrition and long rage' of his marriage. He had spent some time lodging at the Captain Cook Hotel, and had more recently taken a flat. But his writing – another attempt at a novel, this one to be called *The Burning Miss Bratby* – had been the usual painful and less than satisfactory grind. In April he wrote to Frank Sargeson, 'I sit in uneasy and doubtful authority over the cold corpse of Miss Joan Bratby waiting for some sign of returning life'; and to Sinclair, 'Miss Bratby has turned sullen and questions the plans I have for her. Poor dull, poor banal, Miss Bratby.'

But he pushed on and in August announced that a draft was finished – except, of course, that it was all unsatisfactory and would have to be redone. To Sargeson he wrote:

> I've finished the first draft of Miss Bratby … and I will put her by now for a few months … and move in to the next – another short novel, a sort of contrapuntal companion piece. If I ever get that done I'll begin a second draft of Miss B. and after that go back to no. 2. Perhaps! Perhaps! But everything is still to be done to Miss B. What I have I suppose is the frame only … But maybe even the frame is something.

The 'sort of contrapuntal companion piece' was to become 'Riley's Handbook'. It was an act of rebellion against himself, his life, his marriage, his Miss Bratby fiction – an anti-novel with an anti-hero; a brilliant, verbose, plotless, depressive-exalted rave. For the first and almost the only time, Duggan was giving voice to his innermost, most anarchic self. It was self-caricature, a double negative creating a rich and strange affirmative – the affirmation of self through style. Furthermore, a first draft (later considerably expanded) was finished in less than two months, the bulk of it in just three weeks. This was fluency of an entirely new kind. For once he was not working against the grain but with it, and the writing was coming as easily as the leaves to the tree. It was something that would never be repeated except in the writing of

'Along Rideout Road that Summer', which followed.

Ian Richards's biography is workmanlike, thorough, capably written. There are very occasional errors of date and fact (Janet Frame, for example, was not living in Sargeson's army hut until 1955; and Aucklanders called the Avondale Mental Hospital 'the Whau', not 'the Wow'!). There are some encounters/ exchanges/occasions recorded which I find implausible and for which in each case there is only one source. The Kendricks, the Georges, the Christines and the Jacks have enjoyed retelling their Duggan stories – and so they should. It was not for them to hold back; but some of it might have received a larger dash of authorial scepticism. Caveat emptor, however. *To Bed at Noon* tells the story of Duggan's life in broad outline and in some detail; and if I have any hesitation about the book it is only, I suppose, because there is something faintly official and neutralising about it.

What, for example, were the circumstances of that astonishing turnaround in Duggan's habits as a writer in the second half of 1960? Here one must touch on the question of biographical tact. It has been no secret from Duggan's family and friends that he had a very serious love affair in Dunedin. In his fiction he never worked far from himself and his circumstances (he used to talk anxiously about 'using up one's fictional capital', meaning one's life experience), and 'Riley's Handbook' stands as a new way of dealing – immediately, summarily, piping hot – with life as it happened. It is at once a comic strip of his life in Dunedin, and a vehicle for what was, after all, his governing passion, *language*. Riley, lapsed Catholic and anti-cleric, the tubercular artist of modest reputation on whom some 'public money' has been spent, escapes his marriage, comes to live and work as rouseabout in a pub where he has an affair with Myra, the chambermaid, but remains obsessed with his mother, Pegeen, whose death in his childhood he experienced as an abandonment, and for whom Nan, the pub-owner's wife, becomes a substitute.

Everything is grossly exaggerated, made at once darker and funnier; but it is no exaggeration of how Duggan felt, and those feelings drove the fiction and found life in the language. There is hardly a sentence that can't be read as Duggan speaking out of the centre of his own experience. Beckett, life in a Dunedin pub, the love affair, and an upsurge of rebelliousness, of 'fuck it all, fuck everything', had freed him for the moment to speak plain and speak fancy, and he did it with astonishing relish and unprecedented fluency.

So there is for me a problem about a biography that leaves out an event so important not only in his life, but in his struggle to find the means, the material, and the emotional drive for getting words down on paper. It's unlikely Duggan's widow can be responsible for the omission, since a later affair with a young painter (the model for Isobel in 'O'Leary's Orchard') is recounted. And if it was the woman herself who objected, why could not her name have been changed, as the painter's was, to conceal her identity?

Duggan fought a life-long interior battle against what he described as 'conventional fiction', for which the local example he most often gave (though not the only one) was the work of Ian Cross. It was not that he wanted to deny those who enjoyed it their pleasure, nor those who wrote it their reward. But to resist its influence, and to hold out against the literary-commercial ambience in which it flourished, was necessary if his own different (and I would say higher) creative impulses were to stay alive. 'It's the proper job we're after, here,' the rebellious Riley tells himself. 'It's enough, all said, to be sweating over making something out of nothing. I'm not in the amusement racket.'

The Burning Miss Bratby was, I'm sure, the very kind of fiction his strongest instincts told him he should not be writing, but which a sense of obligation to those who subsidised his work drove him back to. And when he took his own eccentric path again, the world was quick to remind him what a profitless one it was. When he got together the collection *Summer in the Gravel Pit* for Blackwood Paul, Paul accepted 'Riley's Handbook' for inclusion; but when the collection went to Gollancz for co-publication, the English firm insisted it be removed. Paul, and more particularly Charles Brasch who had published it in *Landfall,* deserve enormous credit for giving Duggan confidence in a work so desperately authentic it was at first shocking even (or perhaps especially) to its author. But how do you sell such fiction at large? The short answer, I suppose, is that in the short term you can't.

There is, I think it's true to say, a good deal of 'conventional fiction' in the work Duggan did publish, and for some of it he is still over-praised by a small loyal following that prefers not to discriminate. But such work (I would suggest 'Blues for Miss Laverty' and 'O'Leary's Orchard' as examples) was often less than satisfactory because it was written to some extent by the man who wanted to please, not himself, but others, and this is somewhere imprinted in the prose, giving it a flavour that is faintly stilted and prissy. These are stories less likely to wear well over time.

'Along Rideout Road that Summer', on the other hand, clearly given a very strong stylistic push by a rereading of Nabokov's *Lolita,* followed 'Riley's Handbook'. It has a similar desperate comic quality; but it seems to come out of confidence that he has for the moment found his own voice and his own mode. It returns to the material of the first of his stories that really pleased him, 'Six Place Names and a Girl', but with ease, sophistication and amplitude. It has Duggan's own self-mocking charm, his wit, his social confidence, his mix of comedy and sadness, his anarchic sense of fun; and it tells us something about ourselves, Maori and Pakeha, as few stories do. I have written about it several times,* and for me it is still the greatest single New Zealand short story.

But where was he to go from there? No one could make a living writing

---

* See, for example, my introduction to Duggan's *Collected Stories*, Auckland University Press, 1981, reprinted in *In a Glass Case, Essays on New Zealand Literature*, C.K. Stead, Auckland University Press, 1981.

be a writer's writer; or perhaps one should say a reader's writer, meaning real readers, not the clients of airport bookstalls. After Dunedin he returned to Auckland; to the loyal, tolerant and long-suffering Barbara who always supported him; to his friends; to a successful decade as an advertising executive. But there was an underlying sense of defeat. In 'Six Rileypomes' published pseudonymously in *Mate* in 1961 he speaks in the voice of an Odysseus returning to Penelope, to his son Telemachus, to 'duty', and to 'debts the heart [has] not paid', describing himself as 'sullen and indifferent company', still remembering Calypso – 'in love yet'. They are poems containing the same sense of loss that had found its way into the final pages of 'Along Rideout Road that Summer', where Buster says his farewells to Fanny Hohepa:

> And in the end, beginning my sentence with a happy conjunction, I held her indistinct, dark head. We stayed so for a minute, together and parting as always, with me tumbling down upon her the mute dilemma my mind then pretended to resolve, and she offering no restraint, no argument better than the dark oblivion of her face.

Duggan continued to write, but it seems he knew perfectly well that he was backed into a corner. 'I cannot' (he wrote to Charles Brasch) 'go back from all the furious flow of "Riley's Handbook" to the well-tuned banalities of, say, Chapter. It may be that I cannot go forward either.'

What followed was a decade in which advertising and alcohol slowly but surely defeated the writing and any kind of secure self-regard. I still remember the best of it, the social occasions of the early and middle sixties, with the greatest pleasure and nostalgia. But a point was reached where the writing stopped, and so, soon after, did the socialising. Now there was only work, booze, violence, therapy and shame. Yet 'The Magsman Miscellany', written in the last year of his life, demonstrates that another Duggan – wiser, more tranquil, benign even, but still inventive and witty – might have risen from the burn-out and the burn-up if cancer had not intervened.

His suffering was immense, but he should be remembered also as a man who took and gave pleasure in abundance. His literary talents were not broad and various, but they were extraordinary, and his achievement was to add something different, something no one looking at the makeup of the Kiwi character could quite have counted on.

Eric McCormick – The Scholar Ambulant

Eric McCormick was so much a part of the intellectual life of Auckland that a person like myself, involved in the arts and employed by the university, came to think of him, or rather not to think of him but to accept him without thought, as an item in the landscape. In fact I don't have to move from where I'm standing to see a painting by Louise Henderson, which is a reminder of where I encountered him for the very first time. A good friend during 1951–2, my first years at the university, was Diane, Louise's daughter. Eric, already the author of our first serious critical work, *Letters and Art in New Zealand,* was often a visitor at the Henderson house, as was John Weeks, a member of the group with whom Louise exhibited. That household was, I think, a part of my undergraduate education at least as important as what went on in lectures and tutorials.*

Eric at that time was still living in Grafton Road, and it must have been there that I first saw a Frances Hodgkins. Just the year before I arrived at university he had given up his lectureship in English and was already at work on his first book on Hodgkins, *The Expatriate.*

Eric was happiest working alone as a scholar, at his own pace, able to check and recheck everything, never needing to declare himself until he was sure the job was done – a luxury denied the person who must, ready or not, stand and deliver to classes. As a lecturer he had been diffident and less than happy; and I remember a friend of those years, Peter Goddard, one year ahead of me in English, saying he'd sat beside Maurice Gee in one of Eric's lectures, and that when it ended Gee had looked down at the system of ticks and crosses he'd been making instead of notes and declared, 'That was 40 per cent ums and 35 per cent ahs. The rest was very interesting.'

When I returned from my two years as a lecturer in Australia, and a further two as a research student in England, there was another point of common ground between us. My PhD supervisor was Professor L.C. Knights, who had been Eric's contemporary at Cambridge, and was later King Edward VII Professor of English there. Together they had been involved in founding

---

In March 1999 I was the guest speaker at an occasion for the naming of the E.H. McCormick Research Library at the Auckland Art Gallery. I spoke without notes, but was afterwards asked for a text. This, as far as I could recall, was what I said.

* I have written about the Henderson household in 'Why Do I Like It, Then?' in Part 4 of this book.

Scrutiny, the formidable Leavisite journal which for three decades remained a dominant force in British academic criticism. Kind, encouraging, and deeply serious, Knights spoke warmly of Eric, and it was clear he found it puzzling that he should have returned to New Zealand. He was similarly puzzled when I made the same decision, and even warned me delicately that, like Eric, I too might vanish into obscurity in the South Pacific rather than fulfill my promise in a place able to appreciate and reward it.

Through the 1960s and seventies Eric's path and mine crossed frequently. He was associated with the University Press, and at intervals a research fellow in the History Department, where Keith Sinclair regarded him as a mentor, admired and was even, I think, in awe of his meticulousness, and did everything he could (which was a good deal) to smooth Eric's path so that his researches could continue.

I had read the published version of Eric's lecture *The Inland Eye,* delivered at the Auckland Art Gallery in 1959 while I was overseas; and in (I think) the late 1960s came his wonderful piece in the *Listener* about the visit of Rupert Brooke to New Zealand. The effect of these two together led me to urge him (I'm sure I wasn't alone in this) to write an autobiography. Brooke had been my first model as a thirteen or fourteen-year-old poet; and in the Mt Albert Grammar School library I'd come upon the selection of his letters from the South Seas with an excitement similar (I imagined) to Eric's when he made his discovery that Brooke might even have set foot in his home town, Taihape, while he was a child there. What I failed to recognise at the time was that these two items, as Eric saw them, were only indirectly about himself, and that that was what made them possible. For a person as diffident and private as he was, autobiography could only be sanctioned by having, or seeming to have, a subject other and (as he would have seen it) more important than himself.

Nor did it occur to me how different Eric's interest in Brooke, the young poet famous for his beauty, was from my own. Mine was romantic only in the literary sense. I think I knew from Louise Henderson's conversation, and from Frank Sargeson's, that Eric was homosexual; but he (and even I) belonged to a time when a private life was private. I didn't figure in Eric's so I didn't think about it. If I had, I would have been less puzzled by his response – ironically, almost whimsically, negative – to my urging on him the idea of a full autobiography.

Much later, in the early 1980s, he agreed to be interviewed by Vincent O'Sullivan for the *Listener,* and his regrets afterwards showed how sensitive he was about even the most charitably intended public exposure. There was no tape of their conversations. 'I can only conclude,' Eric wrote to me, 'that when the decision ... was made to publish an article [O'Sullivan] had to rely mainly on his recollections, his impressions, and his own vocabulary.' To Eric, exactness, subtlety of emphasis, were of the utmost importance, and he felt words – quite the wrong words – had been put into his mouth:

I never use 'Oxbridge', I don't sneer (why should I?) at university teachers who also wish to be 'creative artists' (a term I avoid), I don't criticise by innuendo, and certainly, never condescendingly described the Leavises as 'rather simple folk' (*folk!*) Vincent meant well, but the whole thing was a mistake. I should have refused.

—

In 1972, after eight months in Menton on the Mansfield Fellowship, I moved with my family to London for the remainder of the year. One of the things I had done in Menton was to read right through all Mansfield's published work; and it had come to me that her letters and journals, set side by side, often illuminated one another. My thought was that I should make a selection and run them together chronologically, dividing the book into chapters with biographical summaries and notes. In London I put the idea to Allen Lane and Penguin. It was accepted, and a contract drawn up.

I was keen to add significant unpublished letters, which would mean, of course, working in the Turnbull Library where most were held. But some were in the British Museum, and it was there, not in the famous Reading Room where I had worked on my PhD but in the Manuscripts Room, that I found Eric working on what became *Omai, Pacific Envoy,* in which the handsome boy from Polynesia comes to Europe and moves at ease among the rich and famous.

Eric introduced me to his London, or to that part of it which was not private and secret. He liked to discover the grottiest cafes (there was no acute *é* in the pronunciation) where for a few pence the darkest imaginable English tea was served in thick cups with buns and butter. He introduced me to the YWCA, hidden away behind the rather smarter YMCA in Tottenham Court Road, where the lunch was not good, but cheap. Sometimes, when we both took the opportunity offered once a week to work late in the Manuscripts Room, he took me to a serve-yourself Italian restaurant. Here was puritan Eric's ideal – genuine Italian food and wine, prepared by Italians, but cheap, and without the pretensions he so much hated of 'good' restaurant eating.

Sometimes when we were working together he would say there was something he needed to see in the National Portrait Gallery, and we would set off together to look at it. I am used to being told I walk too fast, but Eric, almost thirty years my senior, set a cracking pace. He also knew shortcuts, alleys, underground passageways, and left me with the impression (which can't have been entirely correct) that it was possible to walk most of the way from Bloomsbury to Trafalgar Square without ever coming up, or out, into the main thoroughfares.

We exchanged information about our work; and it was to Eric I showed my discovery of a letter revealing that John Middleton Murry's, and consequently Antony Alpers's, dating of Mansfield's 'A Married Man's Story', was quite wrong – which meant, in turn, that Murry's narrative of the ups and downs of Mansfield's career as a writer was seriously flawed. (Alpers was to reject this finding in a footnote to his 1980 biography; but later, in editing a chronological collected Mansfield, appeared to accept it by placing the story where the letter showed it should go.)

Through the rest of the 1970s I was on the committee of Auckland University Press, which published *Omai, Pacific Envoy* in the same year, 1977, as Allen Lane and Penguin brought out my Mansfield selection.

Reflecting on what I know of McCormick the man, and of his work, it occurs to me not unfair, nor anything Eric would quarrel with, to say that he began as a colonial and a snob. These were the imprint of time, place and circumstance, and his whole intellectual life and writings were given over, not to erasing the imprint, but to correcting it. It had to be possible to inherit our European traditions without being overborne by them, and without letting them distort our local recognitions. In the arts it was necessary to have our own good critics and sound scholars, and Eric set up single-handed as critic and scholar, with the same kind of diligence, courage and practicality that his father had set up McCormick's Boot and Shoe Emporium in Taihape. That's why his life and his work are so important, even though the books themselves vary a great deal in interest and quality. We needed such a person. He filled the post.

To me his masterpiece remains *The Expatriate,* where he wove together extracts from the treasure-trove he had discovered of Hodgkins's letters – so skilfully and tactfully, with such a sure hand and eye, the reader forgets his presence and reads the work almost as autobiography. As a young man Eric had wanted to be a fiction writer and had given up this ambition because, he said, he recognised his own limitations. But here was fiction, not in the sense of something 'made up', but of the imagination working upon factual material to body forth the larger truth, the life, the 'story'. Eric McCormick became Frances Hodgkins, and his pleasure in the role shines forth clearly in the prose.

There is a moment of sad autobiographical truthfulness in Eric's 'Beginnings' article* when he acknowledges that as a child he was teased and bullied for effeminacy, and that he caused his father great embarrassment by always wanting to dress up in women's clothes. Frances Hodgkins's letters were the clothes that allowed him to appear at his best.

---

* *Islands* 22, Vol. 6, No. 4, May 1978, pp. 380-390.

Gregory O'Brien
and Andrew Johnston

Gregory O'Brien is both poet and painter, and latterly a valued, one might almost say a necessary, voice in the public presentation of work by major New Zealand artists (notably Colin McCahon and Ralph Hotere), and in the articulation, not of a theory, but of a language and a set of reference points, for talking about them. He has sometimes illustrated his own poems, and their visual elements are unusually strong.

As poet he has always been confident, fluent, inventive and industrious, beginning as something like a surrealist, where almost everything in the picture was 'real', or had a recognisable foundation in 'fact', but was chosen and arranged in comic and/or disconcerting conjunctions. It was a kind of wit that had great charm, and was happy to risk the charge of whimsy.

But soon the 'real', the natural and recognisable order of things, was being allowed predominance and authority, though still with the underlying sense that its stability was hardly more than a pact dictated by social convenience. That 'natural order of things' was our necessary myth, our convention of representation, causing us to overlook the miracles of absurd conjunction which are around us all the time.

Observant, excited, always on the move, O'Brien was, and remains, a quirky aggregator, maker of lists and connections, teller of tales and tallies. Loquacious and nervous, quick, clever and affectionate, amusing and engaging – *l'homme, c'est le style*. 'The camera is a chatterbox / of the eyes', he writes in one poem, seeming to catch an aspect of self in the characterisation.

There is also, lurking somewhere behind this life-energy, the bleak knowledge that we occupy a universe which is flying apart, and that any slight sense we have of controlling our own destiny is an illusion. So we must keep talking to one another, and perhaps to 'God'. O'Brien's poems all have the sound of a voice, of communication which hopes for communion, of language as the game by which we prove ourselves, the instrument with which we divert ourselves while the sun goes down.

Through the second half of the 1990s his work continues playful and the touch light, but there is a steadying of focus and a gain in ballast as life-commitments (love, marriage, children) make the need for some kind of 'faith' more urgent. In that sense, more than in the sense that O'Brien's Catholicism is important to him (which it is), many, perhaps all, of his poems can be seen

Published in *Contemporary Poets*, Chicago, 2000.

as prayers. But they are neither solemn nor unserious, and have (in Keats's phrase) no 'palpable design' on the reader. O'Brien is a kind of priest who intones, 'Let us play.' And the piety is real.

His poems are also very often stories – unplotted narratives which continue to reveal, as his early work did, how un-ordinary the ordinary is. Deadpan astonishment is his stock-in-trade. The places we inhabit are as absurd as they are beautiful. Seeing is Believing, and the surprise of it seldom wanes or wavers.

These narratives mix disparate elements without apology (but usually with explanatory notes!). He is a huge raider of history (big and small, local and family), of biography, of locations, spaces, landscapes, giving his readers always a sense of rapid movement – through space (these poems travel), and time (things are always happening where things have happened). There is copiousness, untidiness, clutter, jitter. There is also reflection, a reaching beyond the comic, droll, or bizarre, toward the sad shadows of general truths.

What holds it all together perhaps is the consistency with which the painter's eye shapes everything into scenes:

> A woman is kneeling in a stream -
>   the mist is a sponge drawing the town
> up into itself. Dogs lie around the park
>   like battered violins
>   their music scattered ...

In the very best, the absolutely proper, sense (the sense of a Great Tradition) everything in O'Brien's poetry, even the eloquence, is borrowed and reused. He has made his proper connections with those who have gone before, and his lines are open to the future.

—

Andrew Johnston's constant attention is to the word which, as in St John's surprisingly emphatic declaration about what there was 'in the beginning', comes before what it refers to, and calls it into existence. 'Being' is there already in 'begin', needing only a slight rearrangement of the letters.

The word, then, must be 'God', and when you grant it such precedence, it works hard for you. It seems to reverse Allen Curnow's insistence on 'the reality prior to the poem', but the difference is more apparent than real. It's a matter of where the two poets start – from opposite poles, but each working towards the same centre, a world of words, but one as near to 'reality' as we can ever hope to be authors of.

In Johnston's sequence 'Fool Heart' the Dwarf Conifer Collection is 'whistling I wish / IwishIwish'. A dead, or dormant, phrase like 'sensible shoes' suddenly springs to life as footprints reveal 'a toehold on the real'. 'New leaves/put themselves out for you.' A man whose heart, like the conifers, goes 'I wish IwishIwish', 'might need a new frame of mind'. A shag 'dives – for its other name / and comes up with *cormorant*'. 'Old magnolias burst into Latin.' It is to have their being arrested, confirmed, attested, that the conifers and magnolias, the shoes and the shag, are wanting, and this is a miracle which only language can perform for them.

There are two aspects to this: the word as meaning, and the word as sound – and in Johnston's poetry the two have to work unusually closely together. Speaking by phone across continents, 'There's an echo, / it's you, it's euphony, it's funny.' The title of his second collection, *The Sounds* (both place and aural quantity), catches this doubleness perfectly.

There is, one feels, reflecting on his poems at large, a characteristic temperamental movement in them which is an escape from an inner darkness into the neutral light of particulars. There is wit; there is even comedy; but who ever supposed that these can't (and don't commonly) flourish in a sad soil? The poet alone in New York, trying to remember the names of the Seven Dwarfs, remembers Happy last. In London, where the sun 'fades from star to rumour', he tells himself, 'Kneel and pray to the fire instead: / your wishes will be granted, as wishes are, / little by little.' Parting from a lover, loss and grief are there, but pressed down, disciplined to wit:

> When I leave I leave
>
> a lot to be desired.

There are two forms Johnston especially favours: one a poem in five, or more latterly six, loose unrhymed couplets; the other the sestina. The couplet poems seem in various ways to spring from, or attach themselves to, occasions. The sestinas have, rather, the appearance of generating something out of nothing. They reveal hard graft and great technical accomplishment; but not even a master of the form can make any but the first stanza sound inevitable. In 'The Singer', however, Johnston goes close to it. He also likes to use the haiku, not singly but as a stanza form, and its economy suits his temperament:

> along the beach road
> River Glade, Park Avenue
> Oak Bay, Walnut Close
>
> fences and glimpses
> architectural finish
> magazine gardens
>
> gap for the golf course
> Toledo Park Motel, keep
> your options open

Johnston's work has been likened to John Ashbery's. That is one of several influences; and it may be Ashbery's example which has encouraged his fascination with the sestina. But the temperamental difference is huge. With Johnston one doesn't have to take so much on trust. He requires his words, wherever they start from, to make their way towards something we can recognise and begin to understand; Ashbery prefers to stay well clear of 'meaning', while signalling excitedly that it's there somewhere, just out of sight.

Mansfield's F.O.

In 1972, while working on my Penguin selection of Mansfield's letters and journals, I visited her friend Ida Baker. They were born in the same year, 1888, and met in London as schoolgirls at Queen's College, Harley Street, where together they chose their 'professional' names. Kathleen Beauchamp would be Katherine Mansfield, and Ida Baker would be Lesley Moore – K.M. and L.M. They were to be friends for life, Mansfield always dominant, summoning Baker when she needed her, dismissing her when the need was past and she had grown tired of her subservience. Baker never wavered in her devotion, and as Mansfield's tuberculosis required that she spend winters in warmer places while her husband, John Middleton Murry, remained working as an editor in London, the friend's help and companionship became essential. Baker was loved sparingly, teased, mocked, raged at, and sometimes hated with ferocity.

At the time of my visit I had recently transcribed from a manuscript of a letter to Murry a passage, omitted from the published version, in which Mansfield had spoken of her 'hate' of L.M.: '… her great fat arms, her tiny blind breasts, her baby mouth, the underlip always wet and a crumb or two of chocolate stain at the corner – her eyes fixed on me – fixed – waiting what I may do that she may copy it. Think what you would do if you had consumption and lived with your deadly enemy … I leaned over a gate today and dreamed she'd died of heart failure and I heard myself cry out, "Oh, what heaven! what heaven!"'

I wasn't sure that Baker had read such passages, but it was most likely she had, since Murry employed her, after Mansfield's death, to copy manuscript letters and journals. Yet Baker had always put these explosions down to Mansfield's illness, and her fidelity remained unshaken.

The following are notes taken immediately after my visit and only recently rediscovered. (I had just turned forty.):

23.10.72
Took the train from Waterloo to Salisbury, stopped by to look at the Cathedral, and then took the bus to Wood Green, a village off the main Salisbury–Bournemouth road. Narrow roads and bridges, with the bus brushing hedgerows as it went. I got down at the village (no one but me left

---

Published here for the first time.

on the bus by then), the bus went on, and there I was, alone, no one in sight. I walked along the country road, through the village (one shop only and a post office), and found the lane L.M. had marked on the map she had sent me – only a track for walking or riding, not for cars – a bank covered with autumn woods on one side, water meadows on the other, and a pony grazing down a lane.

The cottage was right at the end of the lane, among trees, thatched, very small. A dog came out to greet me. The wooden plank door was half open (kept like that, she later explained, so the tits could fly to and from their nests indoors). I looked in and there she was, struggling out of her chair, a very old lady, her head sunk forward, a pronounced stoop, finding it difficult to get up and come and greet me. She looked all of her eighty-five years and for a moment I felt alarmed that I had bothered her, but she soon put me at ease about that.

The stud of the cottage must be less than six feet – I had to stoop to avoid bumping my head on the ceiling. Books and pictures everywhere. Two rooms downstairs, but at the back a small modern kitchen – 'modern' in 1942. Upstairs, two small bedrooms and a larger one, with tiny windows looking out on the thatch.

L.M. gave me a glass of cider and we talked for a little, and then took everything to the lunch table so we wouldn't need to get up and down. She had cooked me a stew and vegetables, followed by two kinds of pudding. She herself ate a hard boiled egg and cold peas, together with some of the hot vegetables and then a small portion of pudding. We must have sat two hours over lunch, talking almost exclusively about Mansfield and her friends.

She has a distinguished face, is very much an old-fashioned gentlewoman, and doesn't appear to have lost her intellectual edge – though she has very poor eyesight and has the greatest difficulty reading. One can see that she was worthy of being Mansfield's friend – that the impression of her as a nonentity, an insignificant hanger-on, is quite wrong. But she says that at the time she was too uncertain of herself to be an ideal companion for Mansfield. 'What Katherine needed was someone like Anne Rice [the American painter who did Mansfield's portrait] who could breeze in, full of life and high spirits, with flowers and jokes and gossip and laughter. That was what Katherine liked. I was much too tentative.'

She was very good, very fair and balanced, about Murry. She smiled and got a faraway look in her eye when she said, 'Oh, he was a *charming* boy.' She recognised the attraction and felt it herself. But he was too immature, she said, always adopting a pose, a role, because he was uncertain of himself. He was *God*. He was the *Devil*. He was suffering torments of soul because of *the War*. It was all very dramatic; and when Katherine had spent a day on oxygen because she couldn't breathe it was difficult to tolerate his coming in and saying his *soul* was in torment. There was great intellectual companionship, and real love. 'But Murry failed Katherine when she became ill because he wanted someone to support him, not someone needing support.'

I asked what she thought of letters Murry had written to Frieda Lawrence saying he'd only discovered in his fourth marriage what love between a man and a woman could be. L.M. smiled and said, 'Well, of course, dear Mary [Murry's fourth wife] was what he'd always really wanted – nurse, doctor, secretary, companion, lover, all rolled into one. Her whole being was given over to him.' With Katherine there was great love, but at the same time she had her own identity, and perhaps what Murry unconsciously resented (even though he acknowledged it) was that her talent was superior to his.

L.M.'s conversation didn't tell me a great deal I didn't already know, but it made many things vivid. When she spoke with sudden emphasis of Lawrence striding up and down the room, impatient, on the verge of anger (he was waiting for lunch, which poor L.M. was making) she somehow conveyed an impression of his energy and urgency.

'After Katherine's death,' she said, 'there was nothing left of me. I was just a heap of ashes. Then, after a few months, I realised there was something.' She went through the motions of reaching down, picking what was left out of the ashes and holding it up between thumb and forefinger. She said, 'I always thought of it as a little omnibus.'

Murry paid her £10 a month to transcribe manuscripts, and then 'he passed me on to Elizabeth'. [Mansfield's cousin, the Countess von Armin, later the Countess Russell, author of *Elizabeth in her German Garden.*] 'Elizabeth was by this time married to Bertie's brother, the Earl. They lived the high life, but Elizabeth had various bolt-holes to get away and write in.' One was this cottage in Wood Green, and she put L.M. in charge of it. When Elizabeth 'couldn't stand the Earl any longer' she left him and begged L.M. to travel with her, but L.M. declined. She had by that time met the woman, twenty years her senior, who would be her companion for many years. They farmed, travelled, and settled once again in the cottage [which perhaps Elizabeth left to her?] in 1942, remaining together until the friend's death.

I had the impression that this must have been a lesbian relationship. She gave that impression without saying so; but she was explicit and emphatic that there was nothing of that kind with Mansfield, and that she had not even known what the word meant until long after Mansfield's death.

I asked about Mansfield and Virginia Woolf and she said, 'Of course Katherine was always ... *interested* – in everything Virginia did. In her writing ... But there was a barrier. As people say these days, they didn't quite *click.* I never did understand why that fell through.'

I can see why Ottoline Morrell called L.M. 'the Mountain'. (Mansfield, who loved naming people, called her variously the Dwarf, Betsy, and the Faithful One, soon abbreviated to F.O.) She's now stooped but still very tall, with large strong legs and big sensible walking shoes. She dresses in a tweedy countrywoman way.

She said that after Mansfield died she never talked to anyone about her, nor answered letters about her, because she'd promised she wouldn't. Katherine had said, 'When I'm dead people will come and ask about me. Don't tell them anything.' So for a long time she didn't. Then Kot [their friend S.S. Koteliansky] urged her to help Antony Alpers who was writing a life, and for four years, on and off, she did. But when the book came out [this was Alpers's biography of 1954 – he has since written another] she regretted it. She thought Alpers 'hadn't caught the true Katherine', and she couldn't finish reading it.

So for another twenty years she said no more, until recently, when the BBC persuaded her to co-operate in a programme, and a friend helped her record her memories.

I asked why Mansfield insisted she mustn't talk. 'Oh I think I know why,' she said. 'It's because she thought I would be asked about the literary side of her life, and I didn't really know enough – wasn't qualified to speak about it.' But there was a whole life outside books. 'People forget that. That was what I shared with Katherine.'

She explained why she believed the photograph at the front of the 1951 edition of the letters to Murry is not Mansfield but Beatrice Hastings – neck too thick, lips too heavy, curved eyebrows. 'Of course the dress and hairstyle are right, but Beatrice Hastings imitated Katherine's style at that time, so they would be. The little necklace looks like Katherine's, but *her* necklace wouldn't have gone around *that* neck!' I knew already that this was her opinion, and I didn't tell her that I disagreed, that I believed the photo in question was simply the healthy young Mansfield, pre-tuberculosis, who in 1911 had put on a little weight. As for '*that* neck' – I couldn't help remembering Beatrice Hastings as Modigliani had painted her, with a neck like a starved giraffe.

I scrambled around the cottage photographing it from the slope that looks down on it, then from the water meadows (getting my feet wet). The trees on the hill-slope were turning yellow-orange and showering down. We'd had coffee after lunch and we had tea before I left. She said, 'When I knew you were coming I didn't expect it to be unpleasant, but I didn't expect anything. I certainly didn't expect it would be so very *pleasant*.'

We shook hands warmly at that door which remains always ajar so the birds can reach their nests. I felt it wasn't right that she should be left alone but that, no doubt, is what she prefers. I stopped and looked back at the cottage. The sun was shining on it and on the autumn trees. It seemed remote, picture-book, quite unreal. This had been, so to speak, my first living (though at second-hand) contact with Katherine Mansfield, and almost the only one remaining. Katherine and Murry, Lawrence and Frieda, Virginia Woolf, Ottoline Morrell, Bertrand Russell, Mark Gertler, S.S. Koteliansky, the Gilbert Cannans, Tom and Vivienne Eliot, the Gordon Campbells – they were all dead. Just this one frail old woman remembered them all.

Part 2

Four
Public
Lectures

Narrativity,
or the Birth of Story

Roland Barthes opens his essay 'The Death of the Author' by quoting a sentence from Balzac's story 'Sarrasine': 'This was woman herself, with her sudden fears, her irrational whims, her instinctive worries, her impetuous boldness, her fussings, and her delicious sensibility.'

Barthes then asks, 'Who is speaking thus?' And he continues, 'Is it the hero of the story bent on remaining ignorant of the castrato hidden beneath the woman? Is it Balzac the individual furnished by his personal experience with a philosophy of Woman? Is it Balzac the author professing 'literary' ideas on femininity? Is it universal wisdom? Romantic psychology? We shall never know' [Barthes goes on] 'for the good reason that writing [*'écriture'* is his word] is the destruction of every voice, of every point of origin. Writing is that neutral, composite, oblique space where our object slips away, the negative where all identity is lost, starting with the very identity of the body of writing.'

High talk of that kind in the French language moves very fast, like a performance of *Die Fledermaus* on ice. It's a rhetoric that trips off the tongue, issues like a string of pearls beautifully articulated through pouting lips, and is gone before you can say in your clod-hopping anglophone way, 'Hang on a minute, did you just say? Surely you didn't mean ...'

Is it meaningful, can it ever be made meaningful without perversity, to say that writing is a 'neutral, composite, oblique space ... where all identity is lost'? Barthes has a reason for saying so; and I have a reason for disputing with him. He wishes to dispose of the author for the benefit (or so he pretends) of the reader. 'The birth of the Reader,' the final sentence of his essay says, 'must be at the expense of the death of the Author.' I am here to assert that the author is not dead, and that I (not exclusively you understand, but just by way of example) – I am he. I wish to assert further, and quite contrary to Barthes, that the survival of the author is necessary to the survival of the reader – and by reader I mean another person whom modern theoretical approaches to literature have pronounced dead: the Common Reader.

My purpose is not self-assertion or self-promotion, but to remind you that there is a person who sits down with a pen or at a keyboard and who puzzles over the best way something should be told; and that this silent, boring person,

---

An invited lecture delivered to a plenary session of the 27th Congress of AULLA (the Australasian Universities Languages and Literatures Association), University of Otago, February 1993, and published in *Landfall* 186, Spring 1993.

leaves distinct traces of him- or herself which common readers learn to recognise and come to expect, enjoy, admire, and even to love.

Let's get clear – or less unclear – what this means.

I suppose Byron is generally credited with being one of the most colourful authorial personalities to have lived. We know a good deal about Byron's schooldays, his marriage, his amorous life, his lameness, his swimming, his horsemanship, his politics, his passion for Greek national independence; we know (if I'm not misremembering) that he said his literary faults were those of negligence and not of labour and that some of his narrative poems were tossed off while undressing after coming home from balls and masquerades. None of that, however, is quite the Byron those who are his readers feel they know well and recognise instantly. The Byron known to his readers is not a man of action, not a great lover, not a purveyor of opinion, but a characteristic turn of phrase, a kind of imagery, a particular cadence, certain quirks of narratology. He's a man discovered in the action of making linguistic choices, hesitating between one word and another, attempting to find a vocabulary and grammatical structure that will match certain internal colours, appetites, tones, cadences. The state of mind or of undress in which this process was conducted is of interest, perhaps, but of no great relevance to the literary quality. Even manuscripts, when they exist, can show only a very little of a process at the end of which is left, each time, another example of what his readers recognise as the distinct Byronic voice. That authorial voice is what I will keep coming back to in order to challenge the validity of Dr Barthes's death certificate.

Anyone who ventures to write begins by being a reader. You work within an existing tradition. Your own talent and experience of life are never enough. You must be fed by what has gone before. That's the nature of all the arts; and though there must be times when the tradition will seem oppressive and limiting, the merest glance at literary history will show that the writers whose work survives and earns continuing respect have all drawn richly on the literary past. To do that is a talent in itself. To recognise it and chart it is one of your legitimate functions as academic teachers.

But the writer has to make choices, and those choices are made intuitively, long before they become conscious and are rationalised. In my own case I would say that over all the years I've been writing fiction, or perhaps I should say more accurately, not so often writing fiction as *thinking about* writing it, there have been four broad impulses, or inclinations, or directions. I can't call them anything so clear as guiding principles, because they were in operation long before they were recognised and formulated.

The first has been to keep the writing at some distance from what I've always thought of (the term is vague, but my conception of it is not) as 'conventional fiction' – not to abandon it altogether, since on the whole it's what readers expect, but not ever to relax into it either.

The second has been a love of narrative, and of narrative complexity –

quite different from E.M. Forster, for example, who says regretfully, 'Yes – oh dear yes – the novel tells a story'; or from Ford Madox Ford, who I think said 'story' was a dirty word. Forster (this is in his *Aspects of the Novel*) admits that narrative is 'the fundamental aspect'; but he adds, 'I wish that it was not so, that it could be something different ... not this low atavistic form.' To me 'this low atavistic form' has always seemed potentially as subtle and fine and challenging as music.

The third of these inclinations, or directions, has been to keep open and faintly ambiguous the degree to which what is offered can be seen to be 'true'. There can be a very fine line indeed between fact and fiction, and to make the reader more rather than less aware of it seems to me one of those enriching things good writing can do – a heightening of consciousness about the nature of language and reality.

The last, and perhaps the least important of the four, but one which nevertheless has been consistent, has been to push the frame of fiction out wide; to represent not just individuals but a society – which means in my case New Zealand society – at given moments in its history. Which is to say, I suppose, that although I've held myself at a careful distance from the realist tradition, I've never wanted to cut myself entirely adrift from it.

There is one further impulse, or inclination, or ambition – one which may sound faintly fatuous when stated, but which can't be left unstated because it underlies all the others and explains what makes each writer unique – and that is in one's own terms to 'write well'; which means, not to parade writerly skills, not to do something so it will be noticed and admired, but rather to go as near as one can, in whatever way seems to work, towards matching something that exists in the mind before anything goes down on the page. From phrase to phrase, sentence to sentence, paragraph to paragraph, and so on through the larger structure, one is striving to achieve harmonies, dissonances, repetitions, recognitions – God knows what; it would be foolish to pretend that the author (*this author*) knew exactly, or that anyone else could tell him. What he's after can only be measured in the practice. Quite simply he wants to be able to go back and adjust and reread and say, 'Yes, that's better', and adjust again, and finally be able to say, 'That's very nearly *it*. That's as good as I can make it, or as near as I can get.' That is the only true and safe satisfaction to be had from the business of writing, and what results is once again what I'm calling the distinct authorial voice.

Now let me say something about what I've called 'conventional fiction'. Quite early on I recognised that one could sit down and produce something which was an echo of all the other novels currently or recently written; that this was what many, perhaps most, practising fiction writers did – which is to say of course that some did it badly and some did it brilliantly well. It was a literary convention, which like all conventions in the arts, unpractised readers probably mistake for reality.

Ezra Pound's principle of 'Make it new' is not one of innovation for its own sake; properly understood it means that if you don't in some degree 'make it new' then it's not yours. You are imitating art, not life. The desire is not, or shouldn't be, to be avant garde; the desire is to be truthful. In some headachingly complex and difficult sense, I think the object is mimesis, and to achieve that, what has become merely conventional must always be left behind – but not too far behind if one wants still to speak to an audience. The literary writer, as distinct from the merely professional one, goes on ahead up the trail, but not so far that he's out of sight.

As Alberto Moravia puts it (and I will be returning to him) 'Every time the representation of reality declines into a convention, [fiction] makes a move upward to where convention can't follow it. This flight from mechanisation and ready-made formulae is characteristic of all the arts ...'

I will say here by way of parenthesis that this may seem to contradict my insistence upon the tradition which must live on in the new work. That is a paradox perhaps, but not in practice a contradiction. Often, for example, the new is achieved partly by going back – as Wordsworth and his contemporaries regained a life-grip on the language of poetry by stepping back over the heroic couplet, which had become the corset of eighteenth-century English verse, and revived much older ballad forms. The tradition is a canon (dangerous word, I know) of works which have each in their way escaped from the merely conventional.

So what do I mean by conventional fiction? Its opposite, which will help to define it, is also conventional, but much older – the convention of the fairy tale, or folk tale. Here are the opening four sentences of one by the brothers Grimm:

> There was once a Man whose family consisted of three sons, and his property only of the house in which he dwelt. Now, each of the sons wished to have the house at the death of their father; but they were all so dear to him he knew not what to do for fear of offending the one or the other. He would have sold the house and shared the money but it had been so long in his family he did not like to do that. All at once he thought of a plan, and said to his sons, 'Go into the world and each of you learn a trade, and he who makes the best masterpiece shall have my house.'

Those four sentences contain in summary what a modern novel would offer in the space of a long opening chapter or chapters. It's the merest outline; but all the essentials are there. And just to make clear what I mean by 'conventional fiction', I've drafted a small part of how this same story might begin if it were used as the scenario for a novel:

> 'The old man says we can't have the ute tonight.'
> 'I know. Maurice told me.'
> 'Wants to talk to us.'
> 'Dunno why it can't wait, do you?'
> 'Better humour him. He's been funny lately.'
> The two brothers, stripped to the waist in the autumn sun, were taking turns

digging a drain that was to run along the lower side of the orchard. Dan, the one in the drain with the spade, was lean and blonde with shoulder length hair. Rod, who was rolling a cigarette, squinting away into the distance where the far blue hills seemed to rise up suddenly out of golden stubble fields, was perhaps a year or two older; heavier built and darker skinned.

He licked the cigarette paper, completed the roll, and plucked tobacco shreds from either end. 'Something's worrying the poor old sod, that's for sure,' he acknowledged.

Up from the lower paddock came the sound of Maurice's farm-bike, the barking of a dog, and the ...

And the what? The lowing of the cows being brought in to milk perhaps; or the snorting of pigs; or perhaps the yawning of readers settling into the comfortably familiar hammock of conventional fiction. We have soon to meet the third brother, Maurice, and the father – let's call him Frank; probably the mother too, and some neighbours and girlfriends. We will be given some background – family and local history. Characters will begin to distinguish themselves – the angry brother, the gentle one, the ambitious one; the father who has never quite recovered from the war he never speaks about; the mother who never had a daughter with whom she might have shared some of her secrets and dreams and discontents.

And meanwhile, as the picture builds out character and setting, we have that question hanging over this opening chapter: why has the old man said they can't take the ute out tonight? What is it he wants to talk to them about? In fact of course, he's been a heavy smoker ever since he was a soldier in the Western Desert; and what he's going to tell them is that he's got lung cancer ('the big C', he'll call it), that he 'hasn't got much longer', and that there's the problem of how to divide up the farm.

There are quite a number of elements in that opening as I've crudely sketched it which might be analysed and recognised as standard formulae. There's the opening dialogue, for example, in unexplained isolation ('The old man says we can't have the ute tonight', and so on) followed by the discursive location in retrospect ('The two brothers, stripped to the waist in the autumn sun, were taking turns digging a drain ...') – so we *hear* first, and then we *see*; that in turn followed by exposition and explanation opening outward from a centre, so that the simplicity of the original linear narrative is concealed. There are also certain explanatory cadences, comfortably familiar to readers of the modern novel. Then there's *tone* – here a tone of bluff seriousness, typical especially of male New Zealand fiction, which has its female counterpart in a tone of chatty whimsy. One tone is meant to impress, the other to charm; both, because they're conventions, are traps. Fall too thoroughly into one or the other and the author is indeed 'dead' – anonymous – a purveyor, not of individual 'vision' (to use the term as Yeats uses it) but of a marketable convention.

Even dialogue, which can certainly be well or badly done, is a neutralising convention. Well done, it displays one of the greatest and rarest of literary virtues – economy. But the more there is of it – in other words the more truly dramatic the writing becomes – the less excuse there is for anything else. Just as all art aspires to the condition of music, so all realist fiction aspires to the condition of a play-script, and a whole range of *prose* possibilities are logically squeezed out. So even dialogue can turn into a constriction.

It would be quite wrong to deride this conventional patterning of fiction, because it does have its own potential for value; and also because if you elect to be a novelist then I think you signal a willingness to work somewhere within a recognised framework – just as Shakespeare worked within the conventions of the Elizabethan theatre, or Dickens within the conventions of the Victorian novel. But to assume it thoughtlessly, like a comfortable old shoe, is to court anonymity; it is to negate that distinct authorial voice.

There is also the question of form – very difficult to explain, or define, and you find fiction writers have different ways of talking about it. Frank Sargeson used to talk about 'focus' – keeping it or losing it, which made conversational sense anyway as a subjective indicator. Both Forster and Percy Lubbock struggle with the problem. Lubbock says that a novel 'is a thing to which a shape is ascribable, good or bad'; he also talks about 'a single embracing design'; but he acknowledges that this sense of shape, or design, tends to get lost in the linear and sequential way in which the reader necessarily apprehends the work. Forster speaks of 'pattern'. He says, 'Whereas the story appeals to our curiosity and the plot to our intelligence, the pattern appeals to our aesthetic sense, it causes us to see the book as a whole'. And he suggests that novels have shapes, offering the example of one, *Thais* by Anatole France, that's shaped like an hour-glass, and another, Lubbock's *Roman Pictures,* shaped like a grand chain.

I should say that I looked to see what Forster and Lubbock said on this matter of form because I was on the brink of repeating what I've said before: that in fiction I want to be able to see what I'm writing as a single object. I think of it physically – something you can pick up, like a melon, or a baby, or a radio, rather than something linear running away into the distance. I want it to have narrative-with-unity. And I think ideally for me it shouldn't indulge too far the apparently limitless accretion of detail which the realist convention permits and encourages – not, anyway, so much that the story (Ford's 'dirty word', Forster's 'low atavistic form') gets lost and becomes unimportant.

Consideration of what I wanted to say on this occasion has made me review my own history as a reader of fiction, because I hoped to make some direct connection between the reading and the practice. But to approach that in any general way would be too large a subject; and I thought in a broad-spectrum conference of this kind it might be of interest to set fiction in English aside for the moment and say something about each of three twentieth-century writers, Alberto Moravia, Jorge Luis Borges, and Günter Grass, whose work has been of great importance to me – not of course because they're 'better' than anglophone writers, but because, working in another language, they offer something different.

So here some way past the middle of my discourse let me make a second start with an anecdote. At the end of my first university year my brother-in-law got me a vacation job making sand moulds in the Penrose factory of McEwan's Machinery. In the room where the workers changed and had lunch there was a shelf of cheap paperbacks. One had a promisingly lurid cover and the title *Conjugal Love*. I borrowed it expecting sexual excitements. There were some of those, but they were not what made it remarkable. *Amore Conjugale* (as it is in the Italian) is a novel by Alberto Moravia about a novelist, Silvio, who decides he must stop having sex with his wife in order to preserve some essential part of himself for the novel he's currently writing, which is called *Conjugal Love* and which he believes to be a masterpiece. He gives up conjugal love in favour of *Conjugal Love*. While abstinence is being maintained he recognises a powerful sexual presence in Antonio, the bald squat ugly barber who comes every day to shave him. Leda, his wife, asks that Antonio be dismissed but Silvio refuses and so, consciously or unconsciously, paves the way for her infidelity.

Towards the end of the story Silvio begins to have doubts about his masterpiece. He takes it up: 'I did not read it straight through because I did not wish to be caught up in the rhythm of the narrative; but I read pieces here and there, and the more I read the more disquieted I became.'

He sets out a rigorous criticism under six headings and concludes that his novel fails on every one – that it is 'a book founded upon other books', one which might well be published, but which 'does not count'.

The clear-sightedness, momentarily exhilarating, which has permitted him to see its shortcomings now transforms itself into a 'feverish lucidity' as the sense of literary failure brings down the whole edifice of self. In despair he goes looking for his wife but her bedroom is empty. Their house is in the countryside, and he now remembers a threshing floor on raised ground, seen in the moonlight on the previous night, which with its three stacks suggesting Druidic dolmens had made him think of 'panic love', and of the idea that he might have sex with Leda there. He sets off in that direction and catches sight of her walking ahead of him in the moonlight. He follows and what he sees, of course, and watches, is her meeting and making frantic love on the threshing floor with the barber, Antonio.

In the final chapters there is at first despair, then reconciliation. Intending to tell Leda that he knows about her infidelity he tells her instead about his failure as a novelist – so they talk about two things at once, while pretending that they're discussing only his writing. He reads his novel to her and she proves her honesty and love for him by gently confirming his opinion of it – not trying to win back favour by pretending to admire it. She can see that he has been writing about his relationship with her, and she tells him that insofar as his story fails, it's because it idealises her. One day he will tell their story more accurately – which is to say, without saying it, that her infidelity with Antonio will have to be part of it. So it's clear that the novel we've just read is Silvio's later and more successful version of the novel called *Conjugal Love.*

To come back to myself, the nineteen-year-old student working at McEwan's Machinery in Penrose: this novel, I think, had quite a profound effect on my sense of what modern fiction might be, though I'm sure I couldn't then have said exactly what I learned from it.

Let me begin with the things one might observe as a critic and then work towards the slightly different things that might influence a writer. First there is the economy and sharpness with which the scenes are presented, and the consequent symbolic potential, or (to phrase it more exactly) the exemplary resonance, that seems to be released in them without their ever becoming abstract or simply interpretable. On that first reading and thereafter I was always struck in Moravia's fiction by the way for the reader the two senses of the verb 'to see' merge. As one 'sees' visually one is made to 'see' intellectually – to understand – though not to 'understand' anything that could be properly or fully expressed in any other way. For example, the scene in which Leda makes love to the barber on the threshing floor in the moonlight is a brilliantly visual dramatic climax at the same time that it bears the maximum weight of unstated 'meaning' or significance. If it can be said to 'represent', I suppose it represents the hard truth about human sexuality which Silvio's romantic fiction failed to recognise. It represents his failure of representation. But as soon as one states it abstractly something is lost.

Moravia's two great preoccupations, I soon found, were sex and politics; and his way to them was frequently through the medium of the female psyche. And although there was a sense in which his was an intellectual imagination rather than a sensual one, the land- and sea-scapes against which his human dramas were played out were always so rich and vivid they seemed to give body to his work, to lend it an authenticity it might otherwise have lacked.

Then, nearer to the direct practice of the art of fiction, there was the fact that Moravia was clearly concerned with what I would now call *provenance.* What is the source of the story we are being told? Whose is the narrative voice, and what is its authority? This was an anxiety which I felt in my own spasmodic attempts at fiction – why the simple 'eye of God' narration, which worked perfectly well in nineteenth-century novels, should so often give problems in the twentieth.

Much later I found that this was something discussed in Moravia's essays. The twentieth century, he argued, had lost the nineteenth century's confidence in the existence of, or in having a secure grasp upon, objective reality. Consequently third person narrative, with its pretence at knowing everything, now had the effect of '[inhibiting] the illusion and delight of representation in the novel' – an interesting statement because it meant that whatever steps he took to overcome this problem were taken still in the interests of mimesis.

Finally, and of most direct relevance to the concerns of the writer as writer rather than the writer as critic, there was in *Conjugal Love* the conundrum of the novel that seems to be about itself. I know this is something that readers can find irritating; but it is really the source of some of the most profound aspects of twentieth-century fiction – just as the most profound twentieth-century philosophy (which I would call the modern novel's first cousin) has been about itself. It is the way fiction has of being 'philosophical': not in offering packaged wisdom, any more than modern philosophy has offered ethics, but in exploring what is meant by 'truth'; what is meant by 'reality'; what is meant by 'history'; and what is meant by 'meaning'.

I turn now to another, perhaps lesser but more radical, fiction writer, the Argentinean Jorge Luis Borges, whose work I discovered first in the John Calder edition of 1965.

Rather than radical, perhaps I should have said outrageous. In the stories of that 1965 collection, *Fictions,* there were no land- and sea-scapes, no 'real' Argentina. Borges was remorselessly intellectual, formidably scholarly, sinisterly brilliant, and remorselessly formidably sinisterly playful. He made characters and narratives out of what had clearly begun as abstract ideas – often vast generalising ideas about the universe, or reality, of the kind that come to tease and excite the intelligent child or adolescent and are abandoned in what we call maturity.

For example: what if there were a secret sect, the Sect of the Phoenix, or the Men of the Secret, whose members, known to one another by hidden signs, existed in every country and culture in the world?

Or again, what if there should be a lottery in which a ticket might win you a prize but might equally cost you a forfeit or a punishment; and suppose it became compulsory for everyone without exception to participate in the lottery, and to accept that the punishments, like the rewards, were deserved.

Or suppose the universe were an infinite library, in which the books represented every possible arrangement of alphabetical symbols and their consequent meanings, and that when the vast and apparently random aggregation of books came at last to an end, so that every meaningful linguistic arrangement was represented, the whole thing began over again, thus demonstrating that what seemed random was, simply by infinite repetition, orderly.

Or imagine that a man set out to write *Don Quixote* in the twentieth century – not to revise or alter it in any way, and not to copy it, but to recreate it so that he became its author. How would his book, word for word the same as the one written by Cervantes, differ in meaning from the original?

These, as I've described them, are ideas; but they were bodied forth as fictions, made over into stories. Sometimes it seemed that this was an author outrageously satirising not just one society but all societies; and not just all societies, but the universe itself, the nature of reality. There *is*, there must be for each one of us, at least one secret sect from which we feel ourselves excluded. Life, with its rewards and punishments, *is* a lottery, which we try to convince ourselves has something to do with causation and justice. We *are* locked inside something like an infinite library, because language, arranged and rearranged until we have exhausted its possibilities, is the limit of our intellectual grasp upon reality.

And in the narrator of the story about Pierre Menard, author of *Don Quixote,* Borges anticipates and outdoes all those tricks of half-bogus half-real scholarship which were to become the staple of Nabokov's fiction.

And then (if I can tell it like a story) before the decade of the sixties was out, Borges sprang a surprise – at least on this reader. I remember very clearly, and still possess, the issue of the magazine *Encounter* of April 1969 which offered a selection of his work, in particular one story completely different from anything of his I'd seen up to that point, and which appeared to be an entirely new direction.

It was called 'The Intruder' and it concerned two red-haired rough-neck brothers of Danish descent, the Nilsens, living somewhere in the Argentine outback in the 1890s. The older one, Christian, brings home a woman to live with him. The younger one, Eduardo, grows morose. After a time he too brings home a woman, but soon sends her away. It's Christian's woman he wants. She is simply an object, and compliant, so to get over the problem Christian offers her to his brother and for a time they share her. But still these two, whose unity against a harsh world has been their protection, now find reasons – every reason but the real one – to snarl and bicker; and this is made worse as the woman tries but fails to hide her preference for the younger brother, Eduardo. The two men feel their way of life is threatened; so they take her away some considerable distance and sell her to a brothel. Soon they're finding excuses, first one, then the other, to saddle up and go on journeys; and of course it's not long before one arrives at the brothel to find his brother's horse tied up outside. How do they resolve it – this 'humiliation' (as it's described) of being in love, and the consequent jealousy which threatens their unity, and thus their safety and survival?

The solution is as harsh and simple as the telling. They buy the woman back from the brothel, Christian kills her, and they return, lamenting, to their life as it had been before.

Borges is dealing here, you might say, with a certain social-historical Argentinean reality; yet the result couldn't properly be called realism. It's more like a fable or folk-tale. In the work of his I'd seen up to that point he had made the fantastic seem real; now he was making the real seem fantastic – and both came out as stories. More astonishing, the two kinds of story seemed equally and unmistakably Borgesian.

I had never had such a clear demonstration that it's not the material which makes fiction distinct, but intangible, unmeasurable inflexions, quirks of intelligence, turns of narratological sequence, tone – that authorial voice again being a quality which evidently got through the filter of translation from a foreign language, and which marked the presence of the individual writer as certainly as fingerprints and blood group and DNA codes mark the presence of the particular criminal. Whatever the author may have learned from what has gone before – and I've acknowledged the importance of that – the unique mark remains. It's what I think I remember Wallace Stevens called 'the presence of the determining personality'.

My third significant voice is Günter Grass, whose work I began to read in the 1970s. Let me begin by speaking very briefly of a few representative Grass novels as a critic rather than a writer might speak of them.

Dog Years is surely the great novel of facing up to German post-Second World War historical and political guilt, and a book which, without in any way compromising that subject, also manages to be comedy.

The Flounder is that apparently impossible thing, a large-scale comic novel about feminism which is not simply satire nor masculinist special pleading.

Cat and Mouse is a wonderful evocation of childhood at a place and time where the loss of childhood innocence also meant the loss of political innocence.

Local Anaesthetic, perhaps Grass's cleverest novel, sets politically liberal and therefore guilt-ridden Germans, just old enough to have taken part in the war, in juxtaposition with the rebellious young of the late 1960s who had their political guiltlessness easy, by the accident of birth, but whose anxieties about Vietnam were nevertheless real and important. It's a novel not unrelated to Moravia's *A Time of Desecration*: but Moravia's dealing with that subject, though psychologically penetrating, is abstract and analytical compared with Grass's, which again manages to be comic, and to press home the recognition that all our historical and social problems, important though they must be to the responsible citizen, become insignificant from the perspective of eternity.

Now each of these brief descriptions tells something about the novel, but little or nothing about what a fiction writer might learn from Grass; and I admit I've had to think hard to recognise just where lies my sense of owing him a debt. It lies, I think, precisely in relation to that conventional fiction I spoke of earlier, which tends always towards dialogue, towards the playscript, and thus towards shrinkage and a neutralised prose. Grass taught modern fiction how to elaborate without waste. He is the master of texture, of the turbulence of 'things as they are', of circumlocution. No fiction writer of the second half of the century, or none known to me, has been more ingenious in inventing structures which, while maintaining narrative continuity and interest, also create space in which the author can free-wheel, mark time, give himself his head, let down his hair, be himself. He is, I think, though by no means as great a writer, something like a modern Dickens, a comic writer who has put personality back into the centre of fictional prose – the writer who most clearly gives the lie to Roland Barthes's idea of authorless *'écriture'*. And like Dickens he has managed to mix realism and fantasy and hold them in a unity imposed by voice.

So I've come back again to voice, literary fingerprints, DNA: here are three writers – Moravia in Italian, Borges in Spanish, Grass in German – read by me only in translation, and still my sense of the individual voice of each, carrying unmistakably through all their work, is as clear as is my sense of the voice of Dickens, or Joyce, or Faulkner. In what sense then, or in what sense that isn't perverse and unserviceable, can it be said that writing is 'the negative where all identity is lost'?

There is perhaps a strangeness – but no more, I suppose, than a coincidence – in the fact that these three authors who have had such an influence on my sense of fictional possibilities write in languages of which I know nothing. French is the only foreign language I can read capably; and I did try to follow developments in the French *Nouveau Roman* during the 1960s, dutifully pushing myself through some celebrated texts, including two by Alain Robbe-Grillet, but defeated by what seemed to me their dehumanised aggregations of objects and scenes, and their determined ambulation down any path except that of sequential narrative. Of that school of novels I found only one that excited me – Marguerite Duras's *Dix Heures et Demie du Soir en Eté* – and that was surely because it broke all the rules of the movement and permitted itself something like the sequence and suspense of the conventional thriller.

I certainly have no right to dismiss the school of criticism that grew up alongside and subsequent to the *Nouveau Roman* in France, because I haven't mastered it – haven't made serious efforts to master it. But (speaking, remember, as the author who has been declared dead) I will say that the wave of French theory which has swept the anglophone world seems to me more meaningful, called for, or at least intelligible, in France than it is when it reaches our own academies. French society, and even French intellectual life, appear to the Anglo-Saxon both beautifully and frighteningly well ordered, civilised, *propre*; and this is achieved not by imposition from above so much as by social cohesion, the social contract, a general will to conform. The Liberty which Equality and Fraternity confer is distinctly limited. So to have a hope of success, any challenge to academic authority in France must itself be well ordered, well dressed, intellectually authoritative. It must (and surely the French understand this better than their foreign imitators) claim more authority than it believes it has a right to; certainly more than it expects to be accorded.

So, remembering that Heidegger, whom Günter Grass portrays as 'Old Stockingcap' the Nazi sympathiser, lies somewhere behind Derrida; remembering also Barbara Johnson's saying that Deconstruction destroys not the texts it considers but rather their 'claim to unequivocal domination of one mode of signifying over another', let me, as an amateur, try to deconstruct the advent of French critical theory and suggest that it might be seen, not as the liberation it claims to be, but, on the contrary, as the compacting of twentieth-century scepticism, the compressing of its elements and its 'freedoms' back into a form of literary totalitarianism which executes the protesting author, denies that the land of literature was ever anything but a self-enclosed space of black marks on white, or that there were ever 'common readers' with common rights to it, and so finally sets up the theorist critic as literature's new mad landlord, perversely committed to discovering pumpkins in the vineyards and wine in the wells. Every French revolution begins in the streets and ends in some kind of enthronement. This one enthrones the critic at the expense not only of the author but of literature itself.

That is why I say the survival of the Common Reader requires renewed recognition of the continuing life of the Author in the text. It is with the author alone that the reader may have living communication. The intrusion of the theorist critic in recent years, it seems to me, has been like an auto-immune reaction, the cells of the body of literature attacking and destroying themselves.

All of which can be expressed in another, less ambitious way, simply as I'm sure it appears to many intelligent and educated readers interested in fiction and what is written about it. I don't suppose the major theorists – Barthes, Lacan, Derrida, Foucault – can be held entirely responsible for the aridity of some of their followers' prose; but even their own works, compared with the ingenious, humane, open-hearted, and scholarly essays of a Borges or a Moravia, look cramped and unhealthy. The doctor wants the author dead because he hopes for an inheritance; but will he live long enough to get it? I have to say I doubt it.

I didn't really set out to be contentious on this occasion – but I've possibly slipped into it. If so, and if I've given offence, I apologise. What I meant to do was to put before you an authorial presence, and to make a claim for the authorial voice. So let me conclude with an anecdote and a reflection. About five years ago Alain Robbe-Grillet, author of those Barthesian fictions, came to New Zealand. The Nobel Prize for literature had recently been awarded to Claude Simon, a figure in the French *Nouveau Roman* movement little known outside France, and one whose practice many considered followed other writers rather than led them. M. Robbe-Grillet, whom I found charming and congenial, told me one evening over dinner that the Swedish Academy had wanted to honour the movement, but had not been able to award the prize to its acknowledged leader, Robbe-Grillet himself, because he had been closely involved in the making of a movie in which there was sex with a female minor, and this had given scandal to French feminists who lobbied successfully against the award going to him. Consequently this lesser *Nouveau Romancier,* Claude Simon, innocent alike of originality and an interest in sex with minors, got the million dollars.

In the course of preparing this paper, and thinking of Robbe-Grillet's fiction as the fulfilment of, or partly the model for, Roland Barthes's notion of the authorless text, the thought occurred to me that each of my three writers – Moravia, Borges and Grass – would have been able to make fiction out of those events surrounding the award of the Nobel Prize to Simon – and I can imagine the novel or story each would write.

For Moravia the focus would be on the sexual element and its psychology. A neutral and enquiring light would be shone on the mental processes especially of the young actress and of the ageing writer. For Borges the interest would be in the literary aspect – especially the irony, which he would enjoy very much, of the stylistic imitator honoured over the stylistic originator. For Grass it would be the politics that would be grist to his mill – the characters of the feminist, of the movie maker, of the young actress, of the two writers, would all be seen, on the whole benignly, but in relation to a larger politico-historical context.

But what could Robbe-Grillet – the man to whom this happened (or who believed it had happened thus) – have made of it, apart from an anecdote over dinner? It's unimaginable that in fiction as he has been committed to writing it – a system of black marks on white sheets, denied all reference outward to a larger world – he would have been able to make any use of it at all. T h a t seems to me a final irony, needing no elaboration.

Postscript: There was an amusing end to the evening with Robbe-Grillet which I didn't include in my lecture. After the dinner we returned him, rather late, to his motel, across the street from the Parnell Rose Gardens, and found that he was locked out of his unit. As a Frenchman does leaving a hotel, he had taken his key to the office, and finding no one there, had left it on the desk. But the proprietors lived off the premises, and now the office was closed for the night.

I poked around and found an unlocked door to a room full of tins of tuna, jars of jam and peanut butter, loaves of bread, packets of nuts, cartons of fruit juice and milk; but there was also an invoice with a name and address in Remuera. I found the phone number, called, and the proprietor drove over to let the distinguished Frenchman back into his room.

Could he have made anything of that, in his fiction? I don't think so. Too human, and needing too much by way of explanation. Or if it happened in a Robbe-Grillet novel, you would not know *what* was happening.

He was such a nice man – but as a writer, trapped in a theoretical cage of his own devising.

There was also an amusing end to the lecture itself. Professor Ian Read, a New Zealand expatriate to Australia, took huge offence at my remarks about literary theorists and at question time attacked what I had said. Though his tone was extraordinarily aggressive I didn't mind this because I could deal with it (or so it seemed to me) effortlessly, but another Australian academic felt Read had been rude to the invited speaker, and (I was told) at the next session threatened to 'punch his lights out'.

Nationalism, Regionalism and the Tradition in Contemporary New Zealand Poetry

I approach the questions raised by this conference in two roles – as a critic and historian of modern poetry in English; and as a practising poet, born a New Zealander, who has elected for better and worse to continue to live in and write about New Zealand. There is no special problem in this – or not in the sense that it presents itself inwardly as a division of consciousness; but I think on an occasion like the present one it needs to be stated. What it does mean, probably, is that there have been times in the past when I have been more conscious than many poets need to be, or would want to be, of the broader map of twentieth-century poetry in English, and of where my own work and that of other New Zealand poets belongs on it. It means that my sense of what is local in poetry is something always fitted into a larger picture.

The material sent out in advance of this seminar outlining what was to be discussed mentioned national and regional affinities, and perhaps I should begin there, because nation and region may or may not feel as if they are the same. Allen Tate's critical essays deplore nationalism in literature, only preferring it to internationalism, which he cleverly calls 'the new provincialism'. What he favours is regionalism; and this makes perfect sense when you consider the time at which he was writing and his position as a writer of the American South. For Tate and his fellow Southern writers loyalty was to the region as against the nation, which they saw as a union imposed by invasion and conquest. The Yankee nation was unwelcome, artificial, too large to be comprehended poetically, and industrial. The South was older, separate, agrarian, and available to the literary imagination.

In small countries like Ireland or New Zealand, region and nation are not so clearly distinct. In fact they're often closely intertwined and difficult to separate. But the distinction is important. 'Nation' is a political concept. It has to do with who governs and where boundaries are drawn. 'Region' has more to do with landscape, climate, flora and fauna, local habits, and

---

A guest lecture given at the invitation of the University of Tübingen, Germany, October 1990. A small part was published in the *Times Literary Supplement*, 28 December 1990, eliciting an angry letter to the editor from Fiona Kidman to which I replied on 11 February 1991. The full text appeared in Germany in *Regionalität, Nationalität und Internationalität in der zeitgenössischen Lyrik*, edited by Lothar Fietz, Paul Hoffman and Hans-Werner Ludwig, 1992. Part of the material was also used in a lecture delivered to the English Department, University of Stockholm, 10 December 1996.

sometimes dialect. So regional loyalties may be called upon to serve a national cause, as in Ireland, or to stand against it, as in the American South. If the South had won its war with the Yankees and preserved its independence, Tate's regionalism would also have been a manifestation of nationalism.

Nationalism in its more obvious and patriotic forms usually becomes an element in the emotional life of a people, and consequently in their literature, when there is an outside threat. Apart from a few rousing or sad war poems, there is not really a lot of nationalism in the literature of England, because in the history of modern Europe England has seldom been seriously threatened. Irish literature, on the other hand, reflects Ireland's long struggle to achieve national independence from the neighbour that oppressed her. And the partial failure of that struggle is reflected in the fact that the Irish literature of consequence is a literature in the English language.

So why should nationalism be an element at all in the literature of twentieth-century New Zealand – a country remote, surrounded by ocean, and only once and briefly threatened from abroad? Why should Allen Curnow in his Caxton anthology of 1943, which is usually seen as a sort of New Zealand poetic declaration of independence, have invoked the precedents – strange ones on the face of it – of Irish and Polish literary nationalism? The reason, of course, has to do with origins. Literary nationalism in New Zealand has been the expression less of an achieved nationhood than of the desire to achieve it. It has been part of our post-colonial history. We began as a colony. In due course we achieved political independence. But when does political independence become independence of mind and imagination – and at what point does such a condition become desirable? Those are questions to which a number of different answers – each right in its way – might be offered. If I had been speaking twenty years ago I suspect I might have wanted to offer answers different at least in emphasis from the ones I am heading towards today.

Curnow was born in 1911. Writing in 1943 of D'Arcy Cresswell and R.A.K. Mason, two poets older than himself, he said:

> The English tradition, the classics that came with it, was all the poetry they knew. English was their language, but from England itself they were separated, belonging to a new kind of country where the tradition had no deep root in natural scene and people.

I don't know whether Curnow intended to suggest that by 1943 that situation no longer pertained; but I'm sure it was true for him as a young man. And I would say it hadn't changed significantly for me, born in 1932, twenty-one years after Curnow. Or if it was different for me, the difference wasn't marked until I discovered Curnow's own poetry and the anthology of poets he had put together, by which time I was already seventeen or eighteen.

Like those older poets I was, as I began writing, an expression of my place and time, and the place was still in essence a colony, where an educated literary person grew to adulthood inheriting English literature and literary history as an essential part of his own cultural inheritance.

We were New Zealanders – we were not Englishmen. No one in my family, except one of my grandfathers, who was Swedish-born, had ever set foot in the northern hemisphere. Even my grandmother, who lived in the house with us, was the child of parents born in New Zealand. But in the cultural sense we were colonials. The literature we read had been written on the other side of the world, about scenes and people and circumstances we had never encountered. There were two realities – the one you saw and touched, and the one you read about – and it might be said that each was in some degree compromised by the other. The real was less wonderful than literature; but on the other hand literature wasn't real.

It is always assumed that this must have been a disabling circumstance, and in some degree I suppose it was – although if you're born to it, it seems perfectly normal. But I recognise, when I reflect on it, that like most things which can be expressed negatively, it had its positive aspect as well. The sense that literature is something remote, unreal, marvellous – a sort of heaven of the mind – gives the experience of reading an incomparable richness which in turn, I think, creates that unswerving devotion, commitment, and seriousness characteristic of the best colonial literary minds.

So the gap between literary language and reality might be said to account not only for the triviality of bad colonial writing but also for the power it can have when, in writers of real talent, it becomes serious. Colonial ballading and yarn-spinning usually reveal a casualness about the language, which is treated only as a vehicle for the important matter – the facts and circumstances and scenes of life in the colony. When the real writers begin to appear – and there are only a few at any one time that matter – there is something heroic about the tension between the new reality and the old demands of language. There is a gap to be closed and the spectacle of writers setting about closing it is rather like watching a strong man bend iron bars.

I might say at this point that I notice the outline prepared for this conference stresses a recent trend in German poetry towards concrete local detail – villages, landscapes, townscapes, topography, are mentioned. There has been, so far as I know, no parallel contemporary development in the English-speaking world because at least since the English Romantic movement – in other words for the past two hundred years – 'concrete local detail' (accepting that this can mean anything from a Georgian poet's country lane, to T.S. Eliot's dull canal around behind the gasworks, to, let's say, Allen Ginsberg's New York or William Carlos Williams's Paterson) has never been out of fashion. It has not always, invariably and everywhere, been an element in poetry; but it has always been an option, one sanctioned by that Romantic and post-Romantic tradition, and probably favoured more frequently than any other; and it has figured strongly in New Zealand and Australian poetry because part of the function of post-colonial poetry is inevitably (as one of Allen Curnow's poems has it) 'to introduce the landscape to the language / Here on the spot'.

I should make the point too that this strong tradition of concretion and local particulars is not, and never has been, a matter simply of description. What lies, so to speak, 'out there' becomes, by whatever mysterious processes of literary art, the mirror and expression of what lies 'in here' – indeed the only convincing way of giving it expression. In Wordsworth's classic statement of it:

> Therefore am I still
> A lover of the meadows and the woods
> And mountains; and of all that we behold
> From this green earth; of all the mighty world
> Of eye and ear, both what they half create,
> And half perceive; well-pleased to recognise
> In nature and the language of the sense,
> The anchor of my purest thoughts, the nurse,
> The guide, the guardian of my heart, and soul
> Of all my moral being.

– lines in which the crucial phrases are 'the mighty world / Of eye and ear, both what they half create, / And half perceive'. It is this conspiracy between perceiver and perceived, and the literary tradition built upon it, which has been the foundation of New Zealand literature, and possibly of Australian as well. And I say that not meaning to suggest that what is called 'nature poetry' has been, or should be, the only kind of consequence. I mean rather that a Romantic tradition, which has a strong philosophical base, has worked in unity with a local post-colonial imperative to make varieties of literary realism predominate – and I would guess that this must be so wherever a people, in the effort to break out of colonial dependence, create images by which they might be convinced of their own reality.

This means in turn that while recent theoretical approaches to literature which undermine or question the relation between word and thing have made a significant impression on younger writers, and on some who are not young, there is still a strong realist tradition which is resistant to the most radical implications of those approaches.

Elements of fantasy and of sophistication began to come into New Zealand writing as early as the 1960s – a time when I remember my two favourite fiction writers were the Italian Moravia and the Argentinean Borges, and when I wrote a story called 'A Fitting Tribute' which made a real and radical break with Sargesonian realism. Since that time meta-fiction, magic realism, a new self-consciousness about technique, a new awareness of how impossible it is to draw an exact boundary line between fact and fiction – all these have had their effect in New Zealand on the writing of novels and short stories. In poetry there have been corresponding sophistications. Language is no longer seen simply as a vehicle for the real. It is, rather, a living force which confronts Wordsworth's 'mighty world of eye and ear', sometimes seeming to report it, sometimes to contend with it, sometimes to impose upon it. The literature of New Zealand is no longer, if it ever was, a literature only of local record and representation.

Nevertheless, without wanting to underplay the importance of those recent developments, because they *are* important, still I think it's true to say that most of them, when the first excitements have passed, have revealed themselves to be efforts to get nearer to, rather than further from, a perceived reality – nearer to a world which is believed to exist in some sense objectively 'out there', and assumed to be in some degree shared with those around us.

So the direction taken by those escaping from realism (and this may well be true not just of New Zealand) has usually proved to be, not away from the real, but towards it. It has been an escape from forms and methods which have become 'literary' in the bad sense – tarnished with use. It has been a revivifying of language, a polishing of the glass of perception; and the result has been a set of new fresh surprising images of the same local subject.

To go back a step: the Curnow generation of poets were the first New Zealand inheritors of poetic Modernism. That's to say they read and were variously influenced by W.B. Yeats, by T.S. Eliot and Ezra Pound, and by their exact contemporary W.H. Auden. They saw themselves in reaction against New Zealand's poetic Georgians, who had been inclined to decorate their poems with the external and picturesque trappings of New Zealand – tuis, bellbirds, and 'kowhai gold'.

When, in due course and inevitably, significant stirrings occurred, if not against, at least away from, what Curnow and his contemporaries had done, they came mostly in the form of an emphasis on American rather than British precedents. Young poets of the 1960s and seventies were interested especially in various forms of American post-Modernism – which is not, of course, to suggest that these were developments which passed Curnow by entirely unnoticed.

There are two ways of looking at this fact of our literary history – one neutral, the other which may seem to have a negative emphasis. The neutral one is to say that the history of poetry in the English language tends to move along a broadly common path, and that while poets have particular local subjects and preoccupations, they are always interested in the latest schools and fashions and experiments in form, wherever they may be occurring. The more negative, or anyway less accommodating, view might suggest that each new development which declares itself to be a maturing of our national poetry, is only a further expression of our colonial status, since it always owes a major debt to what is happening somewhere else.

I think each of these views has some validity; and I don't believe the second should be any cause for shame or anxiety. Poetry is not an army, or an arsenal, or even a football team. You don't win a World Cup for it, or lose your life or your territory by doing it badly. Poems are written one at a time by persons who are poets and who operate alone – often in the dead of night, but innocently. What matters is first the scale of the talent, and second the use it is put to, effective or otherwise. How does it help to be a poet famous in the Metropolis if at the moment you put pen to paper you find you have nothing to say? And what does it matter that your address is 61 Tohunga Crescent at the end of the world, if you are Allen Curnow and writing a poem which makes new demands on the English language?

I don't think anyone knowledgeable either inside or outside New Zealand would want to question that thus far Allen Curnow and James K. Baxter have been our major poetic voices, and I will speak for a moment about their upbringing and education because these are relevant to what I have to say. Both grew up in literary households. Baxter's mother was the daughter of two notable academic scholars. She went to Sydney to take her first university degree, and then to Cambridge for her second. Baxter's father was of Scots stock, a Keir Hardie socialist and pacifist with a deep knowledge of the English literary tradition. Curnow's father was an Anglican clergyman and minor poet, and poetry was a subject of family discussion. In other words, quite apart from a traditional (essentially British) education, these men acquired early a strong literary culture. A rich loam was laid down before anything else was planted.

Yet these two were New Zealanders – sons of New Zealanders – and the 'New Zealandness' of their work has been in no way compromised by the fact that its roots are deep in a European tradition. Indeed, we might ask why should it be, since New Zealand's historical roots – the foundation of its laws, its government, its education system and its public institutions – are also there. Baxter, as his biographer emphasises, had a 'mythopoeic imagination'. He was forever dipping into what his British contemporaries, the young poets of the post-war Movement, for a brief time took to describing dismissively as the European 'myth kitty'. Curnow's traditional theological preoccupations, combined with a strong grounding in classic English literature and a spasmodic but certainly not superficial interest in European philosophy, have given an intellectual and imaginative framework to the particular brand of sceptical realism that informs most of his poetry. Yet I can't think of any writers whose work gives truer or more vivid expression to the particularities and flavours and nuances of New Zealand life, to its sights and sounds, to its social problems and psychic dilemmas.

Fifty years ago New Zealand celebrated the one hundredth anniversary of the signing of the Treaty of Waitangi, by which the Maori ceded sovereignty to the Crown and were granted full rights as British subjects – 1940 was a celebration of nationhood and national identity. The younger poets and writers, Curnow among them, stressed independence from Britain and from colonial status. Despite the war, or perhaps partly because of it, there was a positive spirit about, and an assertion of great things that lay ahead of us as a sovereign state in the South Pacific. Our poets and fiction writers, though few New Zealanders in those days paid them much attention, seemed willing to lead the way – to insist that we didn't need to be shackled to our colonial past. There was an intense feeling among younger writers who came immediately after Curnow of 'being in at the beginning'.

This year, 1990, has been our sesquicentenary, and the mood has been quite different – subdued, reflective, uncertain, even sometimes slightly sour. Political and economic independence are realities that have occurred naturally with the passage of time, and have even been forced upon us at an accelerated rate by international developments, most notably Britain's entry into the European Community. At home we have had to face the fact that there were two parties to that Treaty of Waitangi, the Crown and the Maori. Under a Labour Government, Pakeha New Zealand has been asked, and in some specific areas required by law, to rethink what the Crown committed itself to when it signed the Treaty in 1840, and to accept responsibility for honouring, as far as may be practicable, that British commitment. At the same time, Maori interests have combined to assert a distinct cultural identity and its priority in our islands. As a consequence, all the 1990 culture talk has been of 'biculturalism'. The official description of New Zealand is that we have two cultures, Maori and Pakeha, and that these must somehow be accorded equal respect.

New Zealand literature, now heavily subsidised and promoted by the state and built into our education system, has acquired semi-official status, and so has become something of an instrument of policy. New school syllabuses are drawn up which attempt to give attention to Maori as well as English-language elements in education. 'Eurocentrism' is frowned upon. Our South Pacific location is emphasised, as if geography were the most important determinant of cultural identity. Anything in the literary tradition which can be called élitism is unacceptable, particularly if critical distinctions seem to favour the Pakeha product or to apply to works by writers who declare themselves as Maori, standards which they consider to be non-Maori.

All of this can be seen as an appropriate post-colonial tidying; a recognition of the facts of our case, and a response to them. Yet with a perversity which a knowledge of history tells me is proper to the literary mind, I find myself as much out of sympathy with official policy now as I was thirty years ago when that policy tended still to colonial subservience. From my perspective the demand for independence, for a distinct New Zealand culture, which once seemed liberating, has begun in recent years to take on the feel of a new provincialism, a constriction, a retreat inward upon ourselves, a closing of doors rather than an opening.

But there is another and contrary element in this complex equation which must also be mentioned, and that is the shrinking dimensions of our world brought about by ease and cheapness of travel and by the speed of communications. Remoteness, which was a huge factor in the New Zealand consciousness fifty, and even thirty, years ago, no longer seems so important. We watch the final of the World Cup as it is happening. The latest New

Zealander to climb Everest broadcasts to us direct from the summit. London, which when I first travelled, was five costly weeks away by sea, is now reached in twenty-four hours flying time. New Zealand writers can commit themselves to living and writing at one end of the earth or the other without feeling, as they once did, that they have made a radical and absolute choice, the ultimate either/or of the colonial literary consciousness.

It is perhaps partly because of this contraction of the world into Allen Tate's vast new province that local differences are being insisted upon so strenuously. When the New Zealand Government Minister of Arts and Culture decided to celebrate 1990 by buying a flat in Bloomsbury for use by New Zealand writers who might want to live and work for short periods in London, twenty-three of our writers, far from thanking him, published a letter denouncing the gift. The choice of London was described as a reversion to cultural dependence; Bloomsbury was seen not as a convenient location but as a symbol of literary élitism. These writers had wanted the money spent on an island off the coast of Whakatane, accessible only by rowboat, where something truly 'New Zealand' could flourish, uncorrupted by the larger world.

This particular brand of 'fear of flying', it seems to me, demonstrates not a strong new independent identity but, on the contrary, a persisting uncertainty. Worse, it represents a failure to face up to, and come to terms with, the world as it really is in 1990. We have tried so hard to make 1990 the year in which we celebrated the sesquicentenary of the signing of a treaty between Pakeha and Maori. There are reasons for this, and they have been stated and restated in New Zealand in an attempt perhaps to persuade a largely sceptical population. Those are internal and complex matters which don't need to be discussed here. But it is surely going to be far more significant, not just for Europe, but for New Zealand too, and indeed for everyone in our world province, that 1990 is the year when the Wall came down; the year in which the century of the raging ideologies in effect came to an end.

My argument then is that the time has come for those who are seriously committed to a New Zealand literature to reaffirm our British and European inheritance, and our consequent kinship to literature in the English language as it has developed in the United States, Australia, Canada, Africa and India; to acknowledge the strengths we have drawn from those old traditions and recent developments, and the resources that remain there to be tapped; to acknowledge above all that poetry, like all the arts, defines itself by means of a tradition. The individual artist is never enough. You cannot do it on your own – you need the help of the poets who have preceded you. That is the nature of a written tradition. There must always be some significant reaching back into the past, a drawing on what has gone before, and at the same time a sense of forward movement giving energy to the present, like the flow of a river. In our New Zealand case that reaching back into the literary past soon takes us (to use a word currently popular in commerce) 'offshore'.

All of this may seem obvious here in Germany: but I think in New Zealand it needs to be reaffirmed. In the cause of expiating the guilts of our history and democratising our education system, we are in danger of cutting ourselves off from our richest cultural resource. New Zealand writers and educators need to be reminded that you don't alter the history that has made you what you are simply by rewriting it; and also that true cultures develop by a process of evolution – they are not manufactured by acts of will consequent upon the deliberations of committees.

So I have invoked Allen Curnow and James K. Baxter as reminders that it is the poets most deeply rooted in the tradition who are best equipped to deal with the present and contingent, with what Curnow long ago called 'the regional thing, the real thing'. The same might be said in fiction of Frank Sargeson, the first of our writers to find a language appropriate for dealing with ordinary non-literary working New Zealanders, yet whose grounding in classic British and American literature was immense, and was conscientiously renewed and extended throughout his lifetime.

The time has come to stop apologising for our European culture, as if it were something that compromised a true local identity; and to stop anxiously inventing things to put in its place. I wonder whether something like that was what Anne French, one of the most notable of New Zealand's younger poets, had in mind when she concluded her recent poem 'Cabin Fever' with the following lines:

> It all depends
> on where you're looking from. The country viewed from an Air New
> Zealand F27 on a misty winter morning, might just resemble a J
> boat, very broad in the beam, sailing bravely south away from
> Europe and towards the ice, or a waka, small as a room, unstable
> in a big swell, blown off course and heading nowhere in particular.

English in Our Schools

Two years ago I was commissioned by the Education Forum of the Business Round Table to prepare a submission to the Ministry of Education on the draft syllabus for the study of English in New Zealand schools.* I found the draft seriously deficient and wrote my report accordingly. The report was endorsed by the Education Forum and sent on to the Ministry, where, so far as I can see, it was ignored.

So I don't apologise for revisiting the subject. English is the subject which sits right at the centre of all our social interactions. Communication depends upon it; and everything depends upon communication. English is to law and commerce what maths is to engineering; when it fails, structures collapse. It is also at the heart of our culture. Whether we live civilised lives depends on it; or if you prefer it the other way about, its use and misuse in public places is a symptom of the health or otherwise of our culture.

What I have to say, then, is not, as some might suppose, merely 'academic'. Whether I'm right or wrong about the new syllabus, whether my complaints are justified or not – these are questions which have profound implications for New Zealand society.

English studies are usually divided into two subsections – language and literature, and I'm going to begin by talking about the language half of the equation.

Traditionally under the language heading was included grammar, syntax, vocabulary, phonetics, etymology, and so on. Depending on how rigorously they were taught, these could seem the most demanding aspects of English – I suppose because there was no obvious sugar to sweeten the pill. Literature tells stories, has human interest, action, characters, drama, emotion. Language studies offered just a set of facts.

Or so it might seem if it wasn't well taught. In reality, since language is the basic tool of our culture, and all of us use it all of the time, how it works

---

An invited lecture given at King's College, Auckland, as one of several to mark the school's centenary, 1996. Published in *Metro,* April 1997.

* I was, and am, entirely out of sympathy with the Round Table's notion of how education should be funded, but was, and am, moderately conservative on the teaching of English, as were J.S. Taylor, Headmaster of King's College, who chaired the forum, and John Graham, Headmaster of Auckland Grammar, who was a member. I was given complete freedom to report as I chose. My submission on the draft syllabus is discussed with Dr Terry Locke in Part 4 of this book.

should be utterly fascinating – and can be made so. But English teachers at all levels have gradually backed off from it in the past few decades – especially from the formal teaching of grammar, a word which hardly figures in our education system any more, except as a name quaintly attached to some of our schools, reminding us of what they once were.

The excuse offered for this change is that in the conventions of language-use nothing is fixed; that the old grammar-book rules don't apply in real language situations; that (to take an obvious example) although the rule-book says the verb to be doesn't take an object, in fact no one speaking the living language can feel comfortable saying, 'It is I'.

Similarly to teach that there is a correct pronunciation for a word when it's not what your pupils say outside the classroom will be seen by the opponents of formal language studies as anything from an irrelevance to the imposition of what I once heard described at an NZATE* conference as 'class colonialism'.

Let me deal with the excuse first. Language does change, is changing all the time – that much is true. The idea that there should be fixed grammatical rules, immutable for all time, is not only a recipe for linguistic stagnation: it could never be made to work. The rules would stay still while the language moved on, rendering them more and more irrelevant.

But what this means is not that formal conventions shouldn't be studied and taught. It means they should be offered with a stronger emphasis on description than prescription. Students should be taught, 'These are the conventions at the present moment; this is where they've come from; this is where they seem to be going.'

But I would add that there should also be a tendency towards discrimination and recommendation. It is no invasion of the child's sense of self to recommend adjustments in speech and writing to accord with conventions which aid communication and clarity. It is not damaging children – on the contrary it is (to use a current buzz word) empowering them – to point out that certain uses will signal, to those who have authority in our society, an educated person, and that certain other uses will signal an ill-educated or uneducated person. It is no disadvantage to help lay down common ground for the use of language. We are teaching English, aren't we? Then we should teach it!

In fact the teaching of grammar, spelling and pronunciation according to an agreed set of conventions is a way of aiding good order and successful communication – as logical and as useful as the agreed convention that we all drive on the left and give way to the right.

Above all, such studies have the effect of raising the level of linguistic awareness. But if they're to be done properly they must include the dread g-word so carefully avoided by the framers of our new English syllabus: they must include *grammar*. It doesn't need to be at a sophisticated level; but there

---

* New Zealand Association of Teachers of English.

must be a basic terminology, otherwise there are fundamental aspects of language that can't be discussed.

Nor do the language components in English studies need to be dull. They may well be demanding. Some will describe them as 'hard', others as 'intellectually challenging'. But so are crossword puzzles full of anagrams and remote or obsolete words – yet people do them without any compulsion. Why? Because we all use language and we all enjoy overcoming obstacles. Surely one of the very worst aspects of modern education practice is the mania for removing difficulties and smoothing paths. The poet W.B. Yeats has a phrase that's relevant here, 'the fascination of what's difficult', and I thought of it recently when I read that chimps in the Auckland zoo had perked up since their keepers had taken to hiding their lunch rather than just handing it out. There was a challenge, there was excitement, there were rewards, there was competition, there was the possibility of success or failure; the food had to be hunted for and found – and when found it was enjoyed more and (it's a reasonable presumption) did the animals more good.

We too are primates. When demands are made of us, when we rise to meet the challenge, then the intellectual food is enjoyed all the more and does us more good. The further we have gone in English studies towards removing the possibility that students may experience at times a sense of difficulty, frustration, and even failure, the further we have gone also towards removing the sense of difficulties overcome, of deserved reward, of success and the pride that goes with it. This is a psychological truth which our current ideologues in the field of education have failed to grasp.

But these same ideologues who resist the idea of teaching rules of grammar, spelling, and pronunciation, all at once turn into sticklers for rules when it comes to matters of what they call 'gender', and matters of race. Their pupils may not use sexist language – in fact they may write ungrammatically to avoid it. They may not pronounce Maori words as they have come to exist in the Pakeha dialect. The great egalitarians, as is often the case, are not really against rules at all. It's only that they want different rules – their own. And these emerge, not out of the intellectual subtleties of linguistic analysis or of literary criticism, but from the crude demands of political correctness.

There is something which has puzzled me about the recent debate over the English syllabus. When Professor Roger Robinson's committee – made up of professionals within the field – came to draw up their draft syllabus, they seemed unable to express themselves in clear simple English. To illustrate this point in the submission I wrote for the Education Forum I quoted from the English syllabus for New Zealand primary schools in 1904, and then from the current one. The 1904 syllabus was clear and intelligible; the 1994 draft was anything but. Here are a couple of paragraphs from each, by way of example:

> (1904) The chief objects of the instruction in reading shall be to impart to the pupils the power of fluent reading, with clear enunciation, correct pronunciation,

tone, and inflexion, and expression based upon intelligent comprehension of the subject-matter; to cultivate a taste for and an appreciation of good literature; and accordingly to lead pupils to form the habit of reading good books. The reading of such books might, indeed, replace all other kinds of homework.

Poetry set for recitation should, while suited to the age of the pupils, be chosen for its literary merit as well as for the interest it arouses. There is such a wealth of simple and beautiful poetry in English literature that there is no reason to select for repetition verse that is not worth the trouble of learning by heart. One of the objects of making children learn verse or prose by heart is that they may have, stored up in their memory, masterpieces that may develop their imagination and may, whether the children are conscious of the operation or not, mould their tastes for good literature ...

The object of the instruction in composition shall be to train the children in the correct and ready use of their mother-tongue, both in speech and in writing.

Those paragraphs are admirably clear, and the objects expressed, and the means to achieve them, still strike me as excellent. Now here is a typical passage from the 1994 draft syllabus:

In planning programmes, and in assessing and evaluating language development, teachers and learners should therefore focus on both the products of learning and on the means by which learning occurs. Learners should develop self-evaluation skills to help them become self-directed in their use of language ...

Teachers will need to develop a variety of learning experiences which will meet their students' needs and the needs of the community. Programmes should provide ways of achieving the objectives that are appropriate for the learner at his or her stage of development. This will often mean drawing on the student's own experiences as a context for further learning.

After quoting these two passages, separated by ninety years, I said those of us interested in the teaching of English had to ask ourselves whether it had been ninety years of progress. The 1904 passage is clear, simple and direct. It says what pupils must be taught – to read aloud, to memorise, to quote, to achieve 'correct and ready use of their mother tongue, both in speech and in writing'. The 1994 passage, by contrast, is abstract, anxious, and unclear. It's as if the framers of the document know, and expect teachers to know, what they mean by phrases like 'products of learning', 'learning experiences', 'self-evaluation skills', 'the needs of the community', 'appropriate objectives' – know what they mean, but are unwilling or unable to say.

Here, to give another example, are the 'Achievement Objectives' for level eight of the new syllabus under the heading 'Visual language – Presenting':

Level 8: Using static and moving images, students should use and adapt production techniques and technologies to communicate information, ideas, narrative, or other messages, integrating verbal, visual and dramatic features to achieve a range of effects.

These statements apparently have to do with film, television and theatre –

but if that's so, why is it not said? Have our educational bureaucrats lost the talent for simple clear exposition; or do we put people on these committees who never had it? The syllabus is written in the worst kind of committee-speak – the kind of language people use when they want to suggest they are professionals who have authority and mustn't be challenged. Perhaps it's also the language of people who have some sense that they are on intellectually shaky ground.

The new syllabus is structured on a division of language into three strands: written language, spoken language, and visual language. Each of these three is in turn divided in two, which might be called transmission and reception. Written language – we write and we read; spoken language – we speak and we listen; visual language – we present and we view.

I take it we all understand that there are *two* kinds of language – written and spoken, one read the other listened to. Both kinds involve words that can be looked up in dictionaries, conventions of grammar by which they're strung together into sentences, local traditions which determine how they're pronounced, and so on. Language is language is language. But what is this third category – visual language?

It soon becomes apparent that it's meant to cover the study of film, television and theatre; but also posters, computer-generated texts, fax machines, e-mail, Internet, and other uses of technology.

My objection to this third category is not that I think film, television, and all the rest of it, shouldn't be part of an English syllabus. Of course at this end of the twentieth century, it's reasonable that they should. My objection is to the creation of a third and completely spurious category of language – and then giving it equal status with written and spoken language.

All of the media which this third category covers involve real language – that's to say language as described by categories one and two. For example a movie begins with a written script, which includes not only what the characters say to one another, but descriptions of the scene. These scripts are then acted – so we move from written language to spoken language. The same is true of a stage play. There are in addition, especially in movies, purely visual elements, but they can be discussed without inventing a new category of language.

In creating this third category the framers of the document shift from literal terminology (written language, spoken language) to metaphorical terminology (visual language). And the unsatisfactoriness of this would have been more clearly demonstrated if, instead of using the word language, they had stuck to their brief and used the word English: written English, yes; spoken English, yes; but *visual* English? What is visual English if it's not *written?* How did this tripartite structure come about? My guess is that it's a piece of recycled wreckage from an older 'New English Syllabus' of the 1970s. That one was drawn up by a committee which did include some teachers of English but was chaired, for reasons which were never clear, by a geographer. (His name was Russell Aitken.) This group drew up a structure for English studies based on what it called the eight modes of language – language divided into verbal and non-verbal modes, four of each. The four verbal modes were writing and reading, speaking and listening; the non-verbal modes were moving and watching, shaping and viewing.

I don't think anything more absurd can ever have been invented in the name of New Zealand education. It's something which gave us the intellectual status of a banana republic. The study of English was formally divided into eight parts, *four of which didn't involve words?* And how you made sense of the difference between, for example, watching as one of the eight modes of language and viewing as another, was beyond comprehension. No one, so far as I know, will now defend that framework, but for most of two decades it was supposed to govern the teaching of English in our schools; and when I gave a paper to the NZATE conference in Christchurch in 1982 and criticised it, I not only aroused anger and protest, I was in fact hissed by a feminist group among the teachers.

I don't mention that occasion because I bear a grudge or feel deeply aggrieved; I mention it because it's an example of how some teachers become more than intellectually committed – they become ideologically entrenched. I believed when I spoke at their conference that by arguing for greater intellectual rigour in the framing of an English syllabus I was doing my duty as a writer, a professor of English, and (at that time) a father of school-age children; but I found myself cast in the role of the savager of the poor, the semi-literate, the underprivileged, the Maori. This reaction, I think, is a clue to how the eight modes structure came about; and since I think that structure is probably the parent of what the new syllabus calls 'visual language', I'm going to pursue the matter a little further.

What lies behind all this is a problem – a real problem, and one for which I don't pretend to have a simple solution. It is that in every society language is power, and that our ability to use it is related to our sense of identity and worth. English teachers feel, therefore, quite rightly, that they have a power which they shouldn't abuse. By belittling a child's use of English they may undermine his or her confidence; by praising it they may perhaps increase confidence. Further, the range of ability in English is quite as wide as the range of ability in maths or physics – or anything else. The problem with this is that we don't all have to be mathematicians or physicists, but we do all have to use the language.

Now if you add to that the fact that there are sometimes levels of affluence, and worse, racial groupings, which may correspond to the differing levels of ability in English, the English teacher can be seen to be in a very hot seat indeed.

So in the 1970s a brand of English studies developed where there was opportunity for almost everyone to do well, no matter what their level of talent. Perhaps it should have been called Democratic English. It said, in effect, here is a description of the modes of language where fifty per cent of them are non-verbal! If you can't manage words, never mind – there are these other modes where you don't need them. You can draw a picture, or watch television, or do 'body language', and we will find ways of assessing you on that basis and giving you credit for it.

The intentions were not unworthy; but the effects were disastrous. When I was a pupil at Mt Albert Grammar I studied *Macbeth* and as a result I can still quote long speeches from it – part of a wonderful linguistic loam that was laid down for me at that early age. When one of my daughters was at Epsom Girls' Grammar thirty-two years later her class got the outlines of the *Macbeth* story from a movie, and then spent many subsequent periods making a model of Macbeth's castle. My daughter, who had no great talent for making castles, and exceptional skill in the English language (she later graduated in law, and is now a novelist) didn't prosper.

During that period I think many talented children who needed an intellectually challenging environment were bored by English as a subject. They became restless or rebellious. They came to see the English classroom – once a demanding academic environment – as a place of forced, self-conscious chat, of endless 'wanking on', of pointless exercises in visual illustration.

Grammar of course vanished from the classroom. Spelling wasn't corrected. Shakespeare was a name that figured now and then in movies and videos. Dickens was an author the 'privileged' kids, whose parents were readers, discovered at home and didn't get a chance to talk about in English classes!

As for the less talented children, the ones who most needed to be brought up to a higher standard – they were encouraged not to worry too much about words but to get on and do something they could manage in the area of the 'non-verbal modes'. It was meant to preserve their confidence, but what it really did was patronise them – rather like the old adage that used to be written into girls' autograph books: 'Be good sweet maid, let those who will be clever'. It did them no favour. If it protected their confidence, it was false confidence, because it wasn't preparing them for the real world – it simply passed the time and deferred the moment of reckoning.

It seems at last to be recognised that the eight-modes-of-language structure was an absurdity; and my reason for raising it here, as I've said, is that I believe a significant remnant of it, a sizeable rump, lives on in the new syllabus in that division of the study of English into three sections – written language, spoken language, and visual language – with no suggestion, by the way, that one is more important than another.

Film, television, theatre, word processors, modern communication technology – let me say it again – all of that could have been incorporated into the syllabus without the invention of an abstract term which means next-to-nothing, and which leads in the syllabus to examples like:

Visual Language: Viewing, Levels 3 & 4 [i.e. for upper primary school and form I]
Example 5
Achievement Objectives
Viewing: exploring language
Teaching and Learning
Context: examining the impact of visual language on consumer products
* Students view two different cereal boxes and discuss what they notice about them
* The teacher lists the verbal and visual features identified by the students, such as images, colour, layout, graphics and message
* The teacher shows the students another cereal box, and, using the list of features, helps them to identify similarities and differences and to view features that they may not have noticed on the first boxes
* The students gather a variety of cereal boxes over several days, talking informally with others about the verbal and visual features they find interesting
Assessment
* Students are presented with the idea of a brand new cereal and, in groups, describe what features should be on the box so that people will want to buy it
* The teacher assesses the students' understanding of the ways in which verbal and visual language features can be used to create particular effects.
Links with other Strands
Speaking. Listening.

Am I alone in thinking that sounds more like a *Monty Python* script than a serious description of a programme of lessons in English? And is it surprising that some of the children spending classroom time doing this kind of 'visual language' arrive at secondary school (as we've heard recently) virtually illiterate?

Now just a brief word about Maori students in our schools, because the syllabus specifically refers to them and to obligations under the Treaty of Waitangi. Personally my view is that the Treaty was something framed for a society and a set of circumstances which no longer exist, and the continual reference to it is becoming an impediment to social progress. Certainly we have an obligation to Maori children in our schools – but because they're New Zealand children.

What specifically, then, is the duty of an English teacher in relation to Maori? Not, I would say, just to make them feel good about themselves, glossing over whatever deficiencies they may have in English. And not to help them recover pride in their own language and culture. All of that, if it's to happen, must happen somewhere else. The obligation of the teacher of English is to teach them *English* – to read it, to write it, to speak it well; to discover the range of its vocabulary, the riches of its literature, and the best uses that have been made of it here in New Zealand. That's the very best gift that can be made to them.

The English classroom should not be used as a therapy centre for those perceived to be in some way socially disadvantaged; and nor should it be seen as the place for teaching correct social attitudes. If there are qualities that an English classroom should aspire to, I think they should be the same qualities that characterise the best literature – linguistic range, intellectual scepticism, imaginative freedom, historical and factual accuracy.

I come now to the literature component in the new syllabus. Like everything else this is set out in such abstract and unspecific terms – set out so *evasively* – it's difficult to say what's there and what's not. But my general criticism of it is the same as for the language component: there's a lack of rigour, a lack of academic content, a lack of clear, unambiguous required reading; in particular, not enough said about what that 1904 syllabus called simply 'good books'.

Part of the responsibility for this I suppose must fall on developments in the universities in recent decades, where the whole notion of a literary canon and the study of literary history has been undermined by attacks from what the American critic, Professor Harold Bloom calls 'the School of Resentment'.

Traditionally the literary canon – the consensus as to what had been the great works of the past – has been seen as a rich inheritance, a treasure trove available to all who learned to read and had an appetite for the best that has been written in the language. In recent decades this notion of the canon, and the literary history that sustained it, has been attacked as an instrument of social, political, racial and sexual oppression; a means of demonstrating, chiefly by exclusion, the inferiority of the poor, the ethnically other, the colonised, the sexually different, and the female. Feminists have called it the preserve of Dead White Males. Marxists have attacked it as a perpetuation of class privilege. Egalitarians have called it élitist. And so on.

It is this onslaught on the canon which has given heart to those who want English to be an easy-going, all-purpose, non-demanding, essentially unliterary subject. There is, after all (these people say) no need to read Shakespeare or Milton or Keats or Dickens. They don't relate to our lives any more. They're too hard, high-flown, unreal, not 'relevant'. And anyway they're Dead White Males. Let's consign the old literary canon to the cupboard of history and use English in our schools as individual therapy and as a means of teaching correct social attitudes.

Of course none of these things are said outright in the new syllabus; but they are everywhere implied. They are the justification for literary programmes which are almost entirely unspecific. The talented child, ready for the enrichments which great writing can bring, needing new linguistic experience and broader imaginative horizons – that child is guaranteed nothing by the new syllabus. There is only, I suppose, the hope that a very good teacher in a very good school will swim against the tide.

This is where I am unforgiving of the framers and defenders of this document – the Roger Robinsons, the Stuart Middletons – who in their own schooling profited from the study of great literature, and yet are willing to design a syllabus in which, if it isn't exactly denied to the young, is certainly not guaranteed to them. Which of us can predict where, among the children coming up through our schools, are the ones who will grasp that literary experience, if it's offered, and profit by it? No one can predict that. Nobody knows until it happens.

Everyone growing up in an English-speaking community deserves the opportunity to discover the best that has been written in the language. Not everyone will profit by it, or even want it – but the chance should be offered. That's what the syllabus should say; that's what it should require of English teachers – that's what the new document doesn't say and doesn't require.

To see again how the syllabus works let me turn, for an example, to the section which should make the highest and most precise demands on talented senior students – Reading, for levels seven and eight. These are the top levels, covering all of the final three years of secondary school, forms five, six and seven. Once again the Achievement Objectives (as they're called) are set out in painfully abstract language; but in general they seem to be saying what you would expect – that students well advanced in the educational process should be well advanced in reading. But not a name is uttered by way of example or suggestion, either of author or of text. So what specifically is intended at this level?

If we turn from the Achievement Objectives to the examples offered of how this part of the programme might look in action in the classroom, we find there are just four suggestions (and remember these are to cover reading in English for all of the last three years at secondary school).

The first example suggests students and teacher 'select a theme, such as youth and age, or city life' and then find different texts on the topic to explore different conventions of writing.

The second suggests teacher and students collect 'a range of feature articles, editorials, columns and essays' as a basis for a study of 'the expression of personal opinion and points of view'.

The third suggests the teacher should read an extract from 'material perceived to be intended for females or males' as the basis for a discussion of 'gender bias in language'.

The fourth suggests the teacher and students 'read together short extracts from prose texts on similar subjects, selected from major periods of English literature' as the basis for investigating language changes reflected in literature.

Two characteristics strike me here, as everywhere in the document. The first is the avoidance of any suggestion that teachers should *teach*; that they should be experts in literature and language, the possessors of special and valuable information which it's their job to pass on to the young. Everything is built on the notion of the teacher as 'facilitator', as if the children already have inherent in themselves the essential knowledge, or the means of access to it. This is an approach to literature and language studies quite as nonsensical as it would be in chemistry or nuclear physics.

The second characteristic is the absolute refusal to specify literary content, or academic content, or level of content. Not only is no author named; the words 'novel', 'play' and 'poem' are not used. Students are to read 'a wide range of texts', but just what that means, what the 'range' is to include, what is understood by the adjective 'wide', is over to the individual teacher and school.

I mentioned *Macbeth* earlier. Will my grandchildren hear of it at all? I suppose it might creep in as part of a study of 'gender stereotyping' – although I should add that if it did, and if it was looked at closely, it might subvert the intended purpose.

It doesn't surprise me that bureaucrats and social reformers are distinctly nervous of great literature and anxious to undermine its authority and minimise its effect. There is nothing new in this. Plato said the poets would be cast out from his ideal state. Shakespeare's company was banished by the Puritan faction and had to build their theatre outside the city walls; and it's the same Puritan type – our New Victorians as I've called them – who have had the strongest hand in the framing of our education policy.*

Great literature is unsafe; it's subversive; the moralist has never been able to depend on it. It teaches that life is more complex than religions and ideologies want us to believe. It mocks empires and scorns bureaucracies. It teaches scepticism. It sometimes sets beauty in competition with virtue, and lets beauty win. It excites the mind and imagination to reach beyond the limits of the ordinary and the good-orderly. It tells the hard truths. It shows life as it really is, not as we think it ought to be.

When I was young New Zealand was hardly out of its colonial sailor suit, and there was a strong desire among intellectuals that we should break the ties with Mother England and develop a proper sense of independence. I felt that very strongly myself. Later, we were precipitated into independence by Britain's entry into the European Community.

Now, as a result of that and subsequent developments, we seem to be flailing about trying to invent an identity. Our Prime Minister, thinking of trade, tells Asians we are part of Asia. Others insist we are part of the South Pacific, part of Polynesia, as if geographical location alone determined a nation's identity. There is a great deal of official talk about bi-culturalism, and obligations under the Treaty.

My own view is clear. We are principally a mono-cultural nation, though with a significant minority, Maori and recent immigrant, who are in varying degrees bi-cultural. We are politically independent, but historically and culturally interconnected with the larger English-speaking diaspora. The picture would have been more complicated, perhaps, if pre-European Maori society had had lines of communication out to a parent culture in the larger world, but it didn't. It was totally insular. The Maori language is local. The English language belongs to the world.

---

* 'The New Victorians', *Answering to the Language,* 1989.

So our predominant culture – that which binds us all and gives us commonality – is the Anglo-Celtic one derived from a British heritage, at the centre of which is the English language and the literatures which enshrine its greatest uses.

There was a time in my life when, if anyone had thought to ask my opinion about the teaching of English in our schools and universities, I would have been asking, 'where is the New Zealand content?' One doesn't have to ask that any more – and that's good. But now one has to ask, 'where is the broader cultural and historical framework?' It seems to me unfortunate if we have shaken off our old colonial/provincial identity only to become insular.

We are told over and over that the recovery of their culture is essential to Maori confidence; yet the same people who tell us this seem to want to dismiss or dilute or marginalise the English language culture which is the common ground on which we stand, and which is also, for a remote island people, a wonderful passport to the world. The predominant tendency of this new English syllabus is just one part of the attempt, conscious or unconscious, to deprive us – certainly Pakeha New Zealanders, but I would say all New Zealanders – of our common intellectual heritage.

As one whose professional life has been in teaching English language and literature, and whose vocation is the writing of fiction and poetry, it seems to me I have a responsibility to oppose that tendency, and to make my opposition public.

English in Our Universities

Forty years ago certain literary matters seemed, and I think were, a good deal clearer and simpler than they are now. 'Literature' was the kind of writing that was meant to last; that was what distinguished it from journalism, and from all forms of writing whose function was to be merely useful or entertaining – to be used and (as Paul Valéry says) used up. The literary works which lasted for several generations, or better still, for one or two centuries, joined something called the canon – the aggregation of great, or major, or significant works which every well-educated person knew at least something about, and some of which they would have read.

The determination that some literary works went on being read while others were neglected and forgotten was made by the applied common sense and good taste of generations of readers, strongly influenced by critics, many of whom were themselves poets or (less frequently) novelists.

The authors of these surviving classics were men and women whose life stories were often exemplary and became adjuncts to the canon. We read the author; but we also read *about* the author. The study of one sometimes enhanced our understanding of the other; and in any case 'the lives of the poets' as Dr Johnson called his collection of literary biographies, could be interesting and instructive in themselves.

So literature was a landscape peopled with actual characters and dramatic events as well as fictional ones; and those who studied it could sometimes seem immensely experienced and knowledgeable and worldly wise without ever having ventured from their desk or chair. Furthermore these great readers could have endless conversation with one another, even on first meeting. Having read the same books, they knew the same crowd.

The canon was not fixed, nor even very precisely defined. It was, rather, a subject for debate; it was continually modified by the addition of new work, and by revision of opinion about works of the past. As T.S. Eliot, the figure who dominated the literary world of my youth, put it, it was not just a matter of the present being influenced by the past; the past was also changed by the present – our perspective on it altered and so our valuations were modified. So the serious study of literature involved not only a developing critical sense

---

An invited lecture given at the Alexander Turnbull Library, Wellington, in 1996, and at Georgian Court College, Lakewood, New Jersey, in 1997, and published here for the first time.

and a continual refinement of taste; it involved also a sense of history.

Let me outline briefly some of the ways in which each of these 'givens' of literary life has been called into question – or, as some would see it, displaced – by the tide of literary theory during the past two decades.

First the author: we have been told that the author is dead. Writing – *'écriture'*, as Roland Barthes calls it in his essay 'The Death of the Author' – has no 'point of origin'. It is 'that neutral, composite, oblique space where … all identity is lost'.

Like so much that springs from modern French critical theory, this is very nearly incomprehensible. But Barthes concludes his essay by saying, 'The birth of the Reader must be at the expense of the death of the Author'; so we may take a short-cut for the moment and suppose him to mean that readers must be free to make what they will of a literary work, without consideration of authorship.

The reader, then, is more important than the writer? That is what Barthes seems to be saying. But as we read further among the new theoreticians we soon see that there is a traditional notion of the literary reader which has also been challenged and rejected. Modern theory has not only announced the death of the author; it tells us that what used to be called 'the common reader' never existed.

When Virginia Woolf addressed 'the common reader' she took the phrase from Dr Johnson's essay on Gray. 'I rejoice to concur with the common reader,' Johnson wrote; 'for by the common sense of readers uncorrupted with literary prejudices, after all the refinements of subtilty and the dogmatism of learning, must be finally decided all claim to poetical honours.'

This passage, Woolf says, pays respect to 'the pursuit of reading … carried on by private people'; and she offers her essays as one such person's response to a selection of books, ancient and modern. The common reader, she says, 'differs from the critic and the scholar … He reads for his own pleasure rather than to impart knowledge or correct the opinions of others.'

It's clear that what Woolf wishes most forcefully to convey is that this person is an amateur, one with no particular axe to grind, *a lover of reading for its own sake.* And it's in that sense that the phrase has passed into common use. The common reader is one whose first commitment is not to an ideology, or class, or race, or sex, but to the act of reading itself; a person who is disinterested – open-minded – and who responds to the literary work on the basis of good taste, and observation, and knowledge of human behaviour, not on some predetermined notion of good morals, or religion, or philosophy, or politics.

But this common reader, modern theory now tells us, doesn't exist and never existed. No one is disinterested. No one is objective. We all have our political bias, our faith (or denial of faith), our ideological commitment, our loyalty to class, race, nation, sex; and these at least influence, and often determine, our response to literary texts. Disinterested reading, aesthetic objectivity – these belong to the mythology of a discredited culture of dominance and privilege.

So the author is dead and the common reader never lived. What about the literary canon – the Great Tradition, as F.R. Leavis called it?

This, we are now asked to accept, was never what it seemed – a treasure trove available to all who learned to read and had an appetite for the best in fiction and poetry. On the contrary, it was an instrument of social, political, racial and sexual oppression. It was an élitist instrument for demonstrating, by exclusion, the inferiority of the poor, the ethnically other, the colonised, the sexually different, and the female.

Associated with the canon is the notion of literary history, itself a branch of social history. Like the canon (the theorists tell us) it too was an instrument of oppression. History was always in the hands of the dominant class, the oppressors, the colonisers, who told the story of 'what happened' to suit themselves and to justify their continuing social and political hegemony. The literature of the poor, the oppressed, the female, and so on, which would have told a different story, was prevented from coming into existence; or where it did occur, it was 'marginalised'. Critical judgements which claimed to be 'aesthetic' were really political instruments for exclusion of the enemy underclasses.

The terminology is essentially Marxist. One effect of the theorising of literature has been to politicise it; and especially to politicise it by saying literature always was political – it only pretended not to be.

There has been another strand in this theoretical revolution which might seem to run counter to the ones I've described so far. Twenty years ago Jacques Derrida, the most radical and impenetrable of the French theoreticians, declared 'Il n'y a pas de hors-texte' – there is no outside text; nothing beyond the text. In other words, writing is not only, as Barthes argues, essentially authorless. It has no reference outside itself. Each literary work is a self-enclosed verbal structure, not to be measured against 'reality', but creating a lexical and grammatical order of its own.

How, then, we might ask, can such a self-referential object also be seen as a political instrument? On this point the theoreticians differ, and we don't need to go into the details of their differences. But one could argue, I suppose, that even a work without reference outside itself could still be a weapon in the armoury of a class. It could be seen as a class accomplishment, a practice signifying status, a domain to which only the privileged have right of entry.

I have simplified complicated issues. What I've offered is an amalgam of modern literary theory, derived mainly from French writers – Barthes, Lacan, Derrida and Foucault – and passed on through their latterday and, most commonly, English-language exponents. The ideas are not all perfectly consistent. Tweedledum doesn't always agree with Tweedledee, and now and then, as in the nursery rhyme, they resolve to have a battle; but the general direction has been towards generalising and philosophising the nature of literary experience. To this end, the particular work – whether it is Emily Dickinson or *Moby Dick, Hamlet* or bus ticket – hardly matters. If there is nothing beyond the text, and if the canon is an artificial hierarchy created partly to serve political and social ends, then what matters is not so much the words on the page, but what the theorist-critic makes of them.

And that has been the effect of literary theory. It has replaced the author by the reader. But not any reader – not 'the common reader'; only the reader as critic. It has denied the special status accorded to what used to be called Great Books; and it has challenged the separateness and authority of literature itself. So in the end we are left with everything in question, all authority undermined except that of the theorist.

Now let me take each of these elements in the amalgam – the author, the reader, literary history and the canon, the literary work and the world outside it – and consider the good and the bad, the sense and the nonsense, in the revolution that has taken place.

(1) The Author

Barthes, and I think Foucault too, has announced 'the death of the author'. Barthes's essay on this subject is difficult; and there is a sense in which it can be said to be wrong-headed, perverse and untrue. The more we read the work of any of the great writers, the more we have the strong impression of a single personality encompassing the whole oeuvre. Dead or alive, the author lives in every sentence; and recognising this, 'the common reader' is likely to feel a certain impatience with Barthes's argument.

But, as I suggested, I think we can also make a kind of sense of it (limited sense) if we suppose that what he means to say is something like this: all consideration of authorship is a distraction, an irrelevance. Once the text is there we should forget where it came from. What matters is what happens when we take it up and read. Not until that moment, that interaction, does the literary experience occur; and so only then does the literary work come into being. When the completed text leaves the author's hand it is still only black marks on a white page. For that item to become a poem or a story, someone must read it; and since that is so, each reader is in part the creator of the literary work he or she takes from the text.

But this recognition that authors can be seen as irrelevant once the work of writing is complete is not new. It was what caused the New Critics (as they were called fifty years ago) to point to what they called 'the intentional fallacy' – the fallacy of supposing you could know what the author intended the work to 'mean'; or of thinking that if the author told you what was intended, that was necessarily a guide to what had actually been achieved.

And long before the New Critics there had been the recognition of something inexplicable, even magical, about literary composition, which separated the author as ordinary person from the completed text. The work was literary precisely because it was not simply the result of an act of will which the author could afterwards necessarily explain, interpret or repeat; and this mysterious fact was expressed metaphorically or mythically. The Muse had descended; the lips of the prophet were touched with a burning coal; Nature (as Matthew Arnold said of Wordsworth) took the pen from the poet's hand.

The problem is that both contrary propositions are true. Each major work expresses as indelibly as fingerprints or DNA the presence and unique identity of its author; and at the same time, each work stands free of its author, whose subsequent understanding of it, though certainly of interest, may not be more authoritative, nor of greater value, than that of any other reader.

(2) The Common Reader

Once again the idea put forward by modern literary theorists is half true. Of course there is no adult alive who is purely objective, open-minded, even-handed, disinterested. So there is a sense in which it's true that everything, including every literary reading, has a bias of some kind – or let's call it an interest. But is it proper, or useful, to call that interest 'political'? This is an argument, or a strategy, which denies the possibility of an aesthetic response distinct from, and sometimes in conflict with, one's interests.

If everything is political, how does it advance discussion at all to say so? How is discourse aided if we are not able to insist there is a distinction of category between a speech in favour of a prime minister's or president's re-election, and a description of a sunset?

As in life, so in literary matters, nothing is pure. There is in each of us a capacity to function, separately, or even simultaneously, in two quite different modes – one political, which tends towards action; the other literary, which tends towards contemplation. In one mode we want to change the world, or see it changed; in the other we accept for the moment whatever is, and *experience* it for what it is – and for all it's worth!

Literature from time to time approaches the political mode and sometimes crosses over into it – but it goes there from its own separate territory; and if it stays there long, it ceases to be literary. Literature defines itself, in other words, partly by being different from politics.

It's not that there are two kinds of reader – the political reader who has an axe to grind and the common reader who has none. It is, rather, that in each of us there is both. When we set aside our polemical self, our political self – the self which is loyal to cause or class or religion or tribe or nation – and give the existential, or contemplative, or aesthetic self pre-eminence, then we become, for as long as that lasts, the common reader.

In his Preface to *The Lyrical Ballads* Wordsworth asks, 'What is a poet?' And he answers (using the generic 'man' to mean humankind – all men and all women – as Woolf uses 'he' to mean both) that a poet is 'a man speaking to men'. The poet speaks (Wordsworth goes on) as one 'possessed of that information which may be expected of him, not as a lawyer, a physician, a mariner, an astronomer or a natural philosopher, but as a Man.'

'To this knowledge,' Wordsworth says 'which all men carry about with them, and to those sympathies in which, without any other discipline than that of our daily life, we are fitted to take delight, the Poet principally directs his attention.'

Directs his attention, that's to say, to what Virginia Woolf and Dr Johnson called 'the common reader'.

(3) Literary History and the Canon

The canon is a kind of summary of literary history. It represents, if you care to see it that way, the winners in the battle for literary survival; and feminist and Marxist critics in recent years have made the point that up to the end of the nineteenth century the winners were 95 (or perhaps 99) per cent white males.

It's true of course that on the whole the conquerors write the history and the defeated are silent; inevitably therefore the truth of written history must be partial. But the recognition of this fact has had an odd effect: it has seemed to sanction historical, and literary historical, writing which makes little or no pretence at objectivity. Historians in the past, however they may have failed to recognise their partisanship, at least paid lip service to objectivity and tried to be fair-minded and even-handed. Now objectivity is declared to be impossible, and it's considered naive, and sometimes even culturally insensitive, to attempt it. The duty of the historian is not so much to get the story right as to compensate for what are considered to have been the wrongs of the past.

It's as if one said, 'Every human being is a sinner; therefore it's naive, or worse, hypocritical and dishonest, to try to be virtuous.' History, and literary history, have become polemical – and this is a development that exactly parallels the denial of the existence of the common reader.

The great problem for those who attack the traditional canon – the School of Resentment, as Harold Bloom calls them – is that they have not been able to come up with a plausible alternative list of works which deserve close attention. Literature is inevitably the preserve of the well educated and therefore, if you choose to see it that way, of an intellectual élite – which is not, of course, the same as an upper class. Writers from any class, from the lowest to the highest – a Blake, a Dickens, an Austen, a Shelley, a Byron (to illustrate the breadth of the spectrum) – might from time to time speak *for* those who were poor; they very seldom, almost never, spoke to them – because the very ability to read the best literature was a symptom that you were no longer a part of the underclass. In this century, particularly in the decade of the 1930s, the Marxist ideal of working-class art setting itself against bourgeois art simply led to posturing and falseness among middle-class intellectuals with guilty consciences.

There have been, of course, at all times, and especially since literacy became widespread, various kinds of popular writing which had no literary pretensions, and some recent critics have tried to make this sort of work a serious object of study, arguing that it has been unfairly marginalised. I suppose it *is* worth looking at if you are a social historian; but if your interests are literary, such studies soon turn into patronising and self-contradictory exercises, arguing simultaneously that the work has merit, and that the notion of merit is irrelevant.

In many different ways, however, during the past couple of decades teachers of literature in universities all around the Western world have been turning their backs on the traditional canon in favour of works considered to be worth study for reasons which are not primarily literary. The intention is worthy. The outcome in terms of society at large may or may not be good. But the damage done to literature is immense. Literary studies have been press-ganged into the service of social and political causes; and far from resisting this invasion of their space, many teachers of literature have encouraged it.

There are always new discoveries to be made. It's the nature of the literary canon, as I've said, to be continually changing – not only the past influencing the present, but the present altering our view of the past. But an all-out assault on the very notion of the canon, a turning of thumbs down, or of backs, on many of the great works of the past – this has been for the most part a wasteful and self-defeating exercise.

The result has been, first, that students miss opportunities for linguistic and imaginative enrichment during their formative years; and second, there has been a loss of that common ground, those common reference points, that shared aesthetic experience, which used to exist among educated people, wherever they came from.

(4) The Word and the World

Traditionally there were two kinds of literature, one symbolised (as M.H. Abrams reminded us many years ago) by the mirror, the other by the lamp. The mirror reflected reality; the lamp shone forward into the darkness, showing us the way. One type of writing was mimetic – it dealt in representation; the other was prophetic or didactic – it taught us lessons. Both were directly related to the real world, and were judged in large part by our recognition of that relationship.

But now Derrida, and the many little Derridas, have told us that there is nothing beyond the text. A poem or story is a self-enclosed, self-referential linguistic machine, not to be judged better or worse by our sense that it matches the world known to our senses.

Once again, this contains a small but important and often neglected element of truth, perversely pushed beyond the limit of usefulness. The grain of truth is best illustrated by poetry, where the language is most highly charged. Most readers, and even most literary critics, pay too much attention to meaning and not enough to the fact that words are to the poet what clay or stone is to the sculptor – the material out of which the work of art is made. Each work of literature does in some sense create a linguistic world which is self-enclosed, which is not only to be measured against the real world, but has its own grammatical order, its own shape and logic, and (perhaps we can say) its own 'virtual reality'.

But once all that has been acknowledged, we are still left with the fact that one of the functions of language – not its only function, but a hugely important one – is reference: to 'mean' in the sense of pointing beyond itself; and one of the ways literary language impresses us is in its conjuring of something we respond to as truthful, accurate, exact, undeniable, and which exists beyond the frame. Literary writing of high quality gives us 'the shock of recognition'. It finds ways of revivifying our sense of what we know at first hand but have ceased to feel acutely.

In other words (and once again!) – yes, the literary work is a self-enclosed structure; and no, that is not all it is. It is also something which reintroduces us to the world we already know. At some times it says, 'This is how it is' (the mirror); at others, 'This is how it ought to be' (the lamp); and in both cases the 'it' is a reality outside the text.

There are, it's true, some few literary works which seem to escape from reference. Some, like the nonsense verses of Edward Lear, are charming; others less so. In France in the 1960s a school of fiction writers, of whom the most notable was Alain Robbe-Grillet, wrote novels which so deliberately refused to make contact with recognisable place and time, one was indeed left feeling that these were purely language constructs; and I think it was on their example that Roland Barthes built his notion of the authorless text.

Similarly the work of the contemporary American poet John Ashbery creates a mime of meaning while declining to be meaningful; and surprisingly Harold Bloom, who has been so staunch a defender of the traditional literary canon, seems to have been enchanted by these texts, and has at once elevated them to canonical immortality.

But whether one wishes to argue for or against these works, they make the larger point simply by being rare and manifestly *different,* in a category of their own – a fiction and a poetry which declines reference and blocks off every path that might seem to lead beyond itself.

Once again we are faced with a paradox. Just as the author is present in the text and yet absent from it, so, in all but a very few cases, the literary text is both separate from reality and yet dependent on it for purpose and sanction – rather as the baby in the womb is dependent on the mother's blood supply for oxygen, yet has its own distinct blood which may be of a different group. To the person who reads always and only for 'meaning' we cannot point out too often how much more the language of a literary work does than mean, what a rich and complex inner life it has. To Derrida, on the other hand, we have to say if there is *'rien de hors texte',* then the text must be at least eccentric, and probably barren of any literary interest other than that of a curiosity or a sport.

In each of these aspects of my amalgam of modern literary theory I have acknowledged a grain of truth and a large element of overstatement.

The author is dead, yes; but the author is also very much alive.

All readers are political, yes; but all readings are not.

Literary history is written by interested parties, yes; but that is a reason for striving after objectivity, not for giving it up as a lost cause.

The literary canon needs to be challenged and revised, yes; but that was always the case.

The literary work is a verbal text which has a life of its own; true, but total severance from reality is the literary equivalent either of cuteness or of death.

I am not saying that these developments consequent upon the rise of literary theory have been always and only bad. Like any intellectual movement, especially when it includes an element of revolt, it has been exciting for those involved, and challenging for everyone. But with its Maoist mania for continuous revolution, its leveller dislike of anything that smacks of hierarchy or of claims to aesthetic superiority, and above all its consistent refusal to speak plainly, the fashion for literary theory has been damaging to the simple practice of reading books, and consequently bad for literature.

The problem, as is always the case with critical fashions, is not so much the originators, who are, after all, clever people asking challenging questions. The problem is with the imitators, who have copied their masters' often near-impenetrable prose, turned their terminology into a clubbish jargon, their ideas into sacred doctrine, and their methods into repetitious routines – the latter frequently including a game called Deconstruction, in which the critic proves his or her superior intelligence by catching the writer out in self-contradiction. So the author is not just dead; the author is stupid as well.

Let me give five samples of the kind of writing that results, each of them written by a university teacher of English. They're taken from a book called *Contemporary Poetry Meets Modern Theory,* published by Harvester in Britain and Simon & Schuster in the United States. Here first is Dymphna Callaghan writing on Pat Parker:

> Such symbols of resistance, transformation, survival, are synonymous with the life of an African-American lesbian in a racist and homophobic society ... It is in this sense that the poem functions as an instance of an atypically political post-modernity, and it is precisely its politicisation which causes it to interrogate and problematise Haraway's formulation of woman of colour as the paradigmatic postmodern identity.

Example two: Thomas Docherty on the subject of Seamus Heaney:
> This trans-historical or mythic Subject is ... no longer easily available to Heaney, for the postmodern has problematised the relation between the Subject and History, or between the 'real' and its 'representation'. If in 'the society of the spectacle' or the 'hyperreal simulacrum', everything now is of the status of the image, then the 'real' has simply disappeared. The reality which is supposed to ground our representations, be it the presence of History as exterior fact or the presence-to-self of the supposed transcendental Subject, has itself become image.

Example three: Helen M. Dennis offers a little self-portrait before getting to work on her subject, 'Adrienne Rich and consciousness raising as a poetic method':

> I am an Anglo-American gynocritic: I prefer to pronounce it with a hard 'g'. Despite the hardness, I would define the gynocritic as she who is motivated by love rather than hatred. But love of female author-texts is sometimes fuelled by hatred of patriarchal institutions and by female anger.

Example four: Peter Middleton describes Ron Silliman's poetics:

> [Silliman] argues that 'when a language moves towards and passes into a capitalist stage of development' there 'is an anaesthetic transformation of the perceived tangibility of the word' and the 'function of reference in language is "narrowed into referentiality", ... Poetry can be 'the philosophy of practice in language', a philosophy which can work out the 'preconditions of a liberated language within the existing social fact', if it recognises the way referentiality has repressed the signifier in favour of the signified, and then relates this to the class struggle.

Example five: Joseph Chadwick on a book called *Reader* by Robert Gluck:

> *Reader* is created as a 'site of bliss' insofar as it responds to the texts it reads with an unexpected, unpredictable, desiring gaze (a gaze that reads 'WWII' with an eye to its formation of categories of sexual pathology, that reads 'Keats' by watching TV). And *Reader's* reader is so created insofar as he is neither the reader whom the volume identifies as its writer ('Robert Gluck') nor the reader whom any specific text addresses ... These transformative encounters between readings and readers thus depend upon the element of unpredictability that gives 'cruising' whatever subversive edge it may have as a practice of gay desire.

These examples are not in the least untypical. They could be multiplied over and over. Such writing would simply not be tolerated in literary journalism, because readers would rebel and editors would be sacked; but universities, it seems, are answerable only to themselves, and this is the language which a significant number of academics in the past two decades have used for literary discourse. It's a cult language, most of it quite unserviceable for ordinary teaching. Some clever students enjoy it and want to join in and prove themselves; many more feel shut out by it or bored and rebellious at what is, after all, a kind of occult practice.

The coercive tendency towards an extreme politicisation of literary discussion has also had the effect of alienating students who are natural readers, and numbers enrolling for courses in English are declining. Those people Virginia Woolf spoke for, who have quite simply a taste for good books, have been squeezed out by others who have, very often, no taste for them at all except as ammunition in the wars of class, race and gender.

So the movement of literary theory which first presented itself as an attack on the institutionalisation of literary studies has ended by institutionalising them more than ever. The test of time for the literary canon is replaced by the test of political correctness and social amelioration; the author is pronounced dead, and the common reader a fiction; and the theorist critic is left unchallenged, pronouncing in jargon from the highest chair of authority.

I'm sure it will be said that I have exaggerated; that in fact in many universities literary studies continue as before, uncontaminated by the worst excesses of theory. But I think that view is too sanguine, and perhaps an excuse for not taking a stand. Poetry and fiction have to exist out there in the public world, unprotected against attack by reviewers and readers, and so should writing which purports to be about poetry and fiction – especially when it is publicly funded and offered as part of an education in the humanities.

At the core of modern theoretical approaches to literature there lies a central cluster of political ideas and prejudices which are not in themselves mysterious or unduly difficult, but which have consistently been made to seem so by the language in which they have been expressed. It is time, I think, to tell the nervous children that the glove-puppet contains nothing more frightening, or more authoritative, than a human hand.

Here is a passage (published in the *London Magazine*) from the recent autobiography of Frank Kermode, one who has made himself truly expert in modern literary theory, as I am not, and who sees very clearly its damaging effects:

> The academy has long preferred ways of studying literature which actually permit or enjoin the study of something else in its place, and the success of the new French approaches has in many quarters come close to eliminating the study of literature altogether; indeed, there are many who regard the word as denoting a false category, a term used to dignify, in one's own interest, one set of texts by arbitrarily attributing to them a value arbitrarily denied to others. This position many find grateful either because it saves trouble or they have ideological objections to the notion that certain sorts of application can detect value here and dispute it there; or because they are, as it were, tone-deaf, and are as happy with the new state of affairs as a professor deaf from birth might be if relieved of the nightmare necessity of 'teaching' the Beethoven quartets.

What kind of fatalism has permitted Sir Frank to join in this game, apparently without complaint, while all the time recognising its dire effects on the very enterprise – the intelligent and sensitive reading of great books – to which his life has been committed, is not, I suppose, quite beyond my understanding, but it is certainly beyond my present scope. He has at least, at last, made his view plain; and if the further implication is, as it seems to be, that it is time for radical reconsideration and change, then it is one I endorse and applaud.

But what is needed, more than for the elderly to recant, is for the young to rebel.

Postscript: In a lecture given at Boston University, 2 April 1998, and published in *PN Review* March–April 1999, George Steiner, one of the great modern critics, signals even more emphatically than Kermode has done, his rejection of the current academic fashion for literary theory, and says: 'It is my conviction on this point that has made me an 'outsider' in the academy, *laus Deo.*'

The pure and applied sciences, Steiner writes, 'are founded on theory in the only proper sense of the word. They work in experiment, falsifiability ...' which have no role in the humanities.

> 'Theory' seems to sing the Siren's song of exactitude, of predictive powers, of encoded expression – those arrows speeding across the diagrammatic page – native to the sciences but radically spurious in the humanities.

Much more extraordinary has been the apostasy of Frank Lentricchia, Gilbert Professor of Literature at Duke University in the United States, famous (in his own description of himself) as 'historian and polemicist of literary theory' who, in an essay in *Lingua Franca* reported in *ACLS Newsletter* of fall 1996, simply turns his back on his own past, in which he has spent most of his energy '[showing] my students that what is called "literature" is nothing but the most devious of rhetorical discourses (writing with a political design upon us all) ...'

> Over the last ten years I've pretty much stopped reading literary criticism, because most of it isn't literary. But criticism it is, of a sort – the sort that stems from the sense that one is morally superior to the writers that one is supposedly describing. The posture of superiority is assumed when those writers represent the major islands of Western literary tradition, the central cultural engine – so it goes – of racism, poverty, sexism, homophobia and imperialism: a cesspool which literary critics would expose for mankind's benefit. Just what it would avail us to learn that Flaubert was a sexist is not clear. It is impossible, this much is clear, to exaggerate the heroic self-inflation of academic literary criticism.

Perhaps the tide is turning. In the *London Review of Books,* 13 May 1999, I read the following from none other than Terry Eagleton, who has surely been, over the past two decades, the best-known expositor, practitioner and fashion-shaper of literary theory in British universities. Mockingly inventing a 'samizdat handbook' for post-colonial theorists, he says its second rule would be, 'Be as obscurantist as you can.'

> Post-colonial theorists are often found agonising about the gap between their own intellectual discourse and the natives of whom they speak; but the gap might look rather less awesome if they did not speak a discourse which most intellectuals, too, find unintelligible. You do not need to hail from a shanty town to find a Spivakian [he is referring to the post-colonial theorist Gayatri Chakravorty Spivak] metaphorical muddle like 'many of us are trying to carve out positive negotiations with the epistemic graphing of imperialism' pretentiously opaque. It is hard to see how anyone can write like this and admire the luminous writings of, say, Freud. Post-colonial theory makes heavy weather of respect for the Other, but its most immediate Other, the reader, is apparently dispensed from this sensitivity. Radical academics, one might have naively imagined, have a certain political responsibility to ensure that their ideas win an audience outside senior common rooms. In U.S. academia, however, such

popularising ∴ is unlikely to win you much in the way of posh chairs or prestigious awards.

Radical theorist, and certainly no 'populariser', Eagleton himself now has a very posh chair – at Oxford. But this call to his own followers for a bit of clarity and common consideration for the reader (as if their readers, all students, were not acquired by compulsion rather than won on the open market!), strikes me as it would if I heard Charlie Manson telling his followers to smarten up their appearance because they were making a bad impression on the public.

Part 3

Meanwhile in the **World**

Barry Humphries – Contemporary

For the celebration of Barry Humphries' sixtieth birthday in 1994 I had a poem in mind but never quite found the time or the focus to write it. It was to be called 'Contemporaries', and the idea came first from the memory of a Manly scene in the autobiography of Australian poet Bruce Beaver: drunken father holding forth to fearful mother and son, the latter burying his face in a comic about one of those flying heroes of the 1930s. Taking offence, dipso-Dad snatches/hurls (one action) the comic. Son, unhesitating, dives after it – out of the window; and his appalled parent flies out after him! Young Bruce bounces on the dunny roof, then down to the lawn, closely followed by father. Dazed, they lie side by side on the grass, staring up at the stars.

And then, same era or epoch, but at the hugely distant (yet very near) opposite side of the continent, there is Randolph Stow (again I'm relying on the memory of something read), allowed to ride with the drovers, lying down dozing in shade after lunch and waking to find himself surrounded by emus, their heads-on-stalks bobbing forward to look, and then back as if discussing what this could mean. The boy laughs out loud and they scatter.

If I could explain, at least to myself, why these two scenes represent for me a particular flavour of time and place, I might have been able to make intelligible the connection with Beaver's and Stow's contemporary and compatriot, Barry Humphries. Is it something to do with the sense that the buried source of comedy may as often as not be pain? Somewhere W.B.Yeats says that we achieve maturity when we begin to see life as tragedy. When I was young and immature I liked that very much. Now that my friends and contemporaries are turning sixty, I prefer to think that if we must have a measure of maturity, let it be the comic vision, or at least the appetite for it.

Barry's autobiography, *More Please,* concludes with a moment in the early 1970s when, having at last overcome his alcoholism and returned to London, he is suddenly assailed in the street by a sensation so unfamiliar he collapses on a doorstep thinking he may be about to die, until he recognises that the strange forgotten feeling which has returned to him is none other than happiness.

Part of this appeared in the *London Review of Books,* 30 January 1992, with the title 'Here to Take Karl Stead to Lunch', and part in *Barry Humphries: Bepraisements on His Birthday,* ed. Ken Thomson, London, 1994. Further reminiscences were added a few years later for a collection of essays planned by Barry's second ex-wife, Rosalind Hollinrake of Melbourne, but never published.

I first saw Barry on stage in the Phillip Street Theatre in Sydney in 1956 or '57, and got to know him in the early sixties after we had each come back from our first visit to London. Barry's second wife, Rosalind Tong, a dancer, was an Aucklander and they came on visits to her parents. I think it was Barry's Melbourne friend, Murray Groves, then a lecturer in anthropology at Auckland University, who arranged for him to put on a lunch-hour show in the university hall. This was where I first encountered the then rather downmarket Melbourne housewife Edna Everage of Moonee Ponds.

Confronting an audience Barry had, even then, an extraordinary sharp-eyed stillness and confidence. You were going to be embarrassed, but never by any failure on his part, only by your own failure of nerve – to be hearing such things in public! To be laughing at them!

There was an evening when Barry took my wife and me to a sort of teen club under the street where there was a band and dancing. (He was, and is, remarkable in the way he finds off-beat places to suit his taste wherever he goes.) We were all aged about thirty and felt out of place; my inclination was to be inconspicuous but with Barry for company that was not going to be possible. The Beatles hadn't yet set the fashion that allowed men to grow their hair long; and in New Zealand the short-back-and-sides was almost a moral obligation, as was the jacket and tie. (I can remember, for example, an occasion at Auckland University when Olly Keys, Professor of French, refused to continue lecturing because there was a male tie-less in his class.)

Barry's hair was long, partly as a social protest (his headmaster in Melbourne had been given to saying 'Long hair is dirty hair'), and partly because at that time this was the hair that came out from under Edna's hat. He wore an overcoat and no tie, rather, as I recall it, like a tramp, and we hadn't been long at our table before he'd made everyone aware of his presence. When the band began something with a strong beat he suddenly launched himself backwards into the crowd.

His dance was extraordinary, jerky, almost spastic, yet rhythmical, with something of that physicality with which Dame Edna still reminds her audience that she's really a big energetic male. Someone shouted angrily at Barry, calling him 'Jesus' (not liking the long hair); there was a precarious moment when the crowd might have turned hostile; and then, by some magic of facial expression, he swung it entirely in his favour. The crowd pressed around clapping and cheering him on, while Barry, still leaning backward in his dance and with the bewildered expression of someone not quite sane, but benign, danced with prodigious vigour. When he sat down I felt as if I'd watched someone go over the Niagara Falls in a barrel and survive.

Not long afterwards I wrote what would now be called a 'post-modern' story, 'A Fitting Tribute', about a character called Julian Harp, who solves the problem of engineless flight. He recognises that when a man lies on his stomach and flaps his arms, the wing-tips point forward instead of back like a bird's, so he must contrive the means to fly lying on his back; and he succeeds, constructing models, and then his final set of wings, out of the struts of umbrellas which he steals, or has his girlfriend steal, from public places. He takes off from the Auckland Domain during a gymkhana, watched by a huge crowd, and vanishes out over the Pacific, never to be seen again. His success in flying is soon hailed around the world, and in his absence, presumed dead, Julian Harp becomes a New Zealand hero. Statues and monuments are erected, works of art commissioned, even a religion founded, around the figure of the first man to fly. The story is told by his girlfriend who has had a child by him. She knows what he was really like and that the sanitised hero who is becoming a national icon bears little resemblance to the real Julian; but when she tries to tell her story she's not believed, and threatened with arrest and prosecution.

The figure of Julian Harp was modelled on Barry Humphries, and the scene I've described in the teen club occurs in the story, as does Barry's remark to me that at night the timber houses of Auckland look like lanterns. The story first appeared in the *Kenyon Review* in the United States, and soon afterwards was translated into Spanish in *Revista de Occidente,* and into Hungarian for an anthology of *The World's Best Stories.* It seemed to me significant that liberal-literary persons in a Fascist and a Communist state of that time should both seize on it. New Zealand and Australia were political democracies; but the sense of moral repression, of the crushing weight of propriety, was very strong. Barry's outrageousness – his dandyism, his Dadaism, his stage transvestism, his arid-voiced repetitions of Australian place-names and products – were all aspects of one rebellion against that social oppression. Whatever he has become since, that's where he begins; and it's possibly the part of his performances least understood in London which might explain in turn the struggle he had to get started there.

My recollection of evenings with Barry and Rosalind at that time is of waiting for something to happen. In a public place it was likely to be extravagant and theatrical. Among friends he tended to lie low at first, listening, and then, when he had enough to go on, and enough in the tank, suddenly commanding attention, recycling it all into something comic, probably embarrassing, but not really unkind – more surreal than satirical. I could usually see it coming, knew that conversational space had to be made for it, and felt sometimes like those sweepers in the game of curling who run in front of the stone as it slides over the ice, brushing a path for it.

After that might come a slump into boozy uncertainty. Of his four wives I think of Rosalind as the heroic one. She worked so hard in those days to revive his confidence, to assure him he *had* been funny, *had* been admired.

I took him once to visit Maurice Duggan, without quite realising how far each of them was down the road to alcoholism. Duggan, large, strong, physical, once summarised his life for a literary magazine, beginning each section 'And the nurse said, "Drink this."'* His limp was noticeable and even picturesque,

---

* See 'The Making and Unmaking of a Maurice' in Part 1 of this book, p. 60.

but the loss of a leg which had caused it was something Duggan was extremely sensitive about.

He was a great Irish-style talker who also tended to peak with a brilliantly funny story that would have everyone sick with laughter, and then lapse into alcoholic gloom, and even sometimes violence.

Barry listened while Duggan explained about toheroa – the season, the limit on the bag, how it was minced to make an incomparable soup; listened too, and looked, while Duggan, quietly proud, showed the books on his shelves, and how many of the modern fiction writers he owned in first editions.

Duggan must have been up on the plateau ready to go into his usual hilarious anecdote-and-plunge when Barry pre-empted the moment, launching into a monologue about his own collection of hardcover toe-he-rowers, and about how short the season was on books and how tight the limit on the bag, but the great soups that could be made by critics who put them through the mincer. I remember it now only in crude outline; but in detail – in performance so to speak – it seemed bewildering and clever. It was the only time I ever saw Duggan driven backwards into sobriety. Afterwards, if ever Humphries was mentioned, Maurice would dismiss him as 'a clever magpie'.

Barry was a charming and inventive companion, and I don't think I recognised just how powerful the urge towards the outrageous was in him – that picking at the wound of suburban niceness – until he called on a visit in 1966 carrying his huge compilation, *Bizarre,* inscribed to the Steads in a flourishing hand with the Edna-ish motto, 'Life is a melody if only you'll hum the Tune.' Helplessly suburban like Edna's New Zealand bridesmaid, Madge Allsop, I found its pictures of deformities, Siamese twins, obesity, bearded women, dwarfs and imbeciles, so disturbing I couldn't get past them to the highly literary texts. I kept the book hidden. Sometimes I thought of tearing out the inscribed page and throwing the rest away. I didn't want it seen because I thought anyone who looked inside those covers would think worse of Barry; and indeed *Bizarre* remains one of the very rare Humphries 'performances' which everyone who writes about him baulks at or stumbles over.

Then for quite a number of years I lost track of him. There was his alcoholism, the break-up of his marriage to Rosalind, but most of all his increasing fame, and my own sense during those years that I was losing touch with what was going on in London.

Some time in the early eighties came Edna's first visit to Auckland in her full commercial glory. We were summoned to a dinner party; there were tickets to the show and references from the stage to 'the little Stead family'; Barry took us to supper afterwards. It seemed that nothing had changed except that there were now no dips into alcoholic despondency; and in fact, for Barry, no alcohol. I told him how a few years previously I had hesitated outside the Theatre Royal in Drury Lane after his show, wondering whether I should ask to see him. He said, 'I was probably in my dressing room asking "Where are all my friends?"'

Several writers have puzzled over how it is that Dame Edna contrives to make her victims enjoy being mocked. In the television studio politicians are made to dance like bears and sing like birds. Husky male film stars wear frilly aprons and carry Dame Edna's drinks tray, or are turned away from her door. The rich and famous are apparently dropped through trap-doors or catapulted out of their chairs. In the stage show women hand over their shoes which are held up to ridicule, or invited up to explain how they come to be dressed as they are. In the Auckland show two women noticed by Edna's scouts wearing the same dress were persuaded to come on stage together.

Part of the trick, I suppose, is that at close quarters the person inside Dame Edna's drag is so clearly present – precisely the same person who looks out through Sir Les Patterson's extravagant makeup. The biggest joke is against himself. In the presence of someone willing to make himself into Edna or Les, why should we want to preserve our dignity? But there is also, under the clever little stabs of malice, something essentially benign about Barry Humphries. Benign, and observing. Nothing is more flattering than simply to be noticed, attended to, and there is never any doubt that his victim, or indeed anyone at all who sits down and talks to the man, is being closely and particularly observed. There is a narcissistic blindness about many theatrical people which Barry entirely lacks.

Another essential element in the magic is language. Bazza Mackenzie's Australian vernacular is a brilliant invention based closely upon reality. So are Sandy Stone's grinding circumlocutions, the best known of which is probably 'Had a bit of strife parking the vehicle'. Edna's genteelisms are also wonderful parodies of something instantly recognisable. Humphries saw Australia more and more clearly by departing from it, returning, departing again. As Clive James wrote in 1983, 'If he had not had his Europe, he would never have completed his rediscovery of Australia.' He represents the dilemma of Australasian and Anglo-African expatriation – the loss and the gain of it. He can only be fully understood at home; but there he's likely to encounter a good deal of sullenness and resentment, which is overcome, paradoxically, by the irresistible force of a fame earned where the comprehension of what he is doing must be less than complete.

Barry is horribly inventive. He loves contrivance and elaboration, and these are apparent in everything from his use of language, to clothing, to stage sets. I remember going to supper at his house in Hampstead in, I think, 1984, and being shown print-outs of the script he was writing for the movie *Sir Les Patterson Saves the World*. It seemed to me a great idea. I imagined (why? I was thinking like Madge again) everything scaled down to the necessities of cinematic realism – a sort of James Bond parody, with Les more modest in scale, less the gross pantomimic archetype he can be on the stage. But of course nothing was scaled down except the size of Sir Les's trouser snake. I suspect the movie was a disaster in every way. There are times when Madge should be permitted a word, and listened to.

On the same visit I was taken up another floor where wife three, painter Diane Milstead, had her studio. She'd been working a long time (my recollection is two years, but that seems improbable) on a single large canvas which was mounted on its easel under lights in the middle of a spacious room. It was a conventional seascape, except that in the foreground was the principal subject, a mermaid on a rock. Diane talked about it, I stared at it, and Barry stared at me. It wasn't just the subject that astonished me, but the fact that she was standing, her bent fish-tail somehow holding her upright. I was trying to think of something to say. How about, 'If Jesus could walk on water, why shouldn't a mermaid stand on a rock'? No, that wouldn't do.

I managed to say something that was nothing, but what I took away from that moment was the sense of Barry as the detached observer. Something was happening outside himself, which he had possibly anticipated, or even contrived – and he was enjoying the spectacle.

Or that's how it seemed at the time. But it's sometimes a mistake to attribute everything to the cleverness of a very clever person. Innocence and simplicity are also possible, and Barry probably has more of both than most of his public would find credible. In a significant exchange with one of his biographers, John Lahr, at the time when Diane was making a very public fuss about their divorce, Barry remarked, 'I was so much into pleasing. I thought I was entertaining her. Isn't that my role? There's a great deal of unlearning to do.' Maybe he had simply brought his wife someone he knew would find something nice to say about her mermaid.

A week or so later he took me to lunch at his club. People were gathering for the presentation of some theatrical awards. Seeing Barry arrive, members of the press gathered around. Was he here to receive an award? No, he replied sternly, as if he didn't wish to be pestered; he was here to take Karl Stead to lunch. He made it sound much more important. I could see that although no one had the least idea who Karl Stead was, no one liked to ask because all were pretending they knew.

We met next, backstage, after a show in Sydney, consisting ('self-indulgently', the programme said) of the Sandy Stone monologues and nothing else. Some of the scripts date back as far as the 1958 recording, *Sandy Agonistes;* some are much more recent. Sandy is now dead, but his ghost shuffles on wearing his dressing gown and slippers and carrying his hot water bottle. Where Les and Edna are loud, energetic, irrepressible and vulgar, Sandy is painfully slow-spoken, low-key, puzzled, gloom-burdened, haunted by language, by the memory of names, and physically so still that the transition from life to death has been accomplished with a minimum of disturbance. But it's in the character of Sandy that Barry's great skill with language, his ear for peculiar turns of speech and his ability to give them a half-turn further into absurdity, are clearest. I treasure especially a set of scripts, *Shades of Sandy Stone,* privately printed in Edinburgh in 1989, which Barry sent me inscribed 'For Karl, who was there when the hottie was warm, with the author's fond regards.'

I suspect he likes to get back to Sandy Stone because he is still in control of the character. He began by being in control of Edna, but she long ago got away from him, and he is now dragged helplessly in the wake of her success. When Barry and Edna were alternated, a few years ago, on the South Bank show, it was Edna who was totally confident and at home. She was the complete showbiz persona, the little housewife he used to keep in her place who now keeps him in his. By comparison, Barry seemed charmingly tentative – a man of letters, bibliophile, antiquarian, scholar, all of which he is in his private life, though in public he is all showman.

That Sydney backstage occasion was when I first met wife four, the beautiful Lizzie Spender, previously known to me only as the angel-faced daughter whose photograph appears among the illustrations to Stephen Spender's *Journals 1939–1983*. Tessa, one of Barry's two daughters to Rosalind, was also there. Across the street in the hotel were Oscar and Rupert, his sons to Diane Milstead. 'Barry,' I wrote afterwards, 'was his usual mix of haste and care, charm and dangerous wit – a rare, elusive, irresistible personality.'

—

Now – many dinners, suppers, lunches later – I run occasions randomly together and recognise that in each there is something memorable, either contrived by Barry, or prompted by his presence.

We have him for dinner in Auckland and the gay uncle of one of my daughters' boyfriends, who perhaps has always imagined the big stage tranny must also be gay, or perhaps simply out of admiration, makes a huge pavlova and sends it with his nephew. We are photographed with Barry and the pav …

In London I'm invited to dinner at Lizzie's flat – Barry is now living there – and meet conductor Charles Mackerras on one occasion, film maker Peter Weir on another …

In Auckland again I take Barry and Lizzie to Karekare where Jane Campion's *The Piano* was made, and where 'the little Stead family' have a bach on Lone Kauri Road. Barry wears a very large hat and I photograph him standing on a rock, the sea behind. Neither us mentions Diane Milstead's painting, but one, at least, has it in mind …

Barry hears of the Dead Poets Bookshop in Onehunga and gets me to take him there. We find, among many things of interest, a first edition of *The New Poetic*. Outside, in a strange precinct, Barry declares the area 'spooky' and suggests if I sit on one of the benches I might be transformed into an old dero and never be seen again. He invents a headline: 'Person Seen in Onehunga Thought to be Karl Stead.' This, I recognise, bears some psychic relation to his Sandy Stone fantasy, which is probably why the name of the bookshop attracted him in the first place …

Kay and I go to his show in Auckland and afterwards have pasta with him and Lizzie in the flat they are occupying – the pasta cooked by Lizzie, who has published a book of recipes called *Pastability*. I am wearing a sober tie. Next morning Barry turns up at our door with a present – a beautiful silk tie, not garish but bold – predominantly orange, with turquoise and darker blues …

In London I take daughter and son-in-law to his show. He has done a matinée that afternoon, but eats with us in an Italian restaurant before the evening performance, arranges drinks for us at the interval, and insists we meet afterwards. When we part in the street, late, he moves very slowly. I can see weariness, and yet efficiency too – economy. This is a man entirely in charge of his own life …

Auckland again. He and I lunch at the Metropole in Parnell. With apologies, aplomb, politesse, he sends back his first choice and orders something different, explaining that he has detected wine in it, and that he's not able to take alcohol. A day or so later he slips away from a dinner in a Parnell restaurant, asking daughter Margaret to drive him to Remuera. He doesn't say where he's going, but I know it's to give the local Alcoholics Anonymous meeting the encouragement that must come from the fellowship of the famous …

In London again Kay and I are invited to dinner. Roy Foster arrives and hands over to Barry volume one, just about to be published, of his official biography of Yeats …

—

But I go back now to a particular place and time – London, a restaurant in Piccadilly – the Caprice – 9 July 1995, I think a Sunday. Barry invites me to supper with Lizzie and her parents Stephen and Natasha Spender. Barry notices that I'm wearing the tie he gave me in Auckland and is pleased. Stephen, now well into his eighties, has broken a hip some months before in New York, and has continuing heart problems. He looks frailer than when I last saw him, but is in good appetite and on good conversational form. It's a wonderful literary occasion, the talk all books, recollection, nostalgia and gossip.

Exactly a week later in Paris I hear on the radio that Stephen has died of a heart attack. I write a letter of condolence to Lizzie. Next day, in Brantome, there is a message at my hotel to say that Barry has been trying to reach me. I phone him in London and we talk about what proved to be Stephen's last supper party. We remark on the poet's conversation and the good stories he told.

'I hope you took notes,' Barry says.

'Of course,' I say, lying.

'What about that story about D.H. Lawrence …'

'Lawrence?'

'In Germany.'

'Oh, Lawrence,' I say, not remembering. 'Extraordinary.'

Already I've been feeling guilty that it's not possible for me to get back to London for the funeral – and sorry not to be there. Now, added to that, is my failure to be recorder of the great man's last conversation. I walk along beside the Dronn, saying the kind of thing one says when burdened with guilt. 'Fuck it, why should I remember. I *never* take notes. I don't keep a journal. That was Stephen's trick. I'm not cut out to be anyone's Boswell.' (And so on.)

And then, stopping on a stone bridge over a mill-race, I remember! The English writer who, in Stephen's anecdote, went on a German walking tour was not Lawrence. It was Hugh Walpole. The date was 1929. Walpole intended to go alone, but German friends asked would he mind taking someone with him – a man, a returned soldier from the First World War, suffering from depression and needing fresh air and companionship to lift him out of it.

Walpole said he didn't mind at all, and so the two, the Englishman and the German, walked for some days together. The German was amiable enough, Walpole reported later, mostly silent, occasionally quite amusing, did clever imitations over drinks in the evenings, and was inclined to get excited on the subject of the Jews.

He had a small moustache, a flick of straight hair angled forward over his brow, and yes, his first name was Adolph.

Stephen Spender – Inside the Great 'O'

In October 1990 I was in Germany, a country I know only a little of, in the university town of Tübingen. My guide was a student, a young woman called Svenja. On the day after those in what had been called the GDR had their first free post-war vote as citizens of a united Germany, she took me to the little garden overlooking the river and under the tower where Hölderlin, because he was mad, or thought to be, was incarcerated for thirty-five years, and where, mad or not, he continued to write poetry. The vines that covered the walls and crept around the base of the tower were turning orange and gold, as were the forest trees that covered an island in the river.

Although it was only mid-morning Svenja had already taken me to a tiny pub or tavern, a single room with crooked wooden beams somewhere in the medieval town below the castle, where we had eaten slices of onion pie and drunk a frothy red wine so new it tasted like a cross between wine and cider. These pleasant things, she told me, were specialties of the Swabian region.

After that we had crossed a bridge, descended to the island, and there, under big trees sending down their showers of leaves, Svenja had shown me a huge statue erected by the Nazis, or under Nazi aegis, representing a nineteenth-century composer of folk music. Out of his bronze pockets and from under his bronze coat emerged armed men, soldiers, showing that the might of Germany sprang from its folk tradition.

As I looked from Hölderlin's garden across the river to the island, it occurred to me that as the autumn advanced into winter the monument would gradually be discovered, first a dark shape, then an unpleasantly explicit symbol. I felt at once that I was 'inside literature', a feeling that comes at rare moments in Europe, and one more complex, intangible, and powerful than the literal connections made when visiting, say, Wordsworth's cottage at Grasmere, or the grave of Yeats near Sligo. Knowing no German (an unfashionable language when I was at school) and only a few translated works of Germany's greatest writers, I wondered what 'literature' I had in mind. Then it occurred to me that what I was feeling was that I was inside a poem by Stephen Spender, one which, like the very best of his poems, has never been written.

Germany at a decisive moment in its history, which meant, in turn, a

---

First published in the *London Magazine,* December 1991–January 1992, and expanded for this book.

decisive moment for Europe and for the rest of the world – that was one element in the equation; but the moment as experienced took its special quality from others – the presence of youth, beauty, falling leaves, the madness of poetry in its locked tower, the river flowing by dependable and imperturbable; and finally, down there among the trees, that hulking shadow which might be of a shameful past or a threatening future.

One other recent recollection springs to mind. A year earlier, visiting London, I was walking back from lunch with my publisher, Christopher MacLehose, when he was stopped in the street by his friend Mark Bonham-Carter who wanted to show him a little book just acquired. Bonham-Carter put it down on the bonnet of a car, at once setting off its burglar alarm. Unruffled by this, the Noble Lord (a Liberal life peer) moved to the next car and opened the book again, while the offended Rover or BMW continued to denounce him. It was a copy of the list drawn up by the German SS of those in Britain who were to be summarily dealt with when England had been defeated and occupied. I think he said that only three of those listed were still alive; and he showed us Spender's name, **Steffan Spender**, the entry looking grim indeed, marked out for death in its black gothic script.

The enigma of Stephen Spender is that he has always been, among the moderns, the most time-bound, the most history-burdened, of visionaries; or to put it more appropriately, he has been the most transcendental of politicos. In this he is a near relative of Shelley's, about whom he once wrote a small book,* and like Shelley he has suffered from a modern criticism which has looked, not for words as wings, but for the precise relation between what are now called signified and signifier. By this I don't mean Spender as poet has been dealt with harshly by the critics, who have for a very long time now treated him with the respect due to the dead; but rather that the poet has been inadvertently overborne and up-staged by the man of letters.

I read him first when I was a student in the 1950s, when he still figured strongly as one of 'the Auden group', 'the Gang'. I could afford to buy very few books, and would have borrowed his from the university library; but I owned one collection of his poems, *Ruins and Visions* (which I see was marked down from 9/6 to 7/6), and the autobiography, *World Within World*. And I had, for six months or so, a friend with amazing red hair and the name Thelma, with whom I had two things in common – a passion for dancing and a love of contemporary poetry. She owned 78 rpm recordings of Spender reading some of his poems, including 'Ultima Ratio Regum', 'I Think Continually of Those who are Truly Great', and 'The Landscape near an Aerodrome'. I need only to open the *Collected Poems* at any of these and I hear at once those intense, softly musical, upper middle-class, vulnerable tones – the whole man right there in the voice:

---

* See 'How to Read Curnow' in Part 1 of this book.

> I think continually of those who are truly great,
> Who from the womb, remembered the soul's history
> Through corridors of light where the hours are suns
> Endless and singing. Whose lovely ambition
> Was that their lips, still touched with fire,
> Should tell of the Spirit, clothed from head to foot in song,
> And who hoarded from the Spring branches
> The desires falling across their bodies like blossoms.

It may have been no more than an Old World well-bred pronunciation (Mansfield records that Virginia Woolf was always finding things *tah-some*) but the word 'fire' as he read it truly seemed to burn – appropriately in a stanza where it is central symbol or fact. The poem is something of a Wordsworth in Shelley's clothing. But the soul of the poet, which in Wordsworth loses, as it grows away from childhood, all memory of its origin, is seen in Spender's lines to remember its immortality, represented by a Wagnerian combination of music and fire.

To press too hard on these images, to require of them an exact logic (how can an hour be a sun endless and singing?) is to undermine the quality peculiar to Spender the poet. Word by word and sentence by sentence the poem makes a kind of half sense which, as in the poetry of the French Symbolists, must be completed by a congruent emotion in the reader. But the Symbolists were bent on wringing the neck of eloquence. In Spender's most authentic poems the reader's complicity is won or lost by eloquence – seen most clearly here in the exhilarating way the lines change gear at the opening of the third stanza:

> Near the snow, near the sun, in the highest fields
> See how these names are fêted by the waving grass …

If you don't feel a strong electrical surge, almost independent of meaning, in the pauses represented by the commas in the first of those two lines, then perhaps you should stick to reading prose – or a very different kind of poetry; and if you do feel it, and want to be fair to Spender, you must let that unfashionable experience have its head.

But Spender was not just a lyric poet. He had the confidence of his class, at a time when class really counted, and the sense of responsibility of one who grew up in a family of distinguished and public persons. (At the age of nine, needing to do number one while his father was visiting Number 10, and kept waiting too long in a taxi outside, he had to decide whether to go to the door and ask to use the lavatory, or make other arrangements. He chose the latter, and peed discreetly into Downing Street through the off-side window.) As a student at Oxford in the 1920s and subsequently and more urgently in Germany in the early 1930s, Spender felt obliged to question poetry itself. Was it justified in those pressing times? And if it was, should it be the kind that came most naturally to him, or some other kind?

World Within World (still immensely readable) records how subject he was to the influence of more decided characters – first Auden, then Isherwood.

No doubt he exaggerates his own compliance. His critical and political prose shows that there was, as Matthew Arnold said of Keats, 'flint and iron in him'. But circumstances conspired to make him measure his native impulses against what 'the age demanded'. He became for a time a pylon poet, a romanticiser of pistons, airfields, factory chimneys, the poor – and of workers talking of 'the World State' as they returned home from the funeral of one 'who excelled all others in the making of driving belts'.

Spender has been the Kate Adie of modern literature – in Germany when the Nazis came to power, in Spain during the Civil War, fire-watching in London during the blitz, an official visitor to Hitler's ruined bunker in October 1945, a delegate to post-war meetings of the great European writers. In 1968 he contrived to be, or circumstances contrived to put him, at Columbia University in New York when students 'liberated' the campus in April, in Paris the following month when students from the Sorbonne took to the streets, in Czechoslovakia in July when Russian tanks turned 'the Prague Spring' to tears, and finally in Berlin when the heady days of Rudi Dutschke's youth revolt were coming to an end.

Spender has met and talked to all the major and many of the minor literary figures of his time, and recorded a great many consequent impressions and thoughts in books, articles and journals. He has been supremely the modern man of letters, interesting to a wider public for whom poetry remains a mystery; and his prose has always had the rare quality of being direct, frank, unpretentious and immensely readable, offering at every moment, not 'objective' reporting, but the spectacle of the poet observing, thinking and feeling. He has never been willing, nor indeed able, to make his writing anonymous. He has never adopted the much-favoured tone which suggests we are being addressed by no one in particular, or a committee, or God.

Certainly not God – and Spender has always been good at telling stories against himself:

> Rose 5 a.m. Went to airport and caught 6.45 plane to Madras. Arrived here ten thirty. Had a moment of sheer horror when I saw a large crowd gathered beyond the barrier, armed with wreaths and flowers and posies. When I approached they burst into clapping. I forced myself to smile, and then a man, walking just behind me, stepped forward and had a wreath placed over his head.

Whether or not he writes poems, and whether or not they are 'good', Spender is always and everywhere the poet – a fact he reminds us of more as a warning of his limitations than as a claim to privilege. He records how he longed to tell Virginia Woolf, but lacked the courage, or the cruelty, to say it, that every time he passed the monument to Edith Cavell in Charing Cross Road, with its Bloomsbury-like inscription 'Patriotism is not enough', he replied inwardly that sensibility was not enough either.

He has always been something of a failure in his own eyes, painfully aware of weaknesses and self-abasement (only a very confident person could have made so much of these), and willing at times to accept the judgement of others that he was not entirely sane. The scene I remember most vividly from *World Within World* is the one in which the student Auden tells him that he is 'one of the Gang' and that he must write 'nothing but poetry':

> This remark produced in me a choking moment of hope mingled with despair, in which I cried, 'But do you think I am any good?' 'Of course,' he replied frigidly. 'But why?' 'Because you are so infinitely capable of being humiliated. Art is born of humiliation.'

Spender has always represented his inner uncertainties and sufferings vividly. About to marry for the first time, he was assailed by terrible doubt and depression:

> Blackness and desolation seemed the truth and all else evasion and escape. My day-to-day activities seemed a process of flight from and awareness of horror; and I despised myself profoundly for ever being happy. My marriage now seemed to me like a prison sentence.

But the marriage brought happiness; and so when it ended there was another plunge into despair – recorded both in his autobiography and in the opening poems of *Ruins and Visions*.

Yet if there is a consequent impression of him as gloom-burdened and tormented, a reading of almost any one of his books, poetry or prose, quickly dispels it. In fact there is a radiance in most of his work, a persistent affirmation. Auden told him once that if he were in love, had good health and sufficient money, he ought to consider himself happy. It registered with Spender and was remembered because clearly it matched something in his own temperament. Unhappiness was 'a condition *which few people [had] a right to claim.*' [My italics.]

In the early 1970s, lunching with Karl Miller*, who was 'discussing his own gloom', Spender was asked why he always seemed serene and happy.

> I found it difficult to answer ... Partly on some kind of Goethean philosophic principle that one ought to be positive and count one's blessings ... Lack of self-pity combined with selfishness. Also gratitude for my family, my children ...

Spender's great and saving grace is observation, of himself no less than of what lies outside himself, and his ability to shape his observations in a way which makes a wry, intelligent, and often amusing commentary upon the event. His humour is part of what makes him so readable, balancing the tremors of sensibility and the rigours of social and moral responsibility. His experience of the Spanish Civil War is treated with all the seriousness such a shaping moment in the history of twentieth-century Europe deserves; but his most memorable anecdotes are often comic. Taken up to the battlefront with a five-foot Indian journalist, Spender, six foot three, was advised to stoop in case he should be hit by a sniper's bullet. The Indian also crouched – bent double in

---

* See introduction p. 11, and footnote.

fact – making Spender more aware of an absurdity than of danger. And then:

> Suddenly the Indian looked around from his bent posture and turned his face up to mine: 'I can see death's great question mark hovering between the trenches!' he said in a hoarse whisper.

Even in telling about being accepted by Auden as a poet, a story in which his capacity for humiliation is both asserted and illustrated, there is a finely judged combination of self-mockery and perfect seriousness, as if he is saying, 'Yes, I am this kind of rather unsatisfactory person, but that is necessary to the kind of poet I am.' And to Spender, being a poet has been more important and more real than the actual production of important poems. When as a young man he told T.S. Eliot that he 'wanted to be a poet' Eliot responded predictably that he could understand wanting to write poems, but he didn't know what it meant to 'be a poet'.

Trying to write a sonnet about the Berlin Wall in the early 1960s Spender records in his journal what he considers to be his deficiencies for the task, including 'lack of ... imagination', 'utter incompetence technically', and 'lack of certainty about form'; but then he adds: 'this is my existence even if I am bad at it, I am committed to finding out how bad I am ... Also I believe I do have an existence and it is poetry.'

In reality the man you meet is precisely the man you have met on the page. That is one of the greatest strengths of his writing. It is something more than 'honesty', which is glibly attributed to all kinds of literary liars. It is authenticity. If Spender had to lie (an unlikely circumstance), he would do it authentically. You would say to yourself, 'Ah yes, without a doubt, *this* is a liar!'

In 1992 an unofficial biography was published which represented Spender as bi-sexual in a way which upset him and his family. He had never concealed sexual feelings for, and interest in, males. Indeed, in *World Within World,* which came out in 1954, he wrote with what was for the time great frankness about it. But this new book presented his private life in a way which he and Natasha considered crude, false, exaggerated and untruthful. And at the same time it brought new and unwelcome publicity – news-hounds wanting to stir the pot.

'We're having a *besiege,*' Natasha said, and suggested Kay and I might occupy their house in St John's Wood, full of precious works of art and treasured manuscripts, while they escaped to their place in the French countryside. She invited us for a meal (it would, she warned, only be 'snackeroodles') so we could be instructed in security measures. 'Snackeroodles' turned out to be soup and a roast with wines; and when Stephen complained at the lack of a pudding, a zabaglione was whipped up on the spot.

A few days later we were installed among the Hockneys and Stanley Palmers, the Rouault, the Picasso, the Matisse and I've forgotten what else, and Stephen and Natasha were on their way to Maussanne-les-Alpilles. Stephen had insisted on clearing a desk for me, and even emptying one of the drawers in it, the contents of which were now jumbled together in a pile in one corner. Manuscript poems stuck out of the pile, and when it was knocked over by the vacuum cleaner, there on the carpet was one of his journals. I had wondered how much was edited out of the published versions, whether it would amount to a great deal or just a few details, and now here, for the sometime scholar and critic of poetic Modernism, was the chance to find out. What I discovered was that nothing at all from this six or eight months of the journal had gone into the published selection – that in fact there was a hiatus at that point. And then it occurred to me that there was a gap in the published selection only because this particular notebook had been lost in the drawer Stephen had cleared for me. It seemed a perfect example of the randomness, the informality so to speak, of the literary life as actually lived, and as distinct from its public record.

I began this reflection with a moment in Germany when I felt I was inside an unwritten Spender poem. There are many such in his prose. Here is one from *World Within World:*

> Once ... when travelling in Greece, I dined out of doors at a restaurant on a small island which lies in the Bay of Chalcis. The tables were under the stars, and a few yards from them lay the sea like a black flapping flag, beyond which in a vast ring around the waters the mountains stood like huge grey-green transparent stones. At the table next to me sat a young Englishman – whose face I could not see – and with him a girl. After we had eaten, this young man pushed his chair back from the table, and, without affectation, looking up at the stars, recited lines which began with a great 'O'. Some vague recollection from my school days told me that these were the address of the watchman to the night in the *Agamemnon*. I did not understand the lines, but the Greek words in the clear English voice were filled with the stars, the seas, and the mountains. This is the effect which was my idea of pure poetry, an invocation which one understands imperfectly but which is yet expressed exactly, filled with the stars, the mountains, the tables, and the chairs.

'Heard melodies are sweet/But those unheard are sweeter.' Here everything is given us but the thing itself, which we must provide out of our imaginations. The face of the young Englishman is unseen, the lines he speaks are not understood; what the passage he quotes may be is only surmised. But the beautiful setting, the exact circumstances, the 'great O', and the guess that this might be 'the address of the watchman to the night in the *Agamemnon'*, have their combined effect.

In reading Spender we become, if not the authors, then at least the inhabitants, of his unwritten poems. That has been his great and peculiar gift.

Postscript: In the summer of 1999 forest fires destroyed the Spenders' home and garden in les Alpilles. Natasha had completed a book about it, *An English Garden in Provence*, which was published by Harvill that year. When I saw her in London in May 2000 she told me the house was being restored and she was remaking the garden.

Ezra Pound's Rapallo

In the Rapallo Post Office a day or two before the opening of the Fifteenth International Ezra Pound Conference I got into conversation with a local, there to collect his pension. He had known Pound; used to walk up the *salita* with him to Sant' Ambrogio. 'He was a very nice man. Very charming.' I said his daughter, Mary de Rachewiltz, would be at the conference. He said he thought Pound had lived at Sant' Ambrogio 'with someone who was not his daughter'. 'No,' I agreed. 'She was his daughter's mother.' 'Ah yes. Well, he was a very nice man.'

A marble plaque over the passage from the Rapallo seafront to the Via Marsala records the many years Pound lived there. If you walk along the promenade, as Pound did every week before the war, and up the steep *salita,* up through terraced olive groves to the church of Sant' Ambrogio sitting high over the town, you find, along the road to San Pantaleo, another plaque celebrating Pound's occupancy. There is some overlap of dates. On the whole Pound lived in the seafront apartment with his wife, Dorothy, and visited his friend (bed-companion, lover – mistress as she would then have been called) violinist Olga Rudge at Sant' Ambrogio. But the exigencies of war were to push the three unhappily together – and even for a time a fourth, Mary, Pound's daughter to Olga, who during her infancy and childhood had been fostered by a peasant family in the Austrian/Italian Tirol.

Also down in the town, on the Corso Colombo, can be found a plaque recording that Yeats spent some part of each year there from 1928 to 1930. It quotes his tribute to Rapallo's beauty, and his question, 'In what better place could I spend what winters yet remain?' The Yeats–Pound connection was first through novelist Olivia Shakespear, the married woman who relieved Yeats of the virginity, or anyway the chastity, which his love of Maud Gonne had seemed to require. Around 1912–13 Pound acted as Yeats's unpaid secretary; and Dorothy, whom Pound married, was Olivia's daughter.

There is nothing on the Corso Colombo building to show that Pound's parents also lived there for a time after the father, Homer, retired; but in the *reparto acattolico* of the town cemetery I found Homer's grave. The headstone, surmounted by what appeared to be a death mask and almost completely covered by ivy, makes no mention of Ezra. It records that Homer was born in Chippewa Falls, 26.8.1858, and died in Rapallo, 25.2.1942, and that his wife, Isabel Weston Pound, now resided at Gais in the Tirol. That was because by

London Magazine, April/May 1994.

the time the stone was ordered the war was over, Pound was in Washington awaiting trial for treason, or possibly already locked up in St Elizabeth's Hospital for the Insane (where he would remain for thirteen years); and Isabel, who until necessity required it had never acknowledged nor even looked upon her son's daughter-out-of-wedlock, was now living with her in the mountains. According to the daughter's book,* Isabel was carried the last stage of her journey to Gais on a 'sedan-like contraption' made 'by passing the long poles of rakes and pitchforks between the slats of a deckchair' – 'stately, erect, like the Empress Dowager, followed by more men carrying trunks'. Isabel spent her last days re-reading *Don Quixote,* instructing her granddaughter how to poach an egg, and planning a canal from Venice to Milan 'big enough for boats to navigate with their cargo'. Clearly she was the mother of the *Cantos.*

Pound's dilemma when America entered the war is characterised by the web of personal connections he had created around himself since moving to Rapallo in 1923 – a wife, a mistress, two aged parents (and he their only child). A supporter of Mussolini, he was making regular broadcasts over Rome Radio, in his bizarre way attempting to prevent his own country from entering the conflict. He might at that point have elected to take out Italian citizenship, which would have removed the possibility of the treason charge later on; but he believed himself a loyal American, serving America's interests. He might have made a last-minute return to the United States, but his old father had broken a hip and couldn't be moved, and how would the wife/mistress arrangement have been dealt with? He might have accepted that silence was now required of him; but he had persuaded himself that by continuing to broadcast he was upholding an American's right to free speech. And in any case, the widening gap between the world as it was and as he wanted it to be was causing him increasing confusion, driving him to a sort of frenzy.

There was a pause in the broadcasts, and then they were resumed – uglier, more impassioned, full of Douglas Social Credit and anti-Semitism (usury was the source of all the world's ills including war, and the creation of credit was the solution); but so confused, random and paranoid that some officials in Rome wondered whether this loyal ally of Fascist Italy might in truth be a secret agent sending messages in code.

Opening the conference in the beautiful municipal *Salone* where Pound organised concerts (Olga played, Dorothy was patron), Professor Massimo Bacigalupo of the University of Genoa spoke of Rapallo's place in the poetry. He described finding, in the Yale Library, a cancelled passage in one of the manuscripts of the *Cantos* recounting how, at the time when Italy first surrendered to the Allies, Pound had borrowed from one Massimo Bacigalupo, the local chemist and the professor's grandfather, a copy he owned of the Rapallo newspaper of 1815 recording the return of Napoleon from Elba. The point was that Pound hoped for a similar return of his hero. And he got his wish. The Germans rescued

* Mary de Rachewiltz, *Discretions,* 1971.

Mussolini and set him up in the north as head of the Salo Republic – 'thus' (Bacigalupo remarked drily) 'condemning Italy to two years of civil war'.

It was at this time that Pound walked, rode the rail-cars, hitch-hiked, sleeping rough, from Rome, where he had been broadcasting, to the Tirol to tell his daughter the truth thus far concealed from her about her intermittent parents – that they were not married, that there was a wife. Then he headed for Mussolini's new centre of power. He was back in Rapallo some considerable time later when the Allied armies arrived. Partisans arrested him, and considered summary execution. As he was marched down the *salita* he picked up a eucalypt seed from a tree still to be seen there, thinking that if he survived it might be all he would take of Italy back to America. It was buried with him in Venice almost thirty years later.

From Rapallo the sixty-year-old poet was taken to the US Army Detention Centre near Pisa and locked in the now famous wire cage. After a period that brought him close to breakdown he was given more space, and the use of the dispensary typewriter at night, on which he composed, or typed up from handwritten drafts, the *Pisan Cantos*. This was during the months that passed before he was flown to Washington to face the capital charge of treason, from which he escaped only by the decision to treat him as insane.

Hugh Kenner was the conference star. I had in fact heard him lecture, and met him, thirty-five years before when I was a graduate student in Bristol and my supervisor, Professor L.C. Knights, had invited him to lecture and arranged for us to meet. Since that time Kenner has become established as the major Poundian, the quirkiest and most interesting historian of poetic Modernism, a man of great intelligence, energy and inventiveness whose delivery as a lecturer is affected, and even somewhat impaired, by a deafness which I think must prevent him from hearing and modulating his own speech.

Kenner's contribution to the conference opening, apart from the picturesque flurry of a late arrival, was to offer 'a fact and a piece of wisdom'. The fact, which I suppose most of his audience knew, was the one about the eucalypt seed picked up under the tree beside the *salita* when Pound was on his way to what was likely to be summary execution. The piece of wisdom was something Pound had written to him many years ago: that ninety per cent of those things we perceive as requiring to be done can be achieved within twenty-four hours of the recognition of the need. It was, Kenner said, a corrective against saying 'I haven't found the time.' It was quite true, I thought; but I also found myself wondering what it was Pound had wanted to bully the young Kenner into doing at the time it was offered.

Kenner might have stopped there but he went on. He said he had no idea why an Australian tree should be growing in Rapallo;* but he offered an

---

* There, at least, as a former Mansfield Fellow at Menton, I was able to help him. Eucalypts were planted all along that coast, once a resort for tuberculosis sufferers, because they were thought to purify the air.

explanation why Pound might have used the seed as a symbol for memory. It was a typical Kenner exercise – intellectually strenuous, mythologically far-reaching, etymologically inventive; a performance I enjoyed, but would have enjoyed more if it hadn't been for the nagging realist in me saying, 'This is clever – but it's not *true*. It's how an academic's mind, Kenner's anyway, would work in those circumstances, not a poet's.' Did more need to be said, after all, than that Pound thought he might never see the place again, and picked up for a memento of it something that was pocketable, durable, and fragrant? And that having survived, he continued to treasure it?

I walked up to Sant' Ambrogio twice during the conference, thinking not only of Pound trudging up and back, his life lived 'between a door and a door', but of the image Mary de Rachewiltz offers of the courageous and persistent Olga Rudge (who died recently, aged one hundred) tucking up her formal dress after a concert in the town, changing out of her best shoes, strapping her violin case to her back and tramping up to the house at Sant' Ambrogio. On those hill paths life has become mythology quite as much as it has along the coast at Lerici, where Professor Bacigalupo and I would later go looking for the place where Byron and Trelawny burned Shelley's drowned corpse on the beach.

On the second day of the conference Bacigalupo invited me, with Mary de Rachewiltz, to his house up in the hills where his German wife, Angela, a former ballet dancer, and a friend, were preparing lunch. Once there we could see the church of Sant' Ambrogio away to the east at a lower level. In the garden, where the table was set under a rattan screen among olive trees, I told Mary de Rachewiltz that I had re-read her book on the flight from Auckland to Rome, and how much I admired its crisp style and the way it was put together. She said with Poundian forthrightness and succinctness that unfortunately most Pound scholars saw it as a resource, not as a piece of writing.

She told me she received an advance for it and had used the money to fly to Africa leaving all papers and source materials behind so that it would be written from memory and thus unified – all but the part she called the 'war diary', which belonged to its time. This accorded with my own theory about the *Pisan Cantos*: that the sense of unity, the superior sense of focus in them compared to other groupings of the *Cantos*, is explained not only by the shock of Pound's incarceration and the sense of loss which the end of the Fascist 'dream' meant to him, but even more by the circumstances of the Detention Centre, which deprived him of reference books. The *Pisan Cantos* are an extraordinary feat of memory. But memory is not just a reservoir; it is also a filtration system. This is a view not always welcomed by Poundians because it implies a negative corollary: that large sections of the *Cantos* lack shape and focus, wrecked by linear accretions of material as Pound returned again and again to his book-sources while engaged in the writing.

At the lunch I mentioned that I wanted Mary to inscribe her book about her father for my daughter Charlotte.* On the way back to town, racketing at dangerous speeds down the steep curving hill roads in Bacigalupo's little Fiat, she remembered and insisted on doing it at once. It occurred to that she had taken Poundian principles to heart, and here was one of them in action – an illustration of the 'piece of wisdom' Kenner had offered. To 'Make it New' one should add, 'Do it Now'.

They were good people at the fifteenth conference – good talkers, good listeners, good carousers; and there was very little of the language of critical theory which has entangled and rendered needlessly opaque so much recent discussion of literature. Pound liked exposition to be concrete, particular, emphatic, and perhaps his devotees learn from his example.

But there is a defensiveness and protectiveness among them. Kenner's *The Pound Era* makes great narrative of the history of literary Modernism, placing Pound at its centre. But for him, Pound can do no wrong. This refusal to recognise limitations springs, perhaps, from the knowledge of how strong resistance is in some quarters to any respectful consideration of his work. But my own view is that resistance is best defused by freely acknowledging the unsatisfactory elements in Pound which promote it. Then it becomes possible to argue plausibly for the much that remains which is good, original, valuable, rewarding – and sometimes beautiful, with the rare beauty of the very greatest poetry.

For Pound, all experience came back to language, and language was unstable. It came in through the ear, in different accents and with different emphases, and every word or phrase carried with it the shadow of other sounds, other meanings, a different history, another language. So verbal structures were like social structures – a set of conventions, a pretence at permanence and stability which might at any moment break down. They were buildings that creaked and swayed when the wind blew. Pun, *double-entendre*, wordplay, verbal shiftiness, represented the universal comedy of our insecure hold on order. And I think this was a recognition much more available to an American of the early twentieth century than to a European. Pound's assertive 'Amurknism', which caused lips to curl and eyebrows to be raised, had an intellectual base. A man could walk on water, but only so long as confidence – which meant health, vital energy, testosterone – lasted. Pound lived on after those vital juices and energies ran out. Those were the last sad years, the years of his long silences, out of which he emerged only rarely, usually to say that his life had been a failure, his work 'botched'.

Pound's philosophical base was scepticism; its principle was uncertainty, indeterminacy; and his talent was correspondingly lyrical, not epic. His great error was to propose solutions to the world's ills, and to attempt to project them on an epic scale. In that he betrayed his own genius.

---

*Now a novelist, Charlotte Grimshaw.

Postscript: The facts of Pound's family life are complicated, and until very recently details remained unpublished, though they were known to scholars – especially the fact that Pound's son was not his child, while Olga Rudge's daughter was.

In July 1925 Pound accompanied Olga to the Italian Tirol, where Mary was born and at once handed over to a peasant woman to be brought up as her child. In the summers Olga and Ezra would turn up and take the child with them to Venice. It was only slowly that Mary came to realise that these two were her parents, and she imagined them to be married. In her book she speaks well of her peasant childhood in the mountains. In conversation she is more circumspect, and it's clear her memories are full of dark shadows.

In October 1925 Pound and Dorothy were together again in Rapallo, husband and wife, but at the end of that year Dorothy went to Egypt, and Olga moved for a time into the apartment in the Via Marsala. When Dorothy returned she was pregnant. To whom, and whether this was an accident, or revenge for the child to the mistress, is unrecorded.

Pound and Dorothy now moved to Paris, he to arrange a performance of his opera, *Le Testament de Villon,* she so that her child could be born at the American hospital there. Both these feats were accomplished. The audience for the opera was small but (seen in retrospect) extraordinarily distinguished, and included T.S. Eliot, James Joyce and Ernest Hemingway. Hemingway was a friend who (it's said) had taught Pound to box, while Ez had taught Hem to fence; and it was Hemingway, not Pound, who took Dorothy to the hospital in Paris for the delivery of her first and only child.

Dorothy's child was named Omar Shakespear Pound – Omar a variant on Homer, Pound's father's name; Shakespear because that was Dorothy's family name; and Pound because Ezra was Dorothy's husband; but Pound himself said with typical bravado that the names were chosen for their 'crescendo effect'. Dorothy took the baby to her mother in England, where she remained for a year, and then he was handed over to a foster parent in the Sussex countryside. The experiment in, or accident of, parenting over, the three – Ezra, Dorothy and Olga – settled down again to their childless triangle in Rapallo, which had many more years, indeed decades, to run. Each summer, however, when Ezra and Olga took Mary from her foster-home in the Tirol to Venice, Dorothy would go to England and take Omar somewhere for an English holiday.

Among the many photographs pinned over the desk where I spend my working days, there is one of the lunch in Bacigalupo's garden with Mary de Rachewiltz, and another taken in a restaurant in Princeton with Professor Gail Holian of Georgian Court College and Omar Pound. Mary has Ezra's sharp features, keen eyes, intent look, and magnificent head of hair. There is nothing obviously Poundian about Omar, who has (one might say to emphasise the difference) a face that lacks point – amiable, whimsical, faintly bewildered, not entirely focused. But he is, as Ezra was, a linguist – a translator of Persian and Arabian poetry.

After our meeting in Princeton, Omar gave me a collection of his own poems, inscribed; and (to my great surprise and delight) a translation from Confucius into Italian by Ezra Pound and Albert Luchino, a rare book indeed, published in Rapallo in 1942.

As for that other 'birth' of 1926, Pound's opera *Le Testament de Villon*: it has not lasted as long nor fared as well as Mary and Omar, but I did see it performed, in 1996, in Brantôme, France – appropriately, perhaps, in an enormous floodlit cave, with bats flitting silently to and fro beyond the lights.

Ezra Pound – A Storm in His Luggage

In a letter dated 22 January 1934 to his protégé James Laughlin, Pound makes passing reference to R.P. Blackmur who had written a long unflattering essay, 'Masks of Ezra Pound', in an issue of *Hound and Horn* (which Pound renamed *Bitch and Bugle*). Next day he refers to it again – '24 depressing pages'. A year later there is an angry letter to Blackmur on the subject, sent, however, to Laughlin, perhaps to be sent on. Blackmur is accused of 'placid and conceited ignorance': 'you pups who are born omniscient ... [are] utterly indifferent to FACT.' Three years later there is a reference to Blackamoor; and in 1949 the article was still not forgotten.

Reviewing the first thirty *Cantos,* Blackmur had argued that Pound was 'neither a great poet nor a great thinker' but 'at his best a maker of great verse'. Attempting to explain and justify this judgement, Blackmur went on:

> When you look into him, deeply as you can, you will not find any extraordinary revelation of life, nor any bottomless fund of feeling ... The content of his work ... cannot be talked about like the doctrines of Dante or the mental machinery of Blake ... It is not to be found in any book or set of books. Only in a very limited way can Mr Pound be discussed as it is necessary to discuss, say, Yeats: with reference to what is implicit and still to be said under the surface of what has already been said.

Is the 'revelation of life' which poetry offers necessarily 'extraordinary', or its fund of feeling always 'bottomless'? Do Dante's 'doctrines', or Blake's 'mental machinery' explain the greatness of their poetry? Yeats's 'content' has given his critics much to talk about, but does that talk explain his superiority (if he is superior) to Pound? Blackmur was saying in his own way what many have felt about Pound, and his difficulty doesn't make that view wrong or untenable. But Pound's work, which demanded such an effort of definition, had forced his critic back in the direction of an old argument about aesthetics: Beauty or Truth? Blackmur won't tolerate an absence, or incoherence, of 'content'; yet he writes awkwardly, as if he can hear a ghostly voice asking 'What is the "content" of a nightingale or a Grecian urn?'

As for Pound: a man so isolated as he was in Rapallo, so precariously placed, and at that time in his life so seldom written about seriously and at length, was hardly likely to be unaffected by this kind of attention. His

---

A review of *Ezra Pound and James Laughlin: Selected Letters* ed. David M. Gordon, in the *London Review of Books,* 26 January 1995.

brassiness has a hollow ring of insecurity; and I feel pretty sure we can thank Blackmur in part for the largely unfortunate increase in 'content' in the forty *Cantos* written over the next seven years.

Pound had come to intellectual consciousness at the time of 1890s aestheticism and its hearty aftermath, and perhaps half-shared Blackmur's view that the early *Cantos* lacked a proper purpose beyond poetry. As if to prove himself no insubstantial aesthete, he took more and more to stuffing his epic with political history and monetary theory, which he persuaded himself would save the world from poverty and war. The problem with these *Cantos* (roughly 31 to 71 – though there are some incomparably beautiful exceptions – 39, 47 and 49, for example) is precisely the reverse of Blackmur's objection to those which preceded them: not that their 'content' cannot 'be found in any book or set of books' but that it can, and, many Poundians believe, must be if the work is to be properly understood.

Pound's experience in discovering and making known the work of Eliot, Joyce, Williams, H.D. and others had taught him (what is still true) that the publishing industry is continually settling into predictable commercial patterns which can't cope with poetry or fiction that is new, radical or unfamiliar. His way of overcoming this was to find converts who might start up a new publication or small publishing house. When James Laughlin, a wealthy Harvard student thirty years his junior, visited him in Rapallo in the early 1930s, hoping to learn to be a better poet, Pound found little good to say about his writing. 'No Jas, it's hopeless. You're never going to make a writer ... do something useful ... Go back and be a publisher.' The advice was brutal, and self-serving, but it was right; and Pound backed it up by offering the names of writers Laughlin could help. New Directions (or Nude Erections as Pound preferred to call it) was born. By 1936, when its first anthology was published, the contributors included Pound, William Carlos Williams, E.E. Cummings, Wallace Stevens and Marianne Moore. For thirty-five years Pound advised, instructed, cajoled, abused, while Laughlin for the most part acted on the good advice, ignored the bad, and behaved with a degree of patrician independence proper to a man who was able to wait almost two decades for his company to trade at a profit.

The style of Pound's letters to Laughlin – abrupt, cryptic, full of jokes, puns, compressions – is the off-the-cuff and off-the-record epistolary equivalent of the 'presentative method' of the *Cantos*. The compulsive habit of linguistic distortion can be irritating, but it is interesting because it shows a mind always conscious of language, one meaning always lying on the borders of another, or others, to be pushed over by a slight shift of orthography or pronunciation – a consciousness increased by a good working knowledge of other languages, and by living in a country where his own was not the common currency. No one to my knowledge has made the parallel between Joyce and Pound on this point, Pound's letters, like Joyce's *Finnegan's Wake,* creating a language of their own which makes sense as much by parodying English as by using it:

as fer Horse/trail/ier?? Gheez you are a glutton fer punishment ... or are you doin' it to allay fambly suspicion??
If Hostrailia cd/sing Bach, muvver!
As fer Murdering the cafeDRAWL ... waal no new england eXcent cd/be slushier than the british squeeze wot went over the rahdeOH from old Lunnon
    BUT mebbe it pays Possum's rent
.....

Yrz 15 ap.
Sazfakery -
also yr v-se improved
c
o
m   E P
p
l
i
m
e
n
t
i
.....

I SURE dew agree re / Aiken. Eliot's low saurian vitality ... when the rock was broken out hopped marse toad live and chipper after 3000 or whatever inclaustration.

For anyone who prefers to concentrate solely on the negative side of the Pound ledger David Gordon's selection inevitably offers material. Pound's tone with those who were trying to help him was often rude and ungrateful, even when his situation was desperate.

you punks NEVER connect ANYthing with anything else ...
do stir the mud in yr cranium
.....

Do you ever meet an ADULT? isn't it time you began to consult one of that exotic genus / Very few specimens in this damnisphere but still not wholly extinct. Not that YOU ever revealed the presence of one TO me.
.....

The lot of you from Eliot
down
appear to suffer from mental paralysis.

Even for one who reads this jitter and gabble with close interest, finding in it the life-energy of an original and hugely talented writer, there has to be the recognition that at times it is serving only as camouflage for intellectual shallowness, irrationality and injustice. Some of his outbursts would be wicked if they were not so powerless to do harm. It is Pound's nakedness that absolves him. He is a Lear who never travels without a heath and a storm in his luggage. When he named Eliot 'Possum' it was in recognition of a cunning, a way with the world, which he himself entirely lacked.

Laughlin is patient with him, occasionally reproachful ('We ... agreed ... it was tragic that you could not understand that we were both trying to do what we thought ... best for you'), seeming to accept that Pound's abuse was meant jocularly; but there are times when he speaks with brutal frankness, especially about how Pound's politics in the late 1930s had alienated potential readers in the United States and caused bookshops to refuse to stock his work.

As Pound's monetary theory got entangled with anti-Semitism and began to appear in the letters, Laughlin put his foot down:

> I think anti-Semitism is contemptible and despicable and I will not put my hand to it. I cannot tell you how it grieves me to see you taking up with it. It is vicious and mean ... Furthermore, in regard to the Cantos I will not print anything that can be fairly construed as an outright attack on the Jews.

The image Pound promoted of himself as embattled purveyor of economic and historical truths which might have saved Europe from a second major war in this century still persists among those who favour his poetry, and on the other hand is the prime target for his detractors. This means in turn that the argument about him, insofar as there is direct engagement, still focuses on what Blackmur called 'content'.

'Poetry', Auden says, 'makes nothing happen.' And in fact, Pound's materials in the *Cantos* – history, myth and memory – are in themselves perfectly respectable. It is the persistence with which he tries to use them to make political and monetarist points that creates the problem. He raids his sources, overloads his lines with examples, banging it all down like an ill-tempered and overworked skivvy with a team of shearers to feed.

On the other hand, when he forgets his worldly obsessions and uses that material well, his compression, ebullience, linguistic economy and freshness, together with a capacity for sudden moments of blazing lyric intensity, remind us that we are dealing with a major poet. What he needed during that decade of the 1930s was for someone to tell him to forget Blackmur's attack and to take to heart, rather, what Keats wrote to Shelley – that if 'Purpose' was the God of modern literature, then it was time to serve Mammon.

There are moments in these letters when Pound comes close to recognition that it's the *Cantos'* energy, their grand affirmation, and not their doctrine, which matters:

> in fak wot DO they say, over 40 years, and 40 vollums Ezept: Wake up and live.
>   very incomprehensible
> in a Freudian era.

But for much of his life he seemed caught in a blind determination to avoid repeating the failures of those 'aesthetes' whose work had so appealed to him in his youth. It took the collapse of the 'dream', the defeat and murder of his hero Mussolini, and the shock of his own rough incarceration by the US Army, before the *Cantos* came back into some kind of focus. The *Pisan Cantos* are, I suppose, as difficult as any; but they have artistic coherence and self-sufficiency. A steady and individual light shines through them. One might even describe their language by borrowing that famous phrase of the 1890s and say it 'burns with a hard, gem-like flame'.

There followed his thirteen-year detention in St Elizabeth's Hospital in Washington DC; and then, only three or four years after his release and joyful return to Italy, energy and confidence deserted him. He fell into the depression and silence of his old age, speaking only to declare his own folly and failure. In a letter to Laughlin he describes his mental state:

/no memory to speak of/
                    no ability to register
either the pitch of a note, or remember sequence
of tones or notes to a tune.

It's of the greatest interest and significance that the loss of memory (Mother of the Muses) and of musical sensibility are singled out as the crucial faculties denied him.

Fragments of Canto 115 were written when Pound's powers were failing, but they contain lines which take us right back to the essence of his best work, that quality of beauty in language, indefinable, unmeasurable, ineffable, unmistakable – as when the old poet describes himself:

A blown husk that is finished
                but the light sings eternal
a pale flare over marshes
        where the salt hay whispers to tide's change.

Pound's weakness was that he attended to what Blackmur and others said of him; and his consequent fault was to put too much trust in ideas, and too little in that uncanny poetic and critical instinct which in his younger days had made him the great entrepreneur of Modernism.

Craig Raine - A Celebration

29.4.94: I wake in a very small first floor room in London with large French windows and a balcony looking out on Mecklenburgh Square, 12,000 miles from my home in Auckland where I expected to be on this day. In the past three weeks I have seen winter, very much here to meet me, pack its bags and stamp off to the other place. Leaves are coming on the huge trees over the road; pink blossom on the cherry trees is already scattering on the grass of the square; every second indifferent-looking shrub has put forth purple blooms and proved to be lilac; daffodils have come and gone, followed by tulips. Today the air is mild and promises to be warm.

What is happening at home I won't learn from the news. I will know about the excitement of the South African elections, the distress of Bosnia and Rwanda, the campaigning for local body elections in the United Kingdom, the burial of Richard Nixon in California, the latest sectarian killing in Northern Ireland, the continuing search for agreement between Israel and the PLO, the *fin de siècle* gloom that is afflicting Paris. The news is predictable, and that in its way is reassuring. New Zealand would need to sink beneath the waves to make the front pages, and then it would not stay for long.

I am writing a novel set in Italy, London and Brittany. Away from the usual distractions of my life in New Zealand I sit at my laptop every morning (Sundays included) writing the London section. Some mornings are good, full of confidence; others are bad, clouded by doubts. This morning has been a bad one, the doubts in the ascendant. That is never a reason for changing one's habit. What matters is simply to get it down on paper, a first draft which can be worked at later.

I have a sandwich lunch in my room, read my novel of the moment (Martin Amis's *London Fields*), rest, try to think what may have gone wrong with this morning's writing, or whether the doubts are groundless.

Le Nouvel Observateur invited 240 writers from around the world to record how they spent 29 April 1994. The results were all translated into French and published in a single lavish collection with photographs, *240 Ecrivains Racontent une Journée du Monde.* As it happened I was in Britain when the day arrived, which explains why I grabbed at every possible New Zealand anecdote in writing my piece – and by lucky chance there were some. Ian MacEwan was another of the 240 writers, but neither of us knew the other was engaged on the same task. Neither's account of the Raine occasion overlapped with, nor contradicted, the other's, though each reported something of the other's conversation.

At 4 p.m. I walk to Russell Square, take the tube to Marble Arch, and catch the bus to Oxford, where I'm to dine with Craig Raine and his wife, Ann Pasternak Slater. Both teach at Oxford. Craig is poet and critic, formerly poetry editor of Faber & Faber (the chair once occupied by T.S. Eliot). Ann (known to her family as Li) is a scholar who is just completing an edition of the poems of Herbert.

The roads are jammed with end-of-week traffic and the bus is slow. The journey takes two hours. I walk to the Raines' house and arrive at seven. Li sits me in the garden with a drink and goes on feeding the three boys, Isaac, Moses and Vasca – three great-nephews of Boris Pasternak. The daughter, Nina – tall, beautiful – will eat later with the adults.

Craig arrives by bicycle down the lane at the back of the house. The basket on his handlebars is full of bottles of wine and champagne – already chilled, he assures me. There is something to celebrate. He joins me in the garden. We are to toast his new book, the one he has always referred to as a narrative poem, but which he now calls a novel in verse. His account of what has happened is complicated, but the essentials are as follows.

On my last visit, in September of last year, the other visitor was Christopher Reid, poet, and Raine's successor as Faber's poetry editor. Reid was to stay overnight and read the finished poem – 300 pages. He read half of it, later read the rest, and admired it. That seemed the end of the matter. Faber was Raine's publisher and would continue to be.

But now enters publisher-turned-literary-agent who takes over negotiations on Raine's behalf. He points out that the work in question is an intensely readable narrative of exceptional public interest, bringing the lives of two families, the English Raines (Craig's father was a professional boxer) and the Russian Pasternaks, into an unlikely panorama of modern European history. Unlike most poetry, this will be highly marketable, and the publisher's bid should reflect this.

The Faber management consider, and come back with an advance of £15,000. They ask that this be kept secret because it is so far beyond what they normally offer for a work of poetry.

To Raine's surprise the agent declines this and goes to Penguin. He pushes the same line, Penguin accept it, and an extraordinary deal is done. The book will be marketed intensively and pushed as a novel in verse, with the Booker Prize in mind. The advance offered and accepted is £60,000. An American publisher is also found.

We have drunk to Craig's and the book's success several times over (the boys have been fed and Li has joined us in the garden) when the next guest arrives. This is the novelist Ian MacEwan.

MacEwan and I have been in the same room before – in New Zealand. At that time I was at the centre of an absurd literary feud about the purchase by the New Zealand Government of a flat in London for visiting New Zealand writers;* and MacEwan was present at a meeting in which I had to deal with criticism of the way the affair had been conducted, and my part in it. He remembers it in more detail than I do because, he explains, when he travels he takes copious notes. I'm embarrassed that he should have been witness to what seems in retrospect hardly better than a domestic quarrel; but I'm touched, and even flattered, by what he remembers of my part in it.

Raine also has a recollection of his one visit to New Zealand. He was to read at the Wellington Festival and was preceded by Albert Wendt, who chose to read a very long extract from a long poem. First, however, Wendt felt he must explain what he was about to read, and the explanation was even longer than the extract. 'I knew I wasn't going to understand the poem,' Raine says, 'because I didn't understand the explanation.'

By the time his turn came to read he felt the audience was exhausted, and so was he. He read two short poems and sat down.

By now the third guest has arrived, Leslie Cunliffe, as beautiful and elegant as a writer for *Vogue* magazine ought to be. She is American by birth but has lived in Britain many years, having once been married to the historian Marcus Cunliffe. We go indoors to eat around a scrubbed table in the Raines' basement kitchen – a setting, Craig explains, which sometimes shocks their guests by its unrefurbished plainness, even dinginess. The peeling paint on the ceiling is pointed out; the brown stains up the wall behind the oven. This grime is something I've hardly noticed before, thinking of it, if at all, as frightfully 'Oxford'. It hasn't occurred to me, on the other hand, that it might be a matter for conscious pride. Clearly none of the £60,000 will be spent on the kitchen.†

We are not finished yet with the subject of New Zealand. MacEwan tells a story about his stay with Auckland writer John Cranna, Cranna's partner of that time, Verna Smith, and their elderly and infirm cat. After a few days in Auckland they set off to take MacEwan to stay at a bach on the Coromandel Peninsula. They had almost reached their destination when the cat had a seizure and appeared likely to die. A vet was found. He administered antibiotics and analgesics, but recommended hospital.

Cranna and Smith withdrew to a corner of a carpark for a quiet talk, leaving MacEwan alone with the cat. The visitor resisted the temptation to put the animal quickly to death. The couple returned to the car and told him regretfully that they must go back to Auckland. So there were three hours' driving back, and the cat was put in intensive care. Its devoted owner remained, MacEwan said, at its bedside. 'In the next bed there was a tortoise.'

MacEwan decided now that he would drive alone to Coromandel. He hired a car, put his bag down in the street, turned away for a moment, and when he

---

* See 'Nationalism, Regionalism and the Tradition of New Zealand Poetry' in Part 2 of this book.
† I was wrong. On a subsequent visit I found the kitchen had been wonderfully refurbished and modernised.

turned back the bag was gone. It contained his laptop and the disks of his current work. Next morning it was front page news: VISITING WRITER HAS BAG STOLEN. It was explained that the theft would mean a loss to literature. Two or three mornings the National Radio linkup phoned and interviewed him. How was he feeling? Had there been any breakthrough? How had the loss affected his attitude to New Zealand, and would it be reflected in his writing? After three days the bag was returned to the street where he left it. Nothing was missing. There was general relief.

There is a point in a dinner party beyond which nothing is quite coherent, or coherently remembered. Alcohol, hilarity and exhaustion take over. But (unlike many such occasions) I register what we are eating and that, like the wines, it is good: a wild mushroom soup, a pasta frutti di mare, an excellent salad, and finally strawberries and raspberries with ice cream.

The English are not a philosophical race, but there was a time when a group of writers could not have spent an evening together that didn't at some point turn to political analysis and debate. We are indeed at the exhausted end of a century of ideological struggle which has collapsed into economic pragmatism. Gossip, always part of literary talk, becomes its substantial centre. I don't deplore the change, believing that on the whole the *Zeitgeist* determines group behaviour; but there is a faint sense of guilt, as if the world, and we with it, have become less serious.

It's after one when the party breaks up. I'm offered a bed for the night in any of three Oxford houses, but I'm determined to be at my desk in London on time in the morning. I catch the 1.30 bus. I am the only passenger, and as it roars through the dark landscape back to London a curious excitement takes hold of me. I feel an intense and unfocused happiness. It's something rare. Not that I'm usually unhappy – but this euphoria is out of ordinary, and I know it's something to do with the personality of Craig Raine, and with the ambience of his family and house.

Allen Ginsberg – King of the May

The night I finished reading Barry Miles's biography of Ginsberg I had the following dream. In an open car or landrover I was driving a neighbour, a religious old man, in search of his son who was gold-mining in a park. The old man's wife was there, a shadowy figure in a red cardigan who seemed to dissolve into the background. He gave directions which I didn't think correct, but they were. Behind a clump of trees we found the mine – very deep diggings covered over with a beautiful domed roof supported by poles, magical-seeming, like the pleasure dome in 'Kubla Khan', although built only of rough-sawn timber.

We got down onto the grass and I had to save the old man, who slipped and almost fell into the mine. His son appeared, a strong confident middle-aged man who kissed each of us (others had arrived) saying that as friends of his father we were welcome. I was surprised by the embrace, but thought it had something to do with their religion, and found it not unpleasant, even strong and reassuring.

When I woke I was sure that though the son didn't look like Ginsberg, he was the Ginsberg figure, and that the old man my neighbour represented his father, Louis, also a poet. The unfocused woman in the red cardigan, the only female present, represented Allen's mother Naomi, whose madness and death are the subject of 'Kaddish', one of his most powerful and famous poems. Their religious sect perhaps represented the Ginsbergs' separateness as Russian Jewish émigrés. The gold-mine deep in the earth but in a very public place, and with its magical makeshift dome, was Ginsberg's poetry. The embrace was not so much his homosexuality as his emotional directness and invasive physicality.

I think the dream told me at one level how I had responded to the poet revealed in the biography. It went under my surface prejudices, embarrassments and distastes to what was clearly acceptance and probably also respect.

Since I first read Ginsberg in the late 1950s I've always thought that to acknowledge his native power has to come before anything else. Yes, he's often boring. At its worst his poetry has about it as much style and shape as a soiled mattress on a rubbish dump. But one has to go past that to what's good and durable.

Ginsberg's unabashed laying bare of personal facts which society prefers

---

A review of *Ginsberg: A Biography* by Barry Miles, broadcast on the ABC in 1990 and expanded here.

should be hidden is what draws attention first. Like his paranoid mother, who used nakedness as a weapon, Ginsberg is temperamentally an exhibitionist. He likes to be seen and he loves to shock. But that doesn't explain the force of his poetry at its best.

He is a builder of structures, very strong, very simple, and quite original. In 'Howl', for example, each of its three sections is built on a different frame. Part I begins with the famous 'I saw the best minds of my generation destroyed by madness,' after which almost every long breath-extending line begins with 'who' –

> who poverty and tatters and hollow-eyed and high sat up smoking
>> in the supernatural darkness of cold-water flats floating
>> across the tops of cities contemplating jazz
> who bared their brains to Heaven under the El and saw
>> Mohammedan angels staggering on tenement roofs
>> illuminated,
> who passed through universities with radiant cool eyes hallucinating
>> Arkansas and Blake-light tragedy among the scholars of war
> who were expelled from the academies for crazy & publishing
>> obscene odes on the windows of the skull,
> who cowered in unshaven rooms in underwear, burning their money
>> in wastebaskets and listening to the Terror through the wall ...

The second section, the most impassioned (and the one that wobbles out of control towards its conclusion) builds on the repeated execration of Moloch, the deity whose worship is marked by the sacrificial burning of children. Modern America is Moloch:

> Moloch, whose love is endless oil and stone! Moloch whose soul is electricity and banks! Moloch whose poverty is the
> specter of genius! Moloch whose fate is a cloud of sexless hydrogen! Moloch whose name is the Mind!

And in Part III, addressed to Carl Solomon in Rockland Hospital for the Insane, there is the repetition of 'I'm with you ... where ...'

> I'm with you in Rockland
>> where you imitate the shade of my mother
> I'm with you in Rockland
>> where you've murdered your twelve secretaries ...
> I'm with you in Rockland
>> where we are great writers on the same dreadful typewriter.

In each section the structure relates to, and is partly responsible for, the tone – exalted in I, angry-aggressive in II, black-comic in III.

In addition to structure and tone there is also, in Ginsberg's best writing, verbal density which is always related (as in Whitman) to momentum. The sheer speed with which the poem is rushed down, the energy of it, burns off excess and ensures a kind of compression. There may be copiousness but there is very little waste.

And finally there are surprises, jokes, quirkiness, and obscurity, so that although the poetry is direct and concrete in its statements, it doesn't entirely give itself up. In its detail it retains mysteries, an area of free play for the mind of the reader.

Of course there was not a generation gone mad in the 1950s. But there was, in many otherwise sedate young literary minds, a reserved space where the idea of it could be welcomed and entertained – the more so because in those years the western world seemed politically frozen in a pervasive and self-defeating paranoia, sourced in Washington and leading, by an inexorable logic, to some bad end which, when it came, proved to be Vietnam. Ginsberg gave voice to a decade's repressed rebellion:

> America stop pushing I know what I'm doing.
> America the plum blossom is falling ...
> America I used to be a communist when I was a kid I'm not sorry.
> I smoke marijuana every chance I get.
> I sit in my house for days on end and stare at the roses in the closet ...
> My mind is made up there's going to be trouble.
> You should have seen me reading Marx ...
> I'm addressing you.
> Are you going to be let your emotional life be run by *Time* magazine?
> I'm obsessed by *Time* magazine.
> I read it every week ...
> It occurs to me that I am America.
> I'm talking to myself again.
> Asia is rising against me.
> I haven't got a Chinaman's chance.

These lines are simple in statement, subtle in their humour. They are self-mocking. But more important, they mock a society in which what ought to be childish rebellion is seen as significant and threatening, demanding correction. And one needs to have lived through that decade to know just what it meant to be obsessed with *Time* magazine's distortions, and the knowledge that they represented the collective American mind – even, sometimes, the collective mind of the West.

Like Ezra Pound, Ginsberg was a great discoverer of talents that would match and support his own. Barry Miles reveals the extent to which he charmed, cajoled and bullied publishers to take the work of his friends – especially Jack Kerouac, William Burroughs and Gregory Corso. He and they were the Beats, precursors and mentors of what became in the late 1960s a social revolution advocating drugs, free love, gay rights, flower power and the wisdom of the East. Like any liberation, it was wonderful for those strong enough to cope with it, dangerous for those who were not.

In his darker moments Ginsberg must surely have asked himself how many young people whose minds or lives were blasted by various kinds of excess might have survived it they had not been buoyed up and swept along by that reckless Beat romanticism. The precarious Peter Orlovsky, whose long-lasting gay marriage to Ginsberg has been much publicised, gradually succumbed to various addictions. Kerouac abandoned a daughter who became a drug addict and a prostitute; and Kerouac himself died of booze. Burroughs's son to the wife he shot dead while drunk, died of drugs and alcohol. Those opening lines of 'Howl':

> I saw the best minds of my generation destroyed by madness,
>   starving hysterical naked
> dragging themselves through the negro streets at dawn looking for
>   an angry fix,
> Angelheaded hipsters looking for the ancient heavenly connection
>   to the starry dynamo in the machinery of night

read now less like a statement of facts than a prophecy of what was to come.

Ginsberg was a great publicist for poetry and for himself. He became a jet-setting Buddhist-American-Jewish gay-poet guru, giving readings and advice everywhere, including where possible (shades of Ezra!) to heads of government. This was one big 'unacknowledged legislator' looking to be acknowledged.

Invited to Cuba not long after the Bay of Pigs invasion he was soon expelled for saying, among other things, that he thought Raoul Castro, Fidel's brother, might be a fairy and that he would like to go to bed with him. Because of difficulties with airlines from Cuba he had to fly to Czechoslovakia where he found royalties and a welcome, only to be expelled again for overt gay activities after having been elected King of the May by one hundred thousand students. It was his reputation as a rebel that got him invited to these places, and his rebelliousness that got him evicted.

From the Outsider and mind-terrorist of the 1950s he went in the space of a decade to being an international symbol and spiritual leader for a generation in revolt. 'Bliss was it in that Dawn to be alive', but to be young was absolutely necessary, and that wasn't going to last. By 1970 his energy and originality, and his ability to focus on the task, were already seriously depleted, and running out fast. Put in Ginsberg-ese the message of his life might be, 'Don't fuck with your brain or it will fuck you.'

Another Contemporary — Thomas Keneally

One of the few occasions when I've met Thomas Keneally was a visit he made to Auckland in the early 1980s. This was after *Schindler's Ark* had been Bookered, but before it was Spielberged, so Tom was on an upward trajectory that was to continue – a fact which only made him more than ever the beaming diplomat, the Happy Man of Aust. Lit.

This was the time when radical feminism was at its most rampant in the universities of Australasia and went about stoking its angers and looking for trouble. Inadvertently, it met Tom Keneally at the very doors of the Auckland English Department. He and I arrived there, two fiftyish bald-heads, and I, the host, opened the door for him and waved him ahead of me. At that same moment, one of the warrior princesses of the new dispensation arrived on the other side. A man of his generation, Tom stepped back, smiled his broad charming smile, and signalled her to go through. She hesitated, frowning, then went through, hissing as she went, 'Sexist!'

'Ah, Tom,' I said. 'Welcome to the academy.'

Seen from WC1 New Zealand looks just 'offshore' from Australia; and the significance of the real 1,200 mile gap diminishes in the world of modern transport and communication. But it has been considerable. The differences are historical and social as well as climatic and topographical.

Australia at large is all drama and exaggeration. Two memories come to mind: one a 1950s newsreel showing sheep dying of drought under dead trees high in the branches of which were the skeletons of animals left there in the last flood; the other of flying over the red central desert which seemed to go on for hour after hour, and seeing away below, on either side of a thin straight line that must have been the road through, minute silver squares set out in rows, the unpainted roofs of a mining town.

In their native state the Aborigines burrowed into a condition of identity with the land. The European mind, unable to achieve this coincidence with heat and rock and dust, and in any case (quite reasonably) not wanting to, has had to struggle to give mythic expression to what it feels – and more, to what it knows – exists beyond the coastal fringes where it has made itself at home. In the visual arts, Drysdale's red landscapes and 'blackfellas' among rickety wooden verandahs, Boyd's eerie waterholes and ghostly figures, Nolan's square

---

A review of *Woman of an Inner Sea* by Thomas Keneally in the *London Review of Books*, 24 September 1992.

Ned Kelly heads like a prison out of which the eyes stare at barrenness, are examples.

In literature the mythic scale has been as courageous, though not always as successful. I find it hard to enjoy the florid extravagances of Patrick White's *Voss,* while respecting the attempt to make word match fact. Xavier Herbert tried to meet size with size, insisting that his *Poor Fellow My Country,* close on a million words, be published in a single hardback volume which one day may fall on and kill a frail person trying to read it in bed – but a remarkable narrative, animated by an epic-scale will to do justice to its continental subject.

My first university job after graduating in New Zealand was a lectureship in Armidale on the northern tableland of NSW, which is no doubt the university where Alec Ramsey, central character of Keneally's *The Survivor* (1969), is Director of Extension, and where Keneally himself (some time after me) spent a few years as a tutor in drama. The University of Armidale did all the extramural work for the State, and that meant going out on weekend schools. One of these was at Dubbo. There had been heavy rains, direct rail links were cut, so to give a few classes to a few students I had to travel 350 miles to Sydney, then a further 250 to Dubbo – all of it through an unvarying bluegum landscape. The rains continued and the Macquarie River rose twenty-four feet in the twenty-four hours I was in the town. It was just running into the gutters of the main street as I got on my train to leave. The Macquarie, or its near neighbour the Bogan, must be the unnamed river that figures, and floods, in Keneally's new novel.

Keneally too has mythic ambitions. His heroine, Kate, born Gaffney, married Kozinski, is escaping from a failed marriage and a consequent disaster so appalling we are not told what it is for fear disclosure might 'unbalance the little tale with grief and fill the mouth with ash'. Since Kate has been the mother of two children we have (and are meant to have) a fair notion of what it might be. The narrative strategy is to keep us waiting for the confirmation and the details.

Meanwhile Kate sheds her middle-class identity, leaves Sydney, and travels somewhere on that line through and beyond Dubbo to Narromine, Trangie, Nevertire, Mullengudgery and finally Myambah, where she eats a great deal of white bread and steak, works as a barmaid, and becomes involved with the townsfolk and in the drama of the flood. She's brought back, in other words, to the heart of the old Australia – another (and equally serviceable) version of Les Murray's bush-romanticism:

> She wanted to be back among those country faces ... She wanted to *feed* numbly on them. From the present, poisoned world, she wanted to track back with the help of those faces to the safer Australia ... where people called lunch *dinner* and dinner *tea*; where they referred to their suitcases as *ports*; called all dairyfarmers *titstrippers* and *cowcockies*; cooked on wood burning stoves which had belonged to their grandmothers, and might ... give you a comparative rundown of the drought or flood of 1964 as against the drought or flood of 1986.

Kate's adventures return her to something like sanity and equilibrium, despite the scars, physical and metaphysical, which remain. And what the catastrophe which sent her to the interior has been is not only revealed; it is also explained. By the end, the domestic drama has taken on the colour of a detective story in which villainy is exposed and villains punished.

Keneally has considerable narrative powers. His novels are like pieces of strong rough carpentry (somewhere between Maurices Shadbolt and Gee); and the metafictional apparatus of this one doesn't alter that basic quality – the tone of voice of a confident, genial personality, an uncomplicated and outward-looking ego; and a brisk competence with language which does its colourful and energetic work while falling short of absolute finesse, or fineness.

His strategy is to address us in the opening sentence as 'Dear bookbuyer' (something we have to put up with 57 further times in 280 pages), and to speak in the role of the author of a novel – though there's nothing in the text to say that the novelist is Keneally. This novelist has been told a story by a rich young woman in a foreign city, and for his own purposes he has transferred it to Australia. Thus the primary fiction is that there was a reality which occurred somewhere else in the world and which our unidentified narrator has made over into an Australian story. I'm willing to entertain this fiction, to suspend disbelief, but not for an instant to believe it. It is, in fact, a strategic cover for what is scarcely believable at the core of the novel Keneally (as distinct from his fictional novelist) has written.

All this is confused by what I take to be an unwarranted intrusion by Keneally's publisher, who has provided a blurb in which it is said that *Keneally* heard this story from a young woman … etc., inviting, I suppose, a quite inappropriate comparison with the way *Schindler's Ark* came into being.

The least convincing part of the novel is its mythic structure, drawing on an early belief that the continental interior contained the 'inner sea' of the title. When the river floods, a symbolic 'inland sea' is created. Myambah is threatened with inundation because its system of levees has been devised in large part to protect the pastures of corrupt shire president McHugh. Insufficient to hold the waters back, the stopbanks let them into the town and then contain them on two sides, while the railway embankment and the road form two further sides of a huge enclosing parallelogram. Kate's Myambah friend, Jelly (so named because of his expertise with gelignite), attempts to repeat a success of years before when he saved the town by blowing a hole in the railway embankment, releasing the waters onto McHugh's land. Jelly's explosion does its work again, but this time it kills him.

This fatality sets Kate wandering further inland with Jelly's friend Gus, proprietor of a tame emu and a tame kangaroo, named Menzies and Chifley after the Prime Minister and Leader of the Opposition of the 1950s. She is being pursued by her rich husband's hired thug, Burnside, intent on making her sign away some of her matrimonial property rights. At the dénouement the peaceable Chifley's powerful clawed kick will deal out a deserved and terrible, though not fatal, punishment to Burnside.

Most of this is implausible. Kate's behaviour, which her personal loss is meant to explain, is only marginally more believable than Gus's success in persuading a full-grown emu and a full-grown kangaroo to ride with him in a dinghy. And although its mythic pretensions invite us into the complicity of 'interpretation' (Woman seeking Purgation traverses an 'Inland Sea', as much mental as topographical, accompanied by the two emblematic animals of the national coat of arms) these are blandishments at a rather low intellectual level. What keeps the novel alive is tone, its refusal of that undue solemnity which often afflicts national epics, an insouciance in the narrative voice, even conceding 'the threadbare trickery of it all', but reminding us, 'dear bookbuyers', that as readers of fiction we are accustomed to contrivance, require it and even contribute to it by an imaginative filling of gaps.

Less ambitious and more interesting in the structural framing is the contrast between two kinds of corruption – the good old cosy familiar Sydney Irish Catholic kind with which Keneally, the one-time novice priest, is entirely at home; and the post-war 'New Australian' European Catholic kind, which he, or rather his narrative, maligns so thoughtlessly and cheerfully one takes that, too, as part of the contrivance. 'History is everything. People will not in the end forgive you for not having shared theirs.' That's Keneally, surely, speaking through his narrator-novelist, who is thus licensed to be unforgiving.

The simple system of good lawlessness and evil lawlessness which results is interesting not because it's true, or fair, but because it represents so precisely one local and secular point of view. It's something I recognise as 'Sydney' – old Sydney – as particular as the Harbour Bridge and the Manly Ferry; or as the Catholic Cathedral with its statue of an Archbishop inscribed, 'A Worthy Son of Ireland and Her Gift to Australia.'

Kate, our heroine, is of an Australian-Irish Catholic-Labour family. Her villainous and unfaithful husband, Paul, is Polish-Australian scion of Kozinski Constructions (their 72-foot motor-launch is called *Vistula*), 'big developers', destroyers of the old Sydney, under investigation by the National Securities Commission. Paul's mother wants her granddaughter called Gosia or Danuta or Maja rather than Siobhan; and when her grandson is named Bernard instead of Casimir, she remarks, 'I never went along with Hitler. I bled under Hitler. It doesn't mean you need to dance with Jews, or name your children after them.' Her worship of the Black Virgin of Czestochowa (quaintly) appears to Irish eyes something akin to black magic.

Kate's favourite relative, her uncle Frank O'Brien, is a priest, and (as the press describes him) a 'well-known racing and sporting identity', who in partnership with his mistress, Mrs Fiona Kearney, widow of a Sydney alderman 'named by the Independent Commission Against Crime as a notable operator of SP bookmaking outlets', has gone extensively into real estate. He's determined not to 'let a load of Dago gobshites in some congregation in Rome force me out'; and when his Eminence Cardinal Fogarty takes legal action to remove him from his presbytery, O'Brien's friend, mortician Patrick O'Toole, responds publicly with what one instantly recognises as authentic old-Oz circumlocutions: 'Though I am a loyal son of the Church, I have to say that in this case Cardinal Fogarty has again shown that generosity of spirit is not his strong suit.' (In reality this would be delivered with an 'uh' between every third or fourth word.)

This is high church comedy, and needs no excuse; but late in the novel some twitch of conscience prompts Keneally to offer one. SP bookmaking 'was as old as the anarchic continent [Really?] and as ancient as convictism.' [Acquitted by geography and history!] 'It was harmless too, in some lights, part of the unofficial democratic rights of the Australian working men and women.' [A form of social justice, even!] In Father O'Brien's world 'corruption ... did not exist if it were among the friendly and the loyal and was a token of love. He was not ashamed, in fact shamefully unashamed, to ask for favours.'

There must surely be a matching sentimentality, or special pleading, by which the Kozinskis and the Krinkovichs would justify their corruption and even their murders. But this is a story, not a moral exploration; and though there are always insights to be gained, discoveries to be made, stories go better, run faster, when we know who we are supposed to like.

Father O'Brien's mortician friend O'Toole is not there just for local colour. When Kate, far inland, is in need of rescue, a blue helicopter with O'TOOLE painted on its side drops down out of the evening sky, and out steps uncle Frank. It's another fine moment of comic extravagance; and if you are resisting it, wondering how a mortician comes to own such a machine, that too is explained. It was used for 'rare ash-scatterings over the sea, now that Catholics were permitted to cremate themselves. This had enabled him to get the whole thing off tax.'

When I read Peter Carey's *Oscar and Lucinda* it seemed to me Carey had begun with an ambitious concluding image – the glass church floating down the Bellinger River – and worked backwards to contrive it. I have a similar uneasy feeling about this novel – that Keneally has asked himself how he could contrive to have symbolic 'Australian woman', flanked by those emblematic animals, marsupial and flightless bird, visit the mythical inland sea, and what might be made of it. In the course of contriving this piece of symbolism he has written something perhaps remote from his intention – more nearly, for all its metafictional levers and push-buttons, an old fashioned realist novel in the line of, say, Dal Stivens.

There is a lot of 'thinking' along the way; but what Keneally knows, remembers and sees is (as with most novelists) more interesting and convincing than what he thinks. Nevertheless, that sometimes strenuous, sometime naive or innocent, 'thinking' is an aspect of a strong personality and an authentic Australian voice.

Ted Hughes, Sylvia Plath and the Ironies of Literary Reputation

An English friend, Anthony Thwaite, a poet of established reputation there, writes that his selected poems came out recently to a 'muted reception'. 'In the wonderful world of poetry,' he goes on, 'Taddeo Grande has swept the board.' By Taddeo Grande he means, of course, Great Ted; and the work that is carrying all before it is *Birthday Letters*, eighty-eight poems addressed to the late Sylvia Plath, written, the blurb says, over a period of more than twenty-five years, but giving this reader, at least, the impression that they are all of a piece and that the majority are very recent.

Much of the story is widely known. Hughes married Plath and fathered two children, and then, in 1963, left her for Assia, wife of the Canadian poet David Wevill. Plath, American-born poet and novelist, was brilliant, tough but erratic, given to extremes of gloom and ecstasy, and in her teens had tried to kill herself – not a person to be so hurt and left with two children in the harshest of English winters. Some of her last and strongest poems come out of the pain of that desertion. *Ariel,* published in 1965, two years after her suicide, made her famous. Some years later Assia killed herself with Shura, her child to Hughes.

By the 1970s Plath had become an icon of the women's movement while Hughes, its demon, came under something like a feminist fatwa. He was attacked and reviled, hounded, heckled in public and panned in the press. On top of his private griefs and guilts was loaded this general obloquy.

Hughes's position has been in some ways similar to John Middleton Murry's in relation to Katherine Mansfield – including having a second wife who repeated the manner of death of the first. By judicious publication of her work, the copyright of which he inherited, Hughes, like Murry, has created, sustained and fostered his first wife's reputation, at the same time profiting by it, and feeding the appetite of any who wished to see her as victim and him as predator. Any word against the Martyr would only compound his guilt.

Hughes's silence on the subject of their marriage has been wise. His treatment of her was probably indefensible; but over time the repetitious fury of those who wished to make use of her for reasons that had little to do with literature has almost worn itself out. An interest in the human truths begins to supersede moralism and ideology.

And now comes *Birthday Letters,* Hughes's first public statement on the

A review of *Birthday Letters* by Ted Hughes in the *New Zealand Listener,* 4 April 1998.

subject. It couldn't have been better timed. Readers possess the facts necessary to make sense of these poems and a keen interest in their subject. If the same book had been issued to a public knowing nothing about the author's life it could easily have passed relatively unnoticed. But it's as if we've all attended a series of seminars to prepare us. How could it fail? Taddeo Grande sweeps the board.

I was a postgraduate student in England when Hughes's first book, *The Hawk in the Rain* (dedicated 'to Sylvia'), was published to acclaim. I bought it hoping perhaps for the kind of excitement I'd had two years before from Philip Larkin's *The Less Deceived,* but read it thinking 'Which hawk? What rain?' He was praised in England especially for his animals, but they seemed to me animals in the head, or at best in a zoo. I was squeamish about some of the violence in his work, which struck me as gratuitous, distasteful, and in a way pretentious – faked.

When *Crow* came out in 1970 I was somewhat awed by its raw force, and the sense that something genuinely horrible lay behind the sequence, out of sight. Since it was dedicated to the memory of Assia and Shura, this is not surprising; but at that time I knew nothing of his second tragedy. I had got to know David Wevill during the Commonwealth Festival in 1965; but not well enough for such intimate matters ever to come up. I had not, in other words, had the kind of briefing we've all had for *Birthday Letters.* So I registered simply a force beyond the immediate subject, or apparent occasion, of the poems. And that was as near as I was ever able to go towards admiring Hughes, whose work seemed to me always to aspire to strengths which Plath, in those last poems, had achieved without trying.

Some cruel Frenchman (was it Mallarmé?) said of Tennyson's *In Memoriam,* 'When he should have been broken-hearted he had many reminiscences.' What struck me reading *Birthday Letters* was that many of the poems were not even reminiscences. They seemed distant from the real Plath, as if Hughes too had attended that series of seminars. He too has read the biographies, and the journals, and the letters, and they are now his source, more real to him than she is. Of course here and there genuine memories pop out, and they are of great interest; but these only serve to underline how second-hand much of the material feels.

Economy is unknown to Hughes. When in doubt, he adds, never (or so one feels) subtracts. And then there are those characteristic attempts to explain something by means of an extended image – some poor misshapen metaphor dragged in off the streets, required to testify, and finally beaten to death for refusing to come clean with answers it doesn't have. English muddle not infrequently confuses obscurity with profundity, and Hughes has always (innocently – since he's too confused to be aware of it) profited by this.

The wrong thing admired (Hughes), and the right thing for the wrong reason (Plath) – that may seem a gloomy picture, but it's certainly not uncommon in literary history. So much reading of new work is in terms of the foreground, the 'subject', and contemporary interest in it; but as the foreground recedes and the interest wanes, then only the quality of the writing will preserve the work.

Time, we can be sure (or if we can't be sure, we can hope) will sort it out. Meanwhile only the hardest of hearts will grudge Taddeo Grande, Poet Laureate, his late enhanced fame and public forgiveness.

Postscript: Hughes died a year or so after this was written and was buried in the Poet's Corner of Westminster Abbey with full literary honours.

E.E. Cummings – Petal by Petal

In the Woody Allen movie *Hannah and her Sisters,* Eliot (Michael Caine) contrives to cross paths on a Manhattan street with his sister-in-law, Lee (Barbara Hershey), with whom he has fallen in love. He pretends to be hunting for a bookshop; she shows him the way to it and there he finds, as if by chance, E.E. Cummings's *Collected Poems,* which he insists on buying for her. Putting her into a taxi he tells her, twice, to be sure to read the poem on page 112, which he says makes him think of her. Later we see her lying on a bed with the book, and hear her, voice over, reading the second and final stanzas of 'Somewhere I have never travelled …':

> your slightest look easily will unclose me
> though I have closed myself as fingers,
> you open always petal by petal myself as Spring opens
> touching skilfully (mysteriously) her first rose
>
> …
>
> (i do not know what it is about you that closes
> and opens; only something in me understands
> the voice of your eyes is deeper than all roses)
> nobody, not even the rain, has such small hands

Along with the poem whose opening two lines must have stuck like burrs to the memory of everyone who ever read them –

> anyone lived in a pretty how town
> (with up so floating many bells down)

– the love lyric Allen uses to convey his character's foolish and unstable passion is probably Cummings's most widely known. I find it in four of five anthologies on my shelves that represent him. It is his 'Break, break, break …'; his 'Lake Isle of Innesfree'; his 'Love Song of J. Alfred Prufrock'. Like all good anthology pieces its vehicle is a cadence which sweeps right past the intellect on its way to the emotions, ignoring as beneath contempt such questions as why the rain should have small hands rather than, say, large feet.

Also much favoured is the elegy on his father, beginning

> my father moved through dooms of love
> through sames of am through haves of give,
> singing each morning out of each night

A review of *E.E. Cummings: Complete Poems 1904–1962* ed. George J. Firmage, in the *London Review of Books,* 27 May 1993.

>   my father moved through depths of height

where the reader makes a sense (any one of several will do, since they are all the same) of the thing line by line, lulled into unawareness that the primary linguistic action is not towards meaning at all but towards the patterning of sounds – 'move' echoing 'love', 'have' and 'give', 'doom' echoing 'same' and 'am', for example, in the first two lines. As for meaning – 'My father was a good man and I loved him' is what the lines are reiterating through seventeen samely inventive, and ultimately wearying, stanzas.

This, though he is not fairly called a sentimentalist, is the Cummings who appeals to sentimentalists, and was cited by them against the detractors (in his lifetime, 1894–1962, there were many) who jeered at his formal experiments, his lower-case poems, his inventiveness (or perverseness) with grammar, punctuation, typography. Armed with the assurance his capacity for strong and wholesome emotions provided, his supporters saw him, as he perhaps came to see himself, as one of Modernist poetry's victims in the vanguard.

He also saw himself as a victim of the political Left who, he believed, controlled American poetry publishing and did not forgive him for *EIMI,* the eccentric prose work of 1933 in which he recorded his angry-contemptuous response to five weeks in the Soviet Union; and this sense of victimisation added to the curmudgeonly tendency of his later years. Cummings was not a political poet, but there are at intervals (and reading through the 1,100 pages of this new *Complete Poems* they are important in creating variety and widening the picture) satiric or otherwise 'engaged' poems reaching outside his usually closed circle into a wider world. These are anti-war ('I sing of Olaf glad and big'; 'My sweet old etcetera'; 'Plato told / him'), anti-commerce ('A salesman is an it that stinks excuse'), anti-bourgeois ('The Cambridge ladies who live in furnished souls'), anti-Left ('Kumrads die because they're told'), even anti-American ('Next to of course god america i / love you'). But, it has to be said, they could also be anti-Semitic in the plainest Poundian manner ('A kike is a most dangerous / machine').

Between the love poet and the satirist there is a third, the experimentalist – overlapping with the other two, but distinguishable, I think, by the fact that in this mode his energy source is not primarily in the love or the hate but in the language:

>   Buffalo Bill's
>   defunct
>   who used to
>   ride a watersmooth-silver
>   stallion
>   and break onetwothreefourfive pigeons justlikethat
>   Jesus
>   he was a handsome man
>   and what i want to know is

>how do you like your blueeyed boy
>Mr Death

This too is an anthology piece. Cummings once visited a girls' college in Vermont and the whole school rose and chanted it in unison. Its success lies in its spareness – how much more it signals than it says – and in the way it both utters and rounds upon its own romanticism.

Cummings grew up in a Cambridge Mass. academic and Congregationalist sanctuary, with vacations in the New Hampshire countryside, cosseted by a mother who kept everything he wrote and painted from his earliest years, confident he was destined to need an archive. He had literature from family as well as from (and before) schooling, his early years including a great deal of uplifting New England poetry (Longfellow, notably) along with traditional English poets and novelists – an aggregation that would have put most of his English contemporaries to shame.

At Harvard he learned, not from courses but in the way exceptional students learn from one another, about the new art (Cézanne, Matisse, Duchamps, Brancusi), the new music (Satie, Schoenberg, Stravinski, Scriabin), the new literature (Amy Lowell, Stein, Pound, Eliot, Joyce), and was bold enough to give a graduation address in 1915 referring to most of these.

In 1919, when America entered the European war, he joined an ambulance corps in France, the great adventure of his life. Remarks considered by the French censor to be anti-French and pro-German in letters by his friend William Slater Brown, and Cummings's staunch refusal to dissociate himself, or say that he 'hated the Bosch', resulted in their being incarcerated together for three months while the possibility that they were spies was looked in to. *The Enormous Room,* the 'faction' Cummings made of this, has been, over the decades since, a writers' book, praised by T.E. Lawrence, Graves, Hemingway, and other notables, but selling modestly. Hemingway describes it in his letters as 'the classic example of the really fine book that could not sell', and suggests that its problem was 'a style that no one who had not read a good deal of "modern" writing could read'. In fact its style, shifting effortlessly between conventional past-tense narrative, and a present-tense, occasionally verbless, impressionism, is not the problem; nor are the events and characters in the least uninteresting. The limit lies, I think, in Cummings's lack of what the narrative writer needs before all else – a clear direction forward, the promise hidden in every sentence of an outcome, an upshot. *The Enormous Room,* interesting, admirable, alive with that charming and sometimes irritating chutzpah which informs the best of the poems, is not a book that seems to require you to read it all, or return to it soon.

Cummings's poetry is full of intuitive felicities ('The mind is its own beautiful prisoner'), or felicitous accidents:

>Humanity i love you
>because you would rather black the boots of
>success than enquire whose soul dangles from his
>watch chain

That deliberately naive opening line could be Frank O'Hara (and probably signals an important O'Hara source); but the lower-case voice of the little nobody, the Chaplinesque charmer, together with the strong cartoon image of Success (boots and a watch-chain), half-conceal, without spoiling its effect, the ambiguity of the statement, which means 'Humanity I love you for your moral failure' – with the further implication, 'because it matches my own.'

When unvisited by whatever mysterious servitor it is that lays their rare and brilliant best effortlessly out for poets (and it's a facility that deserts him as often and as long as it deserts anyone who writes regularly through a lifetime), Cummings spent much of his energy in constructing what I think of as puzzle poems. In some of these there was a system of typographical gates locking one statement inside another. Others, like the one below, were simpler:

    (fea

    therr

    ain

    :dreamin

    g field o

    ver forest &

    wh

    o could

    be

    so

    !f!

    te

    r?n

    oo

    ne)

The statement is not difficult to unravel (Feather rain dreaming field over forest & who could be softer? No One). It is in itself rich, evocative – words conjuring a world. So why the complications of typography? Only I think (but an important only) to delay arrival at what lies beyond language; to ensure we're prevented from doing what we do in most of our reading – rush straight through the medium without noticing it. Language is the vehicle bringing out of us a world we already possess (mimesis depending upon re-cognition), and Cummings's tricks of style force us to work with it, as he has done, experiencing it as plastic and malleable. We have been given a kitset, not in order to become carpenters, but to learn the feel of wood. He also likes to conceal small rewards for those alert enough to notice them. So in this example we have discovered in fact a haiku:

    feather rain dreaming
    field over forest and who

> could be softer? no-one

Challenging in a different way are those densely textured poems in which some kind of inner, and not always penetrable, struggle goes on between drive and discipline, sense and form:

> by god I want above fourteenth
>
> fifth's deep purring biceps, the mystic screech
> of Broadway, the trivial stink of rich
>
> frail firm asinine life
>   (i pant
> for what's below. the singer. wall. I want
> the perpendicular lips the insane teeth
> the vertical grin
>   give me the Square in spring,
> the little barbarous Greenwich perfumed fake.

Man and Manhattan, location and lust, seem interlocked here. What's less obvious is that this is the octave of an irregular sonnet, rhyming *a b b c c d e f* (and the *a d e* and *f* will find pairings in the sestet). One's uncertainty about meaning may be less important than the conviction that there is one, a conviction which springs, paradoxically, from the poet's difficulty in taking hold of it. The language is alive, active; and it's in that sense of action more than in 'meaning' that verbal composition becomes poetry.

It's a surprise to recognise that Cummings must be one of Modernism's most notable sonneteers, and interesting to compare with Lowell whose 'open sonnets' did away with rhyme altogether. Cummings fought free of the old iambic (though often it echoes, like a ghost on the stairs), put the form into casual dress, and let it speak popular demotic so that it could (and did) pass, in any crowd of Modernist poems, quite unrecognised. Only a second and informed look revealed that this relaxed and informal language had been wrestled into a tight traditional scheme of rhymes and half-rhymes. Here, for example is his tribute to Ford Madox Ford (to whom Lowell also addressed a sonnet):

> possibly thrice we glimpsed –
>   more likely twice
> that (once crammed into someone's kitchenette)
>
> wheezing bulgily world of genial plac-
> idity (plus, out of much its misbutt-
> oned trouser fly tumbling, faded five
> or so lightyears of pyjamastring)
> a(vastly and particularly)live
> that undeluded notselfpitying
>
> lover of all things excellently rare;

> obsolete almost that phenomenon
> (too gay for malice and too wise for fear)
> of shadowy virtue and of sunful sin
>
> namely(ford madox ford)and eke to wit
> a human being
> – let's remember that

It hasn't come easily, and it isn't by any means perfect; it may depend too much on the reader possessing knowledge of, and even affection for, Ford; but no practitioner could be uninterested in the tussle that has gone on between linguistic informality and that perfect sonnet scheme, *a b a b, c d c d, e f e f, g g*.

In such a large output there is inevitably a lot that's weak, unsuccessful, unsatisfactory. It's also, even for the reader who knows Cummings reasonably well, full of surprises, discoveries, unanticipated pleasures. One for me is the translation of Aragon's long poem 'Red Front', where the effect is not unlike that of some of Pound's translations. The original provides the material, which is therefore beyond question, and all the poet's skill goes into the writing-into-English.

Other pleasures are fortuitous and challenge one to question one's own response. On pp. 426 and 427, for example, I find two poems, entirely different except that by the standards of the 1990s they will give offence. One is a tightly packed set of stanzas:

> the boys I mean are not refined
> they go with girls who buck and bite
> they do not give a fuck for luck
> they hump them thirteen times a night
>
> one hangs a hat upon her tit
> one carves a cross on her behind
> they do not give a shit for wit
> the boys I mean are not refined

… and so on. Are these bully boys deplored? I'm not sure that they are. Are they celebrated? Damn near! Should they be? Well no, but … It's an interesting (Brechtian?) challenge.

The poem on the facing page is a rhapsody on how *alive* that group are which in my lifetime were first Negroes, then Blacks, and are now African Americans. The poem calls them, unacceptably in all those phases (except now, when Af.Am.s may use the term to one another), niggers –

>   Not jes
>   livin
>   not Jes alive But
>   *So* alive (they
> s
>   born alive) …

So the lines continue, concluding

                                                           niggers
                                  is
                        born
              so
   Alive)
              ump-A-tum
                     ;tee-die
              uM-tuM
                  tidl
                          id
           umptyumpty (OO————————
                                            !
                            ting
                    Bam-
          :do)
       ,chippity.)

Did you laugh? No? Well, I'm sure one shouldn't. But who is being set up here? African Americans, or those who are awfully good about how *alive* they are?

Cummings suffers from the Arnoldian paradox. Life may be a bitch, but poetry's business is with beauty and energy – to manifest, register, and affirm them. Where circumstances bear too heavily on the Arnoldian poet, life is squeezed out, energy fails, and so does poetry. So he is full of bounce, or he is silent. This is not so much a philosophical position as the expression of a temperament. Even at his rare best (and that means perhaps two or three dozen poems) a poet like Cummings will always be half-resented by those of less positive cast, to whom his buoyancy will seem an affront and suggest, quite contrary to the facts of his life, that sympathy and suffering were beyond him.

David Malouf Goes Elliptical

Gemmy Fairly appears at the edge of a small mid nineteenth-century settlement out of the 'empty' Queensland hinterland. He is twenty-nine and has spent sixteen years among Aborigines who rescued him after he was cast overboard from a passing ship. He has almost forgotten his own language, and has acquired the semi-mystical consciousness of the tribespeople.

He's taken in by the McIvor family – Jock and Ellen, their small daughters Janet and Meg, and nephew Lachlan Beattie. Soon his presence is causing concern. The community lives in a state of apprehension (what is feared is not at all clear) about the Blacks, and it's thought Gemmy might still be communicating with them. There's also a feeling that his 'whiteness' has been compromised; that he's in some sense 'unclean'. The McIvors' nearest neighbour and friend, Barney Mason, is particularly anxious, and his unscrupulous rouseabout, Andy McKillop, who sees two black men visit Gemmy and talk to him, plays on these fears.

There's a night raid. Gemmy is abducted, beaten, and only saved from drowning by Jock. He's removed to the care of a woman, Mrs Hutchence, the only one in the settlement who has a 'real house'; but his own fears are now such that he feels he must reclaim the pages on which were transcribed as much as was understood, and misunderstood, of his account of his previous life. Once he possesses what he (mistakenly) believes to be these sheets of paper, he feels released. He vanishes from the community. Nine years later Lachlan, working on a road gang, convinces himself that Gemmy's bones are among the remains he's shown of eight or nine blacks ridden down and killed three years previously in a 'dispersal' – but there's no certainty.

In a coda to the narrative, Lachlan and Janet meet in old age and reflect on how Gemmy's appearance among them affected their lives and their view of themselves.

When Gemmy comes into the settler community they notice not only his loss of English but physical changes that have made him seem closer to an Aborigine than to a European, and they wonder inwardly, 'Could you lose it? Not just language, but *it. It.*' The space between their sense of duty to a White who has endured such misfortune, and their response to one who looks and smells and behaves like a Black, is the screen on which the nature of racism is projected.

A review of *Remembering Babylon* by David Malouf, in the *London Review of Books*, 10 June 1993.

But Malouf is more deeply concerned with the relation of humankind to the Australian landscape. By becoming 'aboriginal', Gemmy has crossed the divide which separates white Australia from the land it occupies.

The clergyman, Mr Frazer, has some sense of this. He uses Gemmy's knowledge of the local flora and fauna to assist in compiling what he thinks of as a 'report'. His vision is of an Australian continent which would provide for its settlers as it has provided for its aboriginal inhabitants – not by introduced crops and animals, but by the hunting and gathering of what is already there. When he offers this report to the Governor, Sir George Bowen, the latter's incomprehension is meant, it seems, to illustrate another aspect of the settler failure to come to terms with the true inner reality of 'Australia'. The exact nature of the potential native vegetable- and meat-supply is not spelt out; and that may be as well for the novelist's purpose, since it's indicated that Sir George's estate grows strawberries, grapes, peaches and asparagus; grazes deer, Breton cows, and an Arabian bull, and runs peacocks and pheasants.

There's an oddness about the shaping and tone of this novel. It sketches interestingly the background of the schoolteacher George Abbot, and offers the beginning of his relationship with Miss Leona Gonzales, but then leaves him, and it, undeveloped. It suggests more about Gemmy's childhood than it reveals, as if the author had thought it out and then decided against using it. It seems to promise a Victorian-style development of character, leisurely and ample, and then fails to deliver. In tone it seems to shape towards tragedy, for Gemmy and the local Blacks, and perhaps for the McIvors, but turns aside from such dramatic potential in favour of a more life-like shading away into uncertainties and inconclusions.

Perhaps a much larger novel has been trimmed down; or perhaps the first draft proved to Malouf that his larger intentions were flawed, but not before they had been signalled in the writing. If these guesses of mine are wrong, the fact that the novel prompts them at least indicates something about its structure – one with more elaborate foundations than seem appropriate to the final design.

A good deal of what happens goes on below the surface. The settlers are neither frank nor articulate, so the forces of thought and feeling among them – liberal and good-hearted on one side, racist and violent on the other – are delivered to us in generalised abstract by the novelist himself, and through the perceptions of Gemmy who must also stand for the shadowy absent tribespeople:

> And in fact a good deal of what they [the settlers] were after he [Gemmy] could not have told, even if he had wanted to, for the simple reason that there were no words for it in their tongue; yet when, as sometimes happened, he fell back on the native word, their eyes went hard, as if the mere existence of a language they did not know was a provocation, a way of making them helpless. He did not intend it that way, but he too saw that it might be true. There was no way of

existing in this land, or making your way through it, unless you took into yourself, discovered on your breath, the sounds that linked up all the various parts of it and made them one. Without this you were blind, you were deaf, as he had been at first, in their world. You blundered about seeing holes where in fact strong spirits were at work that had to be placated, and if you knew how to call them up, could be helpful. Half of what ought to have been bright and full of the breath of life to you was shrouded in mist ...

Whose sermon is this? Not Gemmy's – not really – but the author's. The novel has many such passages – decently written, perfectly in step with the moral precepts of our time, worthy but leaden – lacking fictional life and veracity.

Jock McIvor is the only adult male in the community open to Gemmy's influence, and he begins to recognise this fact in the following passage, where he acknowledges his separation from 'them' – his fellow-settlers:

Was he changed? He saw now that he must be ...
When had it begun?
When they agreed to take Gemmy in ...
He had never been a thinker, and he did not now become one, but he began to have strange thoughts.
Some of them were bitter. They had to do with what he saw, now that he looked, was in the hearts of men – quite ordinary fellows like himself; he wondered that he had not seen it before. What the other and stranger thoughts had to do with he did not know.
It was as if he had seen the world till now, not through his own eyes, out of some singular self, but through the eyes of a fellow who was always in company, even when he was alone; a sociable self, wrapped always in a communal warmth that protected it from dark matters and all the blinding light of things, but also from the knowledge that there was a place out there where the self might stand alone.

Once again this is not the character thinking in character, but Malouf thinking for him. It's ventriloquism, and bogus. And now, as if to illustrate instantly the new man Jock has become, he begins to see things in the natural world previously unnoticed – green insects on grass tips, a bird drawing long silver threads out of the running water of a stream. These perceptions are 'like a form of knowledge he had broken through to. It was unnameable, which disturbed him, but it was also exhilarating.'

The change affects his marriage too, beneficially. Here is Jock's wife noticing the improvement:

He had turned his full gaze upon her – that is what she felt. He wanted to know now what her life was beyond what he saw and had taken for granted, a shirt washed and shaken to make it soft, food on the table; to enquire into her affections. It was amazing to him – that is what his tentativeness suggested – that he had known so little and had not looked. There were times now when the intensity of his looking made her blush.
It was as if they were at the beginning of a courtship.

Here we're told what we haven't been shown; even what we may have no good reason to find credible. Gemmy is an unfortunate stick figure who brings, says and does next-to-nothing. Why should his arrival among them prompt this radical change, this self-discovery, turning a hardy forty-year-old settler into a Sensitive New-Age Guy? There's nothing to explain it or make it plausible. It's there because it serves Malouf's moral purpose. Don't ask why. Take your medicine!

Settler societies breed two phases of myth. In the first the settlers romanticise themselves and their heroic fight against the untamed and the uncivilised. In the second, their somewhat-educated descendants, enjoying all the benefits of settlement, represent their forebears as ignorant destroyers, and romanticise the unique character and spiritual identity of the culture which colonisation damaged or destroyed. The second phase is strong in fiction by Australian males. In varying strengths it's found in White, Herbert, Keneally, Carey and Malouf. Since all such myths contain their share of truth they needn't be damaging and may even be fruitful; but the fiction writer needs to hang on to his sense of probability – how human beings *really* behave – and of irony.

In pre-publication (and pre-Booker) publicity the Big Guns have been wheeled out. Doris Lessing has welcomed this novel's 'really impressive achievement' which is to compress 'the myths, the poetry, the history of a vast and ancient continent'; Michael Ondaatje has likened it to 'a spirit painting in a 19th century locket – full of wisdom and magic – the most delicate tracing of a profound and elliptical history, thrilling in its style and adventurousness'; the marketing director of Waterstone's has called it 'visionary', 'a combination of Coetzee, Ondaatje and Okri'; and the publishing director of Picador has called it 'inspired, magnificently poetic and elliptical ... a world novel in every sense to rank alongside the best of Coetzee, Salman Rushdie ... and Gabriel Garcia Marquez.'

Does Malouf deserve such backers – and perhaps the Booker as well? Maybe he does; maybe they all deserve one another. Here are his final paragraphs:

> Out beyond the flatlands the line of light pulses and swells. The sea, in sight now, ruffles, accelerates. Quickly now it is rising towards us, it approaches.
>
> As we approach prayer. As we approach knowledge. As we approach one another.
>
> It glows in fullness till the tide is high and the light almost, but not quite, unbearable, as the moon plucks at our world and all the waters of the earth ache towards it, and the light, running in fast now, reaches the edges of the shore, just so far in its order, and all the muddy margin of the bay is alive, and in a line of running fire all the outline of the vast continent appears, in touch now with its other life.

What is happening here? Well, nothing really. But it's 'visionary' – isn't it? Even 'elliptical'?

The Death of a Book

The New Poetic, my book on W.B. Yeats, T.S. Eliot and the Georgian poets, had a commendably (for an academic study, an exceptionally) long life, but a protracted dying. I wrote it in my late twenties as a PhD thesis under the supervision of Professor L.C. Knights while I was Michael Hiatt Baker Scholar at the University of Bristol. It was first published in 1964 in the Hutchinson University Press series edited by Basil Willey, King Edward VII Professor of English Literature at Cambridge, a chair to which Knights succeeded, followed by Frank Kermode. Its next incarnation was in the United States as a Harper Torchbook in 1966, where it acquired its longer title, *The New Poetic: Yeats to Eliot.* Pelican brought it out in its first British paperback in 1967, and again in 1969 with a new cover. Hutchinson reclaimed it, and reissued it at intervals through the 1970s and on into the eighties as a handsome trade paperback. The strangest form it took (described it in the accompanying brochure as 'a late classic of Imagist criticism') was as a hardcover in the AMS reprint series Des Imagistes, along with books by Pound, H.D., Richard Aldington, F.S. Flint, John Gould Fletcher, Amy Lowell, Ford Madox Ford, Remy de Gourmont, Wyndham Lewis, T.E. Hulme, Herbert Read, Arthur Symons, Harriet Monroe, and others. In 1987 the Pennsylvania University Press republished it as 'a classic in its field of scholarship', and encouraged me to write a brief reflective introduction.

By this time it had sold many copies – I don't know how many, but well over 100,000. It had been prescribed, cited, quoted, especially in discussions of Eliot. Bits had been reprinted in four different Macmillan *Casebooks* and in several collections of essays on Yeats. I accepted when I visited Britain that I was likely to be identified as its author;* and on two separate occasions, while I was still in my late forties or early fifties, a young academic at a conference expressed surprise that I was still alive and not terminally ancient.

I didn't expect the book to go on for ever, and wouldn't have felt more than a passing twinge of regret to see it go out of print. But the way this happened, and my spasmodic attempts to hold onto some sense of proprietorship, illustrate the difficulties of authors at a time when publishers

---

PN Review, November–December 1996.
* While I was putting this collection together my friend Professor Mac Jackson sent me the *Times Literary Supplement* crossword in the issue of 18 June 1999, with the anagram clue 28 Across: New Zealand critic gets dates mixed (5).

are behaving collectively like an illustration of the marine food chain. That, and not the book itself (about which, of course, I could write a great deal) is my subject.

In August 1988 I received a letter from Stephen Warshaw, Chairman of Hutchinson Education, to say that they were transferring Hutchinson's education list to Unwin Hyman. 'The decision has been a difficult one to make and one in which your interests have of course ...' (etc.) A week later came a letter welcoming me to Unwin Hyman. 'Your book will be immediately in the hands of an experienced specialist in your subject area ...' (And so on.)

The experienced specialist turned out to be Ms Claire L'Enfant who had worked for Hutchinson and had, I suppose, changed ship when she found one to be sinking. Recognising that the letters I'd received were formulae meant to cover all cases, I wrote to say that there had been some talk of letting the book go out of print, and asking whether this was still the case. In January 1989 Ms L'Enfant confirmed that it was. 'I regret this very much, as I am a great fan of the book ...' (etc.)

For two years I gave it no further thought, but in March 1991 I received a letter from Michael Brozicevic, Group Royalties Director of HarperCollins, saying no doubt I was aware (I was not) that Unwin Hyman had become a subsidiary of HarperCollins, and enclosing a royalty statement.

I replied thanking him for '£18.63, being 75% of subsidiary rights payment' (source undisclosed) on *The New Poetic.* But I pointed out that I had been informed in January 1989 that the book was going out of print, and had asked for a reversion of rights. 'That being the case, there are no grounds for Unwin Hyman to accept any part of a payment for subsidiary rights, whatever their source, and it appears that the balance of £6.21 is still owing to me. This sum is less important, of course, than that any returns on the book should now be made to me in full.'

Mr Brozicevic replied, 'I'm afraid I don't have any details to hand on whether there has been a formal reversion, and normal publisher's practice is that sub-rights income is shared until there is such a reversion.'

I replied giving him details of my correspondence with Claire L'Enfant and quoting my Memorandum of Agreement to the effect that if the publisher should let the book go out of print, and within nine months of receiving written notice has not reprinted, all rights forthwith revert to the author.

'That,' I went on, 'covers the present case, and I write to make clear to you my understanding that rights have reverted to me and that any income earned after 17.10.89 belongs to me. I should be grateful to have your confirmation of this.'

This received no reply, and since this book from my past was of no great interest or concern to me, I forgot about it. But at the end of March 1992 Mr Brozicevic (still of HarperCollins) wrote to express his pleasure in sending me a further royalty statement. This, if it came, doesn't appear to have survived in my file; and perhaps it didn't come, but was only preliminary to a letter dated a week or so later from David Croom, Managing Editor of Routledge, who had pleasure in enclosing a statement of my earnings for 1991, and telling me that as a Routledge author (I had never had anything to do with the firm) I was 'entitled to buy all Routledge books directly at trade terms'.

The royalty statement, bristling with code numbers, was headed Routledge Chapman and Hall, and showed that 'The New Poetic: Yeats to Elliot' [sic] had earned £9.17.

By now I was irritable. My reply read:

Royalty Department
Routledge, Chapman and Hall (etc)
                     Account number RSTEAO64
                     Your ref 488679
                     0090713516
Dear Royalty Department,

Thank you for sending me your 7926/327 sales earnings of £9,17 representing PROO37 AMERICAN ROYS on my book *The New Poetic Yeats to Elliot* [sic].

Your system of referencing is overpowering, and I hope I have got the numbers right; but I'm sure you will understand my bafflement in that to my knowledge the book is out of print and throughout its long history has never been published by Routledge.

Can you help me?
        Yours sincerely,
            (007) C.K. Stead

On the same day I wrote to Mr Brozicevic saying that he had not replied to my letter of June the previous year. I pointed out that, though HarperCollins published my fiction, it had 'no right to give permission for use of *The New Poetic*, nor to negotiate payment for such use, nor to accept payment on my behalf'.

He replied to tell me that my book, though out of print, was part of the Unwin Hyman Academic list sold a year previously to Routledge. How, in that case, did HarperCollins remain in the picture? This was not explained.

'I think you should be aware,' he went on, 'that the rights do not automatically revert to you if the book is out of print but usually there are formal procedures which require a written confirmation that the rights have reverted.'

It was 'written confirmation' I had been seeking. What other 'procedures' than my writing letters were required? Secret rites for the rights? I didn't ask this question, however, but waited to hear from Mrs Gill Taylor, Routledge Royalty Manager, who 'will be writing to you separately'.

Her letter came. It was headed International Thompson Publishing Services Ltd. 'You are probably not aware,' she wrote, 'that Unwin Hyman who held the publishing rights to your book under your contract with Hutchinson, sold their academic list to Routledge in July 1991.' She hoped this would 'clarify the position'.

What seemed clear was that a book published by Hutchinson, and allowed by them to go out of print, had somehow passed, without reissue or reinvestment of any kind, to one publisher, then to another, and finally to a third, while the author, who had been imperfectly advised and never consulted, struggled to hold onto his rights as owner of the copyright.

Bewildered, I said none of this, but wrote to point out that it was now four years since Unwin Hyman, never publishers of the book, had allowed it to go out of print, and that in that time I had been attempting to obtain reversion of rights.

Mrs Taylor replied:

> If you refer to the rights granted under the contract with Hutchinson under clause 1, the term 'sole and exclusive right to publish etc *for the legal term of the copyright*' and read in conjunction with clause 16 'without prejudice to any existing contracts —————— here', you will see why in law all rights have not reverted to you. The legal term of the copyright is life plus fifty years after death [mine, she meant] and the subsidiary rights were extant at the time when the Hutchinson edition went out of print in 1989.
>
> There is no doubt that the rights in the Hutchinson edition of your book have reverted to you under clause 16 but the subsidiary rights remain with Routledge.

I did not accept this interpretation (the important clause had said that *all* rights would revert) but rather than argue I waited for a letter from Routledge's publishing director, a Mrs Janice Price, since Mrs Taylor's letter had concluded 'I am sure Mrs Price will be in touch with you soon.'

But no letter came, and once again, since this was not in itself a matter of importance in my life, my mind turned elsewhere. I think I must have assumed that my first book, like an old workhorse, was lying dead somewhere in the back paddocks. Almost two years later it whinnied at the door, this time in the form of a royalty statement from Routledge for *The New Poetic: Yeats to Elliot* (TSE's extra *l* must have got built into the system) showing it had earned me £22.44. But there was no cheque. 'IN VIEW OF EVER INCREASING ADMINISTRATIVE COSTS OF SENDING OUT SMALL SUMS OF MONEY,' a note on the statement said, 'WE WILL CARRY FORWARD TO THE NEXT ACCOUNTING PERIOD ANY ROYALTY PAYMENTS UNDER £25. WHEN A BOOK IS DECLARED OUT OF PRINT ANY SUMS HELD WILL BE PAID TO YOU.'

In other words, 'You are a pain in the neck with your piddling earnings, so we'll keep them.'

Weakly assertive, I demanded my money; and then, once again, tramped through the same old story, pointing out that the book was now out of print not only in Britain but in the United States, and claiming that all rights belonged to me.

How would it go as a bedtime story? 'Once upon a time there was Hutchinson; there was Allen and Unwin; there was Edward (was it?) Hyman; there was Collins; there was Croom Helm (the name Croom occurred somewhere in the correspondence); there was Routledge and Kegan Paul; there was the Thompson organisation; and in America there was Harper. And there was an author and his book ...'

How the Many became the One; how the book went out of existence but its ghostly 'Rights' remained to be owned, on-sold, claimed and counter-claimed; and how the author was driven through bewilderment to exasperation and beyond into a sense of the absurd, would be the substance of the tale. Perhaps it could even be a murder mystery, involving a series of deaths through the interlocking and overlapping chain of publishers, with the book author as prime suspect.

And in the end? In August 1994, six years after the sale of the Hutchinson list and five after the book had gone out of print, I received a cheque for £22.44 and a note on Thompson International Book Services letterhead from 'G.M. Taylor (Mrs), Royalty Manager of Routledge, Chapman and Hall', formally reverting all rights in *The New Poetic* to its author.

Postscript: The story continues. Shortly after this article appeared in *PN Review,* the *Times Literary Supplement*'s NB Column (13 December 1996) summarised it, and remarked,

> Professor Stead deserves congratulations on having had the courage to make these distressing events public. While the papers are full of commissions, advances and prizes, no attention is ever paid to the inevitable conclusion of the process, leaving the obsequies to be conducted in shame-faced privacy.

This kindly farewell, however, alerted the Athlone Press, formerly publishers to London University, to the fact that *The New Poetic* was out of print and available. A modest offer was made and accepted, and it has been reissued, with a substantial quotation on its back cover from Seamus Heaney's discussion (in *The Government of the Tongue*) of the effect the book had on his own and others' reading and understanding of T.S. Eliot.

One other fact is of interest. I'm told that copies were sent to New Zealand newspapers and literary journals by Athlone, whose editors were sure that the reissue of a book with such an interesting international history, and praised by a Nobel Prize winner, would attract attention in the author's home country. It didn't. To my knowledge no mention of it was ever made.

Theroux's Naipaul and New Zealand's 'Malcolm'

New Zealand novelist Maurice Shadbolt recently published what he called a 'memoir', explaining that this was a form, or mode, differing from autobiography in that it claimed only to be events as remembered, with no promise of accuracy. Since Shadbolt had announced publicly, a year or so before, that his current mind problems had been diagnosed as the onset of Alzheimer's disease, the excuse for inaccuracy and invention was complete. An expectation was aroused which the book didn't disappoint.

Earlier we'd had an autobiography in three instalments from Lauris Edmond, winner of the 1985 Commonwealth Poetry Prize. Edmond offered no disclaimer as to accuracy, and reviews of the volumes as they appeared commonly praised her honesty. What this meant, I suspect, was that Edmond wrote about matters customarily passed over – for example explaining how and why her former husband, the headmaster of a primary school and father of her six children, had been a failure both professionally and domestically.

By the time the third volume appeared, the ex-husband was dead and couldn't answer back. But when a reviewer again praised Edmond's honesty two of her daughters wrote to a Wellington newspaper protesting. 'How can [the reviewer] possibly know whether this is an "honest" account of events or not? Was she there? Has she talked to any of us who were?'

I thought of these examples of the problem of truth and accuracy in autobiographical writing during the past week while I was reading *Sir Vidia's Shadow,* Paul Theroux's book about his thirty-year friendship with V.S. Naipaul. I don't think my reaction was unusual. The intended negative image of Naipaul was convincing. Yet, while believing much, and deploring some, my admiration for Naipaul survived; and I finished the book feeling I would probably like him a good deal more than I would the man who was exposing his faults and his fads.

Sir Vidia's Shadow is distinctly readable. But elements of invention and contrivance are obvious, especially in the dialogue – in some chapters glaringly so, to the extent that they undermine credibility altogether.

Chapter 10 recounts a lunch party at Naipaul's house in the Wiltshire countryside. Theroux arrives by train and is met by a car sent, as promised, by Naipaul. His gratitude is short-lived. When he reaches the house the driver, 'Walters', asks for £4 – quite a large sum in 1974. (The book is full of stories

---

London Review of Books, 27 April 2000.

of Naipaul's meanness, his unwillingness to pay the bill in restaurants, and so on.) Other guests are Julian Jebb (unkindly caricatured), Hugh Fraser ('tall', 'lopsided', with an 'aura of helpless authority'), and his wife, Antonia, whose charms and 'sexiness' are unstintingly acknowledged.

Then arrives a couple from New Zealand, 'Malcolm', an academic who has looked after Naipaul on a recent lecture tour to their country, and 'Robin', his wife, 'wearing a soft, unnecessary hat, as New Zealanders seemed habitually to do'. They have come in a taxi from the station. Malcolm is a ruddy-faced farming type; both have extreme New Zealand accents.

It was here that my unease about the facts became more marked. Malcolm compliments Theroux on his study of Naipaul with, 'Beaut book, Paul.' He explains that he is 'on the English faculty at uni'. An American would say 'on the English faculty'; an Australian would say 'at uni'; a New Zealander would say neither.

Robin says, 'It gets dark here so early. Listen to that wind.' Theroux remarks, 'If I had not heard New Zealand in her nasalised *dahk* I would surely have heard it in her *weend*.' Nasalised *dahk* is right for New Zealand speech; *weend* is Australian. We New Zealanders have the Northern Irish flat *i* sound: *wund*.

But who were these two? The others in the scene were real people, widely known. A New Zealand academic and his wife ought to have been people I could recognise.

After the lunch provided by Pat Naipaul (including a separate, and superior, dish just for her husband), snuff is offered, which leads to talk of erectile tissue in the nose, sneezing and its relation to orgasm. This increases Theroux's already intense excitement at the proximity of Antonia Fraser, and he describes at some length his inner fantasy of being alone with her on a Carribean island, she wearing a white see-through dress with nothing underneath.

In Malcolm the talk of erectile tissue prompts a quotation from the poet Rochester, which leads to an argument with Lady Antonia about whether or not Rochester is 'porno' (Malcolm's word), during which the New Zealander '[sticks] his pink face into Antonia's pale one', and is described as 'beaky', 'in the throes of pedantry', 'angry,' 'rigid', his 'eyes glassy with rage', 'fussed and breathless and indignant', while Lady Antonia deftly defends her view that Rochester is 'a lyric poet with heaps and heaps of charm'.

The chapter was not getting more believable. Malcolm is said to have written a thesis on 'Augustans and court wits', and is expert enough to quote Rochester insistently (boorishly, in fact). I couldn't imagine such a person taking such a morally disapproving tone about Rochester, nor using the word 'porno' at all. But this argument, Theroux decides, 'was probably less about Lord Rochester than it was about class and accents. It created a staleness around the lunch table and an awkwardness for all that remained unspoken.'

This staleness is dispelled by Naipaul himself who, agreeing with something Hugh Fraser has said about the 'odd racial contradictions you get with so much intermarriage', takes a copy of *The Mimic Men* from his shelves and '[reads] the concentrated paragraph about the fable "The Niger and the Seine".' This in itself is odd, because in *The Mimic Men* this fable, summarised in a paragraph which must be the one Naipaul is supposed to have read out, seems to satirise proponents of racial intermarriage, and is quite unrelated to anything that has happened at the lunch party. But Theroux presents it simply as a rebuke, Naipaul 'giving a lesson in recitation to Malcolm, who had blurted out the rude Lord Rochester stanzas':

> When Vidia was done, he shut the book like a vicar shutting a Bible after a homily.
> 'You see?'

Now the guests go for a country walk. Robin, attempting to reassure the 'still ... flustered' Malcolm, is joined by Pat, the 'pleasant peace-making hostess'. Theroux walks with Lady Antonia, extending his fantasy: 'A hot island and idleness, clear sky and a blue lagoon ... the white dress, the parasol, the hat – and the thrashing legs and damp flanks.'

'I wanted to hug her,' (he goes on) 'and bury my face against her neck – she looked so soft and warm, her lips so pretty. I wanted to clutch her shepherdess costume ... I wanted to tell her how I imagined the two of us on a tropical island.' When, back at the house, there is tea out of doors and shooting at a paper target with an air rifle, Theroux remarks, 'When she raised the rifle and pressed her lips together, I wanted her to spin around and shoot me.'

The Frasers are first to leave, and Theroux 'wants' again. This time: 'I wanted to go back to London with them in their car, to be with her. But it was useless yearning. They did not offer anyone a lift.'

Now, with the party breaking up, there are further puzzles for the sceptical reader. When Theroux says he must go, Pat says, 'I'll call Walters.' So another £4, presumably; but this time money isn't mentioned. Jebb goes by taxi; and since Malcolm and Robin arrived by taxi from the station, it must be assumed they returned the same way. So why don't they all share a taxi? Or share Walters? And how do they avoid meeting on the platform, or on the train?

But it's insisted that 'we all left separately'; and now we see Theroux on the train back to London, trying 'to look out the window, but all I saw was my own reflection, framed by the night, looking in: my other self staring at me for one and a half hours.'

The chapter ends with sad reflections on what lay ahead for those present. Hugh Fraser 'died of a broken heart' when Lady Antonia left him for Harold Pinter. Pat died of cancer. Jebb 'committed suicide with a mixture of vodka and pills'. Of himself Theroux says, 'I left my wife, I lost my family.' And what of Malcolm and Robin? He concludes, 'No news of the New Zealanders'.

Well, I have some, Paul.

All the time I was reading this I was remembering that my former colleague, Michael Neill, now Professor of English at the University of Auckland, had looked after Naipaul on his visit to New Zealand in 1972, and that he used to include a lecture or two on Rochester in some of his courses. But otherwise the person portrayed was unrecognisable. A few days ago I ran into him at the supermarket. Had he read Theroux's book about Naipaul? No. He'd meant to, but hadn't got around to it.

Was he at lunch at Naipaul's house in the country, with Theroux? Yes, he was.

Who was there? Neill listed the same guests.

I told him Theroux had renamed him 'Malcolm' and was extremely rude about him. 'He says you had an argument with Antonia Fraser.'

Michael looked surprised and amused. 'Really? I thought we got on rather well. We talked about snuff and sneezing – and orgasms.'

'He says you quoted Rochester.'

Michael shook his head slightly. 'I might have. I don't remember that I did.'

'He says you were with your wife. He calls her Robin.'

'I was with Pek.'

Ah, Pek.

Now let me tell you about Michael Neill. He was born in Wales of an upper-middle-class English mother and a New Zealand-born father educated at Harrow and Sandhurst. Michael was sent to what he calls 'a ghastly Anglo-Irish prep-school in Co. Wicklow', but was rescued at the age of twelve when his father decided to go back to New Zealand. After graduating from the University of Otago, he went to Cambridge and did a PhD on the Jacobean dramatist John Ford.

Michael has no New Zealand accent. His is one of those neutral international accents. He is an actor, has a fine voice, and if he quotes poetry he does it well. If you have seen and heard his brother, the movie actor Sam Neill, their voices and accents are almost interchangeable.*

As for Pek-Koon, who was Michael's partner at that time: she is Malaysian Chinese, and has very markedly that accent.

In other words the whole drama of the occasion was invented. Why, and why with such animus towards the New Zealander? Perhaps Michael Neill was getting on too well with Antonia Fraser, while Theroux was having to make do with his damp flanks fantasy. Perhaps Theroux was anxious that he was losing his place as Naipaul's junior proprietor. On p. 219, for example: 'I saw [Malcolm] as Vidia's protégé and seemed to be looking at my younger self.' And on p. 227: 'My protégé days were over ... Malcolm was perhaps the new protégé, but it seemed to me he would not last; he was too contrary.'

'Should I read it?' Michael asked me.

'If I were in your position,' I said, 'I wouldn't be able to resist. But be

---

* In the same year Sam Neill had lead roles in *The Piano,* which won the Academy Award for Best Picture, and *Jurassic Park,* which was the year's record box-office picture. Recently he had the title role in the BBC's mini-series, *Merlin.*

warned, it's exceptionally unpleasant.'

He thought for a moment. 'What an ungrateful bastard. Pek and I drove him all the way back to London.'

'Are you sure?'

'Quite sure.'

'He says he went back by train.'

I've wondered since about the way the facts were altered. Given the image of the New Zealander Theroux was aiming for, a supportive little Kiwi wife in 'a soft, unnecessary hat' was a better match for such a person than the rather formidable Chinese intellectual Pek-Koon was. (She is now a professor of South-East Asian history.) And to acknowledge that 'Malcolm' and 'Robin' gave him the lift back to London which the Frasers didn't offer would have made ingratitude manifest.

Also the separate departures made it possible for our last glimpse of Theroux to be the sad one of him alone in the carriage, staring at his own image in the window of the train, 'framed by the night'.

Part 4

Thinking Aloud
—Thinking Allowed?

The View from Mt Eden

If I go to the top of Mt Eden and walk around the crater looking out over Auckland city and suburbs I can see most of the locations of real significance in my life. I was born somewhere down there, and so were my parents, my wife (we may have been delivered in the same private maternity hospital), and my children. Parents, grandparents, even a great-great-grandfather, are buried there. I can pick out the house in which I spent the first twenty-one years of my life. In a different direction I can see the headland above the house where I have spent most of my adult life, and the bay it looks out on. I can see the three schools I attended – primary, intermediate and secondary – and the first university I graduated from, which employed me for more than a quarter of a century until I resigned to write full time.

Fiction and poetry are arts whose material is language. A beautiful soul, immense erudition, something important to say – none of these will help if you lack that basic talent with the language. Good writing offers a grammatical dance, a verbal music. But because part of its function is to refer, or to 'mean', language points beyond itself. One of the greatest and least obtrusive of the writer's skills is to recreate a world we know already. Where fiction is working well, the reader should be aware simultaneously of language which has on it the stamp of that author and no other, and yet which is producing the sense of a reality out there, recognised as if with your own eyes, and almost without the intermediary of language.

If there is, inevitably, a strong regional element in my work, it alone is not enough to explain what I write or what I look for in writing. Those schools and that university I attended gave me access to something more than my own region; or perhaps I should say they taught me I *had* access to it – in the language I grew up speaking and reading. That larger something was the Anglo-Celtic culture of Britain, together with the wider European culture of which it was a part. It was also the diverse culture of the diaspora of English which imperialism had created, so that elements as different as modern Hollywood and India under the Raj were attachments that came with our language and history. We all know these days, with the same kind of simple historical certainty satirised in *1066 and All That*, that the Empire was a Bad

---

Originally written in 1987 for a book of photographs of New Zealand writers by Adrian Dirks, with accompanying short essays by the writers. So far as I know the book never appeared. This text has been updated.

Thing. No one any longer notices that it was also, being a kind of internationalism and cross-cultural fertilisation, a Good Thing – a fact symbolised for me by the banner carried by a group of British-born Muslims in a recent rally in London: 'We are Here because You were There'.

I began writing at the age of thirteen under the influence of English writers – first Rupert Brooke and John Buchan, then Keats and Wordsworth, Dickens and Sir Walter Scott. Soon I was discovering New Zealand poets and fiction writers who were mapping our country in literature; and as a student I began to read more of the Americans.

In those days New Zealand was still wearing its colonial sailor suit and people were Britishly patriotic, inclined to fall to pieces at the onset of Royalty, and to sing 'God Save ...' at the drop of a hat. It seemed necessary – indeed one felt honour-bound – to stand up to all that; to insist we must stake out and proclaim our independence, political, cultural and literary. Now we have that independence, and it may be time to remember kinship and history. A new distinct 'New Zealand' culture can't be created only by acts of will. It has begun, and it will happen.

When I stand on the top of Mt Eden and see the region in which so much of my own life and work are contained I know there's another sense in which they are not 'contained' at all. My feet are on this ground. My mind is at large. My readers may be down there, or a thousand, or twelve thousand miles away. The books I read may be written here or there. The satellite links are open, the fibre optic cables working, the messages going to and fro by phone, fax and e-mail. The planes fly in and out, and often I fly with them. It is highly unlikely that a series of university winter lectures would now be given like the one I contributed to forty years ago, on the theme of 'the effects of remoteness on New Zealand'. The world is more available to us than it was then, and our minds should be likewise open and available.

Every serious writer will tell you that writing is hard work requiring conscious application. The temptation to straighten the pictures, tidy the house, go out to the mail box, make another cup of coffee, lie down and sleep, is enormous. Frank Sargeson required of himself a page a day. It was a small page of green paper, on which he could put down three hundred words. Others can go much faster. The important thing is to keep it up. But even writing a novel is not all hard and unvarying grind. It has its highs and its lows. The day when you decide to ditch a month's work and start again is one you won't forget. But there are those almost equally rare and memorable times when you feel the story has begun to write itself, the sentences spinning out like thread from a spool. It's as if your ordinary self is simply hanging on and watching. The other self – the artist – has taken control, giving directions, saying what stays and what goes.

In New Zealand we incline to the Roundhead tradition which pays too much attention to the purpose and the message and not enough to the art. That's why the great periods of Matisse and Picasso fascinate me – because there is in their paintings so much of the presence of the artist as artist, so much physical energy, life-force, bravado, panache. A clear artistic purpose cuts through all others like a blade. In the meeting of the artist and his world, a moment of purest life – subjective and objective – is arrested and given some kind of permanence. The result can't be other than affirmative.

That is not to say I'm sanguine about human life or the human race, nor always temperamentally buoyant. Our life is an accident of chemistry and physics on a planet in a solar system that won't last for ever. One way of looking at it, one kind of truth about it, is that we are in this boat together, not behaving very well to one another nor managing very effectively, and the boat is sinking, will sink whatever we do. But that recognition, like every aspect of human consciousness, is a gift as well as a burden.

Literature has two basic modes – tragic and comic, each essential, neither intrinsically superior. My own inclination is towards the comic, or at least towards varieties of wit. I've reached an age when I can say, and defend with confidence, that my preference is for Shakespeare's comedies over his tragedies. And I like S.N. Behrman's statement in the Foreword to one of his plays:

> ... my point of view on the whole tragedy [of human life] is comic. Must one apologise for this? If man is the only animal who can laugh, need he apologise for his distinction?

What I Believe

A discussion of what one believes usually begins with or leads to the question of 'God'. 'Do you believe in God?' Through many European centuries it has been at least socially unacceptable, often dangerous, and sometimes suicidal, to answer in the negative. The freedom to answer no is therefore something to be affirmed and protected; and if I am to give a short rough answer, that is what mine must be.

My dislike of the short rough answer springs, not from uncertainty, but from a disinclination to give the question the status, which such an answer confers, of something entirely meaningful. What am I saying I don't believe in if my answer is no? To concede that one understands this is to turn the negative into a form of denial: 'God may exist but I refuse to believe it'. I prefer to see 'God' as a word to which there is nothing objective corresponding – a word which usage over time slowly defined, and then knowledge over time rendered a nonsense.

I know, and accord qualified respect to, the traditions which pertain to the word. I see no reason to question the authenticity of subjective experiences which many distinguished, and many more undistinguished, persons have reported, and which give the word force and significance in their lives. That tells me something about the human psyche and about how language works; it tells me nothing at all about the larger facts of the universe we occupy. If every person on earth believed the moon was made of cheese that would not make it so.

So my intellectual position is subtly, but I think significantly, different from both atheism and agnosticism. The atheist denies God exists; the agnostic doesn't know. For me the word 'God' lacks a referent; lacks objective meaning; and consequently uncertainty about, or denial of, God's 'existence' are equally without meaning.

All human cultures have invented a God or gods. For centuries Christians scorned, mocked, despised as primitive and barbaric, and sometimes attacked and destroyed the structure and icons, but more important the intellectual respectability, of religions other than their own. We all flinch when we see the devotees of a particularly militant Moslem sect beating their heads until the blood flows; or when we hear an account of some barbaric tribal sacrifice or

What I Believe, the Personal Philosophies of Twenty-Two New Zealanders, compiled by Allan Thompson, published 1993. The postscript, an earlier piece, has been added.

ritual. I suppose few Christians stop to consider how barbaric and primitive a religion whose central symbol is a man nailed by hands and feet, dying in agony, and whose central ritual is the eating of his flesh and drinking of his blood, must seem to those not brought up in it.

Religion rests, not on rationality, but on faith in the ability of certain rituals and symbols to evoke a higher-than-human power, and on the consequent superiority of those who share that faith and understand its secrets. It is one aspect of tribalism and tribal bonding. One of its practical functions has been to strengthen the warrior will against enemies; another to enforce social conformity at home. But there is always a personal as well as a social function. Christian prayer and confession are practices clearly soothing to the disturbed or distressed personality. Various kinds of mysticism develop out of prayer. Eastern religions have taught techniques of inwardness, contemplation, escape from time, some of which seem more sophisticated than anything in the Christian tradition, and less fraught with the difficulty of requiring faith either in 'God' or a life beyond death.

The Book of Genesis, like all creation myths, is entirely man- and earth-centred. God creates the planet we occupy, and all the rest is background, ranged round about for our convenience. The sun is 'the greater light', the moon 'the lesser light'; the stars are small lights in the background. Short of knowledge, the human imagination manufactures such stories, which are then treated reverently as if their source were divine.

As knowledge erodes parts of the myth, the residue is clung to all the more desperately. What was believed literally shrinks to metaphor, but its importance is insisted upon at the same time that it seems to fade before our eyes. Heaven no longer has a location. Hell becomes unimaginable. God, depersonalised and neutered, loses his beard and is of uncertain skin colour. The life after death becomes a matter of debate, even among believers. Religion reduces to traditional ritual on the one hand, and on the other to a wash of good feelings, good deeds, and arguments about what is and isn't a moral act.

People must be free to believe and worship as they choose; only their actions consequent upon belief must be limited by the general good as that is expressed in the laws of society. But believers should not be spared our negative opinions. For too long in our society Christianity has been sheltered by privileges and pieties.

If for myself I reject religious belief – all religious beliefs – I don't then describe myself as a rationalist. One must aspire to rationality and respect intelligence. But we have all seen high intelligence and rational argument put to irrational and foolish ends; and conversely, we have all observed men and women governed only by intuition and goodwill, living harmonious and beneficent lives without any clear understanding of why their behaviour is as it is. Rationality or intuition may equally arrive at ends which serve well the individual, the society, and the race – or to ends which serve them ill.

To say this is to acknowledge that one has no more faith in ideologies and social programmes than one has in religion. For most of my life I have been a supporter of the political Left; but that has been less the expression of an ideological conviction (the theory of Marxism never had more than passing interest) than of a temperamental rebelliousness which has seemed to receive its sanction, if not always its first impulse, from the recognition that all human institutions tend quickly along a path from complacency, through laziness and cynicism, to corruption, and must therefore be subject to continuous criticism and even attack. If I had lived my life in Soviet Russia I am confident I would have been, to the extent that circumstances and my courage permitted, a critic of the institutions of the socialist state. The great virtue of democracy is not so much that humans are collectively wise, but that they keep changing their minds, and consequently their government. Someone should have told Chairman Mao that his principle of 'continuous revolution' had been achieved, not in China under communism, but where he thought it least likely – in the democratic West.

The astonishing and exhilarating collapse of repressive governments in Eastern Europe since 1990 has demonstrated, I think, not so much the defeat of communism by capitalism, but rather the defeat of ideology by pragmatism. Capitalism has its mad ideologues; but in the West they have never had complete dominance. In the East the ideologues of the Left had it all their own way, protected by the terrible engines of the state. Totalitarianism is to be feared because its end is always a rational programme, and human reason alone, permitted to sweep aside common sense and traditional wisdom, is an insufficient and indeed dangerous instrument for the organisation of our lives.

Prescriptions of all kind are unsafe. It is more useful to observe and describe than to prescribe, because an accurate report lets faults reveal themselves, while opinion merely evokes its contrary. We need especially, I think, to recognise that we are earthly animals, governed by the same instinct for survival that governs all the species, programmed to protect and foster ourselves as individuals, as families, as tribes and societies. Our strongest drives relate to food, sex, the protection of the young, and the defence of the group. Any behaviour which conflicts radically with these will bring unhappiness. Our most basic and secure happiness will come from their fulfilment. Morality is their social codification; law is their protection. There are always areas in which individual fulfilment conflicts with the social good; but a sound morality needs no transcendent sanction. It is self-justifying and rationally explicable, though reason alone will not provide a sufficient motivation for it.

Because the twentieth century has grown up under the influence of Freud and (beyond Freud's responsibility) popular psychology, we tend to over-estimate environmental influences and under-estimate what is in the genes. The fact is that a few years, or even decades, of social conditioning can't compete with evolutionary determinism. We can't, for example, simply eliminate tribalism from our psyches; and though in the modern world it is potentially dangerous, it is also the source of social bonding, loyalty and charity.

Similarly, while birth control has revised the role of women in society and liberated them in many ways, it is idle to suppose that we can suddenly eliminate strong, and significantly different, drives in women and men, some of which conflict with the kind of society present circumstances seem to call for. At the moment the most painful dilemma among younger adult females seems to be the recognition that women's liberation has also been men's liberation, and that traditional forms of social bonding which the feminist movement has seen as female bondage were in fact quite as powerfully restricting to men. This general liberation may be inevitable; there is no point in trying to turn back the clock. But the hard lesson is that it has not led to general happiness. It has merely shifted the areas of pain.

Somehow we have to be realistic and pragmatic, recognising that there is a strong and ancient life-force at work in each of us, and that while it may be curbed, to 'cure' it entirely may be less a liberation than a form of self-destruction.

In society every correction of a past error seems to involve the creation of a new one. To assert this is not to suggest that we should all become passive. Man is a social animal, with social responsibilities. We must make decisions and choices and take consequent action – even if it is only to cast a vote in an election. Our role in life, it may be said, is to make mistakes!

But there is a wisdom which stands separate from action. Religion once provided it, and still enshrines much that is durable. The writings of the great Zen Buddhist teachers, for example, still seem to me a strange and rich source of instruction. But as the force of religion has receded, contradicted and eroded by the revelation of what might be called its errors of fact, the respect given to the arts has advanced. As I wrote in my last big book on modern poetry (*Pound, Yeats, Eliot and the Modernist Movement*), 'There is in Western civilisation a large minority of sensitive, intelligent, and usually productive people whose lives are given shape, order, meaning, a sense of elevation and a certainty of purpose, by the pursuit of the best in music, painting, literature and film. These works of art are their shrines and their chapels, their source of enlightenment, order and hope.'

I have gradually come to separate two modes of thought and action, each of which has its place in what I conceive to be the good life. One is the political mode, the other (for lack of a better word) the existential. It is as though we need to be involved in the folly of politics, because what is permitted to happen should be the fullest possible expression – a balanced consensus – of opposing wills, opposing opinions, opposing interests in society. But if we are not to be frustrated, either by not getting what we want, or by getting it and seeing it fail to produce the expected improvement in social conditions, there must be that other, wise, contemplative self, which stands back and recognises that in a well-balanced society the opposed forces frequently cancel one another out, and very little has changed.

Literature often represents politics, and sometimes expresses political passion; but it belongs to the existential mode. It cannot be the instrument of politics. I have had periods of serious political involvement, and I believe they are an essential part of my experience as a writer, and of my duty as a citizen. But I know there is a wisdom beyond politics which must govern the best in poetry and fiction.

In New Zealand at the moment I believe we need to learn to be less officious, less self-important, less impatient, less sure that we know better than our forebears. We need to do our own thinking, instead of letting the world's current clichés about, for example, race and gender, do our thinking for us. We need to recognise that in many ways human societies are self-correcting over time; that 'Men may spare their pains where nature is at work' (as the poet Andrew Marvell wrote) 'and the world will not go faster for our driving.'

Because the world of this new *fin de siècle* is the one we know, while that of earlier times seems alien, we delude ourselves into believing too much in human progress. There is a certain measurable material advance in parts of it; and our modern technology, which seems at times a threat, deserves the credit. But the planet is grossly over-populated, and there is no solution to its major problems which does not include a curb on human increase. Here, at least, it seems plain, is something to be aimed for, something to be done – and to do it we may have to combat local pieties of many different kinds. If it is not done by our own actions, then ecological disasters will do it for us. There are simply too many of us, increasing too fast, for the earth to sustain.

As for moral progress – I see very little evidence of it. While I was jotting down the framework ideas for this article [i.e. in 1991] a war blew up and blew over in the Persian Gulf. If Iraq's invasion of Kuwait was unsavoury (and it was), the spectacle of the United States once again casting itself in the role of world policeman, moraliser and savage avenger, was worse. Countries which invaded smaller neighbours, President Bush told us, had to be stopped. But in recent decades the United States had paid for an army to undermine the legitimate government of Nicaragua, had subverted Chilean democracy, bombed Libya, invaded Panama and Granada, and tacitly supported Israel's invasion of Lebanon. We were subjected to massive disinformation about the size, strength and danger of the Iraqi army; and the slaughter of this rag-tail horde of unwilling, ill-equipped conscripts in the operation called Desert Storm was hailed as a great victory – one for which we were privileged to watch the President praying, invoking a God who, if He were listening and still in business, ought to have responded with a thunderbolt or a plague of locusts. In all of this New Zealand played its customary inglorious role of supporter-on-the-cheap.

I usually describe myself as intellectually a pessimist and temperamentally an optimist. What this means is that I am by nature hopeful – sometimes naively so. My imagination usually favours the lucky outcome when in terms of the cold facts of the case, the unlucky one is more probable. If I had been a German Jew in the 1930s, for example, I would probably have thought 'The Nazis wouldn't – they couldn't – not *really* ...' with fatal consequences for myself and my family.

But intellectually I see the human condition as bleak – though it is a bleakness that has a certain tragic glory. We are burdened, each of us, with an individual ego, and with the knowledge that we must die. And added to that has come in this century the further knowledge that our particular star, the sun, will one day cool, and that the peculiar and apparently unique phenomenon of earthly life in all its forms, will die too. Then the universe, or our corner of it, will go back to being a vastness of light and darkness, fire and whirling masses, unseen, unrecognised, without a soul to name it or admire its beauty. It is that emptiness which hurries the human mind to put 'God' back – but without any reason except that an absence of consciousness can seem terrifying, unthinkable.

Religions lay claim to the mystery, and you will sometimes hear clerics say that those without faith lack a sense of the mysterious. On the contrary, it has always seemed to me that religions are designed to remove the intolerable mysteries by explaining them. The great mysteries are great because they cannot be explained – infinite space, infinite time, the apparent uniqueness of life on our particular planet, and the human consciousness which can 'know' these facts intellectually, but cannot imagine them, and therefore cannot grasp them as aspects of everyday reality.

Our limits in all this are the limits of our language, the tool of communication and thought. Language is at the centre of our culture. Our understanding of ourselves is dependent on its exact use. It serves both reason and passion. It is both a clear light by which we may see reality, and a dangerous one which can blind us. To use it well, to understand how it works, and to teach those uses and that understanding, are not marginal activities. They are central to a good society. For most of my life I have seen myself, first as a New Zealand writer, and second as a teacher of English language and literature. That is how I identify myself. In those pursuits I seek my personal Zen.

Postscript: In a 1987 notebook I found the following entry, which perhaps says 'What I believe' in another way:

Statement:
There are only appetites and the ego to sustain us. When they are gone we are worn out and ready for the scrap-heap.
Love satisfies an appetite and sustains the ego.
'Spiritual experiences' are the ego depersonalised. 'God loves me' is the socially acceptable face of self-love.

Counterstatement:

Why do I want to help my family, cuddle babies, protect small animals, comfort the unhappy (until patience runs out!), save birds and mice from the cat, put spiders outside rather than suck them up in the vacuum cleaner? That is the kinship of the living on this planet. It has nothing to do with 'spirituality'. But neither does it satisfy an appetite – and it's doubtful that it does anything for, or is driven by, the ego. I think it is (i.e. it feels) quite impersonal. I don't expect thanks or gratitude from the mouse or the spider. I don't feel I am being 'virtuous'. I don't want anyone to know. It pleases me to stroke the cat, and to contemplate, or where appropriate to cuddle, the infant. It gives me a sense of relief that the hungry animal is fed, the spider saved from destruction.

Conclusion:

I don't think anything in the counterstatement eliminates the truth, however limited, of the statement. But it needs to be said in addition. We are programmed to reproduce and to cling to life. There is no 'good' except life itself, and that which fosters it. So there is a sense in which the good is always defeated, and always renewed.

All this leaves out the sense of *beauty* which is indeed mysterious.

It also leaves out the sense of comedy. And it's perhaps comedy rather than morals which truly distinguishes the human animal. Morals are only group behaviour generalised and codified. You could draw up the morality of a cat, or a rat, but you couldn't teach either the kind of intelligences that produces laughter.

Remembering the Fifties

The early 1950s was the time when I discovered that modern New Zealand literature and art existed and that our writers and artists were a challenge to the then-dominant culture of Royalty, rugby, racing and beer.

It was good beer, but until someone spoke up for what was probably indifferent wine, how were we to make a start? Painters like Dennis Knight Turner wore beards and berets. Louise Henderson spoke of Cubism in the appropriate Parisian accent. Rex Fairburn wore sandals and talked about compost. Pipes were smoked. Coffee was drunk in Somervell's in Queen Street. Frank Sargeson carried his knapsack, and sometimes loaded it with vegetables for friends on the North Shore which, before the Harbour Bridge opened it to the property developers, was where a number of these people lived.

It's difficult not to romanticise them. They romanticised themselves. A lot of the goings on – the Lowry parties, the strenuous bohemianism, the artiness, the riding of bicycles in seventeen lovely colours – must have been tiresome to serious minds with work to do. But New Zealand at large was, or seemed, incorrigibly philistine. Art of whatever kind had to fight for space, needed to be assertive if it was to begin to believe in itself and be noticed. The many false notes in Fairburn now seem to me those of someone indelibly colonial (as we all must have been) bravely trying to live up to an idea of how 'real' writers and intellectuals did it in London and Paris.

I was conscious that there was a lot of fakery about, a lot of posing; and though I'm sure I wasn't proof against it, the natural scepticism of the critic was some kind of protection against its worst excesses. I used to put my latest poem to the test by dismissing it from my thoughts and then suddenly surprising myself with the recollection of it in the middle of a soccer game. I played centre forward – what would now be called striker – for the university, and somewhat lazily used this position to hang about doing nothing up front when the other side were on the attack. If the poem didn't seem in that instant of recollection to fade into 'literariness', it might be worth working at.

'Hard' was a word I used quite often ('Sky is hard in which the hawk hangs fire') – along with images of rocks and thorns. Donne's intellectual toughness, Eliot's critical sharpness, were touchstones. Effort was essential – and this is something you see surviving in everything Allen Curnow says about the business of writing. The idea that you might in some sense relax

Landfall 185, April 1993.

into the discipline of your gift is still incomprehensible to him. It is something that makes sense to me now – but not in that climate of the 1950s.

Of course I wanted to be published in *Landfall.* Monte Holcroft's *Listener,* and Lou Johnson's *Poetry Yearbook* were important starting places. But just as the young Wilfred Owen wrote to his mother when his work was accepted by Eddie Marsh for publication in *Georgian Poetry*, 'I am a poet's poet; I am started', so a young New Zealand poet of the 1950s whose work was smiled upon by Charles Brasch could consider himself launched.

In *Landfall* Brasch gave us common ground on which we could meet. His 'good taste' had its limits, and the young especially railed against it when their work was declined. But no one remained indifferent; no one walked away. Everyone who wrote wanted to be published there; and everyone worth reading was, sooner or later. The files of *Landfall* are the best guide to the state of New Zealand letters in the immediate post-war decades.

Around 1965, it seems to me, everything changed. American troops were committed to Vietnam, and simultaneously the social and sexual revolution one thinks of as 'the sixties' began to be felt in New Zealand. Poetry changed, and I think Brasch, though he continued to produce a first-rate literary journal, didn't quite understand or keep pace with what was happening.

When I compare the 1950s with the present I'm conscious of the huge gains, but of some losses as well. There's a gain in confidence, which renders strenuous literary nationalism unnecessary. But at the same time I recognise that being 'colonial' was at least a broad perspective. The writer looked outward to a larger world, and was unlikely to over-estimate the importance of local problems in the scale of things. From colonial to provincial (or should I say from provincial to insular) is not a huge advance.

Then there's the ambiguous gain represented by official acceptance. Of course it's more restful not to have poets and painters always setting fire to the tails of foxes and letting them loose among the haybarns of 'conformity'. But isn't there a reverse danger now, when the arts are selectively cropped by the education system to promote various kinds of worthiness? Moralism can be the death of art. Are the Old Bohemians to be replaced only by the New Victorians?

Second Thoughts on
The Death of the Body

My previous novel, *All Visitors Ashore,* had been 'clever' – those who liked it said 'very clever', those who didn't said 'too clever'. I decided my next would tell its story simply and directly. It concerned Harry Butler, Professor of Philosophy at a New Zealand university, expert in 'the mind/body problem'. His house is invaded by the police drug squad watching the couple next door, one of whom, Mandy, is already known to him. His wife has become a Sufi and turned his study into a shrine where she sits on the floor chanting 'I am not this body'. His relationship with a senior student is causing the Philosophy Department's Women's Collective deep concern. And his colleagues are worrying that he might be losing his grip, or his edge, as an academic.

As I set down these basic facts I can see at once that there ought to have been enough in them to satisfy my appetite for complications. Well, there was. But in writing fiction I have always been bothered by the question of provenance. Who knows all this? Who is telling the story?

I was writing in London, alone, away from my family. I had only three or four months in which to do it. I didn't care how long it might take revising and rewriting; but before I returned home to New Zealand I wanted a single unbroken draft from beginning to end. I wrote all day, every day. At the end of the first month I became depressed.

I set out one morning from Mecklenburgh Square, along Oxford Street and across Hyde Park. By the time I got back I knew I had to scrap everything. I hadn't thought out what was wrong, or how I would do it differently. I just knew I had to make a new start. A whole month wasted! I ought to have been cast down, but I wasn't. I was elated. My depression was gone.

So I began again with a description of my room in London. I adopted the voice of someone away from his home in Auckland, telling Harry Butler's story. That voice became the authority by which so much was known; and whose voice it was would be one of the questions a reader might hope to have answered by the end of the book.

I had been in Rapallo with my wife and daughters before the writing began; and while it went on I had to make brief visits to Milan and Turin, then to Kiel and Copenhagen. I simply gathered all these places into the narrative. It continued to tell its primary story – that of poor harassed Harry Butler, his

---

Written for the *Independent* (London), 16 November 1991, to accompany the Harvill Press reissue of *The Death of the Body.*

Sufi wife, his mistress Claire, the police drug squad and the dealers next door, and the mysterious death of his friend Jason; and at the same time it kept up the story of the unnamed narrator moving about Europe, trying to get it all down on paper, and for some reason unable to do it without the co-operation of Uta, wife of a Danish Consul – a sort of Nordic goddess figure, both Muse and Moral Monitor. Gradually the two – the story, and the story of the story – converged, came together and became one. All, or almost all, was explained.

An old friend, Roger Donaldson, whose first movie had been made from my first novel, and now a Hollywood director, got in touch with me when he read *The Death of the Body*. On my next trip through Los Angeles on my way to London he sent a large white car for me. Over lunch he said, 'There's a movie here.' (In fact, this being Hollywood, it's almost certain he said, 'There's a great movie here.')

I'm sure my face lit up.

'Yes,' he said. 'First we drop the European stuff.' I think I was still smiling. 'Then we start at chapter eighteen, and move forward.'

No, this Harvill re-issue doesn't make me dream of Hollywood. It reminds me of walking in Hyde Park in winter, deciding to scrap seventy pages and begin again – and how good that felt.

The Treaty and the Emperor's Clothes

In Hans Christian Andersen's story 'The Emperor's New Clothes', two conmen claim they can make a cloth whose supremely fine quality will be apparent to all except those who are stupid or not fit for the work they're employed to do. Consequently, when they dupe the Emperor into letting them make him a set of clothes, his highest officials, and finally the whole population, pretend to see them and admire their fineness, fearing that if they admit he seems to them to be naked, they will only be revealing their own incompetence and stupidity.

This story makes me think of the discussions which have gone on in recent years about the Treaty of Waitangi. Like the Emperor's officials, our politicians and bureaucrats, our educationists, historians, intellectuals and literary persons, and finally and most surprisingly, our jurists, not least Mr Justice Cook, President of the Court of Appeal, have seemed to trip over one another in their eagerness to see in that informal and expedient document, made to serve the needs of a time long gone and a situation no longer pertaining, a force and authority which a more candid appraisal might acknowledge it cannot possess. It's as if anything less would signal incompetence on their part, ill-will to the Maori, racism and stupidity. Our professional community, it seems to me, has been mesmerised by the murmured repetition of Delphic phrases – 'the principles of the Treaty', 'founding document', 'partnership', 'tangata whenua' – while the ordinary person in the street has looked on, unconvinced but silent.

The Treaty was constructed upon the fiction that these islands in 1840 could be treated as a single nation state occupied by one people who thought of themselves as title-holders to all land, and whose collective will was represented by any plausibly large gathering of those who plausibly claimed to be 'chiefs'. The fact that tribes were in a more or less continuous state of warfare with one another, that only some chiefs signed, that there was no way of establishing the authority of those who did or how far it extended, that many opposed the Treaty and then signed it in return for gifts – none of this was allowed to affect the pretence that a constitutionally significant event had taken place.

Nor was it really the Treaty which established British authority in these islands. What entrenched that authority was the weight of Pakeha numbers,

---

Metro, April 1992.

and the lack of any noticeable opposition in the earliest days to the influx of migrants. By the time a significant number of Maori wanted to call a halt it was already too late; and in any case Maori opinion had always been, and remained, divided.

What the Treaty did do was to curb for a time the sale of tribal land, by insisting that such sales should be made to the Crown; but soon the tribal elders, alert to the realities of the marketplace, demanded the right to sell as, and to, private citizens. With that they gave up the largest single protection offered by the Treaty. They became New Zealanders, land holders, capitalists. If that was a mistake, it was not one for which they can be blamed. Like everything that happened, it was part of an irreversible process. Europe had come to New Zealand. One can argue over whether this was more misfortune or good fortune for the Maori people; what seems unarguable is that in one form or another it was bound to happen, and that in this instance Europe was wearing one of its least malevolent faces.

Which of us now, Maori or Pakeha, believe in our hearts that the right of Parliament to make the laws which govern us, and of the courts to interpret and enforce those laws, depend in any way, or are truly consequent upon, those marks of dubious authority on documents of uncertain meaning, drawn up by amateurs to fit a world one hundred and fifty years different from our own? But who is willing to say as much?

In 1840 the Crown was an authority located in London. Today, the Crown for the purposes of the Treaty means the Government of New Zealand, elected by and representing all New Zealanders, Maori and Pakeha. A treaty now between Maori and the Crown would mean a pact between Maori as Maori on the one hand, and all New Zealanders, including Maori, on the other. No such pact has ever been agreed to; and calls to 'ratify the Treaty' are really sly attempts to make the old one over into something entirely new, privileging a minority on the basis (however flimsy in individual cases) of racial origin.

No Maori claiming rights under the Treaty has ever volunteered at the same time to give up his or her claims on those things the state provides for us all; and in that sense such claims are demands for rights over and above those enjoyed by all. For Courts of Law, encouraged by Parliament, to uphold such claims as right and reasonable is to uphold a form of racism and call it fair-dealing.

Since the 1984–90 Labour Government embarked on its programme of giving the Treaty new and quasi-legal authority, there have been many murmurs of discontent, but few voices like that of the child in Hans Andersen's story who was heard saying that the Emperor was naked. One such, however, has appeared in a surprising place. In a paper published in the *New Zealand Law Journal,* July 1991, distinguished lawyer Guy Chapman analyses the 'judicial myth-making' which that government programme has set in train, and in particular that part of it which has its source in judgements from the Court of Appeal.

In several statutes the Crown has laid on itself the obligation not to act 'in a manner inconsistent with the principles of the Treaty', thus leaving it open to the Courts to interpret or devise what these 'principles', nowhere stated in the legislation, nor in the Treaty itself, might be; and Mr Justice Cooke has not been slow to accept the licence this has seemed to offer, and to declare that his will be 'broad, unquibbling and practical' interpretations, that 'what matters is the spirit' rather than the letter, that the Treaty is 'an embryo rather than a fully integrated set of ideas' which should be 'interpreted widely and effectively as a living instrument', and that 'Treaty obligations are ongoing [and] will evolve from generation to generation as conditions change.' Already, in the case where the Maori Council laid claim to the airwaves, the Court has moved outside of legislation which makes specific reference to the Treaty, and permitted an appeal to its 'principles' to hold up the sale of licences to FM frequencies. 'In other words,' Chapman writes, ' the new wave has already broken on new ground, and taken pure common law form. The radio case should stand as a warning or a portent. If the trend is not stopped ... the problem will surely magnify and compound.'

What troubles Chapman is that this extension of reference to the authority of the Treaty is giving it the force of a Bill of Rights or a written Constitution – something alien, unwanted, and doubly dangerous because it takes a form which gives to a racial minority powers and privileges which the majority do not have and cannot alter.

At first glance it may seem surprising that a traditionally conservative body like the Court of Appeal should be hastening this process. But all human institutions favour the increase of their own power at the expense of others'; and there has surely never been a time in our history when our judges have been offered such an instrument to frustrate the will of the elected representatives of the people. That some of them should have accepted it, naively persuading themselves that their 'broad, unquibbling interpretations' of whatever the mood of the moment persuades them is meant by 'the spirit of the Treaty' will be for the good of all, is not surprising. But it is something Parliament, which is the only forum of the people as a whole, should be concerned about and should look to.

Why Do I Like It, Then?

Imagine an Auckland child, an eight-year-old, in whose home there is no television, no telephone, no refrigerator, no washing machine, no car. In winter there is only a fire in the sitting room, or an electric heater, neither used in daylight hours except perhaps in the weekend. There is no insulation between ceiling and roof, no wall-to-wall carpets. In cold weather the bedrooms are like ice boxes.

How is it possible to assert that this child experiences no sense of poverty or deprivation? Only, of course, because I am going back half a century, and because I was that child. None of my friends' houses had those amenities either – not until I was in my teens, by which time my own family too had begun to acquire them.

The fact is no comfort to those currently designated as 'poor', but none the less it is a fact that poverty in Western societies is to a significant extent a state of mind, and of comparison. A person suffers 'poverty', not by lacking the necessities of healthy living, but by having less than others round about. We live in an age unlike any other in human history – one the Australian Les Murray (whose poetry I admire, but whose politics, I hasten to say, I dislike intensely) puts into a new perspective when he writes, as if looking back at it from some point in the future:

> The poor were fat and rich were lean.
> Nearly all could preach, very few could sing.

At that early age, then, I experienced no sense of poverty or deprivation. But two more or less continuous states of feeling were intellectual boredom (which lasted until I went to secondary school) and aesthetic distaste. These were so constant I was not aware of what I was feeling until much later when I acquired a language that could express them.

What weighed against these, and compensated immensely, was the physical environment – Mt Eden, the Auckland isthmus and its beaches, and a farm north of Auckland where holidays were spent. Recently back from England I have been struck again by the wonder of the light, the air, the water, the colours and scents, the pale blue planes of the Gulf, the dark blue of the Waitakeres, the dashing changes of weather. In my childhood these, like the intellectual boredom and the ungratifying interiors, were so normal and

---

Metro, January 1992.

permanent as to pass, if not unregistered, at least unremarked. If I had the choice for a child, quite a few calories would be foregone sooner than the pleasures and splendours of our physical location. But how are these to be weighed against things of the mind and imagination?

All of which springs obliquely from my delight in the Louise Henderson exhibition at the Auckland Art Gallery. Forty years ago I emerged from my Mt Eden home and Mt Albert Grammar to enrol at Auckland University College (as it was then) where a fellow student Diane Henderson, who became a good friend, was Louise's daughter. When I walked into the gallery last September and saw those familiar paintings, I was more than ever impressed by their qualities of orderliness, colour, imagination and grace which draw on a significant individual talent and a great European tradition. But there was for me, in addition, a powerful nostalgia in being reminded of the Henderson household as it was during my student years – the polished floors with rugs, paintings on the walls by Louise and her associates, white shelves full of books in English, French and German, good talk, interesting visitors (painter John Weeks, poet Rex Fairburn, scholar-critic Eric McCormick, gallery director Eric Westbrook).

Louise in those years was beautiful, frank, charming, intolerant of cant. Her husband, Hubert, Director of Education for the Auckland region, was also a remarkable personality. From a New Zealand farming background, he had taken degrees in both arts and science and was educationist, army officer in two world wars, intellectual Leftist, a man whose energy and goodwill seemed boundless and whose readiness to put his wife's artistic career ahead of everything springs to mind when I'm told that 'in those days' women writers and painters were obstructed by home and family.

It was a high bourgeois household of a kind one read about in European literature but didn't expect to meet in New Zealand. When I declared myself Left of Labour, Hubert asked had I read the Communist Manifesto. I hadn't. He took a copy from his shelves and gave it to me – this at the height of the Cold War and McCarthyism – not to convert me, but because he thought it better I should know what I was talking about.

In the late fifties Kay and I were visited by Louise and Hubert in Bristol, and we borrowed their bed-sit in Kensington while they went to Paris. Stacked there were her paintings and sketches done in Beirut (where Hubert had been serving as a UN expert in education) some of which were displayed in the recent exhibition.

Louise's Cubist phase, which preceded and followed her 1952 sojourn in Paris at the studio of Jean Metzinger, was perhaps her most unified and concentrated. For a time she seemed to have fought her way past the obstacle of New Zealand conservatism about 'Abstract Art'. Then in the sixties came Hubert's death – a heavy personal blow – and a new nationalism in the visual arts which tended to push her to one side. I remember Hamish Keith, flushed with a proper zeal for Colin McCahon, and a more problematical enthusiasm for what he was promoting as 'the art of the Pacific Basin', arguing that Louise Henderson was a Parisian, a decorator, whose work had no relevance for us.* That remark illustrates the kind of distortion which gets into critical discourse when the politics of art over-rides aesthetics. McCahon himself (whose sources of inspiration were largely European) appreciated Louise's talent and valued her work; but that was not enough to save her from a period of relative eclipse, which she lived long enough to see pass.

Modern critical theorists like to argue that there is no such thing as a pure aesthetic response because there are always hidden agendas when preferences are declared, each of us biased in terms of race, sex, class and personal history. There must be a grain of truth in this. But to elevate it into a principle, dismissing aesthetic preferences as nothing more than conditioned reflexes, is a cultural folly and an intellectual disaster, pushing out of serious consideration one of the subtlest and best of human responses – that critical recognition, and articulation, of pleasure or discomfort, or of the two in combination, which is important precisely because it arrives independent of any particular conditioning or allegiance.

Man does not live by bread alone. The eight-year-old whose home, judged by the standards of the present, would be found wanting in modern amenities, was never troubled by the lack; but he was troubled by an aesthetic response for which he had no language. If we are merely the products of our cultural environment, how is it that we are able to feel distaste for it, and discover preferences for something other and better? And how are we to profit by those preferences if we allow theorists to deny them value and authority?

---

* My good friend Hamish has recently (1999) bought a share in a Paris apartment. Was it financed with the sale of some of his McCahons? Cultural history is rich in ironies.

Te Papa – A Linguistic Approach

I think I've seen some disagreement about what 'Te Papa' means in Maori. Let that argument continue, as I'm sure it will, until the end of time, but meanwhile could the term not be taken over (the English language is famous for its borrowing habits) as a Pakeha word in its own right?

As a noun 'Te Papa' would mean, first and foremost, 'White Elephant'. A 'Te Papa' would be something expensive, an ongoing cost for no useful return. There might be the implication too that no one knows how the mistake that put it there came to be made, nor how in the world we will ever be rid of it.

More specifically, a 'Te Papa' would imply the spending of public money, planned in Wellington, for Wellington's benefit, at the expense of those places where most of us in fact live. Another way of expressing this particular sense of the term would be to say a 'Te Papa' was something that was 'national' as to the paying of the bills, and 'absolutely positively Wellington' in all other respects.

As a further overtone or implication, 'Te Papa' would suggest not only waste, but extreme bad taste. It would imply kitsch, visual clutter, confusion, a lack of direction, an absence of logical or any other order, and a refusal of maps. To enter the 'Te Papa' experience would mean stumbling about with thousands of other bewildered people, tripping over one another in a confused search for no one knows what, until one of several food 'outlets' is sighted, and that settles the matter.

In general the term 'Te Papa' would signal the Disneyfication of the arts – Maori and Pakeha – and an unwillingness to distinguish between high and low. It might suggest, for example, that the best place for a major McCahon is beside an old refrigerator, in case anyone uppity and élitist thought McCahon deserved special treatment or was in some way 'better' than the rest.

A 'Te Papa', or anything that might be considered Te Papa-ish, or Te Papa-fied, would aim itself not so much at the lowest common denominator as at the shortest possible attention span. It would justify itself in terms of the latest critical theory of the 1960s and seventies, and express its conception of itself verbally on a scale graduating from baby-talk right up to the language of the primary schoolyard – 'Awesome Forces', for example, and 'Home is where the Art is.'

To 'Te Papa' something would mean to justify it by numbers. It would

Art News, Winter 1998.

signify a purposeful vulgarisation of the arts, so that you would come away from the 'Te Papa' experience realising that everyone in the world, yourself included, was an artist, that anything and everything made by human hand was a work of art, that the whole human world was a museum/art gallery – and consequently (and what a relief!) that you would never have any need or occasion to go back.

Left, Right, Left ...

Around a table at Writers and Readers Week in Wellington it was explained to an American visitor that I was known not only as a writer but as a defender of certain 'right wing' positions. The visitor asked what 'right wing' meant in my case. I suggested he should be the judge of that, and gave him my political CV, which went roughly as follows.

I am the son of a man who was a trade union secretary and chairman of the Auckland Labour Party (LRC), and I have never voted anything but Labour. My earliest bitter and abiding political lesson was learned in 1951 when New Zealanders re-elected a National Government which had invoked the 1932 Emergency Regulations to take away basic democratic freedoms while it dealt with a recalcitrant union.

I spent much of my best intellectual energy for at least three, possibly five, years in the campaign against the American intervention in Vietnam and New Zealand's contribution to it. My one criminal conviction is for being on the Hamilton Rugby field in 1981 when the game against the Springboks was stopped.

Throughout all the decades of the Cold War I thought, and still think, that American nuclear posturing, its bullying of smaller nations, its unlawful interventions in Central and South America, its brinkmanship everywhere, made the world a more dangerous place. And if the collapse of the Communist empire has largely removed the danger, so that the world's primary problems are now environmental, which means in effect the excessive growth of human population, nothing has happened which has made me seriously revise the positions previously held.

On economic matters I have been willing to accept that New Zealand lived too well and too long on borrowed money, and that an opening of the doors and windows of protection was necessary to economic good health. But I always said, and meant, that I was glad to be heavily taxed, and to have the charity which I thought I owed to the less fortunate taken from me rather than left to my own not always dependable goodness of heart.

I still hold to that. But at the same time I've recognised more clearly that governments create wasteful and inefficient bureaucracies, and that quite apart from its brutal totalitarian repressions, the appalling condition of the 'infrastructure' (buildings, roads, factories, hospitals) in eastern European

Metro, February 1992.

countries is a warning to us all about believing the state can be relied upon to serve the public good and that free enterprise is always and only self-serving.

In that sense, and in common with most westerners of liberal-left persuasion, I have shifted my ground, moving, as the Labour Party has moved, away from the last vestiges of hard-line Marxist ideology and towards economic pragmatism – a pragmatism motivated, however, by something other than self-interest, and opposed to the notion that anything, from a hospital to a university to an arts council, can and should be run like a business.

So where does the designation 'right wing' come from? It comes, I suspect, from a degree of intransigence I have displayed on the issues of racism and sexism; and also, in literary and academic matters, from an unwavering conviction that talent and excellence are not equally distributed, and that to blind ourselves to that fact, blurring distinctions between better and worse because inequality is socially inconvenient, does harm to a precious intellectual heritage and no good to anyone.

I am unable to accept that racism or sexism can, or should, be effectively opposed by policies which are themselves racist and sexist. You cannot create equality by acts of will or Acts of Parliament. You can only create opportunity, and let time and individuals do their work. Equality of opportunity is the moral principle. Inequality of talent, energy, commitment, intelligence, strength of purpose, is the fact of life.

An official version of our history is becoming generally accepted which is at least as false as the imperialist and patriarchal one it replaces, and this new official view of ourselves becomes the justification for policies by which people are appointed to jobs, admitted to teachers' colleges, given special grants and special privileges, not because they are the most able or best qualified, or because they are talented and poor, but simply on the basis of their race or their sex.

I agree with Iris Murdoch that the effect of Women's Studies and Black Studies has been to put women and blacks into academic ghettos, leaving them uncertain whether they have really done well or merely profited from an official bias. But the matter is more serious than that. It is a matter of principle, of intellectual probity. Even if the outcomes could be shown to be for the collective good, there would still be no moral excuse for a favourable discrimination on the basis of a person's skin colour or sex; and I agree with Doris Lessing when she describes positive discrimination as 'that ultimate *trahison des clercs.*'

I believe the relentless politicising of relations between males and females, and between people of different ethnic background, and the consequent tendency to let ideology rather than natural feeling determine the way we interpret one another's behaviour, has had a coarsening effect on those areas in our social life which call for the greatest subtlety, delicacy and flexibility.

There are very large numbers of intelligent young persons growing up in modern New Zealand who believe their baby-boomer teachers in schools and universities (and especially, I regret to say, teachers of English) are purveyors of official cant. They accept it as something they have to live with, and mostly don't complain; but they are not persuaded – merely, and for the moment, compliant.

Nor am I able to believe that the policies which spring from the new moralism are doing more than a very little good to the truly disadvantaged. In fact it's not unreasonable to see the anti-sexist, anti-racist lobbies as self-serving middle-class élites, gaining advantages for themselves while claiming to act for the good of the larger group who in fact have nothing whatever to gain from anything that goes on in the higher reaches of the education system.

How one is labelled hardly matters. But if to hold to the views I have outlined here is to be 'right wing', then it is the terminology that has changed. I have not.

Part 5

In Conversation

With Harry Ricketts, 1986

HR   Do you think of there being a tradition of New Zealand poetry?
CKS   We inherit the whole tradition of English literature. But there's a sense in which everyone is immediately struck by things which overlap with their own experience. So there's a special excitement in those parts of our poetry which are recognisably 'New Zealand'. There must be an extra dimension in Yeats for an Irish person, and in Hardy for an English person. This is a bonus, but it's more than that. Being brought up in New Zealand when I was – and it would have been even more extreme in Curnow's case – most of what you read related to things you'd never seen or experienced. And this could give you the feeling that literature …
HR   Happens elsewhere?
CKS   Well, not so much happens elsewhere but that it doesn't deal with the real world. To me, to be confronted with reality in literature – with a recognisable reality – for the first time was very exciting. Suddenly there was an immediacy in the writing that there had never been before.
HR   When did you first read something and think, 'this is about the place where I live?'
CKS   The earliest would have been fifth or sixth form, probably reading John Mulgan's *Man Alone*. And round about that time discovering New Zealand poets. I remember an English master coming in one day and quoting, 'This short straight sword/I got in Rome/when Gaul's new lord/came tramping home:/It did that grim/old rake to a T-/if it did him,/well, it does me'. And asking, 'Who wrote that?' Nobody knew it was R.A.K. Mason. By then I'd been writing poems for at least three years and I had no notion that there were New Zealand poets. I became an avid reader of the *Listener,* and read all the poems there. When you're young and purposeful, you go out hunting until you find what you're after, and I found the Curnow anthology [*A Book of New Zealand Verse, 1923–45*] and read that, and read Curnow. By the time I was nineteen I knew a lot about New Zealand poetry.
HR   And by that point there was already a lot to find out about …
CKS   I was only really interested in the moderns. I wasn't interested in

---

From *Talking About Ourselves: Twelve New Zealand Poets in Conversation with Harry Ricketts,* 1986. The interview took place in Wellington, 12 March 1985. It has been edited since first publication. Harry Ricketts is a lecturer in English at Victoria University, poet and biographer of Rudyard Kipling.

the nineteenth-century New Zealand poets.

HR   It must have been a very exciting time!

CKS   Oh, tremendously exciting!

HR   I remember Ian Wedde talking about the difficulties he had in the early sixties with getting hold of American poets and finding there was only one bookshop in Auckland that stocked them.

CKS   Was it Progressive Books? Because that's where I picked them up. I have a first edition of, for example, O'Hara's *Lunch Poems* and I have some first editions of those *City Lights* books – Ginsberg's and Ferlinghetti's. I picked up a lot of American poetry there in the early sixties.

HR   Of course, there would have been American poetry to pick up on in the fifties; Olson and people were well under way.

CKS   I never remember encountering Olson at that time.

HR   He seems to be a poet who …

CKS   He's a cult figure.

HR   I've tried to read the 'Maximus' poems.

CKS   I have read them and I find them interesting but enjoyment in the ordinary sense doesn't come into it, I don't think. And that cult aspect of American poetry irritates me: this feeling of 'We know better, we're one stage ahead of you.' It's like Alan Loney saying in an interview that Stead was 'cluttering up the fast track'. And what this was supposed to mean was that they were all really going faster, but I was pretending to be on the same track and I was just getting in the way. I remember writing a little note to Roger Horrocks saying that there were an awful lot of ramshackle trolleys on the fast track. Loney is the chief proponent of a particular modishness and paranoia, and Roger Horrocks and Wystan Curnow, I suppose, are its academic gurus. But I don't altogether exempt Wedde, either. Well, maybe it's necessary in order to get the best out of themselves to believe that they're doing something for the first time. But how you can be doing something for the first time when it was done twenty years before in America is a puzzle to me. I'm all for anything that gives people a kick along, but you can't erect it into a critical position, can you? I know people think I did that with the essay 'From Wystan to Carlos'. There were two reactions to that. The younger poets, like Wedde and his contemporaries, thought I was pre-empting what they knew much better and ought to have been allowed to say. And then there was the reaction of people, like Lauris Edmond and Vincent O'Sullivan, who felt that somehow they'd been left out, and *ruled* out. Whereas I saw it, and I still see it, not as *pre*scriptive but as *de*scriptive – an exercise in New Zealand literary history – trying to mark a shift that had occurred. The reaction to that essay has really surprised me. Everybody's read it; everybody complains about it; everybody argues about it; everybody talks about it as if it shouldn't have happened. But at the beginning I said very clearly what I was doing. The terms in which New Zealand poetry had been discussed for twenty years had been the terms of Curnow's introductions – and there was nothing wrong with that – but why not shift the terms? It's just like saying, 'Instead of standing here and looking at it, let's go over and look at it from that angle and see what we see.' So I took up that position and described what I saw and it seems to me it can't be argued with – in the sense that I'm only describing from that position what I see. I can't understand what all the fuss is about.

HR   It suggests just how little of that kind of critical writing there has been here.

CKS   There's been a lot of talk but not much serious attempt to get it down on paper.

HR   I imagine that elsewhere it would have been taken as part of a discussion. I suppose *Parallax* and *AND* would see themselves as trying to take up positions and carry on. Would they see it as carrying on or as starting something quite different?

CKS   They would see themselves as developing something that was already well under way here, I think. They see all that as having begun in the sixties and seventies when they were young – that it began with them.

HR   Thinking of New Zealand literary magazines, one thing that would particularly interest me to ask you about would be your feelings towards *Landfall* and Charles Brasch.

CKS   When I started as a student in Auckland in the early fifties, *Landfall* was *the* literary magazine. That was quite good in a way because it wasn't a very large literary scene. You could get poems in the *Listener* or in *Landfall* and there wasn't much else. *Landfall* was a hurdle to be cleared – and that was how I began. When you're very young, you don't necessarily question the standards of an editor. You just think of him as being right. But pretty quickly that goes and you realise what, from your point of view, are his limitations. You know what kind of poem, of the kinds of poem you write, he will like and what he won't. But I feel mostly positive about *Landfall*. That doesn't mean I share, or shared, Brasch's taste. I was irritated by his preciousness both as a person and as an editor …

HR   And as a poet?

CKS   Oh yes. I'm no great admirer of Brasch's poems. He had a sense of cadence. He could roll words out beautifully and he had a voice to match, a rich rolling kind of delivery. But it's not to my taste at all. It's very precious and uneconomical and a lot of it's half-baked and naive. There's a lack of sharpness.

HR   Talking about impressions of people. I can't help noticing what different impressions people have of Baxter and his work. I know you've written about him but what have you felt about him and/or his work, and what do you feel now?

CKS   When I was discovering New Zealand poetry, Baxter was the most impressive young poet coming on, and he had the image to go with it. I remember him coming up to Auckland in 1953. In fact, there's that description in *All Visitors Ashore* of him being carried into a reading – which is true, except that the people who really carried him were Curnow and Fairburn. But the fact of the raincoat, the galoshes, and the feet not touching the floor, that happened at the Auckland University Hall. I shifted it to a house in the novel. The drunkenness just seemed picturesque; it didn't spoil my notion of him as a poet.

Then, later on, as I began to get established, I got drawn into the fight between Wellington and Auckland – Curnow with Louis Johnson and the Hounds of Wellington. There were probably faults on both sides, but right through I'd regarded Curnow more highly than any other New Zealand poet. By this time I'd got to know Curnow and felt loyal to him, so that rather soured my attitude to Baxter, and in the thick of the literary battle – which was heated at times – it probably clouded my view of his poetry. There was more than a decade when nobody was saying a good word about Curnow. There he was, writing brilliant poems and getting no positive response; and being attacked by younger men, so I felt defensive on his behalf. But what makes me guilty about Baxter is that I feel that I joined in the cutting down that happened to him. There was a period when everyone was saying negative things. Brasch and others would be dismissive. What we *should* all have been saying was, 'Well, Baxter may be an irritating person in all kinds of ways, but aren't we lucky to have someone so brilliant!' I realised this in the sixties and I kept thinking, 'I *must* write something.' I wanted to write something that Baxter would read so that I had committed myself publicly rather than just seeing him and saying, 'Jim, I immensely liked your poems' – because that's the easy thing to do. And then he died before I'd done it – although actually in my Fairburn piece I'd brought Baxter in at the end and he was still alive then – so I felt glad that at least I'd signalled something very positive.

Of course I have mixed feelings about a lot of Baxter's work. He wrote so much and a lot of it isn't his best. How could it be? I see Curnow and Baxter as being two kinds of New Zealand poet and I go back and forth between them, according to mood and circumstance. I'm closer to Curnow, in that we both tend to be more scrupulous with the individual word and tend more towards wit and less towards preaching. My relationship with Curnow has been much closer than it ever was with Baxter. I only used to see Baxter from time to time. Whereas with Curnow I think it's true to say that since 1955 every poem he's written I've seen in typescript before it was printed. We've lived across the road from one another for thirty years and when he writes a new poem it goes in my letter-box.

HR Yes, he mentioned that. I thought at the time how good it must be to have someone you feel that ease and confidence with – not that from the outside anyone would imagine that you or Allen Curnow needed ...

CKS Oh, but you do, you see. The sense of precariousness just continues with every new thing you do. I think anybody who grows into total confidence is probably not writing well. It's all right to look back and pick out things you've done and say, 'Well, I feel reasonably confident about this or that.' But

I don't think you can feel that about what's on the typewriter.

HR   One thing that you touched on when you were talking about the fifties was the sense of a debate (perhaps even a row) between Auckland and Wellington. Do you think this is still going on? Does it have any bearing on the response to that Curnow poem, 'Dichtung und Wahrheit'?

CKS   The dispute in the fifties was quite particular. It was a younger group of poets who thought they should be better represented in Curnow's *Penguin Book of New Zealand Verse,* and I think on balance they had some ground for that – Baxter particularly was under-represented. But it's almost axiomatic that every anthologist has his blind spots, and his own view of things, and the only way to deal with that is to have a lot of anthologies. The problem then was that there were very few. A new anthology took on a special importance. So, they felt left out and it happened that they gathered around Louis Johnson in Wellington. Louis Johnson – I must say I like him enormously. You can fight a battle like that and when it's over, it's gone – there's no bitterness at all.

Anyway, the fact that they gathered round him gave the dispute a sort of geographical location, but that was largely accidental. After all, Curnow had come from Canterbury to Auckland in 1951 and there was a group of young poets in Auckland like Keith Sinclair, Kendrick Smithyman, Bob Chapman, who had their own grudge against Curnow for what they called 'The South Island Myth'. Whereas Curnow had said, 'We're all uneasy settlers in an alien land', they were saying, 'We're entirely at home here' – which seemed to me something you don't assert when it's the case. So the geographical thing was really rather complicated, and I don't know that Auckland and Wellington has all that much to do with it. Glover about that time moved to Wellington and he was a close associate and continuing friend of Curnow's; and Curnow was not really an Aucklander. I suppose he's become one. But he was newly arrived then, and on the other hand Smithyman and Sinclair and Chapman in many ways felt closer to Johnson and Baxter than they did to Curnow. But you mentioned in particular the argument about the Curnow poem, 'Dichtung und Wahrheit'. You see, the subject of that poem was also an Aucklander, M.K. Joseph. It's not as though he'd savaged a Wellington writer. And after all, even O'Sullivan and Bertram were Aucklanders originally. So what I'm saying is that it's all very complicated. There are, however, geographical loyalties and something like a different perspective in each centre – including Christchurch and Dunedin – on the whole picture of New Zealand writing.

HR   One question that I've been asking, and it's a general one, is whether you think of the poet as having a role.

CKS   Are you talking about a social, political function in the poetry itself, or of the poet outside his poem? Or are you leaving that to me?

HR   I'm trying to put it in such a way that you can shape it as you like.

CKS   Well, just to take it at the level of poems: if you try to make a literary work simply a *vehicle* for an opinion, then you're heading for trouble.

Because politics is one of my preoccupations I like to think that politics can get into the poems, but it has to happen on its own. And I think the only way it can happen is that the preoccupation, of whatever kind, has to become part of your whole emotional self. The longer you've had the preoccupation, and the more deeply embedded it is in your personality, the more likely it is to find ways to express itself.

I have a view of writing poetry which is – I say this to my students in my Creative Writing course – that it's no good working on the poem, you've got to work on yourself. A conscious effort, saying, 'Okay, there's an hour before midnight and I haven't written a poem for three weeks – I'll really push myself along' and then deciding at the end of that time, 'Well, that's a lousy poem; I must work harder' – that's no good at all. You've got to work on yourself and the self will write the poem. It's a kind of Zen Buddhist attitude. So if the coloration – political coloration – is deeply part of your personality and part of your preoccupations, then it will, as it were, float into the poem and be intrinsically part of it. I don't know if that's an adequate answer but it's the best I can do, because all answers to questions like that seem unsatisfactory once you've made them.

As far as the poet as an individual goes, I just take the view that everybody is a private citizen and has some social responsibility. A responsible citizen is aware of politics and social issues, has opinions on them and where possible – even if it's only in the simple act of voting – participates. In that sense you have only the same responsibility that every citizen has – neither more nor less – except that writing in some small degree gives you a public identity, and the more successful you are, then the larger the public identity, and therefore from time to time you will actually be in a slightly more public posture. So if you get arrested on a football ground it will make the news. That's all. The public aspect of it is just an offshoot of having 'a public', but the question of how much politics gets into the poems seems to me an entirely different question. It's a question the thirties left-wing poets got terribly confused by and hung up and self-contradictory over. On the one hand the Left was urging them to use their poems as instruments, and on the other they inherited a quite sound anxiety about turning poetry into propaganda.

HR   One question that seems an inevitable one to ask you is how you feel the different sides of your work feed into each other. There's the fact that you earn your living as a university professor, but at the same time you're writing poetry and fiction as well as criticism. It seems to me that the most appropriate description of you would be that you were a writer rather than, say, a poet or a novelist, which is also the way I'd want to describe someone like Hardy, for instance. And I think it's fine to be a writer; I don't see any problem with that. You seem to manage to keep these different kinds of writing going in a very admirable way. Have you always been able to do this?

CKS   When I write fiction, I think of myself as a fiction writer, and when I write poems, I think of myself as a poet and I become slightly removed and uninterested in the other function. I never do the two together. The university teaching is the way I earn my living and although it can be a very enjoyable way, it's also very arduous, and for a lot of my life it's got in the way of my writing. So, to some extent, although I think it's true to say that I've been a conscientious and quite a good university teacher, much of it has been working against the grain. Partly, my critical writing has been an offshoot of being a university teacher, but not exclusively. *The New Poetic* obviously was because that was my PhD thesis. If I could have arranged my life to suit myself – which very few people are able to do – I would have written a lot more fiction. And I would still like to, because I agree with you – traditionally people talk about it as if you must be a poet or a fiction writer and think that if you try to be both you can't be serious about either. But Lawrence was serious at both. So was Hardy. When people say, 'Is it a good idea to do both?' as though you're wasting your available talent over a broad field, I always think of Goldsmith. If you talk about the novel in the eighteenth century, you're not going to say *The Vicar of Wakefield* is the greatest novel, but you can't leave it out. If you talk about the theatre, you can't leave out *She Stoops to Conquer.* If you talk about poetry, you can't leave out 'The Deserted Village'. There are the three major available literary forms and he contributed to all three. People seem to have accepted that painters can work sometimes in oils and sometimes in watercolours and sometimes switch to sculpture and I don't see why it shouldn't be the same in literature. One is a writer and one does different things at different times.

With Dennis McEldowney, 1991

DMcE   What I would like to do first is to take Julian Harp from 'A Fitting Tribute' as an image of the young C.K. Stead. The marvellous boy with his self-made wings catapulting off into the blue and soaring over Rangitoto – not disappearing, though, since you did it again and again.

CKS   I wasn't thinking of Julian Harp as myself, of course. His appearance and his behaviour were modelled on Barry Humphries, who was a friend of those years, before he became famous.

DMcE   No, not Stead as the original of Harp, but Harp as a metaphor for Stead. Look at the record. Here's this boy from the scoria garden on Mt Eden going off to do his PhD in London on *the* central question of twentieth-century literature, and having it published and very soon going into Pelican and used everywhere as a textbook. Then, almost simultaneously writing what I think was your first published story, 'A Race Apart' –

CKS   Apart from a tiny story published in *Arena*.

DMcE   – using as a narrator an upper-class Englishwoman, and having it published in England, launching the Hutchinson New Authors series, having it praised by Englishwomen. Then there was your poetry, and twisting Brasch's arm to publish 'Pictures in a Gallery Undersea' in *Landfall* – this twenty-six-year-old successfully twisting Charles Brasch's arm! – and then it was chosen by *Landfall* readers as the best poem in the first fifteen years of *Landfall*. What all this looks like is enormous self-confidence.

CKS   The effect it has on me is rather depressing. I feel it's been downhill all the way ever since. You want me to respond to that description?

DMcE   Was it self-confidence, and if it was, what was the source of it?

CKS   I'm not sure. While all that was happening each thing was exciting and remarkable but I didn't see *myself* as remarkable. I was probably a mixture of energy, which is a kind of confidence, and lack of confidence.

There must have been belief in myself, yet when I look back on it I don't know where it came from. I notice it when I compare young people now, that they seem so lacking in direction or certainty about what they want to do; or they have some vague notion that they want to do something but they don't

---

From *In the Same Room: Conversations with New Zealand Writers,* ed. Elizabeth Alley and Mark Williams, 1992. The interview took place in Auckland, 9 July 1991. Dennis McEldowney has published journals, biography and short stories. He was first Managing Editor of Auckland University Press.

find out how to do it; and when I think that I didn't know anybody who could tell me, and yet I found literary periodicals … For example, my very first poem was published in Australia in the *Jindyworobak Anthology*. It was a poem I wrote when I was eighteen. Well, how did I find out about the *Jindyworobak Anthology* in Auckland, New Zealand? I don't know. So I was purposeful; but the purposefulness and the energy came out of a passionate interest, first of all having discovered works of literature at school and second having discovered the wish to write things of that kind. My whole life was focused on that, and no doubt I was energetic. I suppose there must have been confidence: but lots of people have that. It's either confirmed by success, or it's not.

DMcE   I'm interested that you used the word purposefulness, because that's another thing I had in mind, that there does seem very early a sense of purpose almost as if you had planned a career, and these were stations on it, prearranged.

CKS   I certainly didn't plan a career. All I knew at secondary school was that I wanted to be a writer and I assumed that a person of my kind would be a schoolteacher; and then when I went to university I realised that a lot of New Zealand's most notable poets were university teachers and I thought that was probably what I would like to do but that I wouldn't do well enough academically; I didn't expect to.

I was regarded at primary school as rather slow and not very bright by my parents, so, for example, when it came to secondary school my sister was put into a Latin class but it was thought that Latin would be too difficult for me. I was put into French but not Latin. The first thing I really succeeded at was chemistry, and that was because there was a very intelligent teacher I responded to, J.L.D. Woolloxal. But gradually I did start to do well, not brilliantly, and it wasn't until I got to university that I began to show my real abilities. But my primary ambition at that stage – and it isn't even quite right to call it an ambition – the thing I wanted to do was to be a writer. I certainly didn't have confidence early on in critical writing. I remember saying to Allen Curnow when I was an MA student that I was sure of myself as a poet but not in critical writing, and Allen said reassuringly, 'Well, it's always *interesting* what poets have to say about works of literature', as though I didn't need to worry. So I thought I was going to be a poet and fiction writer: I didn't think I was going to be a critic. To be a critic was something I learnt, I suppose.

DMcE   Other people's image of C.K. Stead is often of one who is primarily a critic and has derived his fiction and poetry from the criticism.

CKS   That's certainly not the case; but I did come to intellectual and academic consciousness and maturity at the time when the great figure in English literature was Eliot, who was poet and critic, and so there was no notion that a poet should apologise for being a critic as well; quite the reverse. Eliot exemplified the great critic who was also the major poet of the time; and he in turn made you aware that this had always been so, that some of the major poets had been the great critics of their age, going back through Matthew Arnold, Wordsworth and Coleridge, Dr Johnson, Dryden.

DMcE   Let's go back to the origin of your intention to be a writer. I don't know that one can ever explain why this happens in certain locations to certain people, but I presume that those it happens to have nearly always grown up among people who are interested in words, and aware of books, not necessarily books one would now approve of. In the essay on John Mulgan you gave a list of novels you were reading as a teenager; which were almost precisely the ones I was reading.* They may not be ones we would now look back on with pride; but I think something of the kind is essential.

CKS   Not with pride? You mean not with admiration? We might go back and find they were worth admiring, mightn't we? – particularly as books for people of that age. I didn't grow up in a very bookish household. My father read quite a lot, and owned books, especially Left Book Club things, the red-backed Victor Gollancz series. He was a Labour man and he subscribed. I still have some of his books down there. My mother didn't read a great deal, though I found when I was older that any time I pushed a book her way and she read it, for a relatively uneducated woman she had very sharp things to say about it. She was a music teacher. But I suppose the point is that when I got to secondary school and was introduced to the standard classic works of English literature, which in those days were put in front of pupils if they were able to read them, all of a sudden it gave my whole life focus. Nothing else was so important to me. I was a keen chess player at school and a keen sportsman: I was a senior rep. in athletics, soccer and tennis and those things were tremendously important. But once I found this passion for literature it didn't stop the other things, but it was more important. And then as for wanting to write, I suppose you begin by imitation. I began by imitating Rupert Brooke. But I think the important thing is that I felt as though up to that point my life was random, and from that point on it has never seemed random. From the age of thirteen or fourteen –

DMcE   That's very early, isn't it?

CKS   Yes, but it happens earlier with some people. It happened with Baxter at the age of about eight.

DMcE   One difference between you and most people who were reading Left Book Club books, as hundreds were of course, is that your father was. So often it was a reaction against the parents that led to reading Left Book Club books.

CKS   Another thing that was marvellous for me was that my father subscribed to the *New Statesman.* It came surface mail and so was a little out of date, but he would read it for the politics and then hand it over to me and I would read the book reviews and the poems.

DMcE   Your father started from the front and you from the back?

CKS   That's right. That was when I was at Mt Albert Grammar, and it

---

* C.K. Stead, 'John Mulgan: A Question of Identity', *Islands* 25, 1979; reprinted in *In the Glass Case,* AUP/OUP, 1981.

gave me my first sense of an ongoing literary world in London that I wouldn't otherwise have known about until I met Frank Sargeson.

DMcE   You've never, as far as I know, written up your meeting with Frank Sargeson. Presumably you are going to at some time?

CKS   I hope to, yes. I sometimes think in terms of doing something specifically on Frank as a memoir and including a selection of letters, because I had many letters from him; or at other times like everybody else I think about writing autobiography.

DMcE   What age were you when you met Frank?

CKS   I would have been a third-year student, I think, so – twenty, or twenty-one.

DMcE   And who introduced you?

CKS   I had some poems published in the *Poetry Yearbook,* and he wrote to me and said how much he'd liked them. I remember sitting in Somervell's coffee shop with Kay and another friend and reading it out because it was so exciting to get a letter out of the blue from Frank Sargeson. I wrote back, we exchanged letters, I invited him to talk to the student literary society – I was secretary, I think. The talk he gave was printed in *Kiwi* in 1955, which I edited with Rob Dyer, and it's in his selected essays. I met him a few times that year, 1954; and then Kay and I were married at the beginning of 1955. We got a flat on Takapuna Beach and called on him. We visited him often and he came to us, and Janet Frame was writing *Owls Do Cry*. The whole of that year we saw Frank at least once a week, probably more often. In fact I found the other day a set of notes he'd made for me. I was studying for my MA and one of the papers was on Milton. I'd said to Frank that I couldn't keep up with all the reading, so he read one or two books – one on Milton by G. Wilson Knight, and I think another one, and simply made a set of notes on his green paper. They were very eccentric and not a lot of use from the point of view of an MA student, but it's an example of the way Frank would throw himself into whatever you were doing, and how helpful he always wanted to be.

DMcE   There's a point near the beginning of *All Visitors Ashore* where Melior Farbro is concerned that Curl Skidmore is going to be buried or smothered in marriage and domesticity; which is an interesting remark, because it seems to me possibly truer of Stead than of Skidmore at that point. That I suppose is a trail we shouldn't follow: your private and domestic life is something your readers don't learn much about; but obviously it hasn't smothered you.

CKS   Well, Frank always had that view that the whole life of the artist should be devoted to his art, or her art, and that marriage was counter-productive and so was the academic life. So I should avoid at least the university. In general his attitude was that writers were better not to marry. I think where problems set in between Frank and me was when I came back from overseas and went into the university and for a while *was* virtually smothered. I was under tremendous pressure working very very hard trying to keep myself alive as a writer and at the same time trying to learn to be an academic, and I was rather irascible with Frank whenever he got on to this particular hobby-horse, because it just didn't seem very helpful to tell me that I was making a mistake with my life and that I was ruining myself as a writer and that the university was a terrible place to be – even if he was right! From time to time that was a source of tension between us. And when there was friction of course Frank would always be very very – I mean he has a reputation for being a wonderful and helpful and saintly character and in some ways he was, but he was also sharp-tongued and difficult.

DMcE He could also be very devious and manipulative.

CKS Yes. He would set traps for you; he would decide that he was going to bring up a difficult subject and you learned after a while that he was capable of planning out a conversation in advance and leading you on a certain path, having dug a big hole at the end of the path. The hole that Frank dug! He did this with all his friends in Auckland and a lot of writers in those days gave up visiting him because there would be some kind of a row and Frank would be really bitchy and they wouldn't go back. But I would have a bit of a row with him and then I'd think Frank's company is too good to give away just because of one incident and so I'd let a little bit of time pass and then I'd go back. I don't mean by that that Frank was solely to blame, because I was also no doubt very prickly and sensitive on some issues of difference between us.

DMcE Frank always referred to you, to me, as the exception, as someone who had actually survived the academic life.

CKS He didn't acknowledge that to me.

DMcE I found when I reread *All Visitors Ashore* that while I enjoyed it immensely the first time, I enjoyed it in a different way the second time because I was no longer preoccupied with noting resemblances and differences between the people you were writing about and the people I'd known. I was able to note that to me the most fully rounded character was the one whose origin I knew least about, the girl Patagonia. This made me to some degree envy your readers in Britain and the United States who aren't worried by these resonances, while at the same time they've obviously missed some things you've intended New Zealanders to get: like Farbro waiting for Ken on the last bus, with its echoes of the story 'An Affair of the Heart', and Skidmore with his Bruce Masonish piece, 'Consider Takapuna'.

CKS I suppose the 'Consider Takapuna' passage might be almost meaningless without Bruce Mason. The waiting for the bus is a bit different: it draws on what Frank told me about waiting for his friend Harry, but then Frank's own story draws on that as well. But people assume all kinds of things are literal that are not. I talked to a group of students once who were concerned about the fact that I seemed to have portrayed Janet Frame, and then it emerged in the course of their questioning me that they assumed Janet Frame was very interested in Zen Buddhism. If she is, I know nothing about it. I'm the person who's interested in Zen Buddhism. It's the one kind of philosophy/religion, if it can be called that, that has really engaged my mind and imagination at periods right through my life. The point is that characters in a novel may begin with particular people but in my mind they separate out, and there are two people; there is Frank Sargeson and there is Melior Farbro.

DMcE   Who is a painter – conveyed very successfully as a painter, as someone who sees visually rather than in terms of words.

CKS   That's right; but it's also more to do with the personality in your mind. I've come to recognise that *every* character in fiction is more the author than anybody else. So if, for example, there is the framework of Frank Sargeson, it's only, or principally, something into which you put some aspect of yourself. As for *All Visitors Ashore*: insofar as Melior Farbro could be said to be Frank or Cecelia Skyways to be a well-known and living writer of the moment, they're also rather idealised, aren't they? But I know that people have reacted negatively and said that it's an intrusion on the life of the person who's said to be portrayed –

DMcE   David Young tried to work up a controversy about that in the *Listener*, I remember, but Janet wasn't having any.

CKS   She said it was a 'masterpiece of creative writing', which seemed to me typically clever of Janet, because it so decisively emphasised the separation between fact and fiction, while at the same time paying a tribute and so defusing any possible use of herself against me.

DMcE   I also found on rereading *The Death of the Body* that since I was no longer preoccupied with wondering when the Mervyn Thompson bits were going to come in, and what they would be like, I could give more attention to other aspects: the whole business of narrative, for one thing.

CKS   Of course there are no 'Mervyn Thompson bits'. One of the things that *The Death of the Body* is about is narrative and narrative frames. It says here are different frames that you can put around these events. You can say it's a murder mystery; that's one frame. It's an academic novel, that's another. It's a domestic novel. The picture is there and you pick up one frame and you pick up another. One idea behind it is just this fact, or it seems to me a fact, that we're all forced to construct narratives or else we're subject to the chaos of unordered impressions, so that in the simplest way if I tell you an anecdote, I tell you that I went up to the dairy and such-and-such happened, somebody said this and somebody else did something else or something fell off the shelf, it's an unconscious but very careful selection, from all that happened, towards a narrative conclusion. To that extent we falsify all the time, to ourselves and to others, because we tell these stories to ourselves as well, and we shape them usually to our own advantage. But the choice is either that kind of falsification or just chaos. If you can't make narrative of your life, I should think the alternative is madness.

DMcE   There's also a sense, though, in *The Death of the Body* that which of the narratives it is to be has already been determined by the voice from the blue folder. Although all these different frames seem alternative ways of looking at the same events, and there could be alternative ways of proceeding with the story, and the narrator thinks about them and sometimes seems about to take them, the blue folder won't let him.

CKS   Just listening to you then I thought of something I hadn't thought of before, which explains something about that novel. In the past I've thought it through to the point where I tend to say that the authority of the blue folder is the authority of *art*. It won't allow the story to deviate too far from a kind of artistic unity. Uta, on the other hand, who's a semi-comic figure, is perhaps muse, but she's also a moralist – probably more moralist than muse. So there's conflict between them. But what I thought of just now is this: after *All Visitors Ashore* I was aware that there were people who reacted negatively to the metafictional aspect of it – the kind of reaction I got in the *Listener* from Ian Cross, for example, who said it was too clever for its own good and so on; and I think I thought, well, I would write a more conventional novel. I was in London and I worked on it for a month. I only had a limited time in which to try and get the draft of a novel down, so a month was very precious. One day I was unbearably depressed and I went for a walk from Russell Square to Oxford Street and right along Oxford Street to Hyde Park and back, and by the time I got back I knew that I had to ditch everything I'd written up to that point. I hadn't analysed why: I just knew that it was no good. I began again – it was one of these courageous things you do which give you more courage next time, because you know it's possible and the outcome can be good. So it's easier next time to face the fact that something's gone wrong; that you've put a lot of work into something and you've just got to scrap it. But the point is that it was then I introduced all the complexities to the story – the story-within-the-story, and Uta, and all the rest of it. Now in a way, the voice from the blue folder, which is so dictatorial, is like that impulse which came from wherever inside myself, which first of all, when I wouldn't listen to it, made me depressed, and finally when I went for my long walk and did listen, said, 'Scrap everything you've written and start again'. I'd never thought of it until now that the voice from the blue folder is the personification of that moment.

DMcE   Does it ever depress you that having spent hours writing a page or two of beautifully constructed scene-setting such as often occurs in *The Death of the Body,* the reader skims over that in a moment and probably forgets it almost immediately? Even though it adds to the general impression of the book as an enjoyable read. You can't very well say to a novel reader, as you can to a poetry reader, that it is really necessary to read it two or three times.

CKS   Yes, that thought is depressing. There are a number of ways around it. One is that you are not writing for the reader who treats your work cavalierly. But if the reader does race through those passages, I think you just have to hope that they lay down something essential even if the reader is not conscious of it. And there have to be strategies to trap and hold attention. If you get onto one conventional mode of fiction and you pedal along and never change then you're not really exercising as well as you might the possibilities for prodding the reader awake, and one of those is to make frequent changes of tone and pace. One of the things about *Smith's Dream* as a novel, I thought after I'd done it, is that it's a long smooth surface and that the reader can just skate over the surface. Fast. You've somehow got to break up the surface; you've got to have cross-threads all the time. One of the intentions in writing *All Visitors Ashore* was to give it a verbal texture that would keep the mind alert, rather than just a smooth narrative passage.

DMcE   Even critics often seem unable to cope with or even be interested in aspects of a novel or of writing in general that are very important to writers when they are actually writing. For example, the emotional impact of reading and even the physical impact is something you don't often get any impression of from critics. When I'm reading a novel by Karl Stead I can laugh aloud, which I often do, I can cringe with horror or terror, which I don't often do with Stead, I can thump the arm of the chair with delight, I can be sexually aroused, I can weep. One sometimes gets the impression that these are even regarded as illegitimate and manipulative uses of writing.

CKS   My feeling is that any writer who hears that he or she is producing these reactions is delighted because that's what it's all about. It means that you've created an imaginative world and you've done that partly by representation and partly by the use of language, including all kinds of subtleties in sound, which is what makes *literature,* as distinct from the kinds of writing that are not literature. I'm not really interested in a criticism that gives you no sense of the personality, the presence, of the person who read the book and reacted to it. I don't necessarily want to be told these particular physical things – it's perhaps difficult and even too primitive to go right back to that; but I do want to feel that there is a person there whose discussion of the book is based on having had these initial primitive and absolutely essential reactions. More and more – I don't mean just in the present: all the time I was at the university I felt this – academic criticism works at a sort of abstract and impersonal level which leaves all that out. The more abstract and analytical it becomes, the less a writer feels that criticism is offering anything that is relevant or helpful. You tend often to get much more commonsense and useful and interesting reactions from untrained but really literate readers than from trained readers. You often feel that people in the university get some of their best reactions trained out of them and they don't recover them until they've gone away for some time, and have had time to get back to books as books.

DMcE   You made the point in one of your essays, I think it was the lecture 'The Poet's View', that critics usually have little to say about what you feel is the most important aspect of poetry, the music, because for one thing it's very complex and difficult to grasp – what's going on is so difficult to analyse – but also because they don't seem to have the language for it; and possibly don't have the language for it because they're not very sensitive to it.

CKS   Yes, and often people who are sensitive to it don't have the language either. The question when it comes to poetry is almost whether there *is* a language for it. You can only point to it and say it's there. For me the musical aspect works in anything which is literary, it works from sentence to sentence and in poetry from line to line at a close level; but it also operates on a much larger level, a structural level, so that ideally in fiction, as I was saying earlier, there should be a sense of, say, one kind of scene, one kind of density balanced against another kind; there should be contrast, there should be light and shade, and this is a kind of musical structure over a big expanse of writing.

DMcE   And movement, from one to the other?

CKS   Yes. These musical things operate in ways which are very powerful – you're *very* aware of them if you *are* aware of them. I don't know whether you saw the three documentaries about Richard Nixon. I was astonished because I had the anti-Vietnam person's view of Nixon, which was simply that he was an evil person. He'd been a Communist baiter and then he prosecuted the war in Vietnam having said he'd end it, and so on. And it isn't that the documentary persuaded me that any of my negative views were wrong; but it showed a whole aspect of Nixon that I'd never imagined. One of the things was that final speech he made to his staff when he'd resigned. You get some of it at the beginning of the first documentary, and some more at the end of the third. There was a moment – and I can imagine a lot of people, not without some grounds, would dismiss it as either sentimentality or cynicism or both – where he quoted from something that Theodore Roosevelt had written when his daughter died, and to me the whole timing of that part of his speech, the light and shade, the long pauses, everything about it, was music. You know, you can think what you like about Nixon – but how can you analyse that? All I can say is that because of the pace of the speech, the emphasis given to one word and not another, the pauses, the light and shade, the things said, the whole complexity – to me it had a musical quality, all the more astonishing because it was coming from this person I'd always thought was some kind of a bug. Well, I don't think that anyone has a language to deal with that; but people need to acknowledge that it's there, to point to it, not let other things crowd it out, and not to think that, say, the moral content of a work is why it is a great work, or that it's a great work because historically it's something or other. Often an academic analysis of a work of literature will tell a lot about its 'content', and you're left with the feeling, yes, well, the same 'content' could make a great novel or a great poem, or a bad novel or a bad poem, and you're no nearer to knowing why this one is great.

When it comes to the question of narrative skills – the disposition of facts and information, the feeding out of information, the withholding of information, the giving of incorrect information and later correcting it – the whole tactics of narrative, this is something which I think people possess innately or they don't . People are either good storytellers or they're not. You can tell a story to one person and hear them tell it again and ruin it; and you can hear another person make a good story out of almost nothing. That is a very basic and very important element, too. I always give the example of

Wordsworth's *Lyrical Ballads*. Critics writing about it never mention that an enormous part of the success of the *Lyrical Ballads* is just that they're tremendously well-told, well-managed stories.

DMcE   My first impression on rereading *Sister Hollywood* was the same as when I read it first. It surprised me as a C.K. Stead book, partly because of this immersion in the Hollywood of the time, but also because it is a much more straightforward narrative than anything you had written since *Smith's Dream;* and a story that you can read as a story without being conscious of meanings or resonances. Though the resonances arrive. Stead, it seems to me, often overturns the expectations people have of him. After all the talk about the importance to Stead of the European tradition and what the Europeans in New Zealand have brought from Europe in their heads, we have Stead here confronting the fact that people's heads in his generation, but not only in his generation, were lined with images from Hollywood. The Edie/Arlene character, like so many characters in New Zealand fiction, escapes to the source of what's in her head, only this is not to Europe, not to London, but Hollywood. Having got her there, Stead is very serious about Hollywood. Hollywood is not just in our heads farcically as it is in some of Ronald Hugh Morrieson's novels.

CKS   It's perhaps not so much what is put into a head that's important as the head it's put into. That's the crucial thing. You can subject a rather inferior head to high culture with little effect – and vice versa. That's the first thing. The second is that there was an idea that somehow I didn't get into the novel in the way that it existed for me beforehand – the idea that the brother and sister both had the same capacity with language and interest in language, and the brother goes the traditional path, which is English literature and an academic career. The sister, being a woman of those times, follows her husband, which takes her to Hollywood; but because of circumstances she discovers a capacity as a scriptwriter. My idea originally was that they were exercising the same talent in different milieu. But I always have a problem with characters who might be identified as myself, and particularly with showing them in a good light. Because the character of the brother in *Sister Hollywood* has so much in common with myself I was inhibited about building him out, so he remains rather insubstantial; whereas I always find it easy to develop women characters, partly because women have been the dominant presences in my life, far more than men, so I feel fairly confident writing about women, but also because if I'm dealing with a woman character nobody's going to think I'm writing about myself. So in terms of *personality* (as distinct from external facts) there is far more of me in the sister than there is in the brother.

DMcE   The life Arlene is leading and what she is doing comes across as far more real than what the brother is doing.

CKS   Yes, he becomes more or less the vehicle for telling her story, and it becomes her story rather than the story of both of them. Except, I suppose the retrospect back to childhood.

DMcE   Yes, that's very different. I did sometimes feel that the Hollywood sections of the book were written in a slightly Hollywoodish way. The language and the kind of narrative is Hollywood. Whereas the New Zealand sections are not at all.

CKS   I'm not sure whether it's altogether successful, or whether the two halves fit together. It's a novel I don't feel entirely clear about in my own mind.

DMcE   It's very enjoyable. And in her own way and of her own time Arlene is almost Katherine Mansfield. There's still a lot of New Zealand in her; even to the fact that though she loves kidneys she doesn't want to eat them for lunch. Lunch is a bread meal. But she wouldn't contemplate going back. How has that book been received by American and in particular Los Angeles readers?

CKS   First of all, individual reactions, including people who are actually in Hollywood, like Roger Donaldson and his wife: they thought it was spot on; they thought it was a terrific image of Hollywood as they knew it even now. The *Los Angeles Times,* which is the big paper in Los Angeles and reviews just one book each day, gave it a big positive review. Other reviews have been good. I haven't had a lot of reviews from America – not as many as from England; there may have been some I haven't seen, but I haven't had any negative reviews.

DMcE   To revert to the image of Julian Harp and 'A Fitting Tribute', I can imagine that story written from the perspective of several decades later, say in 1990, when Harp's career has been further overlaid by legend, by suspicions and jealousies and paranoias, and multi-layered media manipulation, until it becomes menacing and dark, from being comparatively simple and joyous –

CKS   This is the image of Julian Harp as somehow the image of me, is it? What you seem to be pointing to is the degree to which I've become what's called controversial.

DMcE   That's one thing; but another thing that interests me about any person who has become a public figure is what effect this perception of them by the world outside has on their own perception of themselves.

CKS   I think my conception of myself is fairly clear, insofar as anyone can be clear about himself. Of course, unless you're a very prominent politician or something, you don't really know what others think of you; but every now and then you get a little glimpse of it, and insofar as I do and it's negative it's always a bit of a shock – the recognition that in the degree to which you've become a public persona … Actually, it does relate to Julian Harp, doesn't it, because the thing about him is that at the end he's become public property and if the public want to say that he had short hair and was clean-shaven and looked like an army officer then he damn well did, whatever the woman who knew him says. And of course that works negatively, too – if people want to think you're racist, sexist, it's no use denying it because you've been slotted into what is really a political context and you've become a symbol within

that.
DMcE Abrasive is another word.
CKS Yes. And insofar as I am controversial or whatever, it can't be totally unconnected with me; it must come partly from my temperament. On the other hand I think that if people who have a negative image of me actually met me they might find it difficult to match the real person with the public image.
DMcE But what I'm really interested in is what effect this kind of thing has on your work.
CKS I don't think it affects my work at all. It affects me personally, and over recent years I've felt oppressed by New Zealand and glad to get out of it at regular intervals – most notably, I suppose, when the shit hit the fan over the London flat. I was roundly angry with a lot of people in PEN, because I had undertaken something not in the spirit of self-interest at all but because I wanted other New Zealand writers to share the pleasures of London which I experience annually. So I cut myself off from PEN and my fellow writers and it had a marvellous effect. I felt suddenly liberated. I felt much more acutely than I ever have before – though you might think I've always felt this – that I didn't have to please anybody; that it wasn't any good trying because they weren't going to be pleased; and the only thing was to get my head down and write. So I got back to a new novel. I think what I'm saying is that as far as I'm aware, this doesn't affect my writing, except insofar as I choose to let it get into things like essays. I can't see how it affects my fiction.
DMcE The novel isn't going to be Stead's revenge?
CKS No.
DMcE The title, *The End of the Century at the End of the World:* in what sense the end of the world?
CKS Well, just New Zealand being at the end of the world, with whatever overtones … It's an old one, isn't it? – Allen Curnow's 'here is the world's end where wonders cease', for example.
DMcE In the lecture I referred to before, 'A Poet's View', you said that poetry comes from a head of steam and that the poet needs to be in a state of euphoria. You described yourself in the fifties as auto-euphoric. I wondered whether in your own late fifties you still find it possible to get up that head of steam and be auto-euphoric.
CKS You mean, as a poet? I think that for me the way back into poetry is through reading poetry; but lately I've been so continually obsessed with fiction that I haven't written much else, except that I wrote those 1990 commissioned poems, *Voices*. That was an interesting exercise for me. I did it very conscientiously, worked hard at it; but the way I did it was to go back to the forms I would have used when I was young. There's a lot of half-concealed rhyming, quite tight verse forms, and a basic regular five-stress line; so it's more conservative – there isn't the kind of technical excitement that there has been with other things I've written. I suppose I felt intuitively that to mix that

sort of historical material with technical experimentation wouldn't have been quite fulfilling the commission.

DMcE   One of the problems with the Julian Harp image is that the umbrellas from which he made his marvellous wings were stolen. This brings up another opinion sometimes expressed of Stead, that much of his poetry is derivative. You were saying that reading poetry is your way into poetry and obviously there are a lot of echoes of poetry in your poetry. How do you react to that kind of comment when it's made seriously?

CKS   Insofar as Julian Harp is the image of the artist and the umbrellas are stolen, the idea is that every artist, every writer, is stealing umbrellas all over the place. If you don't steal umbrellas you've got no material to make your wings. I was thinking of the material.

DMcE   Only Julian Harp could make those particular wings from those umbrellas – or only Julian Harp did, anyway.

CKS   As for my poetry being 'derivative' – well, I don't know. It's the sort of thing that once irritated me, but now I'm prepared to let the thing work itself out, let people decide yes or no to that. It seems to me it derives from the fact that people know that I was a Professor of English, that I knew a lot of literary history, and that there are conscious connections between poems I wrote and poems I read. But it's hard for me to think of any poet of consequence of whom this isn't true. For example, everybody treats Kendrick Smithyman as a great original, but for most of Kendrick's career, although he's always Kendrick, you can pick the poet he was reading when he wrote one poem and the poet he was reading when he wrote another. He wouldn't deny this, I'm sure. The same is true of Curnow: you can see the influence of Dylan Thomas at one point, of Auden at another, Wallace Stevens at another, but no one says that Curnow is being 'derivative', he's just being 'influenced'. It's true of all the poets who matter. Eliot began by speaking with a voice that was almost indistinguishable from Jules Laforgue; and Yeats began speaking with a voice that was almost indistinguishable from William Morris. That's the nature of a tradition. It's a kind of modesty – you can't do it on your own. You're in the stream and the thing is handed on. If you step out of the stream it's not art; it might be craft but it's not art. And insofar as you let the voices of the past speak in your work, that's part of belonging to the great tradition. Of course there might be a point at which there is too much of another voice and not enough of your own. That's for other people to decide. Whereas once I would have been bothered by that accusation, now I probably just look at the credentials of the person who says it and think, well that's somebody I don't have to worry about.

DMcE   This is something you have often emphasised in your criticism, that the unifying principle of a poet's work is the poet's own voice and personality coming through quite disparate things. I don't ever myself have difficulty in hearing Stead's voice. Do you think it's time for a collected Stead?

CKS   Yes, it's time, if there's time. Maybe. I'm old enough for a collected

Stead, but I would like to have time first to settle down and think what I'd like to go into a selected. With a collected it would be good just to shovel it all in. I don't like older poets rewriting their younger work. I think it's a mistake in every case – even Yeats's. I think it's better left alone. Put it all in and let it stand or fall.

DMcE   I'd like to try out on you a quotation from your story 'A Quality of Life', where the narrator says, 'I speak not only to Nova but to the world. In all my writings this is so, because if I spoke to Nova only, Nova would not believe what I had to say was worth listening to. Therefore I speak to the world in order that Nova will listen.' That sounds a lot more sententious than I can imagine Stead being, but I was wondering whether there was any kind of Stead feeling in that.

CKS   I reread that story recently, and felt a certain embarrassment, because it's about a novelist of about the age I am now. But I wrote it when I was young and hadn't published a novel – so I certainly wasn't writing about myself. And if in some ways I've 'grown into the role', nonetheless the distinction between us should be clear. I am not the person who entertained that thought. That said – there's some relationship between 'A Quality of Life' and 'A Fitting Tribute' in that they're both about *reputation* in New Zealand.* But let's shift over to your question, whether I write for the world in order that Nova should listen. I suppose there might be some element of that, but the primary fact is that writers want to be widely read. I don't believe that any writer wouldn't prefer to be read by two thousand people rather than two hundred, or two million rather than two thousand. And so to be published in England and New Zealand is better than just being published in New Zealand; and to be published in New Zealand and England and America is better than just being published in New Zealand and England. And being translated into European languages is another bonus. But the other thing is that for me personally, I feel that I'm not the sort of person who's going to have an easy path in the New Zealand literary scene. Who is? you might say. Well, somebody like Maurice Gee, who's a very competent writer, and a conscientious, uncombative, modest person. His path will be smoothed, much more readily than mine will be. So I feel that publishing outside New Zealand is a kind of protection. I never feel safe on the New Zealand literary scene. I don't know what you think about this, Dennis, you might think it's paranoia, but I always feel I might be just quietly buried here if I didn't have my lines out.

DMcE   I don't know if it's paranoia; I'm not sure it would happen, but I can see your point. The New Zealand literary community is just too small. Every issue tends to become personal. I reread your essay on John Mulgan recently. It seemed to me sensible and sympathetic and just; and yet it aroused tremendous emotion among some of his friends, who felt not only that Stead

---

* Both stories appear in *Five for the Symbol*, Longman Paul, 1981.

was wrong but that Stead was writing to some kind of agenda.

CKS   That's the sort of thing that puzzles me. There are a number of things I've written that have created controversy where I can't understand the source of the irritation. I was writing positively about Mulgan. If anything, a strictly critical view might be that he doesn't deserve the attention I gave him. But in the course of it I questioned a bit of mythology about whether he'd been unjustly deprived of the Rhodes Scholarship –

DMcE   Which is something a biographer must do anyway.

CKS   – and introduced facts which hadn't previously been considered, and this was felt to be some kind of – well, what? I don't really even now understand it. A disturbing of the peace? I picked up the *Penguin History of New Zealand Literature* the other day and found Patrick Evans saying that I had written a 'provocative' essay on Mulgan. Well, it *was* in the sense that it 'provoked' a lot of angry replies; but was it provocative intrinsically? I think not. And again, there was a recent interview with Albert Wendt on the occasion of the publication of his new novel, and the *Star* rang up and said, 'We've got an interview with Albert Wendt; he says you're a racist. Will you take us to court if we print that statement?' And I said, 'I don't know whether I will or not. You'll have to publish it and find out.' So they didn't print that I was a racist; but Wendt did say that I had no sympathy for the damage that had been done to the Maori. And the basis for this was a review I did for the *Listener* of a book by Raj Vasil. I went away and read the review, and also something in my essay 'The New Victorians' which Wendt had objected to. Well, of course it's possible to disagree with me, but my statements were so cautious and careful, I'd been so circumspect, the idea that I should be called a racist for them – it's an example of what I mean by not feeling safe in New Zealand. There are certain givens, and if you don't pay respect to them, if you question them, you're in danger. However, I also believe it's good to live dangerously. Necessary, in New Zealand, if one isn't to become just another intellectual parrot.

DMcE   You've often said your views come primarily from an anxiety for language. I had a friend once who maintained that the only social responsibility of a poet, *qua* poet, was to the state of the language; and obviously the language is in great danger in many of the more fashionable expressions of opinion. I agree with you about that even if I might disagree with some particular statement.

CKS   Also I think that to be concerned with language is to be concerned with everything. You can't measure the language unless you measure it against what's being said and what it's referring to, so concern with the language is politics and society and everything.

With Fleur Adcock, 1991

CKS   To lead off and see where it takes us I thought we might think of ourselves as polar opposites or mirror images – both in some sense New Zealand poets who have made a choice, you to live and write in England, I to live and write in New Zealand, but we each move in the opposite direction from time to time. Then there's the male/female difference. And we've also been at times on opposite sides of what verges on being an argument or debate about form – 'open' form and more traditional forms. So we occupy positions in which each might have chosen the other alternative. There have been times when we've fired shots at one another but it has never seemed to me that either of us has felt it's deeply contentious or difficult to deal with. Perhaps the New Zealand thing first.

FA   I'm used to being attacked by New Zealand critics for my treachery in having decided to live somewhere else and adopt another style, so I don't take that very seriously – and I think half the time it's not intended with hostility, it's just people going through the gestures of examining what it is to be New Zealanders. But we couldn't entirely have chosen to play each other's positions. I couldn't change my sex.

CKS   No, that's true.

FA   That's a start. And also I couldn't change my upbringing, my childhood which took place in England from the age of five to the age of thirteen, and that is one of the basic things I don't think New Zealand critics take on board sufficiently when they talk about my having sold out and transferred my allegiances. I've talked to you about this before haven't I? – about bluebells and all this stuff: that the natural energies of my childhood are not beaches and pohutukawa and ti-tree and bush. They are bluebells, English woods with squirrels, and English seasons – Christmas in winter with carol singing in the dark.

CKS   The things which in New Zealand are seen as traditionally literary and therefore artificial.

FA   Yes, and to me they are not at all artificial. Those are what I grew up with. We used to go and play in the woods – that was where you played

---

Landfall 181, March 1992. The conversation took place at Fleur Adcock's house in London, 26 August 1991. Fleur Adcock, New Zealand-born poet, permanently resident in London since 1963. Stead and Adcock are the only two New Zealand writers to be elected Fellows of the Royal Society of Literature.

when I was a kid in various places. We moved around a lot, but there were always these constants of the leaves falling off the trees in autumn and the snow coming. Then the spring coming and the primroses coming out, and going to the woods and picking them. Also I was away from New Zealand in a much larger, much more difficult sense because I was here during the Second World War and I felt very involved with the patriotic feelings that we had at the time – the air raids and things that were happening on the fringes of our lives. So I was probably a most unpleasant teenager when I arrived back at the age of thirteen. I think I was despised for my English accent and my skinny legs and my inability to play any kind of sport. I was different.

CKS   I, of course, spent all my childhood in New Zealand, came to England for the first time as a post-graduate student having taught for a year and a half in Australia first, and took away from New Zealand a romantic notion of being a New Zealand writer – a sense almost of being in at a beginning. I was fortunate enough to have had Allen Curnow as a teacher at the university and to have got to know Frank Sargeson while I was still a student, so I had those two mentors.

FA   Well, I can understand that. I mean to me it seems perfectly logical that you should have made those choices. Rather enviable. You *were* in at the beginning. It's like having been in there with Shakespeare and Marlowe, with New Zealand literature having begun when it did. And if I had grown up in those circumstances I might have felt the same. *Of course* it would have been a romantic choice. I'm sure you did the right thing in view of your work, what's come out.

CKS   Well, I don't know about that. I think there's a whole other scenario, but the trouble is you can only ever live one of them.

FA   Yes, but surely you have lived two, though. You've got your critical self as well and that's on an international field.

CKS   I always wanted to write fiction and couldn't really write it substantially until I left the university, or consistently, and I think with fiction you do have to put down a body of work regularly and gradually build up a readership. If I had been really daring I could have done that much earlier here in London. But I always thought in terms of going back to New Zealand, and it wasn't possible to be a full-time writer in New Zealand. That was where the academic employment came in. I enjoyed that for a long time, although I stopped enjoying it some time before I stopped doing it. What about you now? You came over here and worked as a librarian for quite some time?

FA   Yes, fifteen years. I came in 1963 and I worked as a librarian until 1979 with one year off in the 1977–78 academic year. I had a fellowship in the Lake District at a teachers' college – an Arts Council fellowship – and that more or less ruined me for going back to work. So I dropped out after a year and dropped into the Northern Arts Fellowship in Newcastle and Durham which gave me two good years of a grant. I built up freelance contacts I suppose – made it clear that I was available for this, that and the other. And it's been a struggle but then it's worth it.

CKS   Now to change tack: I've been asking you about your reaction to my 'Wystan to Carlos' lecture which caused a great deal of, I was going to say irritation but I suppose I have to admit it also caused a lot of interest, and one should never complain if one's work is noticed. But there was a distinctly negative tone in your references to it, so this seems to me a point where we have apparently differed and we should talk about it.

FA   I didn't really feel that I was attacking it so much as referring to it and using it as a useful exposition of what had been happening in New Zealand while I was away. It was during the time I was compiling *The Oxford Book of Contemporary New Zealand Poetry* and I'd missed a lot of years. I had been reading such poetry as came my way or that I could get hold of when I was in England but when I went back and started seriously doing more reading your article just seemed to help to fill in some of the gaps. And I suppose it wasn't hostility that I felt so much as a kind of bemusement that the literary inhabitants of New Zealand seemed to be obsessed with whether or not something was in 'open form', which, to those of us who live in a world you also inhabit where poetry is written in all kinds of forms, seems a very limited way of examining things.

CKS   To me it was a piece of literary history. It was an attempt to change the terms, because there has to be a set of terms, some kind of structure, there have to be points of reference. The terms in which New Zealand poetry had been historically discussed had been Curnow's and all I did was to say let's propose a different set of terms and see what the picture looks like if we do that. But the other thing was that at that time I was writing a book, my last big literary-historical book – I mean by 'last' that I would never do it again – in which Pound figured. It was an attempt to look again at the area I had covered in *The New Poetic,* but this time putting Pound into the picture as the central figure. So that was why those were the terms I chose, because they were ready to hand.

FA   Yes, and I do recall being rather leery about Pound, or that he figured too large for a natural map. But a lot of it I just found interesting – New Zealand seemed like a very foreign country to me, which it does increasingly now every time I go there; it seems more and more foreign and hard to understand and I need to learn more, the language is changing. Everything is changing.

CKS   I think New Zealand has become more in-turned and in that degree provincial. It's odd that along with what's supposed to be national self-confidence has come an in-turning of consciousness, a preoccupation with local problems. It struck me particularly during 1990. This was the year in which some of the great events of modern history were happening, the year in which the Berlin Wall came down and the Cold War came to an end and democracy began to emerge in Eastern Europe. And New Zealand was obsessed with things which in terms of the great issues of the twentieth century and in terms of the great sufferings and injustices that have been inflicted upon human beings, were minor.

FA	I feel and have felt passionately about what was happening in Eastern Europe. I have spent time in Romania, I have translated from Romanian poetry, I have a lot of Romanian friends who were all writing me letters once they could write without being censored about what it was like under Ceaucescu, and exploding with all the experiences they had to relate – 'at last we are free', 'I saw a truckload full of dead soldiers', 'blood on the snow' – all of these things. What was New Zealand going on about during that time? I don't know. So, yes, it's the nationalism thing. It's also another thing in New Zealand which you come up against, the Polynesian thing. I was bewildered the first time I heard a government minister beginning a speech with … some sort of Maori chant or introduction, and all the audience obviously understood. They'd been going to evening classes, had they, or how did everybody suddenly learn Maori?

CKS	Well, there's a certain amount of pretence isn't there? A great deal of pretence. All I would say about that is, yes, we're talking about degrees of change and there's been a huge one there, but one which we couldn't embark on in this conversation or we would get way off what our problem is.

FA	Yes, right, let's stay in safe waters.

CKS	No, it's not so much safety as relevance. Let's just acknowledge that's a characteristic area of change. Coming back to the question of form, it would be interesting if we could talk a little bit more about this. We don't have adequate terms, but let's for the moment talk about closed and open forms. I have never felt prescriptive on this issue, particularly because I wouldn't want to be prescribed to. My most recent book of poems in fact was commissioned for 1990, I was commissioned to write a poem. What I finally wrote was a sequence of poems which is published as a book and the only way I could see to do this was to write an historical sequence in which I took characters from every phase of our history from the beginning right through; I felt this very much had to be conscious work, you know. It was a commission that had to be met, and the only way I could do it, because the material was going to be historical, was to go back more to what you might say were the forms that most people wrote in when I was young, more like the forms that I would have written in in the 1950s, basically five-stress lines. A lot of them were sonnets. I worked in fairly unobtrusive rhyme patterns, so that the rhyme scheme for example in most of the sonnets is very tight but they're not obtrusive, they're not rhymes which clang on the ear, so they're there for the expert reader of poetry more than for the casual reader.

FA	Well, that's what rhymes should be there for. That's what most of mine are for.

CKS	I really enjoyed doing that. It was hard work and I often found that the work on getting the thing into rhyme improved the quality of the writing.

FA	This is what poets have been saying ever since the Middle Ages.

CKS	But what I'm doing is acknowledging that though I have

experimented in the other way – and there are very good reasons for that – I don't want either possibility to be closed off, and I don't see why anybody should want either possibility to be closed off.

FA   Nor do I, and I try to write in as many styles as I can, and I have tried to write in, well not experimental styles which you would perhaps regard as such, but I also write in rhymed forms when I happen to be in that mental state, and one of the things that affects it is translations I have been doing. I've spent the last couple of years on and off translating medieval Latin poems which rhyme into more or less rhymed English. But I would hate to think that people could predict what kind of poem I was going to write next or what the form was going to be – I think we should all be able to turn our hand to anything. The last thing I wrote was a little rhymed set of verses about hedgehogs for a children's anthology. Of course something like that has to be in rhyme if it is for kids. But on the other hand sometimes I think my most profound utterances come out in free verse of some kind because that is what speaks out of the depths of your – wherever it comes from.

CKS   There's another thing that comes into this question for me and that is the motivation for experimenting with longer poems. Again this is not an absolute, it's not a prescription, it's simply describing a feeling of restriction, or artificiality, about short poem after short poem, each of which is shaped from a beginning through a middle to an end. Sometimes you want something which gets nearer – since I think a lot of the impulse is a mimetic impulse – a bit nearer to life as it really happens. So that's the whole notion, I suppose, of the process poem, where it isn't shaped in that way; it tends to run on, and there's more of a feeling of … the best analogy I think is the one of feeling more that you're inside the artist's studio than that you're in the gallery with the pictures finally hung and framed.

FA   Ah, yes. I see it in different terms. I see it in terms of the long poem being more like a relationship or a marriage or a long affair, and the short poems have been described to me as 'all those little one-night stands'. With the short poem you begin with this passionate impulse, you fulfil it and it's over, whereas with the long poem you can get up at breakfast time and there it still is. That's something I would like to have waiting for me at my desk. Yes, I can see that and I don't discount such poems by any means. I enjoy reading them and I would like to be able to write them – they just don't seem to happen so much.

CKS   Now maybe we can move on to something else. I was thinking of the situation of being a woman writer, a woman poet. Can I first of all ask, do you feel that in your lifetime as a writer you've been discriminated against because you're a woman?

FA   I'm sure I have in the past without really noticing it, and looking back now I can see it constantly. It is apparent even now although the bookshops are full of books by women poets and so are the festivals and readings. The very fashionable thing to do is to have lots of women at any festival or reading, but if you hear some male critic talking about the poets who mean something to him in his mental map you will find they are all male apart from Emily Dickinson, and possibly Elizabeth Bishop if you are talking to Craig Raine. It's still somehow assumed that the top spots are occupied by the guys and the women are somewhere on the lower slopes.

In other words, I think we're just not taken quite so seriously. People think it's a good thing that we're all doing it, but it doesn't have to impinge on them. But in professional terms I don't think that, as far as I can tell, any poems or books of mine have been rejected because I was female. I've certainly found that I identify far more with other women. I'm delighted that there are so many women writing and I expressed that by doing an anthology of them which was very important for me.

CKS   Well, you probably know I've said I don't believe that in New Zealand any editor in my lifetime has ever discriminated against a woman on the basis that she was a woman. I think the only thing I could be persuaded of is a possibility – but it would have to be illustrated in particular cases – that there might be a notion of excellence which is long established and is essentially a male notion; and that there are other possible notions of excellence.

FA   This is what feminist critics talk about as the line of the patriarchy.

CKS   Yes, and that's a plausible possibility but very difficult to demonstrate and extremely difficult to prove. And of course one could take the view that there is something in the scope of the major poets which has to do with masculinity – which might really be saying the same thing in a different way. But you know it doesn't seem to me there has ever been a problem about seeing, say, Katherine Mansfield as the major New Zealand literary figure. One has never seen any sign that Janet Frame ever encountered any problems at all in getting herself recognised as a writer.

FA   Ah, yes, but these are prose writers, and women have always been recognised as good at prose fiction – Jane Austen, the Brontës – that was something that they had established they could do. It was poetry where there was this vatic relationship, with the prophet figure and the relationship with the muse – all of that.

CKS   Can I really pin you down on this one? You did an anthology of New Zealand poetry in which you chose seventeen men and three women. If I had made that anthology I would never be forgiven and it would be held against me as a demonstration that I was sexist and couldn't see the merit of women writers.

FA   There just weren't so many in New Zealand at that time. This is ten years ago we're talking about. There just weren't so many. Nor were there in England. The great flowering of women's poetry began – and even Lauris had hardly started writing then – about 1980. The same here with the Motion/Morrison anthology, *The Penguin Book of Contemporary British Poetry*, it came out about that time and there weren't so many women in that – there were five out of twenty-five – more or less the same ratio. The editors of that were attacked and if they ever did another edition, which they haven't, they said they would try to include more women. There would be more to include now. It's just that we have taken longer to get off the ground. There is also this other phenomenon which I mentioned in the introduction to my Faber anthology, of the late starter – and Lauris Edmond is the perfect example. But there have been so many examples, it's almost taken for granted that this is the way women's lives develop – whether it's to do with family or to do with confidence or to do with other things.

CKS   Or to do with the climate.

FA   Or the climate – that they have felt 'I can't be bothered going on with this because nobody is taking any notice and nobody is interested'. Now people *are* interested, they are all writing and bringing it out and going on to write the next one because the one before has been published. I think there must have just been a general heavy fog of discouragement settling over a lot of women poets ...

CKS   Writers of every kind and particularly poets always have to overcome, to surmount obstacles, to create a readership, to persuade editors that they are worth noticing, and the career characteristically of a poet who has any success is a gradual overcoming of these obstacles. If you take this sort of view of a generalised and pervasive gender bias, then every obstacle that you have to overcome gets interpreted in terms of that.

FA   Well, in that case you can't win.

CKS   Well, it can be put around the other way – that the male can't win, because every obstacle he encounters is a fair one, it's just a literary opinion. But every obstacle that the woman writer encounters is a gender bias. It's like the problem of if there is anti-Semitism then every time somebody doesn't like a Jew it must be anti-Semitism.

FA   Sure. Yes. No, I think these things are changed with history and I think there are different obstacles to be overcome now; one of them is the fact there is this avid appetite for poetry from women, so a lot of poetry that isn't maybe as good as it should be gets welcomed and published. But if we talked again in five years' time even – it moves as quickly as that – I think we would find that the climate was probably different. I've seen it changing so remarkably.

CKS   The trouble is that as soon as these categories get introduced they have a negative as well as a positive effect. As soon as it becomes kosher to balance up the sexes and the races in an anthology the question then is, is somebody in the anthology because he's a Maori, or because she's a woman?

FA   Yes, exactly as in some of your 'Clodian' poems, the one I think you got attacked for – who was the woman? Suffenia or somebody, going off with all the literary prizes. Oh, yes, sure; positive discrimination's a bad thing in any area.

CKS   It's interesting to hear you say that because it always gets blurred with equal opportunity and we have EEO committees – equal opportunity committees – which then bring in positive discrimination and it seems to me in logic that positive discrimination contradicts equal opportunity.

FA It's different in the field of employment because everybody has to earn a living and it's fair that women should have equal goes at getting a job, but not everybody has to get published.

CKS It's fair that everybody should have equal goes at everything, but that doesn't mean the result is going to come out numerically equal. We had better not get into the general area, but perhaps we could take this a bit further. Do you feel that there is a generalised feminine sensibility? I mean, when I think of the field of male writers in New Zealand, what I'm most conscious of is how different I feel from all the rest.

FA Yes, I suppose we all feel different from all the rest of everybody, but I'm glad that I have discovered I was a woman. I've said this before – it sounds ridiculous – but for a lot of my first years of my writing career I didn't think of myself as a woman and my models were male poets because that was who you read, that was all there was to read, and I thought Catullus and Donne were the people who lay behind my work perhaps at some point, and they happened to be male because in those days poets were. But I'm now glad that I've got an audience of women that I'm writing for, in a sense, and in some of the poems I write I'm happy to think these will make sense to women. They may also make sense to men, but I can do without that, whereas twenty years ago if I hadn't made sense to men I wouldn't have got into print.

CKS Again I'm just feeling my way towards this, but the writers in New Zealand that I feel some sort of kinship with, in terms not so much of what's actually down on the page as of the kind of sensibility that's there in the writing, are women – with the exception of Curnow. And although Curnow and I respect one another so much and are such good literary allies, we're very different kinds of writers. This doesn't mean that I feel in the least a feminine writer. I feel as though I'm entirely a masculine writer. But the question of a kind of sensibility it seems to me is slightly separate from the question of sex.

FA Yes, yes. Well, I would have to stop for a long time to think about examples, but of course there are a lot of good male poets with whom I feel that kind of kinship. But then I'm used to feeling kinship with male poets because they're what I've been reading since the age of six …

CKS I've taken issue with feminists, and I've teased them in my novel *The Death of the Body,* but when I'm writing fiction I always feel that I do women characters much better than men characters. Really I've come to the conclusion in writing fiction that all your characters are yourself, but if you're male you can be a woman character without the fear of self-identification.

FA Because if you're in drag they can't pick the bits that are you.

CKS I think drag's a bad analogy, actually, because I'm thinking of the representation of those areas which are not specifically sexual – which men and women have in common.

FA Another thing, though, there is the famous cliché, almost, that women are easier to get to know, women talk about themselves, women let their emotions come out; men are far more guarded and don't talk about their feelings. It is generally recognised that men and women speak different languages, that men talk for competition, in fact, and women talk for closeness and intimacy. I remember a television programme where there were three men and one woman talking about literature – the woman was Patricia Beer. She was hardly allowed to get a word in and when she could they looked rather condescending and waited for her to finish. Then when they started – sparklers, fireworks, it was all real show-off stuff. It was to impress the television audience and to impress each other. I felt very sorry for Patricia Beer, who was saying sensible things but not sounding quite so exciting. I realised afterwards of course it was because she was female and it is how it is ...

CKS   Well, I think that's just a cliché ...

FA   It is a cliché, but it's a *true* one.

CKS   No, because it was Patricia Beer. If it had been Germaine Greer ...

FA   Oh, well she's ...

CKS   ... if it had been A.S. Byatt or Iris Murdoch. I mean there are redoubtable women and mousy men. But if you find a mousy man, you say that's untypical, but if you find a ...

FA   I wouldn't say Patricia Beer is mousy.

CKS   Well, I don't know Patricia Beer, but I think that could simply be put in reverse.

FA   This is just one instance of something that is so common that I would hardly have bothered to put it into words before ...

CKS   Well, while we're on this contentious issue, I remember you read a poem once, about a case, a law case.*

FA   Oh yes.

CKS   And I remember thinking, now that's one of the traps of thinking in gender clichés. It was about how the whole courtroom setup was meant to intimidate women.

FA   But it *did*. It was a case and this is actually based on fact, I was there, and we all felt intimidated.

CKS   Sure, but don't you think the court is equally set up to intimidate men, and does?

FA   No, the man in the case was not intimidated enough. But in the end the judge gave him – it was a custody case, and the judge made a judgement which was a compromise, and granted the mother not total custody of the child but care and control, because the judge seemed to think the father who was a very violent man would mend his ways. Well, violent men don't mend their ways, only a male judge would think *for a moment* that that was likely to happen. It was a deep emotional problem this man had. He was never going to change, but a female judge would discern that.

---

* 'Witnesses', in *The Incident Book* by Fleur Adcock, OUP, Oxford, 1986.

CKS   But he didn't get custody.

FA   No, but he got a lot of access. He was given so much access that that family has been having problems ever since.

CKS   You mean he shouldn't have had any access.

FA   He shouldn't have had the kind of access he had. Care and control means that he still had a say over the child's future. If the woman had had custody, he would have had a limited kind of access which was that he couldn't make any decisions about the child, that he could just visit occasionally. It just happens to be a poem that a lot of people including male critics … John Lucas, in the *New Statesman,* singled out and said it wouldn't have meant so much to him if he hadn't recently come up against something very similar and realised how true it was.

CKS   I just think, leaving aside the question of who got custody, because I seem to remember that didn't emerge in the poem, and that I asked you afterwards …

FA   I usually tell people afterwards.

CKS   Because the poem gave the impression that the man got custody, when in fact he didn't. But what I remember was thinking that part of the point of the poem was that the panoply of the court is designed to intimidate women when in fact it's designed to intimidate *everybody,* men and women; and the further you are down the social scale the more you're intimidated. A well-set-up confident educated middle-class woman is going to be less intimidated by the court than say a working-class, cloth-capped man.

FA   Sure, but there was also the fact that this was a case of domestic violence to which the male establishment is notoriously unsympathetic – women are still regarded as chattels in a very real sense in a lot of situations. Another thing in the poem that I was trying to bring out was the way to make ourselves be respected and taken seriously. We had to disguise ourselves as men, so we were wearing dark respectable clothes, conforming to the male idea of respectability. If we had turned up in short skirts and scarlet t-shirts then we would not have been taken seriously as witnesses. So I said something about 'We three in our dark decent clothes, unlike ourselves'. You have to dress like men.

CKS   How would the man have been treated if he'd arrived in shorts and jandals? You see my view of all these things is, not that they're totally wrong, or that there isn't an element of truth in them, but as soon as something has been parroted by everybody my natural scepticism goes into operation …

FA   Well, I'm not supposed to deny it because it happens to be generally accepted? The fact that a lot of other people feel it too doesn't mean that it's not valid.

CKS   No. No, no. I don't think you should deny it. Obviously you believe it. But I'm just explaining why temperamentally my scepticism goes into top gear when it seems to me that the issue is in fact complicated and is being expressed simply.

FA   Of course it's complicated. We haven't got time to write treatises about the situation of the sexes in 1991.
CKS   Well, this has been a good topic to get on to because obviously our views of it are different and it would be terrible if we agreed on everything.
FA   Well, I suppose we would have nothing to say.
CKS   Perhaps we should stop for a minute now and ...
        [A break here for a walk in the woods. Tape begins with talk about translations.]
FA   I'm interested in the way you've used Catullus and classical authors in your poetry, particularly the 'Clodian Songbook', and how you take off from a poem of Catullus which is really quite unlike what comes out in the end. How did you work on those, how did you go about that?
CKS   They're obviously not translations and I can't pretend to know Latin. I occasionally did something that was *like* a translation, not of the words but of the situation, into a New Zealand and personal context. Other times the poem just takes off from some point in Catullus and goes in its own direction. But it's again a question of first-person poetry and difficulty in creating male characters – the inhibition about anything that might seem to be making claims for oneself. So the speaker in the poem becomes a persona somewhere between myself and Catullus. That allows me a freedom to use personal experience, to invent experiences I've never had, and to adapt experience of Catullus's, in a mixture which is determined by the poem. The poem gets in control instead of either me or Catullus or facts.
FA   Yes, it gives you the opportunity for some lovely literary digs such as the one about the Book Awards that I'm sure everybody was convinced was Stead speaking, when you talk about the feminist and statutory Polynesian winning the prizes. I haven't looked at the original.
CKS   Yes, well every one of these poems has its source in Catullus, but they differ in the degree of closeness or distance. Once I've established that 'Catullus' voice, I can do that sort of thing with a freedom I wouldn't feel if I was speaking in my own.
FA   Oh, yes, and it's much more effective too. It's funnier.
CKS   What about yourself? You really *are* a Latinist.
FA   I'm a very literal-minded translator because, I suppose, I'm bringing something out of obscurity, something that I want people to know about which is not part of the standard repertoire of classical literature. The Latin poets I've translated have been medieval so they are not all very well known. And I've also been doing two poets I was commissioned to translate for Cambridge University Press for a scholarly edition which has caused me great toil and anguish because I had to write footnotes as well and I'm no good at that. These are twelfth-century Latin poets. Well, they are not Latin of course – they are writing in Latin. We don't know what nationality, but possibly one of them is French and one is German. Then the other language I translated from was Romanian and again this was a matter of trying to show the world

something that it hadn't read in English before; these were poets of about the post-war generation, born round about 1950. There were two I have translated to book-length and another one I have translated a few bits and pieces of. I had learnt Romanian, but I made sure that a native Romanian speaker saw my versions after I had done them so that I didn't have too many howlers in the text.

CKS   It is a Latin language, anyway.

FA   It's a Romance language, yes. That's why it was not impossible to learn. It was fascinating doing it; I love learning languages. You forget them very quickly if you learn them quickly but it was an entry into another culture.

CKS   My only experience of the kind of thing you're talking about is when I translate from French because that's the only language I can claim to know in the sense that I know its grammar and its structures and have a decent vocabulary and that I read easily. So translation is *real* translation. The original has to dominate, and you have to be faithful to it. My freedom in using, say, Latin or Japanese is the freedom of ignorance. It's the kind of freewheeling use of something for your own purposes, rather than serving it.

FA   Yes, in one instance you did what Zukofsky did, you played with the words – in the poem about those rude words *pedicabo et te* ... puns on the words.

CKS   There's another where I pun on the *sound* of the Latin words – 'and is it/are you wanting/when darkness knocks/perpetual dormitory', (*'Nox perpetua dormienda'*). But there are two poems in the *Quesada* book that are from the French. One is the 'Pont Mirabeau', the Apollinaire poem, and that has such a beautiful form in the French that the only thing you can try to do is to find an equivalent for that form, the first stanza of the French goes (from memory):

> Sous le Pont Mirabeau coule la Seine
> Et nos amours
> Faut-il qu'il m'en souviens
> La joie venait toujours apres la peine
> *Vienne la nuit, sonne l'heure*
> *Les jours s'en vont, je demeure.*

So you have to try and repeat the pattern, with an equivalent refrain. The other one is the Baudelaire poem, 'The Swan'. I think they have to be judged as translations, and I know they're not such good poems because I was so constrained by the original. But it's an exercise that I've always loved doing. I remember as a student I used to love trying to push a French poem into exactly the same form and rhyme scheme and sense in English.

FA   That's just what I was doing with the Latin ones. The craft, the techniques, the thing you are supposed to be able to do, like the way visual artists have to learn to draw before they can start launching out like Picasso and Matisse. You have to have the basic ... skills.

CKS   The other thing that this might lead on to is the question that I was talking to you about earlier of people of our age having grown up with a particular and fairly stable notion of literary tradition which is breaking down everywhere but perhaps at double speed in New Zealand, because as well as the general breakdown there is the post-colonial rejection of the parent tradition. I still think that it's a great help to have some common ground, and that it should be a rich common ground.

FA   Yes, otherwise you're up on your own and it's terribly sad. I remember a friend of mind who had taught in Australia had a student at school complaining and saying, 'Oh we don't want to read Milton – aren't there any seventeenth-century Australian poets we could read?' They had no idea of what tradition there was, it was all ...

CKS   ... of their own history ...

FA   ... no idea of their own history or the history of the world or anything. Of course if you live in the moment, if you live in your post-colonial moment, then you've lost everything up to wherever it is. So, yes it was certainly a very straight up and down standard Eng. Lit. tradition that we had when I was in school in New Zealand. I went to school here as well of course but back there, when I went back in 1947, it was Milton and Browning and Shakespeare ... We had a little bit of Ursula Bethell and one or two poems by living New Zealand poets ... but that was about it. Mostly they were British and dead, but you have got to read them, yes; where would you be if you hadn't? And of course I didn't get all of them at school, a lot of them I just found for myself. I almost forget now which ones – I used to sit in the school library at Wellington Girls' College – it wasn't bad, the school library – and I read people like MacNeice and Day Lewis, pretty modern poets then, and Eliot I was besotted with. We had had him in class. And then all sorts of other things just filling in gaps, reading people like Ibsen and educating myself and reading what was in the bookshelves at home. So, it was all the classics I suppose ...

CKS   The only New Zealand poet I encountered at school, I mean the only one that was introduced by a teacher, was R.A.K. Mason. Very shortly after that I discovered Curnow's anthology. But the same teacher introduced us to T.S. Eliot. We were having a class – it's interesting that I remember where it happened, we were in the library not in the classroom – and he suddenly began to read,

> The river's tent is broken; the last fingers of leaf
> Clutch and sink into the wet bank. The wind
> Crosses the brown land, unheard. The nymphs are departed.

I thought, 'What is this?' It made my scalp tingle.

With Terry Locke, 1996

TL   In your submission on the Draft Curriculum on behalf of the Education Forum, you describe it as having the flavour and emphasis of a document designed to foster social accommodation and amelioration rather than excellence. What do you mean by 'social accommodation and amelioration'?
CKS   Putting it briefly, the consideration of the social outcome of what goes on in the classroom rather than the academic outcome.
TL   Did you see a kind of a social agenda or a particular ideology operating in the draft?
CKS   Not quite an ideology; rather it is a value system. It's a question of whether you consider the study of English primarily as an instrument for producing certain social outcomes.
TL   There's quite a big continuum between the study of English as an academic object and English for social use. Let's come back to another word you use. 'Excellence' is a word that resonates right through your submission. In your view what is excellence in English?
CKS   It's using language excellently and it is reading excellent examples of it in a way that comprehends and makes the best of them. Everything I say on this is based on the premise that the teaching of English should foster better rather than worse uses in the child's writing and speaking, and foster acquaintance with better rather than worse uses in literature. Excellence is what you strive towards – not necessarily what you achieve. I'm aware that this can cause problems because better and worse uses of the language and capacity for using the language may have a correlation with social stratification. My view is that your job as an English teacher is not to consider those questions too closely but just to get on with your job.
TL   I'm wondering what sort of common ground we can find here. I don't personally use the word 'excellent' very much but I do use words like 'effective'. For me literacy and literature has to do with the ability to be effective in one's use of language in a wide variety of contexts. Have we got a quarrel?

English in Aotearoa (the Journal of New Zealand Teachers of English), May 1996. The conversation took place in Auckland over two sessions. Many of the points made in my submission, and discussed here with Dr Locke, can be found in the third lecture, 'English in Our Schools', in Part 2 of this book. Terry Locke was a senior school English teacher, and is now a lecturer in language education at Waikato University.

CKS   When you talk about better and worse you're talking about a spectrum, and at one end of the spectrum is excellence.
TL   If this keeps going we're going to have sets of criteria for excellence. I'm just wondering whether behind your view there's a kind of aestheticism which separates or compartmentalises a particular kind of language use – let's call it literature – from life, and that allows itself to judge excellence without reference to other kinds of considerations such as the social purpose for which a piece of writing might have been produced.
CKS   Well, that statement, to my mind, confuses kinds of language which have a purpose extraneous to themselves, and works of literature which don't. The piece I wrote for the Education Forum has a clear purpose which is to influence the final form of the English syllabus. If I write a novel it hasn't any clear extraneous purpose other than to be a work of art in its own right, irrespective of what uses may be made of it. I don't see that to make that distinction is correctly described as 'aestheticism', although aesthetics – the art of the novel – is relevant and important.
TL   We've moved a little bit away from my mixed ability fourth form English classroom here. There may be some shades of difference between you and me as to how we might want to define excellence of a literary text.
CKS   The question might be whether you should have a mixed ability fourth form.
TL   Well, I want to come back to streaming because it's something you're hot on.
CKS   I'm not hot on it, but I think that not having it must create enormous problems.
TL   I would say it creates interesting opportunities.
CKS   Well, yes, you might say that. We could debate this.
TL   I want to come back to critical literacy and the question of the status of literature. Clearly this was something you felt was being endangered by the drift of the document.
CKS   I don't think the status of literature is endangered by the curriculum, but I think the curriculum is endangered by not giving literature its proper status. Literature is literature. It's not endangered by what you do in a syllabus. It's there anyway, but if you don't give it its proper status then the syllabus is that much worse.
TL   My position is that literary texts have a place alongside other texts in terms of the development of the student's critical literacy. I would define the major goal of an English programme as critical literacy which involves mastery of a range of linguistic practices over a range of linguistic contexts. It seems to me that what the document was attempting to do was to acknowledge the potential range of texts rather than in some way to diminish the value of literature.
CKS   The literary requirements weren't specific enough and weren't clearly enough set out as requirements. It was too easy for teachers to avoid

them if they chose. And the focus is largely on the less talented. It's as though you can leave the more talented to look after themselves. They're not presented with the demanding opportunities that they would once have been presented with, when English was a more, one might say, narrowly academic subject.

TL	When I was at school English was narrow but it wasn't necessarily academic. In fact, I would say that it didn't really encourage a great deal of curiosity about language.

I want to ask you about some of the expressions you used in your rather passionately written submission, expressions like 'the intellectual life of a community'. In a statement about talented students you wrote, 'On their talent will depend the level of civilisation our society is collectively capable of in the future.' That smacks of élitism.

CKS	Oh, yes. I'm an élitist. Just as a rugby supporter believes that the best players should go into the All Blacks. You have to use the best talents in society by recognising, promoting and rewarding them. Otherwise society falls down around your ears. For some reason we recognise that in some areas and we try to blind ourselves to it in others. We don't say anybody can be a nuclear physicist, or anybody can do advanced mathematics.

TL	You've said, 'On their talent will depend a level of civilisation.' My reaction to this is that some fairly terrible things have been done in the name of civilisation. As I see it, civilisation is a cultural construct and it's often constructed upon premises that may well be agreed upon by people in power but not necessarily by those who aren't.

CKS	The fact that people sometimes do bad things in the name of civilisation doesn't alter for me the truth of what I was asserting.

TL	I mean, élitism is who's best.

CKS	If élitist means recognising excellence, promoting it and rewarding it, then I'm an élitist. As I say, we're not democratic about who goes into the All Blacks.

TL	Well, in that sense I'm an élitist too. I strive very hard to ensure that students I would call talented are given extension. I suppose my question with respect to civilisation is, would you rather be governed by the best minds in the country or the best hearts in the country?

CKS	Well, it's an unreal choice, isn't it? I mean, if you're saying to me that people can be highly intelligent and dangerous, that's obviously true. But if that's used as an argument against what I said, then the logic would be that you would suppress intelligent people because they were potentially dangerous – as Pol Pot did in Cambodia. The question you're raising is really totally irrelevant. All I'm saying is that there are various levels of ability in the study and teaching of English which is your profession and has been mine. We should pay a great deal of attention to the people who are of higher ability, promote and encourage them. Encourage them to see the study of English not as easy and cosy but as something which is intellectually demanding, so they're drawn to go on with it; and do all we can to make them articulate and useful and recognised in society.

TL	Right. I don't think we're afraid of extending our best pupils. I think we are wanting pupils to question very broad constructs, like civilisation, which has been used in the past to oppress. So again, I'm back to the idea of critical literacy. I mean, I think we're in agreement in terms of wanting to ensure that our most gifted people intellectually don't go to sleep in our classrooms.

CKS	Look, you're getting hung up on this word 'civilisation'. Just think what the Nazis did in the name of order. What's the logical consequence of that? That we should promote disorder because Nazis promoted order?

TL	Not at all. Just ensure that we keep questioning these, what you would call 'pieties'.

CKS	Yeah, well *[laughs]* okay.

TL	Grammar. What grammatical knowledge do you think a junior secondary school student should have? How would you teach it?

CKS	They should have a simple set of grammatical terms and a few basic rules about how language works. We all know that grammatical terms are in some sense illusory. The language develops its own rules and then we apply them. So long as you see grammar as descriptive rather than prescriptive – that's what I think is important, because you do have to allow for the fact that the rules, the conventions, are always changing. The best way to get grammar is studying a language other than our own. Our grammar is built into us and we're not conscious of it. It becomes much clearer when you learn a foreign language. But I still think in English it should be taught.

TL	Most English teachers would say, 'Yes, students need a basic vocabulary – metalanguage – to talk about language. But to make sense it has to be taught in a relevant context of use, rather than as an isolated set of facts.'

CKS	That's for teachers at the appropriate level to say rather than for me to say.

TL	You write that there is no significant evidence to suggest that the ability to speak basic English and to watch it and understand it on television is diminishing, but there are signs that literacy is being lost. On what do you base the claim that literacy is being lost?

CKS	Partly on the evidence of students coming to the university and how much they appear to have read. It's an impression, but not of mine alone. It's an impression of a lot of people at the university, including my wife who's a librarian and deals across the counter with students a lot of the time, and of some of the school teachers I speak to. I suppose it is inevitable in a television age.

TL	What actually do you mean by literacy?

CKS	I was talking about reading and writing.

TL	So you wouldn't see literacy as extending to a person's ability to conduct themselves in an oral situation.

CKS	No.

TL	Rather ironically the issue of *English in Aotearoa* this interview is appearing in is devoted to oral language. A feeling that I got from your submission is that you believe that oral language will develop anyway ... so our job as English teachers is to focus on reading and writing. For my part I dispute that, but I wanted to check with you that I'm interpreting you right.

CKS   I do believe in teaching and encouraging spoken English, but I think the reading and writing part of the subject is far more important and shouldn't be put on the same level.

TL   How do you react to the term 'oracy', as a kind of a parallel to literacy?

CKS   I don't particularly like it, but I don't have any strong objection to it.

TL   Just extending this a little bit – in the address you gave at the New Zealand Association of Teachers of English conference in Christchurch in 1982 you said, 'In all reading that has any literary element the ear is more important than the eye.' Now I extend that myself to lots of non-literary argumentative texts also. Doesn't this suggest the real importance of spoken language or the oral component of language or even to the primacy of these things?

CKS   Not to the primacy. The ear component in literature is important because, as well as conveying precise meaning, the work of literature is also a verbal composition which is meant to be heard either in imagination or in fact. The words are arranged in ways which balance and echo one another, most obviously in poetry where you hear the rhymes, but there are many other and subtler aural elements. You don't actually have to hear it read aloud but you must at least imagine hearing it in order to get that sound component. But that's not the same as talking.

TL   How important do you think talk is in an English Language programme?

CKS   It's important. You have to encourage students to express themselves and to have a vocabulary that they can call upon reasonably quickly and proficiently. But I'm not sympathetic to the idea of the English classroom as a place where people sit around expressing feelings and emotions and opinions. The emphasis in the classroom has gone over too far towards that, away from the student receiving information from an expert person who is a teacher.

TL   You wouldn't be particularly sympathetic to the current vogue which defines a teacher as a facilitator rather than an expert.

CKS   No, no I'm not.

TL   Do you support streaming as a teaching strategy?

CKS   I realise there are social problems particularly where, having an A, B and a C class might throw up, say, racial distinctions. It comes down, I suppose, to whether you decide that the academic problem is the one to be solved or the social problem. Where you have to choose between those, my predisposition is to solve the academic problem and let the social problem be sorted out somewhere else.

TL   On the matter of social problems, in the submission you wrote you compare the promotion of gender equity with the promotion of racial purity in Nazi Germany. That seems a fairly extreme analogy to me.

CKS   Well, it would be an extreme analogy if that was the form in which I put it. What I did was to list a number of societies quite unlike our own, where there were at a given time current wisdoms which went unquestioned. I was arguing that the person who is an English teacher, who is highly aware of literature and what it does, should always encourage questioning of the conventional wisdom of the moment rather than promote it. Rather than that happening, often English classes become places where the conventional wisdom is promoted. Now the conventional wisdom of the moment is that there should be gender equity and that there shouldn't be racial discrimination. To say that these should be questioned is not to say that they're wrong. I'm not saying that I think that males and females should be treated differently or that people should be treated differently according to race. I'm just saying that the way these policies *come into effect* can be legitimately questioned.

TL   But if a curriculum document inevitably has implicit social values, isn't it desirable that those social values, if you like, attempt to empower people who may be disempowered in the society.

CKS   I don't think it is desirable. It's a complex issue and all I can say on this question is that a person interested in what I think about it should read precisely what I said in that submission and the examples that I referred to, because I was fairly brief and to the point there and it took many pages. I can't cover it in less space here.

TL   I guess I would wonder whether the things you point to are in fact the conventional wisdom of the time. I want to bring up the idea of 'political correctness' here. One of the things that I felt disturbed by was that your submission played into the hands of those who would brand educators as being part of some 'politically correct' group in society. But I would argue that the real political correctness in New Zealand at the moment stems from the legitimisation of new-right ideology.

CKS   I think there's a difference between what is politically dominant and what is dominant in the intellectual and education community. I would say that in the sphere of politics and economics and commerce, new right ideology is dominant. In the sphere of education, the universities, the arts and other intellectual endeavour, the thing which is called 'political correctness' is dominant. Politicians are prepared to give that away because they don't care about it. So there are clear territories, and I would say the educational field is the largest and most obvious of them, where what's called political correctness is totally dominant; and it's against that, against that view of things, that a lot of my criticisms were directed.

TL   I would argue with you about your identification of dominance there. But what I would like to do is to refer back to your 1982 address to NZATE where you said, 'If I learned radicalism anywhere I learned it from literature; and what it taught me especially was to question every piety – the liberal piety no less than the reactionary one.' I have begun this interview with you as a social critic with the national English curriculum as your target, but I wonder if we can use this statement as a key to understanding your writing. How central to your writing is the desire to question pieties?

CKS   It's central to my expository writing – to my essays and social criticism and even, to some extent I suppose, it gets into the literary criticism. Once you get into the area of fiction and poetry a different self seems to take over. It's mysterious to me what does happen, but it seems that the poetic imagination and the fictional imagination are much more accepting of the whole spectrum. It doesn't mean that they are uncritical but they reveal 'things as they are' as Wallace Stevens writes. The work doesn't so much make a judgement as present the reader with a set of recognisable facts and the reader makes a judgement. I don't really see my fiction and poetry as instruments at the disposal of my ideas.

TL   Would you say a work of art is the greater the more polarities it can encompass?

CKS   As a general statement that seems reasonable. The famous phrase that Keats used was that the poet had 'negative capability', and wasn't 'irritably reaching after fact and reason' but presenting an image in all its richness.

TL   Something I've always liked and feared about you is the sense of your polemicism. I've always got a sense that you find it easier to define yourself in opposition to something than as an advocate for something.

CKS   I can see why I might easily give that impression. I think that's because in the role of social critic or discursive commentator on New Zealand society, it's more important to point out what seems to be wrong and why it seems to be wrong than to linger over the things that are right. The things which are right don't call for comment, they can be accepted; you pass over those and you focus on the things that need correction. That's inevitably the way any social critic works.

TL   I'm just thinking of some of the books of yours that I've particularly enjoyed. If I think about *The Death of the Body* it appears to have been stimulated by what happened to Mervyn Thompson. If I think about *The End of the Century at the End of the World* it appears to be a revision of 1970s liberal politics. *Smith's Dream* is another obvious example of a novel that has grown out of a sense of the fictional possibilities within the New Zealand political situation. It seems from the way you have chosen your subject matter that you're using the novel as a very pronounced outlet for political ideas.

CKS   I'm a person who's always been interested in politics. I grew up in a political family and I've been on the fringes of politics all my life. So when I come to write fiction, politics is part of my subject matter because I've observed it so closely and the people involved in it, and to some extent been involved myself, but I still think there is an enormous difference between what I would write about those events as a polemicist – as an essayist – and the way I deal with them as a fiction writer. The nearest to being a polemical novel is *Smith's Dream*. I tried to make it polemical. But to some extent even there the fiction resisted what I was setting out to do, so that it contains really two contradictory positions which are unresolved, one which says the human animal has a social responsibility to be involved and to be committed and to take action, and the other point of view which is saying, *Look, when things are as bad as this the best thing is to opt out.* Both those positions are there even though I began writing a novel which I thought would be expressing only one of them. But when you get to a novel like *The Death of the Body,* the Mervyn Thompson events are there in the background and it's clear that I take a position of sympathy towards the harassed male harasser. The male is clearly a harasser and I don't make any apologies for him. He does have it off with his student on the floor of his office and so on. None of that is concealed. I don't say, look he's a really nice guy and he never did this. So, again it's a case where you're presented with the facts and people of different persuasion can react differently to them. I'm not insisting on one position or another. And that's what I mean by the difference between myself writing as an essayist and myself writing as a fiction writer.

TL   So you would believe that in the act of writing you can suspend that sort of judgement?

CKS   I know that in the act of writing that kind of judgement is suspended. It's mysterious to me but once I go into the fiction mode or the poetry mode, it's a different self that operates. I think of myself as having a political self and an existential self. It is the existential self that controls the fiction and poetry.

TL   One last question. What is currently shaping our identities as New Zealanders?

CKS   What's currently shaping our identity as New Zealanders, I suppose, is the attempt to shape our identity as New Zealanders.

TL   Can you elaborate on that? That's been around for a while hasn't it? I mean is there anything particular about the 1990s?

CKS   I think independence has been forced on us. We always said we wanted it but it was a bit of a shock when it came. When I was young, intellectuals wanted to break the apron strings and not to be a colony. But then suddenly Mother England said, *We don't want you anyway; we're really part of Europe.* That was when it was a bit of a psychological shock. It was good in that economically it forced us to diversify our markets and to discover new products – to be more inventive. But intellectually it meant we had to rethink our identity more in relation to the South Pacific.

All that's happening, but there is an element of self-consciousness about it and I feel that in the effort to create this new identity for ourselves, we are tending needlessly to cut ourselves off. The richest cultural inheritance still is our European one. We're told that Maori confidence depends at the moment on a recovery of their sense of their own culture, and yet we're rather cavalier about cutting ourselves off from our own.

Part 6

The Scholar Persists

Shelley's 'Constantia'

Claire Clairmont was, briefly, Byron's mistress, and the mother of his child Allegra. But was she also Shelley's lover? Did she become pregnant by him? Did she give birth to his child?

From the journals, also edited by Marion Kingston Stocking and published in 1986, it seems clear she was in love with Shelley at the age of sixteen. After the deaths of the two poets she never spoke well of Byron, nor ill of Shelley. In old age she took the name Constantia, which Shelley had given her in his poems, and asked that the shawl he had given her be buried with her. Her passion for Byron, she said, burned out and left nothing but waste and ash; her love for Shelley, about which she said next to nothing, survived the Byron episode and persisted.

Flexibility about names suggests concealment of origins and uncertainty of identity. Jane Clairmont became Clare, then Claire, sometimes Clara, and added Constantia. Her mother married William Godwin twice in an afternoon, once as 'Jane Clairmont, widow', a second time as 'Mary Vial, spinster'. She brought two children to the marriage, almost certainly by different fathers. Godwin brought Mary, his daughter to Mary Wollstonecraft, and Fanny, who was Wollstonecraft's by an earlier partner. When Godwin and Jane produced a child there were five siblings none of whom had the same two parents. It was a household in which, Claire said, if you couldn't run up an epic poem or a brilliantly original novel, you were 'a despicable creature not worth acknowledging'. Literary figures came and went as often as the bailiffs. Claire remembered Coleridge reading 'The Rime of the Ancient Mariner' to the parents while the children listened from behind the sofa.

But it was Claire's sister Mary who had the intellectual pedigree Shelley found so compelling. Godwin had written *Political Justice,* and Wollstonecraft *The Rights of Women* – two of libertarian Shelley's holy texts. What could their daughter be but brilliant and enlightened? Leaving his first wife, the unfortunate Harriet, he eloped with her in July 1814. He was just short of twenty-two; she five years younger. Claire, sixteen, went with them.

Mary was indeed brilliant, intellectual, literary; she was also cool, sometimes sharp-tongued, and inclined to be depressive. Claire sang beautifully, was witty, energetic, high-spirited, and given to tantrums. Some

---

A review of *The Clairmont Correspondence* (two volumes) ed. Marion Kingston Stocking, in the *London Review of Books,* 22 February 1996.

years later Shelley, his longings temporarily directed elsewhere, would characterise them as the 'cold moon' and the 'fiery comet'.

For the sake of posterity, it must be supposed, Claire doctored her journal of that first venture abroad to remove anything that might suggest impropriety – alterations which can now be seen under infrared light. Consequently entries which, had they been left alone, might have signified nothing in particular, seem, because of the attempted erasures, to point to Claire's growing attachment to Shelley. A typical example, the entry for 9 October 1814, originally read:

> Mary goes to bed at eight – sit up with Shelley over the fire – get rather in a horrid mood – go to bed at eleven cannot sleep all night.

With erasures and additions this becomes:

> We go to bed at eight – get in rather a horrid mood – thinking about ghosts cannot sleep all night.

In the entry for 14 October, after recording a quarrel with Shelley, she writes, and later (the editor tells us) 'did her best to eliminate':

> Can't think what the deuce is the matter with me – 'I weep yet never know why – I sigh yet feel no pain.'

From the entry of 16 October she later scores out:

> Mary goes to bed – Shelley explains he thought I despised him – We talk till nearly one.

From this time onward there were tensions between Mary and Claire, and between Shelley and Mary about Claire. It was always Mary who tried to be rid of her, to achieve 'absentia Claireae'; Shelley who called her back. When he died in 1822 they were still, all three, together. In fact Godwin believed the three sisters – Mary, Claire and Fanny – were all in love with the poet, and even suggested that Fanny's suicide (two months before Harriet, the abandoned wife, drowned herself) had been caused by Shelley's 'preference for her younger sister'.

This is the background to the most daring action of Claire's life, her raid on Byron. Mary had bagged (or de-bagged) a poet; Claire would have one too – that way Mary's cause for jealousy would be removed. Sixty years later, talking to Edward Silsbee, Claire still put those elements together. Pale Mary had been jealous of her 'bright colour', of the attention Shelley paid her and the hours he spent walking with her. After her adventure with Byron, she told Silsbee, 'Mrs Shelley was no longer jealous.'

Byron, a noble lord and already famous, was about as accessible as a modern movie star. Everything would depend, first, on what she wrote to him (the letters survive), and, if she got past the first barrier, what impression she was able to make in person. That she persisted and succeeded is a measure of her audacity, cleverness and allure. But she was seventeen, this was her first sexual experience, and Byron was a man women found it easy to love. Claire's insincere expressions of love, 'made with a beating heart', caught up with her. Fiction became fact. The 'little fiend', as Byron called her, would soon be writing, 'Do you know I cannot talk to you when I see you; I am so awkward, and only feel inclined to take a little stool and sit at your feet.'

Claire's letters to Byron after they became lovers are sincere and eloquent – honest, diplomatic, realistic, but with a painful undertone of hope. There were a few happy months in Geneva together with Mary and Shelley; but when Claire became pregnant Byron acknowledged paternity ('she has had a good deal of that same with me') and refused to see her again.

Although for a long time Claire's letters to him (he doesn't reply) continue to express love and friendship, and to be moderate in their demands, one can see the slow waning of passion and in its place (she would soon have the child to consider) intelligent calculation mixed with the beginnings of rebellion. Even in a letter written before the hope and the passion are spent (September 1816) she can write '[Kinnaird] told Shelley Lady Byron usually called your *Wife* was in good health on a visit to Mrs Leigh.' Since Claire knew quite well (he had told her) of Byron's incestuous passion for his half-sister Augusta Leigh, the sentence is surely a nicely judged double blow. A few pages on she writes, 'Don't look cross at this letter because perhaps by the same post you expected one from Mrs Leigh and have not got it. That is not my fault dearest. I am not the postman.'*

It is this cleverness of Claire's that was so appealing to Shelley, so appalling to Byron. Shelley's women were intellectual companions; Byron's were (in)conveniences.

By the time Allegra was one year old (January 1818), Claire was living at Marlow (on the Thames just out of London) with Shelley and Mary and their two children, William and Clara. Shelley had completed his longest poem, 'Laon and Cythna', there; Mary had completed *Frankenstein,* which was just published; Claire, whose Italian singing teacher described her voice as 'a string of pearls', had been accompanying herself on a grand piano Shelley had 'bought' (he hadn't paid for it) for her; and they were preparing to return to the Continent.

It was at Marlow that Shelley wrote 'To Constantia Singing', a poem which, like Byron's 'There Be None of Beauty's Daughters', is a tribute to Claire's singing, and (unlike Byron's) a signal of his own deep feeling for her. Shelley published it under a pseudonym, and Mary never saw until after his death. Claire's emotional compass had almost certainly swung back to its true north; but there was now, and more importantly, her deep attachment to her child.

There had been an agreement in Geneva that Byron would take Allegra when she was old enough to be parted from her mother. 'I felt,' Claire wrote

---

* I wondered why this kind of clever teasing in her letters seemed familiar until I recognised that it is exactly like Mansfield's.

in old age, 'that I ought not for the sake of gratifying my own affections deprive her of a brilliant position in life.' But now Claire was beset with anxieties. Byron had written proposing that a nurse should bring the child to him. Claire wrote back:

> Do you think I would trust her with such a person? She is all my treasure – the little creature occupies all my thoughts, all my time and feelings ... You might as well have asked a miser to trust his gold for a sea voyage to a leaky vessel. Besides various ceaseless misgivings that I entertain of you. Suppose that in yielding her to your care I yield her to neglect and coldness? How am I assured that such will not be the case? ... I so fear she will be unhappy. I am so anxious ... Poor little angel! – in your great house, left perhaps to servants while you are drowning sense and good feeling in wine and striving all you can to ruin the natural goodness of your nature – who will there be to watch her?

Claire, now nineteen, had grown up. She had achieved detachment. She dared to criticise. In the same letter she reproached Byron for things he had said of her, reported back, 'which mark an utter want of discrimination in you':

> Indeed I ought to be better ... I have no Hobhouse [Byron's friend] by my side to dispirit me with an easy and impudent declaration of 'the villainy of all mankind' which I can construe into nothing but an attempt to cover over his conscious unworthiness. I must be the veriest wretch if I were wicked, placed in such a situation as I am. I have faults. I am timid from vanity; my temper is inconstant and *volage*. I want dignity. I do not like Mary sail my steady course like a ship under a gentle and favourable wind. But at thirty I shall be better and every year I hope to gain in value.

This was the independent spirit which Byron, in his unworthy and self-serving exchanges with his fawning friend Hoppner, would describe as Claire's 'insolence'.

Shelley with his household now left England for the last time. In April they were in Milan and Claire was persuaded the time had come for Allegra to be sent, in the company of her own nurse, Elise, to live with her father in Venice. Claire's letter to Byron at this time, full of grief, anxiety, and attempts to win his compassion and compliance, are the most painful to read. If, as Elise asserted, Claire was the mother of a child born in Naples in December 1818 and christened Elena Adelaide Shelley, then the conception would have occurred at this time. It was in the December of the child's birth that Shelley wrote his 'Stanzas written in Dejection near Naples'; and it was in Naples, according to Trelawny, that he attempted suicide.

These volumes don't settle this vexed question, but they do offer (well buried in the notes) new evidence. Shelley's reference to his 'Neopolitan charge' in letters of 1819, and to her death in 1820, were puzzling until 1936 when Newman Ivy White discovered in Naples the registrations of the birth of Elena Adelaide Shelley (Shelley and Mary given as the parents), and of her death there in 1820. She had been left in Naples in the care of foster parents. Since the child was not in fact Mary's, and since Shelley had kept certain correspondence about her secret from his wife, it seemed reasonable to conclude that Elise's claim that Claire and Shelley had been lovers, and that Claire had given birth to a child in Naples, must be true. These assertions had previously been dismissed because they were part of an attempt by Elise's husband to blackmail Shelley. Now, however, they could be seen to be based on an actual birth; and the question which all along had lain there unconsidered had to be asked: how do you blackmail someone on the basis of sheer invention?

On reviewing all the evidence, however, White, in his two-volume life of Shelley (1947) concluded that Elena could not have been Claire's. How, he asked, could Claire, so deeply attached to one child and still grieving at the necessity of giving her up, have been persuaded to leave another behind? It must, he decided (the evidence is lengthy and complicated) have been a child adopted by Shelley, without Mary's knowledge, to replace their little Clara who had died the previous year. Mary had rejected the new child, and Elena had been left with foster parents, though still legally Shelley's responsibility.

There were terrible weaknesses in this argument, as there are, however, in recent alternatives. In his *Shelley: The Pursuit* (1974) Richard Holmes decided that both Claire and Elise had been pregnant to Shelley. Claire's pregnancy had aborted, and Elena was Elise's baby. Claire Tomalin, in *Shelley and His World* (1980), argued that the child was Claire's; and in a recent review she sticks to that. Returning to the question in *Footsteps* (1985), Holmes concluded once again that Claire was pregnant and aborted in Naples, but now accepted White's argument that Elena must have been an adopted foundling.

A new element in the editing of these Clairmont letters is that Professor Stocking has been able to consult and, where relevant, work into her annotations, notes taken by the American Shelleyan, Edward Silsbee, whose insinuation of himself into the elderly Claire's household in the 1870s became source and subject for Henry James's *The Aspern Papers*. Shelley, Claire told Silsbee, 'got into a scrape' (a phrase she uses elsewhere in the letters to indicate a pregnancy outside wedlock) with a married lady who followed him to Naples. Pressed by Silsbee for more information, Claire refused, saying she was sworn to silence; but Professor Stocking puts this hint together with others to conclude, entirely plausibly, that Elena Adelaide was the child of an Englishwoman, Adelaide Constance Campbell. This is very probably the hard fact behind the romantic and soft-focus tale Shelley told both Medwin and Byron about an English noblewoman, an admirer of his work, who fell in love with him and followed him about Europe. In Shelley's version, which he seemed to intend turning into a narrative poem, she reached Naples and died. In reality, having reached him in some other place, she followed him to Naples bearing his child.

So were Shelley and Claire lovers? When scandal threatened, Shelley wrote to Mary asking her to assure Mrs Hoppner that Elise's story about the abandoned child was untrue. Elise, he wrote, 'has persuaded the Hoppners ... that Claire was my mistress – that is very well and so far there is nothing new; all the world has heard as much and people may believe or not as they think good.' Is this casualness based on confidence that Mary knows the rumour to be false, or knows it to be true? Either seems possible.

Physical lovers or not, what becomes clear, I think, is a sort of submarine constancy in Claire's love for Shelley, and a corresponding jealousy of Mary, which doesn't rule out sisterly loyalty and intellectual respect. She rejoices in Mary's success with *Frankenstein,* even though it makes clearer to her the failure of her own attempts as a writer. Through the later part of their lives, after Shelley's death, she is constantly anxious about Mary's health and welfare. 'I cried all the day after your departure ... my house felt so terrible without you.' A year later she writes, 'You are so much worth seeing. When you are in a humour to reveal all the vastness of your intellect, one observation of yours, one thought, is worth travelling all over Europe to hear.'

Yet she also constantly, perhaps consciously, torments Mary. Knowing her propensity for anxiety ('Knowing how you hate melancholy') she writes longer and longer accounts of her miseries as a governess in Russia, half-blaming her sister for her situation, even asking 'Cannot you do anything to get me out of it?' Her health is always failing, or worse. She is always announcing – thirty and forty years before it happened – that she will soon be dead.

Claire was always the adjutant. In a late letter (1871) to Trelawny she remembers how, when Shelley was courting Mary, 'They always sent me to talk [walk?] at some distance from them, alleging that they wished to talk on philosophical subjects and that I did not like or know anything about these ... I did not hear what they talked about.' 'Claire is timid,' Mary wrote to Mrs Hoppner; 'she always showed respect, even for me – poor dear girl!'

I think Claire recognised something noble in Mary, and in Shelley and Mary together, which she revered and knew she was too unbridled to emulate. On the other hand, as time went by Shelley could confide in her things which would have disturbed Mary; and this, rather than their being lovers, might possibly account for Shelley's secret letters to her, and hers to him addressed, poste restante, to 'Mr Jones'. She was an ally, the keeper of his secrets. She was more resilient than Mary, accompanying him on his rambles (he was a prodigious walker and small-boat adventurer), a less daunting presence, an easier and more amusing companion. But she was not Mary's intellectual equal. Nor was she his wife and the mother of his children; and I think the finest thread of sibling malice in the letters to Mary is the one which subtly represents as a hypocrisy, or apostasy, these two roles of which in truth Claire was deeply envious.

Claire has been celebrated as a liberal and a feminist. No doubt those inherited convictions were genuinely held; and in isolation a small number of her ringing statements of principle can give the impression that she was right up there in the vanguard. But in the full context of the letters to Mary in which they occur, they take on a different colour, seeming like a means of scoring off her sister – as if claiming that she is the true 'daughter' of Wollstonecraft and Godwin, the real 'wife' of Shelley. Even Mary's role as a mother (one child, Percy, survived) is represented as inferior to her own, and in a way tormenting to Mary because it evokes so deliberately the spirit and doctrines of her famous mother:

> A legitimate child to its mother is nothing but a task that was imposed upon her, a labour extorted from her by a sense of her helplessness to resist her imperious Master; she sees in its face the dismal Necessity to which it owed its birth. You might as well expect a negro to have a passionate attachment to the sugar he raises upon the ground of his Planter. An illegitimate child on the contrary calls forth the maternal feelings in full force; it is the offspring of freedom and love, of Beauty and Strength in their most exalted aspect, when the beastly world is banished far and two hearts beat with mutual and unselfish devotion.

And then, in the same letter, thus far amiable and disinterested in tone if not in substance, she all at once whacks Mary hard, blaming her (that is what Mary would have understood her to mean) for the fact that Allegra was handed over to Byron, and to her death. Claire is writing of Mary's assurances that under Shelley's will she stands to inherit £12,000 when Sir Timothy Shelley ('the great unmentionable' she calls him) dies. She says she has about this advice 'the most cruel doubts':

> Would I had had them twelve years ago, I should have acted quite otherwise but then I was young and I had not got rid of my respect for your judgement. I thought you odd – how odd – but I thought nothing could equal your wisdom – on certain points I still think you very wise, in metaphysics, in making horrid catastrophes in a book, in writing prose that is the beau ideal of prose; but not in judgement of worldly matters – you have about as much as a poet that is drunk with inspiration.

But the subtlest wound inflicted on Mary is hidden in a letter of March 1836. Mary has discovered that their friend Jane Williams has spoken ill of her, and Claire is telling her she must forget it, not let it spoil their friendship:

> How can you expect dear Mary, not to be traduced by your friends? What mortal can you point out, either alive or dead, that was so privileged? Neither genius, nor goodness, the two principal exciters of love, can preserve from this evil. Accept of friendship all that it has of sweet and bury the rest in oblivion.

So far so good; but now she goes on:

> I had once a friend whom I loved entirely and who certainly loved me much; yet immense were the lies he told of me: I regard this not – he was great and above all fair-minded and I love him still as if he had never spoken ill of me: to be sure he told me himself in his calm voice and with the gentlest looks that it was absolutely necessary he should traduce me and that he expected I should submit without a murmur to it – and I do with the greatest cheerfulness. So much

frankness and honour would redeem any calumny let it take what root it may – and besides one feels ennobled in being the victim of necessity.

The 'great and above-all fair-minded' friend cannot be Byron about whom, after the death of Allegra, Claire only ever spoke with hatred and contempt. Professor Stocking's note says that she has not been able to identify this person. But who could it have been other than Shelley? And that, surely, was what Claire intended Mary to understand – that he had never told her the truth about their relationship, and that, because he had been honest with her about the need for misinformation and deception, it was a dishonesty she could accept.

There is an incoherent journal entry of 1858 which for a long time baffled me but which, once understood, perfectly catches the conflict of Claire's feelings for her step-sister, describing first Mary's beautiful hair, acknowledging 'the surpassing beauty of her mind', then blaming her for compromising the Shelleyan ideal, and finally describing her as one who 'watched the spectacle of a child led to the scaffold' and then shook hands with the executioner. 'I never saw her afterwards,' she goes on, 'without feeling as if the sickening motion of the Deathworm had replaced the usual flow of blood in my veins.' My confusion came from reading this literally, a result of remembering something Blake wrote after seeing the execution of a child. But of course, what she must mean (once again) is that Mary was to blame for the fact that Allegra was sent to Byron, who neglected her, sent her to be educated in a convent where she contracted the illness that killed her. Allegra is the child, and Byron the 'executioner' with whom Mary shook hands. In the same passage Shelley, with his 'ardent mouth, his exalted being, his simplicity and enthusiasms', is exempt from blame.

'She poisoned my life,' Mary wrote to Trelawny in an uncharacteristic outburst. 'I would not go to Paradise with her as a companion … Years ago my idea of Heaven was a world without Claire – of course these feelings are altered – but she still has the faculty of making me more uncomfortable than any human being – a faculty she, unconsciously perhaps, never fails to exert when I see her.'

Claire's sufferings were immense, but so were Mary's. Together, in the space of three years, they saw the deaths of their three adored children – William, Clara and Allegra – and then of Shelley. Claire grew up in Mary's shadow. Her attempt to escape from it led to Byron, and disaster. The separation from Allegra and her death was a bitterness she never shook off. Her enduring love for Shelley probably caused her rejection of other suitors and lovers – Peacock, Trelawny, Henry Reveley, and the obscure German composer and poet Herman Gambs who published his poetry under the pseudonym of his 'Muse', C. Clairmont.

She was very well read, a good linguist, a fine musician, a brilliant and enlightened teacher, a witty letter writer and journal keeper. A Russian admirer described her as 'English in her pride and dignity but Italian in her liveliness and ardour'. As an elderly woman she could still charm her male visitors while appearing to her nieces and nephews bossy, suspicious, and a pain in the neck.

She is at her best in these letters when she is in a mood to entertain:

> All the life that is left in the house is now concentrated in Nerina, and I am sure she cannot complain of a dearth of sensations for she takes good care to feel with every thing around her and if the chair does but knock against the table she shudders and quakes for both and runs into her own study to write it down in her journal.

That too is very like Mansfield (one of whose characters shudders as a fork breaks through the crust of a meringue). But her best and most amusing letters are not dependent on quick wit; rather, on a slow winding of herself up into comedy over several accelerating pages, as she perhaps wound herself up into her towering black humours and despairs. Comedy was a kind of relief from a life that could seem at times so terrible she more than once said (before her late conversion to Catholicism) her greatest fear was that it might persist after death.

Were Shelley and Claire lovers? Thus far, and probably for ever, scholarship can't finally determine the question – in which case common sense and knowledge of human character will have to serve. Some years ago, writing in the *London Review of Books,* Paul Foot described a prolonged debate on this question conducted at a meeting of the Byron Society in Albemarle Street, London. On and on it went, citing and interpreting evidence pro and con, until a woman in her late seventies rose to rebuke the academics. 'If *I* had been alone with Shelley,' she said, 'as Claire was at Este in the Spring of 1818, I jolly well would have slept with him.'

Postscript: Shelley and his 'Heart's Sisters'

Shelley's last residence was the Casa Magni at San Terenzo in the Gulf of Spezia. The house is still there and my friend from Rapallo, Professor Massimo Bacigalupo, who knows its current owner, took me to it. It has a large central room on the first floor, opening on to a terrace. A road now divides the house from the sea which once, on days of storm, beat up almost to its lower doors. To the right, looking from the terrace, can be seen the headland of Portovenere; to the left another headland hides the town of Lerici. One of Byron's great swims was the six kilometres between the two, a fact which is commemorated by a plaque at Portovenere; and the plaque itself and the fact that Henry James visited it are mentioned in one of the cancelled drafts of Ezra Pound's *Cantos.*

To sit on that terrace in June sunshine is to be swamped by the vividness of literary history – its richness, its complexity, perhaps its absurdity. Here Claire Clairmont and Jane Williams played their guitars and sang while Mary Shelley, weak from a recent miscarriage, lay on her couch in the eastern room, looking out to sea. Here the young household (they were all still in their twenties) played chess, and in good weather took their meals. Here Shelley walked in his sleep and saw terrifying visions of a dying child, of flood and blood. Here the women waited for sight of a sail that would bring the two husbands, Shelley and Edward Williams, back to them. Here Edward Trelawny brought finally news that bodies had been washed ashore; and from here he went to organise the cremations on the beach at Viareggio that would be watched by Byron and Leigh Hunt.

Shelley's relations with women lie at the centre of his work, and perhaps of critical reactions to it. His map of human society, one feels, must have been indelibly traced on his consciousness during his early years at Field Place in Sussex, where his grandfather the baronet and father the heir represented authority and hence tyranny, his mother perhaps the female principle in its conservative manifestation, and his sisters, all younger, the victims who were also companions and objects of his dawning sense of sexual love. As the sole and older brother he saw himself as the protector of these sisters against unjust authority. ('Say, my heart's sister, wilt thou fly with me?' he writes many years later to Emilia Viviani in the poem 'Epipsychidion'.) When he eloped with his first wife, Harriet, it was to rescue her from the 'tyranny' of her father and her school, and the couple were soon joined by her sister Eliza, and then by his intellectual 'sister' Elizabeth Hitchener.

When the idyll broke down he eloped with Mary Godwin, taking Claire along as well. Throughout all the ups and downs of her feelings for Mary, Claire's attachment to Shelley remains constant; and when, having rejected Trelawny's desperate overtures after Shelley's death, she left Italy in 1822, she wrote in her journal, 'I remembered how hopelessly I had lingered on Italian soil for five years, waiting ever for a favourable change, instead of which I was leaving it having buried everything that I loved.'

Byron was not interested in women as companions, as intellectual equals, as collaborators. To Shelley his 'heart's sisters' were all these things; yet it is Shelley, not Byron the noble lord licensed by his station to be careless in these matters, who has been more often condemned. This is unfair – but not entirely. Women knew where they stood with Byron – that they had no standing. ('Byron came down on the chambermaid like a thunderclap,' Polidori records.) With Shelley the confusions of sex and intellect, ardour and infidelity, theory and practice, must have been difficult in the extreme. Mary could accept and understand her relations with him only in retrospect, and it was an understanding which brought a self-reproach no less painful for being undeserved.

—

It was in 1877 that Henry James discovered the Casa Magni. He describes how he hired a boat and had himself rowed across the bay from Portovenere, where he had seen the plaque commemorating Byron's swim, to the 'now desolate' (it was at that time more or less in ruins) villa. 'In that place,' James wrote, and with his genius, [Shelley] would as a matter of course have heard in the voice of nature a sweetness which only the lyric movement could translate. It is a place where an English-speaking pilgrim himself may very honestly think thoughts and feel moved to lyric utterance. But I content myself with saying in halting prose that I remember few episodes of Italian travel more sympathetic … than that perfect autumn afternoon.

James extracts wonderfully the essence of the place and the sense of dark dramas played out there, leaving us with a final image of himself, having climbed to the castle on the headland over Lerici, lounging 'in the fading light, on the vine-decked platform that looked out … upon the quiet sea, beyond which the pale-faced tragic villa stared up at the brightening moon.'

This is typically Jamesian in standing so remote from the human drama which gives the moment its poignancy. Nothing of what went on there, not even Shelley's drowning, is directly mentioned. All that resonates most keenly is left unstated, James taking for granted (as a writer might at that time) common knowledge, shared with his readers, of basic literary history.

Similarly when James discovered that he had spent time in Florence while Claire, an elderly lady still in possession of relics of Shelley and Byron, had been living there, and that he might, if he had cared to do it, have attempted to meet her, the fiction he wrote as a consequence, *The Aspern Papers,* tells nothing at all of the life of the dead poet and his mistress. The scene is transposed from Florence to Venice. Juliana, the aged mistress, gives nothing away. In the end the papers of the great poet, Jeffrey Aspern, are destroyed; and the drama focuses on the consequences of the scholar's headlong thoughtless pursuit of those sacred literary remains. Literature feeds on life; scholarship feeds on literature; and at the farthest end of this strange food chain lies the Jamesian story feeding on all three.

James knew that there had been a Shelley scholar, Edward Silsbee, who had managed to get himself into the aged Claire's confidence, and even spirit some papers away; but he doesn't name him, even in his Preface to *The Aspern Papers* written many years later. What he prefers to reflect on is

> … that odd law which somehow always makes the minimum of valid suggestion serve the man of imagination better than the maximum. The historian, essentially, wants more documents than he can really use; the [writer] wants only more liberties than he can really take.

It was Silsbee who got the documents, James who took the liberties.

Shelley and James, at least in appearance, stand at opposite extremes of behaviour – the social rebel and the social conformist. But what they did in life, what 'really' happened to them, though of immense interest, is of little consequence compared to what the imagination, and that structuring capacity with the medium of language, were able to make of it.

Index

Bold type indicates a major entry.

A

Abrams, M.H. *The Mirror and the Lamp* 42, 120
Adcock, Fleur **247-59**; *The Incident Book* 255n; (ed.) *The Oxford Book of Contemporary New Zealand Poetry* 249; 'Witnesses' **255-6**
Adie, Kate 141
Aeschylus *Agamemnon* 144
Aitken, Russell 106
Aldington, Richard 184
Alexander Turnbull Library 68, 114n
All Blacks 262
Allen, Woody *Hannah and her Sisters* (movie) 173
Allingham, Margery 43
Alpers, Antony 68-9, 76
Amis, Martin *London Fields* 157
AND 227
Andersen, Hans Christian 'The Emperor's New Clothes' 211, 212
Apollinaire, Guillaume 'Le Pont Mirabeau' (quoted) 258
Aragon, Louis 'Red Front' 178
Arena 232
Arnold, Matthew 118, 141, 179, 233
Ashbery, John 72, 121
Ashton-Warner, Sylvia 49
Ati Awa 35
Auckland Art Gallery 66n, 67
Auden, W.H. 97, 141, 142, 143, 155, 244
Austen, Jane 119, 252
Avondale Mental Hospital 63

B

Bacigalupo, Angela 148
Bacigalupo, Massimo 146-7, 148, 150, 279
Baker, Ida (Lesley Moore) **73-6**
Balzac, Honoré de 'Sarrasine' 79
Barthes, Roland 89, 91, 115, 116; 'The Death of the Author' 79, **117-8**
Baudelaire, Charles 'Le Cygne' ('The Swan') 258
Baxter, Archibald 98
Baxter, James K **98-101**, 227, 228, 229
Baxter, Millicent 98
Beat poets / poetry 163
Beatles 130

Beauchamp, Harold 55
Beaver, Bruce 129
Beckett, Samuel 61
Beer, Patricia 255
Behrman, S.N. 199
Berlin Wall 100, 143, 249
Bertram, James 152
Bishop, Elizabeth 252
Blackmur, R.P. 152-3, 156
Blake, William 119, 152, 278
Bloom, Harold 110, 119, 121
Bloomsbury 100
Bonham-Carter, Mark 139
Booker Prize 158, 165, 183
Borges, Jorge Luis 84, **87-8**, 89, 91, 92, 96; *Fictions* **87**; 'The Intruder' 88
Bowen, Elizabeth (ed.) *34 Stories by Katherine Mansfield* 39
Boyd, Arthur 165
Brasch, Charles 22, 23, 31, 51, 58-9, 64, 65, 208, 227, 232
British Museum Reading Room 68
Broad Bay (Otago) 23
Brontë, the sisters 252
Brooke, Rupert 67, 198
Browning, Robert 'A Woman's Last Word' 34
Brozicevic, Michael 186, 187
Buchan, John 198
Burroughs, William 163
Bush, President George 204
Butler, the Hon. R.A. 19
Byatt, A.S. 255
Byron, Lady Annabella 273
Byron, Clara Allegra 271, 273, 274, 278
Byron, Lord George Gordon 80, 119, 148, 271, 272, 274, 275, 277, 278, 280, 281; 'There be None of Beauty's Daughters' 273
Byron Society 279

C

Caine, Michael 173
Callaghan, Dymphna 122
Campbell, Gordon 76
Campion, Jane 27; *An Angel at my Table* (movie) 55; *The Piano* (movie) 192
Cannan, Gilbert 76
Carey, Peter 183; *Oscar and Lucinda* 169
Casa Magni at San Terenzo 279, 280
Castro, Fidel 164

Castro, Raoul 164
Catullus 254, 256
Cavell, Edith 141
Cawley, Dr.R.H. 20-1
Caxton Press 30, 31
Ceaucescu, Nicolai 250
Cervantes, Miguel de *Don Quixote* 87, 146
Cézanne, Paul 175
Chadwick, Joseph 123
Chaplin, Charlie 176
Chapman, Guy 212-3
Chapman, R.McD 51, 229
Chatham Islands **35-7**
Christchurch 40, 43
Christie, Agatha 43
Clairmont, Claire **271-81**; Letters quoted 276, 277
Clutha, Janet (*see* Frame, Janet)
Coetzee, J.M. 183
Cole-Catley, Christine 63
Coleridge, Samuel Taylor 233; 'Kubla Khan' 61, 161; 'The Rime of the Ancient Mariner' 61, 271
Common Reader 91, 115, **118-9**
Condell, Henry 60
Confucius 151
Cook, Mr Justice, President of the Court of Appeal 211, 213
Coromandel 52, 54, 159
Corso, Gregory 163
Cranna, John 159
Cresswell, Walter D'Arcy 94
Croom, David 186
Cross, Ian 64
Cubism 207, 215
Cummings, E.E. 153, **173-9**; *Complete Poems 1904-1962* **173-9** (quoted) 174, 175, 176, 177, 178, 179; *EIMI* 174; *The Enormous Room* 175
Cunliffe, Leslie 159
Curnow, Allen 9, 29, 31, 41, 45, 51, 52, 57, 72, 94-5, 97, **98-101**, 207, 226, 228, 233, 243, 244, 248, 249, 254, 259; *The Axe* 43; *A Book of New Zealand Verse, 1923-45* 225; 'Dichtung und Wahrheit' 229; 'The Parakeets at Karekare' 45-48; (ed.) *The Penguin Book of New Zealand Verse* 52, 229
Curnow, Tremayne 98
Curnow, Wystan 226

D
Daily Mail 19
Dallas, Ruth 23
Daniel 12
Dante 152
Davey, Norris (Frank Sargeson) 56
Davin, Dan 9, 22, 29
Dawson, Peter 57
Day Lewis, Cecil 259
Deconstruction 90-1
de Gourmont, Rémy 184
Dennis, Helen M. 123

de Rachewiltz, Mary 145-7, 148, 150, 151; *Discretions*, 146
Derrida, Jacques 90, 91, 116, 120, 121
Dickens, Charles 60, 84, 89, 90, 108, 110, 119, 198
Dickinson, Emily 117, 252
Dirks, Adrian 197n
Docherty, Thomas 122
Donaldson, Roger 210, 242
Donne, John 207, 254
Douglas, Sir Roger 10
Douglas Social Credit 146
Dowson, Ernest 31
Doyle, Harry 57
Dryden, John 233
Drysdale, Russell 165
Duchamps, Marcel 175
Duggan, Barbara 60, 65
Duggan, Maurice 10, 17, 30, 40, 54, **60-6**, 131, 132; 'Along Rideout Road that Summer' 61, 63, 64, 65; 'Blues for Miss Laverty' 64; *The Burning Miss Bratby* 62, 64; *Collected Stories* 64n; 'The Magsman Miscellany' 65; 'O'Leary's Orchard' 63; 'Riley's Handbook' 61, 62-4; 'Six Place Names and a Girl' 64; 'Six Rileypomes' 65; *Summer in the Gravel Pit* 64
Duggan, Nick 60
Duras, Marguerite *Dix Heures et demie du Soir en Été* **90**
Dutschke, Rudi 141

E
Eagleton, Terry 125-6
Edmond, Lauris 29, 31, 189, 226, 253; *The Quick World* **49-50**
Edmond, Trevor 50
Education Forum of the Business Round Table 102 & n
Eliot, T.S. 76, 95, 97, 114, 143, 150, 153, 154, 155, 158, 175, 184, 188, 207; 'The Love Song of J. Alfred Prufrock' 173; *Murder in the Cathedral* 154; *The Waste Land* (quoted) 259
Eliot, Vivien 76
Elise (servant to the Shelleys) *see* Foggi
'Elizabeth' (Elizabeth von Armin, later the Countess Russell) 75
Elizabeth in her German Garden 75
Elizabeth II 19
Elizabethan theatre 84
Elkind, Dorée 30
English, teaching of **102-126, 260-6**
English in Aotearoa 260n, 263
Epsom Girls Grammar School 108
Eurocentrism 99
Evans, Patrick *The Penguin History of New Zealand Literature* 246

F
Fairburn, A.R.D. 31, 207, 215, 228
Faulkner, William 90
Feminist theory / criticism 11, 119, 165, 252,

254, 276-7
Ferlinghetti, Lawrence 226
Fletcher, John Gould 184
Flint, F.S. 184
Foggi, Louise (Elise) 274-5, 276
Foot, Paul 279
Ford, Ford Madox 81, 177, 184
Forster, E.M. 10, 84; *Aspects of the Novel* 81
Foucault, Michel 91, 116, 117
Frame, Janet **17-28**, 55, 236, 237, 252; *An Angel at my Table* 25, 27; *Faces in the Water* 21; *Living in the Maniototo* 24, 26; *Owls do Cry* 17, 19, 235; 'The Reservoir' 25, 26; 'The Triumph of Poetry' 22
France, Anatole *Thais* 84
Fraser, Lady Antonia 190, 191, 193
Fraser, Hugh 190, 191
French, Anne 'Cabin Fever' (quoted) 101
Freud, Sigmund 202
Friedlander, Marti 23, 53

G
Gadd, Frank 58
Gambs, Herman 278
Gee, Maurice 66, 167
Genesis, Book of 201
Georgian Court College 114n, 150
Georgian poetry 97, 184, 208
Gertler, Mark 76
Ginsberg, Allen 95, **161-4**, 226; 'America' (quoted) 163; 'Howl' **162** (quoted) 162, 164; 'Kaddish' 161
Ginsberg, Louis 161
Ginsberg, Naomi 161
Glover, Denis **29-32**, 51, 229; 'Fool's Song' 30; 'Sings Harry' 30, 31
Gluck, Robert 123
Goddard, Peter 66
Godwin, Fanny (Frances Imlay) 271, 272
Godwin, Mary Jane 271
Godwin, William 271, 272, 277; *Political Justice* 271
Goethe, J.W. 142
Goldsmith, Oliver 'The Deserted Village' 231; *She Stoops to Conquer* 231; *The Vicar of Wakefield* 231
Gordon, David M. 152n, 154
Goulden, Mark 21; *Mark my Words*, 21
Goulden, Mrs Mark 22
Graham, John 102
Grass, Gunther 84, **89-90**, 91, 92; *Cat and Mouse* 89; *Dog Years* 89; *The Flounder* 89; *Local Anaesthetic* 89
Graves, Robert 175
Gray, Thomas 115
Greer, Germaine 255
Grimm, the brothers 82
Grimshaw, Charlotte 9, 108, 136, 149
Groves, Murray 130

H
Halcrow, Thelma 28
Hardie, Keir 98
Hardy, Thomas 231
Hastings, Beatrice 76
Hauraki Gulf 18
Haydn, George 63
H.D. (Hilda Doolittle) 153, 184
Heaney, Seamus 122; *The Government of the Tongue* 188
Heidegger, Martin 90
Heminge, John 60
Hemingway, Ernest 150, 175
Henderson, Diane 66, 67, 215
Henderson, Hubert 215
Henderson, Louise 43, 66, 207, 215, 216
Herbert, Xavier 183; *Poor Fellow my Country* 166
Hitchener, Elizabeth 280
Hitler, Adolph 137, 141
Hobhouse, John Cam 274
Hockney, David 143
Hodgkins, Frances 66, 69
Holcroft, Monte 51, 208
Holian, Gail 150
Hollinrake, Rosalind 129n, 131
Holmes, Richard *Shelley: the Pursuit* 275; *Footsteps* 275
Hoppner, Isabella 275, 276
Hoppner, Richard Belgrave 274, 276
Horrocks, Roger 226
Hotere, Ralph 70
Hound and Horn 152
Hughes, Shura 170
Hughes, Ted **170-2**; *Birthday Letters* **170-2**; *Crow* 171; *The Hawk in the Rain* 171
Hulme, T.E. 184
Humphries, Barry **129-137**, 232; *Bizarre* **132**; *More Please* 129; *Sandy Agonistes* (recording) 134; *Shades of Sandy Stone* 134; *Sir Les Paterson Saves the World* (movie) 133
Humphries, Oscar 135
Humphries, Rupert 135
Humphries, Tessa 135
Hunt, Leigh 280

I
Ibiza 19
Ireland, Kevin 17
Isherwood, Christopher 140
Islands 69n

J
Jackson, MacD.P. 2, 184
James, Clive 133
James, Henry 60, 279, 280, 281; *The Aspern Papers* 275, 281; Preface to *The Aspern Papers* (quoted) 281; *Italian Hours* (quoted) 280-1
Jebb, Julian 190, 191
Johnson, Barbara 90
Johnson, Lionel 31

Johnson, Louis 208, 228, 229
Johnson, Olive 30
Johnson, Dr Samuel 114, 115, 119, 233
Johnston, Andrew 10, **71-2**; 'Fool Heart' 71; 'The Singer' 72; *The Sounds* 72
Joseph, M.K. 229
Joyce, James 61, 90, 150, 153, 175; *Finnegan's Wake* 153
Jurassic Park (movie) 192n

K
Karekare 46, 135
Keats, John 60, 110, 141, 155, 198; 'Ode on a Graecian Urn' (quoted) 144; 'Ode to a Nightingale' 46, 48
Keith, Hamish 215-6, 216n
Kelly, Ned 166
Keneally, Thomas **165-9**, 183; *Schindler's Ark* 165, 167; *The Survivor* 166; *Woman of an Inner Sea* **166-9** (quoted) 166
Kenner, Hugh 147, 148, 149; *The Pound Era* 149
Kenyon Review 131
Kermode, Sir Frank 184; (autobiography quoted) 124
Kerouac, Jack 163, 164
Kidman, Fiona 93n
King, Michael 17n; *Moriori: A People Rediscovered* **35-7**; *Frank Sargeson: A Life* **55-9**
Kings College, Auckland 102n
Knights, L.C. 66-7, 147, 184
Koteliansky, S.S. 76
Kuhfuss, Svenja 138

L
Labour Party 12
Lacan, Jacques 91, 116
Laforgue, Jules 244
Landfall 17n, 31, 58, 208, 227, 232; *Landfall* Readers Award 232
Larkin, Philip *The Less Deceived* 171
Lasenby, Jack 63
Laughlin, James 152-6
Lawrence, D.H. 76, 136, 231
Lawrence, Frieda 75, 76
Lawrence, T.E. 175
Leavis, F.R. 67, 116
Le Gallienne, Richard 23
Lehmann, John 18
Leigh, Augusta 273
L'Enfant, Claire 185
Lentriccia, Frank 125
Lessing, Doris 183, 220
Lewis, Margaret *Ngaio Marsh: A Life* **43-4**
Lewis, Wyndham 184
Listener 67, 208, 227, 237, 246
Locke, Terry **260-7**
London Magazine 18, 19, 124
London Review of Books 11 & n, 125, 279
Loney, Alan 226
Los Angeles Times 242

Lowell, Amy 175, 184
Lowell, Robert 177
Lowry, Robert 207
Lubbock, Percy *Roman Pictures* 84
Lucas, John 256
Lucino, Albert 151

M
McCahon, Colin 70, 215, 216
McCarthyism 215
McCormick, Eric 55, **66-9**, **215**; 'Beginnings' 69; *The Expatriate* 66, 69; *The Inland Eye* 67; *Letters and Art in New Zealand* 66; *Omai, Pacific Envoy* 68, 69; E.H.McCormick Research Library 66n
McEldowney, Dennis 22, **233-46**
MacEwan, Ian 157n, 158-60
Mackerras, Sir Charles 135
MacLehose, Christopher 139
MacNeice, Louis 259
Mallarmé, Stéphane 171
Malouf, David *Remembering Babylon* **180-3**
Manning-Butler, Sir Reginald 19
Mansfield, Katherine 23, 24, 29, **33-4**, **38-42**, 49, 56, 68, **73-6**, 140, 170, 242, 252, 273n, 279; 'At the Bay' 38, 40; 'The Daughters of the Late Colonel' 25; 'The Doll's House' **40-2**; 'The Garden Party' 40; 'A Married Man's Story' 68-9; 'Millie' 38; 'Ole Underwood' 38; 'Prelude' 38, 41; 'The Ring' 34; 'To Stanislaw Wyspianski' 34; 'The Woman at the Store' 38, 39; Mansfield Fellowship 23, 49, 68, 147
Manson, Charles 126
Maori 35-7, 53, 98, 99, 104, 107, 109, 112-3, 211-3, 246, 250, 252, 267
Mao Zedong, Chairman 202
Marlowe, Christopher 248
Marquez, Gabriel Garcia 183
Marsh, Sir Edward 208
Marsh, Ngaio **43-4**
Marvell, Andrew 61, 204
Marxism / Marxist theory 11, 53, 110, 119, 202, 215, 220
Mason, Bruce 43, 50, 94, 236
Mason, R.A.K. 59, 259; 'Prelude' (quoted) 225
Mate 64
Matiora 35
Matisse, Henri 143, 175, 198, 258
Maudsley Psychiatric Hospital 18, 20, 21
Maxwell, Garth 10
Medwin, Thomas 275
Melbourne *Age* 24
Melville, Herman *Moby Dick* 117
Menton 23, 58, 68
Merian 17n
Metzinger, Jean 215
Middleton, Peter 123
Middleton, Stuart 110
Miles, Barry *Ginsberg: a Biography* 161-4
Miller, Karl 11 & n, 142
Milstead, Diane 134, 135

Milton, John 110, 235, 259
Modernism 97, 144, 147, 156, 177
Modigliani, Amedeo 76
Monro, Marilyn 23
Monroe, Harriet 184
Moore, Lesley *(see* Baker, Ida)
Moore, Marianne 153
Moravia, Alberto 82, 84, 86, 89, 91, 96; *Conjugal Love* **85-6**; *A Time of Desecration* 89
Moriori 35-7
Morrell, Lady Ottoline 75, 76
Morrieson, Ronald Hugh 30, 241
Morris, William 244
Morrison, Blake 252
Motion, Andrew (ed., with Blake Morrison) *The Penguin Book of Contemporary British Poetry* 252
Mount Albert Grammar School 67, 108, 215, 234
Mount Eden 197-8, 215, 232
Mozart, Wolgang Amadeus 61
Mulgan, John, 234, 245, 246; *Man Alone* 225
Murdoch, Iris 23, 220
Murray, Les 166, 214
Murry, John Middleton 39, 68, 73, 74-5, 170
Murry, Mary 75
Muse/s 118, 156, 278
Mussolini, Benito 146, 147, 156

N
Nabokov, Vladimir 61, 88; *Lolita* 64
Naipaul, Pat 190, 191
Naipaul, V.S. **189-193**
Napoleon (Buonaparte) 146
National Portrait Gallery (London) 68
Native Land Court 36
Nazi Party 138, 141, 205, 265
Neill, Michael 191, 192, 193
Neill, Sam 192 & n
New Critics/Criticism 117
New Directions 153
New English Syllabus (of the 1970s) 106
New Statesman 234, 256
New Victorians 112, 208
New Zealand Association of Teachers of English 103, 107, 264, 265
New Zealand Literary Fund 20
New Zealand Poetry **93-101**, 235
New Zealand Poetry Yearbook 208
Niagara Falls 130
Nixon, Richard 240
Nobel Prize 27, 91, 188
Nolan, Sidney 165
Norfolk Island 35
Nouveau Roman 90

O
O'Brien, Carol 25
O'Brien, Gregory 10, **70-1**
O'Connor, Frank 41

Ogilvie, Gordon *Denis Glover: His Life* **29-32**
O'Hara, Frank 176; *Lunch Poems* 226
Okri, Ben 183
Olsen, Charles *Maximus* 226
Ondaatje, Michael 183
Orlovsky, Peter 163
O'Sullivan, Vincent 67-8, 226; (ed.) *Poems of Katherine Mansfield* **33-4**
Owen, Wilfred 208

P
Page, Evelyn 43
Palgrave, F.T. (ed.) *The Golden Treasury of Songs and Lyrics* 26
Palmer, Sir Geoffrey 10
Palmer, Stanley 143
Parallax 227
Parker, Pat 122
Paul, Janet 30
Peacock, Thomas Love 278
Pek-Koon 192, 193
PEN 29, 50, 243
The Penguin Book of New Zealand Verse 12
Picasso, Pablo 143, 198, 258
Pickard, Alec (A.P. Gaskell) 57
Pinter, Harold 191
Plath, Sylvia 170-2
Plato, 112
PN Review 124
Poet Laureate (UK) 172
Polidori, John (Byron's physician) 280
Pound, Dorothy 145, 146, 150
Pound, Ezra 10, 18, 81, 97, **145-156**, 163, 164, 175, 178, 184, 249; *Cantos* 152, 153, 155, 156, 279; *Fragments of Canto* **115** (quoted) 156; *Le Testament de Villon* (opera) 150, 151; *Letters* **152-6**; *Pisan Cantos* 147, 148, 156
Pound, Homer 145, 146, 150
Pound, Isabel Weston 145, 146
Pound, Omar Shakespear 150, 151
Price, Chris 10
Price, Janice 187
Prince, Renate 17
Pritchett, V.S. 39
Proust, Marcel 28

Q
Queens College Harley Street 73

R
Racine, Jean *Andromaque* 18
Raine, Craig **157-60**, 252
Raine, Isaac 158
Raine, Li (Ann Pasternak Slater) 158
Raine, Moses 158
Raine, Nina 158
Raine, Vasca 158
Rapallo, 145-151
Read, Herbert 184
Read, Ian 92
Reid, Christopher 158

Reveley, Henry 278
Revista de Occidente 131
Rhymers' Club 31
Rice, Anne Estelle 74
Rich, Adrienne 123
Richards, Ian *The Life and Art of Maurice Duggan* **60-65**
Ricketts, Harry 225-231
Robbe-Grillet, Alain 90, 91, 92, 121
Robinson, Roger 33n, 104, 110
Rochester, John Wilmot, Earl of 190, 192
Roosevelt, Theodore 240
Rouault, Georges 143
Rudge, Olga 145, 146, 148, 150
Rushdie, Salman 183
Russell, the Hon. Bertrand (later Earl) 76

S
Saint Elizabeth's Hospital for the Insane, Washington D.C., 146, 156
Sargeson, Frank 9, 17, 18, 20, 21, 22, 23, 25, 28, 31, 39, 55-9, 62, 63, 67, 96, 198, 207, 235, 236, 237, 248; 'An Affair of the Heart' 25, 236; *I for One* 57; *Memoirs of a Peon* 57; *Never Enough* 58; *Up on to the Roof and Down Again* 57
Satie, Eric 175
Schoenberg, Arnold 175
Scott, Margaret 30
Scott, Sir Walter 198
Scriabin, Alexander 175
Selwyn, George Augustus, Bishop 36
Shadbolt, Maurice 62, 167, 189; *Among the Cinders* 62
Shakespear, Olivia 145
Shakespeare, William 38, 43, 60, 84, 110, 112, 199, 248; *Hamlet* 117; *King Lear* 155; *Macbeth* 108, 112
Shelley, Clara 273, 278
Shelley, Elena Adelaide 274, 275
Shelley, Harriet 280
Shelley, Mary **271-81**; *Frankenstein* 273, 276
Shelley, Percy Bysshe 140, 148, 155, **271-81**; 'Epipsychidion' 45, (quoted) 280; 'Laon and Cythna' 273; 'Stanzas written in Dejection near Naples' 274; 'To Constantia Singing' 273
Shelley, Percy Florence 277
Shelley, Sir Timothy 277
Shelley, William 273, 278
Silliman, Ron 123
Silsbee, Edward 272, 275, 281
Simon, Claude 91
Sinclair, Jack 54
Sinclair, Sir Keith **51-4**, 62, 67, 229; *Halfway Round the Harbour* 51; *The Origins of the Maori Wars* 53
Slater, Ann Pasternak *see* Raine, Li
Smith, D.I.B. 2, 19n
Smith, Verna 159
Smithyman, Kendrick 51, 63, 229, 244
Spanish Civil War 141, 142

Spender, Lizzie 135, 136
Spender, Natasha 136, 143; *An English Garden in Provence* 144
Spender, Sir Stephen 45, 136, 137, **138-144**; *Collected Poems* 139; 'I Think Continually of Those who are Truly Great' 139, (quoted) 140; *Journals 1939-1983* 135, (quoted) 141, 142, 143; 'The Landscape near an Aerodrome' 139; *Ruins and Visions* 139, 142; 'Ultima Ratio Regum' 139; *World within World* 139, 140, 143, (quoted) 142, 144
Spielberg, Steven 165
Spivak, Gayatri Chakravorty 125
Stead, C.K. 134-7; *All Visitors Ashore* 25, 209, 227, 235, **236-9**; *Answering to the Language* 13; 'The Clodian Songbook' 253, 257, 258; (ed.) *Collected Stories of Maurice Duggan* 64n; *The Death of the Body* **209-10**, 237, 238, 266, 267; *The End of the Century at the End of the World* 243, 266; 'A Fitting Tribute' 25, 96, 130, 232, 242, 244, 245; *Five for the Symbol* 245n; 'From Wystan to Carlos' 226, 249; *In the Glass Case, Essays on New Zealand Literature* 64n, 234n; *The New Poetic* 135, **184-8**, 231, 249; 'Pictures in a Gallery Undersea' 232; 'A Poet's View' 239, 243; *Pound, Yeats, Eliot & the Modernist Movement* 203; 'A Quality of Life' 245; *Quesada* 258; 'A Race Apart' 232; *Sister Hollywood* 241-2; *Smith's Dream* 239, 241, 266; (ed.) *World's Classics New Zealand Short Stories, Second Series* 13
Stead, Kay 18, 19, 22, 25, 26, 27, 135, 136, 143, 215, 235
Stead, Margaret 136
Stead, Oliver 22
Stein, Gertrude 175
Steiner, George 124-5
Stevens, Joan *New Zealand Short Stories* 25
Stevens, Wallace 153, 244, 266
Stivens, Dal 169
Stocking, Marion Kingston (ed.) *The Clairmont Correspondence* (two volumes) **271-81**
Stow, Randolph 129
Strauss, Johann *Die Fledermaus* 79
Stravinsky, Igor 175
Svensson, Carin 26
Swedish Academy 91
Symbolism / Symbolists 140
Symons, Arthur 184

T
Takapuna 56, 59
Taylor, Gill 186, 187 188
Taylor, J.S. 102n
Tennyson, Alfred 'Break, break, break...' 173; *In Memoriam* 171
Te Papa (National Museum) **217-8**
Theatre Royal Drury Lane 132
Theroux, Paul *Sir Vidia's Shadow* **189-93**
Thomas, Dylan 21, 244

Thompson, Mervyn 43, 237, 267
Thwaite, Anthony 170
Time 163
Times Literary Supplement 184n, 188
Tomalin, Claire *Shelley and his World*, 275
Tong, Rosalind *see* Hollinrake, Rosalind
Trelawny, Edward John 148, 274, 278, 280
Turner, Dennis Knight 207

V
Valéry, Paul 114
Vasil, Raj 246
Victorian novel 84
Vietnam War 12, 163, 208, 219, 240
Viviani, Emilia 280

W
Wagner, Richard 140
Waitangi, Treaty of 12, 98, 99, 109, 211-3
Walpole, Hugh 137
Wedde, Ian 12, 226
Weeks, John 215
Wendt, Albert 54, 159, 246
Westbrook, Eric 215
Westminster Abbey, Poet's Corner 172
Wevill, Assia 171
Wevill, David 171
White, Newman Ivy 274

White, Patrick 166, 183
Williams, Edward 280
Williams, Jane 277, 279
Williams, William Carlos 95, 153
Wilmers, Mary-Kay 11n
Wilson, Tim 10
Winn-Manson Menton Fellowship 23
Wollstonecraft, Mary 271, 277; *The Rights of Women* 271
Woolf, Virginia 75, 115, 119, 123, 140, 141
Woolloxal, J.L.D. 233
Wordsworth, William 118, 140, 198, 233; 'Lines written a few miles above Tintern Abbey' (quoted) 96; *The Lyrical Ballads* 241; *Preface to The Lyrical Ballads* (quoted) 118-9; *The Prelude* (quoted) 164
World War I 137

Y
Yeats, W.B. 10, 31, 97, 129, 145, 152, 184, 225, 244, 245; 'Adam's Curse' (quoted) 60; 'The Fascination of What's Difficult' 104; 'The Lake Isle of Innesfree' 173
Young, David 237

Z
Zukovsky, Louis 258